Third Wave Feminism

Third Wave Feminism

A Critical Exploration

Expanded Second Edition

Edited by

Stacy Gillis, Gillian Howie

and

Rebecca Munford

First edition published in 2004
This edition published in 2007 by
PALGRAVE MACMILLAN
Houndmills, Basingstoke, Hampshire RG21 6XS and
175 Fifth Avenue, New York, N.Y. 10010
Companies and representatives throughout the world.

PALGRAVE MACMILLAN is the global academic imprint of the Palgrave Macmillan division of St. Martin's Press, LLC and of Palgrave Macmillan Ltd. Macmillan® is a registered trademark in the United States, United Kingdom and other countries. Palgrave is a registered trademark in the European Union and other countries.

ISBN-13: 978–0–230–52174–2 paperback
ISBN-10: 0–230–52174–6 paperback

This book is printed on paper suitable for recycling and made from fully managed and sustained forest sources. Logging, pulping and manufacturing processes are expected to conform to the environmental regulations of the country of origin.

A catalogue record for this book is available from the British Library.

A catalog record for this book is available from the Library of Congress.

10 9 8 7 6 5 4 3 2 1
16 15 14 13 12 11 10 09 08 07

Transferred to digital printing in 2008.

Contents

Part II Locales and Locations

Part III Politics and Popular Culture

Acknowledgements

Third Wave Feminism: A Critical Exploration originally emerged from a conference held at the University of Exeter in 2002. Our thanks go to all those who participated in the event, making it a joyful, fruitful and rewarding conference. We would like to thank those who contributed to the organisation of the event, making it an enjoyable and trouble-free experience: Susie Evans, Anna Hunt, Nina Kelly, Laura Perrett and Becky Stacey. We would also like to thank the School of English and the School of Modern Languages at the University of Exeter for providing financial support. This revised edition contains some new pieces in place of some from the first edition. We would like to thank the contributors to both editions for their hard work and commitment to the project.

Stacy and Becky would like to thank feminist friends, past and present. Particular thanks are owed to Ashley Tauchert, who first suggested organising the conference, and to Andrew Shail, because he always steps up to the mark.

Gillian would like to thank Isobel Armstrong, John Dupre, Regenia Gagnier and Helen Taylor for providing invaluable and generous encouragement for the Institute of Feminist Theory and Research.

Bob Stoate assisted with the editorial work and was a great help.

Many thanks to the *Journal of International Women's Studies* for allowing us to publish revised versions of Agnieszka Graff's and Winifred Woodhull's chapters, which originally appeared in a special issue on *Third Wave Feminism and Women's Studies* 4.2 (April 2003), edited by Stacy Gillis and Rebecca Munford.

We would also like to acknowledge Figure 15.1 from *Persepolis 2: The Story of a Return* by Marjane Satrapi, translated by Anjali Singh, copyright © 2004 by Anjali Singh. Used by permission of Pantheon Books, a division of Random House, Inc.

Notes on Contributors

Mridula Nath Chakraborty completed her PhD at the University of Alberta, Canada. She is trained in literary criticism and postcolonial methodologies of reading the world. Her most recent work explores the role and presence of Third World feminists in the Anglo-American academy in addressing issues of experience, embodiment and essentialism. Her areas of research and publication include postcolonial literatures, diaspora and transnational studies, culinary cultures, translation theory and practice, regional Indian writing in bhasha traditions as well as in global English, and popular Bombay cinema.

Jennifer Drake is an Associate Professor of English at the University of Indianapolis in the U.S. She is the co-editor of *Third Wave Agenda: Being Feminist, Doing Feminism* (1997), and has published essays on women writers and visual artists. Her current book project is entitled *The Misfits of Women's Lit.*

Ednie Kaeh Garrison is a Visiting Assistant Professor at Penn State University in the U.S. She completed her PhD in American Studies at Washington State University in the U.S. She has published on third wave feminism and U.S. Riot Grrrls, and is currently designing a study of the global circulation of the name-object 'third wave feminism.'

Stacy Gillis is a Lecturer in Modern and Contemporary Literature at Newcastle University, U.K. She has published widely on third wave feminism, (post)feminism, cyberpunk and cybertheory, and popular fiction. The editor of *The Matrix Trilogy: Cyberpunk Reloaded* (2005), she and Rebecca Munford are the authors of *Feminism and Popular Culture: Explorations in Post-feminism* (2007). Forthcoming work includes *The Edinburgh Critical Guide to Crime Fiction* (2008) and a collection on the cultural afterlife of the First World War.

Kristyn Gorton is a Senior Lecturer in Media and Popular Culture at Leeds Metropolitan University, U.K. She completed her PhD in English Literature at the University of Edinburgh, U.K. She has published on feminist theory, television studies and Marguerite Duras. Forthcoming work includes *Critical Scenes of Desire in Twentieth-Century Fiction, Theorising Desire: From Freud to Feminism to Film* and *Media Audience: Television, Meaning and Emotion.*

Agnieszka Graff is an Assistant Professor at the American Studies Center, Warsaw University, Poland. Since the mid-1990s she has been active in the Polish women's movement, focusing on reproductive rights and gay/lesbian rights in the context of Poland's EU accession, and is a founding member of the Women's 8th of March Alliance. She has written for Poland's major newspapers and is the author of *Swiat bez kobiet* [*World without Women*] (2001[2004]), a collection of essays on gender in Polish public life. Her current research project concerns rhetorical strategies of feminism in the U.S., but she continues to write on the intersection between gender politics and nationalism in Poland.

Leslie Heywood is a Professor of English and Cultural Studies and Director of Graduate Studies at the State University of New York, Binghamton in the U.S. Her publications include *Built to Win: The Female Athlete as Cultural Icon* (2003), *Pretty Good for a Girl: An Athlete's Story* (2000) and *Bodymakers: A Cultural Anatomy of Women's Bodybuilding* (1998). She is the co-editor of *Third Wave Agenda: Being Feminist, Doing Feminism* (1997) and editor of the two-volume *The Women's Movement Today: An Encyclopedia of Third Wave Feminism* (2005). She is currently working on a follow-up volume focusing on third wave feminism, environmentalism and consumer culture.

Gillian Howie is a Senior Lecturer in Philosophy at the University of Liverpool, U.K., and Director of the Institute for Feminist Theory and Research. She is the author of *Deleuze and Spinoza: Aura of Expressionism* (2002), the editor of *Women: A Cultural Review*'s special issue on *Gender and Philosophy* (2003), and co-editor of *Gender, Teaching and Research in Higher Education* (2001).

Luce Irigaray taught at the University of Vincennes in the early 1970s and was a member of the École Freudienne de Paris. She left on publication of her second doctoral thesis, *Speculum of the Other Woman* (1974). She has since worked at the Centre National de La Recherche Scientifique. A prolific and influential writer, her work ranges over psychoanalysis, linguistics, social theory, law and philosophy. Other notable works include *This Sex Which Is Not One* (1977), *An Ethics of Sexual Difference* (1984), *Democracy Begins Between Two* (1994) and *Between East and West* (1999). She has recently published on architecture and sustainable communities, as well as work on civil rights used by UNESCO.

Amanda D. Lotz is an Assistant Professor of Communication Studies at the University of Michigan, U.S. Her publications include articles in *Critical Studies in Media Communication, Feminist Media Studies, Television & New*

Media, Screen, and *Women and Language.* Her *Redesigning Women: Television after the Network Era* (2006) explores the rise of female-centred dramas and cable networks targeted towards women in the late 1990s as they relate to changes in the U.S. television industry. She is currently researching changes in the U.S. television industry since the 1980s and shifts in the medium's role as a cultural institution.

Niamh Moore is a Research Fellow at the Centre for Research on Socio-Cultural Change (CRESC) at the University of Manchester, U.K. She works on qualitative methodology in CRESC's Qualitative Research Laboratory, and is particularly interested in the methodological issues raised when 're-using' qualitative data to research socio-cultural change. Her other interests cohere around ecofeminism, and feminist and environmental politics. She is currently working on a book based on ethnographic research, including oral history interviews, conducted with women activists at the Clayoquot Sound Peace Camp on the West Coast of Canada in 1993.

Rebecca Munford is a Lecturer in English Literature at Cardiff University, U.K. She is the co-author of *Feminism and Popular Culture: Explorations in Post-feminism* (2007) with Stacy Gillis and the editor of *Re-visiting Angela Carter: Texts, Contexts, Intertexts* (2006). She has published essays on Angela Carter, the cross-channel Gothic, Daphne du Maurier, post-feminism and third wave feminism. Forthcoming work includes *Decadent Daughters and Monstrous Mothers: Angela Carter and the European Gothic* (2008).

Mary Orr is Professor of French at the University of Southampton, U.K., following five years as Professor of Modern French Studies at the University of Exeter, U.K. Her most recent monographs are *Intertextuality: Debates and Contexts* (2003) and *Flaubert: Writing the Masculine* (2000). Her many journal articles and essays reflect her main research interests in the modern French novel, literary translation and French critical and gender theory, especially in their transnational contexts. Her recent work includes a co-edited volume of feminist reappraisals of French and German male canonical writers from Goethe to Gide and her current research projects include a monograph to remap the history of ideas of nineteenth-century France through the lens of Flaubert's *La Tentation de Saint Antoine,* and essays on the roles of early nineteenth-century French and British women in the natural sciences.

Patricia Pender is an Assistant Professor of English and Women's and Gender Studies at Pace University in the U.S., where she teaches courses in early modern women's writing, feminist literary history, and contemporary popular culture. She has published articles on Aphra Behn and Anne Bradstreet as well as a previous piece on Buffy in *Fighting the Forces* (2003). She is currently at work on two book-length projects, *Authorial Alibis: Early Modern Women's Writing and the Rhetoric of Modesty*, and *Girls on Film: Cultural Studies in Third Wave Feminism*.

Lise Shapiro Sanders is an Assistant Professor of English Literature and Cultural Studies at Hampshire College in the U.S. She is co-editor with Amy Bingaman and Rebecca Zorach of a collection of essays, *Embodied Utopias: Gender, Social Change and the Modern Metropolis* (2002). Other publications include 'The Failures of the Romance' in *Modern Fiction Studies* (March 2001) and a chapter in Andrew Higson's collection, *Young and Innocent: Cinema and Britain, 1896–1930* (2002). Her most recent book is entitled *Consuming Fantasies: Labor, Leisure, and the London Shopgirl, 1880–1920* (2006).

Andrew Shail is News International Research Fellow in Film at St Anne's College, University of Oxford, U.K. He is the co-editor of *Menstruation: A Cultural History* (2005). He has published widely on early cinema culture, and is currently working on a monograph on the origins of the modern super hero and a co-edited collection on cinema in fiction, 1895–1915.

Elaine Showalter is Professor Emeritus of English and Avalon Professor of the Humanities at Princeton University in the U.S. Her books include *A Literature of Their Own* (1977), *The New Feminist Criticism* (1985), *Sister's Choice: Traditions and Change in American Women's Writing* (1991), *Inventing Herself* (2001) and *Teaching Literature* (2002). She has lectured widely in the U.S., Europe and Canada and reviews fiction regularly for *The Guardian*, *Times Literary Supplement, London Review of Books* and the *Washington Post*.

Jane Spencer is Professor of English at the University of Exeter, U.K., where she works on writings from the seventeenth to the nineteenth centuries, specialising in feminist literary history. She has edited Aphra Behn's drama and written widely on women's fiction, poetry and periodical writing. Her books include *The Rise of the Woman Novelist* (1986), *Elizabeth Gaskell* (1993), *Aphra Behn's Afterlife* (2000) and *Literary Relations: Kinship and the Canon, 1660–1800* (2005). She is currently working on the representation of animals in the Enlightenment.

Cristina Lucia Stasia is a doctoral candidate in the English department at Syracuse University in the U.S. She works at the intersections of film theory and third wave feminism and has previously published in *The Journal of Bisexuality*. Her primary research interest is in constructions of femininity, the figure of the girl and action cinema. She is currently writing her dissertation on the female action hero film.

Alison Stone is a Senior Lecturer in Philosophy in the Institute for Philosophy and Public Policy at Lancaster University, U.K. She works on post-Kantian European philosophy, feminist philosophy and political philosophy. Her books are *Petrified Intelligence: Nature in Hegel's Philosophy* (2004) and *Luce Irigaray and the Philosophy of Sexual Difference* (2006). She is currently completing *An Introduction to Feminist Philosophy*.

Susan Stryker is an internationally recognised independent scholar and filmmaker whose theoretical writings and historical research have helped to shape the field of transgender studies. Most recently, she directed the Emmy Award-winning public television documentary *Screaming Queens: The Riot at Compton's Cafeteria* (2006) and co-edited *The Transgender Studies Reader* (2006).

Ashley Tauchert is a Senior Lecturer in Eighteenth-Century Literary Studies at the University of Exeter, U.K. and Founding Director of the Institute for Feminist Theory and Research. She is the author of *Mary Wollstonecraft and the Accent of the Feminine* (2002) and *Romancing Jane Austen: Narrative, Realism and the Possibility of a Happy Ending* (2005).

Anastasia Valassopoulos is a Lecturer in Postcolonial Literatures in English at the University of Manchester, U.K. Her interests include Arab women's writing, popular culture in the Middle East and, more widely, the construction and impact of Arab feminism. She has written on the Tunisian filmmaker Moufida Tlatli's work, Nawal El-Saadawi's early novels and their understanding and negotiation of an early first wave feminism, as well as on Lebanese women's novels of the civil war. She is currently working on a monograph entitled *Contemporary Arab Women Writers* (2008).

Melanie Waters completed her Ph.D. on post-war confessional literature and American political history in the School of English at Newcastle University, U.K. In 2005, she co-organised *From Pornography to Politics'* a symposium which brought together scholars from across the U.K. and Europe to discuss the changing relationship between pornography, feminism and the academy. Her major research interests are feminist and psychoanalytic theory, contemporary poetry and popular culture. She has recently co-authored a chapter for *Reading Desperate Housewives: Beyond the White Picket Fence* (2006) with Stacy Gillis.

Imelda Whelehan is Professor of English and Women's Studies at De Montfort University, U.K. She is the author of *Modern Feminist Thought* (1995), *Overloaded* (2000), *Helen Fielding's Bridget Jones's Diary: A Reader's Guide* (2002) and *The Feminist Bestseller* (2005). She is co-author of *Fifty Key Concepts in Gender Studies* (2004) and has edited and co-edited a number of books on literary adaptations, including the forthcoming *Cambridge Companion to Literature on Screen* (2008).

Winifred Woodhull is an Associate Professor of French and Cultural Studies at the University of California, San Diego in the U.S., where she teaches on the Critical Gender Studies and Third World Studies Programs as well as in the Department of Literature. Her publications include *Transfigurations of the Maghreb: Feminism, Decolonization, and Literatures* (1993) as well as articles on French and francophone literatures, and literatures of immigration. She is currently completing a book on French cinema of the interwar period.

Foreword

Imelda Whelehan

In 1995 when I offered an overview of second wave feminism in *Modern Feminist Thought*, my conclusion, in retrospect, seems rather gloomy. In the mid-nineties were we in danger of simply 'reinventing the wheel', I wondered? I was not alone in this fear and I actually quoted Josephine Donovan in my conclusion.[1] This sentiment has become ubiquitous in critical accounts of feminism, especially when looking forward to the possible futures for a feminist ideology, and this volume has several contributors who express identical anxieties. What is the real fear now, I wonder, in reinvention? The third wavers, as I understand them in all their contradictory multiplicity, have reinvented the wheel, but at the same time they have added new features and specifications which are designed to challenge those who thought they knew what feminism was.[2] For so long we (I and other commentators on the second wave) have pointed out that while no one 'owns' feminism, the worst conflicts within feminist politics were effectively about ownership and colonisation. Third wave feminists seem content to move forward on the basis that feminism is not owned – itself refreshing – and in so doing have thrown all the certainties up in the air, perhaps to resolve themselves as something new and challenging. Certainly, I for one am enchanted by the celebration of a feminist life, as well as the accounts of all its pitfalls, that third wave writers have offered.

The younger women writing critically of feminism in the mid-nineties – Naomi Wolf, Katie Roiphe and Rene Denfeld in particular – were only a few years younger than I, but spoke convincingly of the feminist generation gap creating an impasse where 'younger' women simply did not share the life experiences of their foremothers and felt policed by what they perceived as the rigid codes of feminist behaviour.[3] Since the 1960s and 1970s, the world had changed beyond recognition for these young women and second wave feminism's solutions would not allow them to navigate the complexities of their own lives. As someone born, by the trend/marketing categories referred to by Leslie Heywood and Jennifer Drake in their chapter in this collection, in the last year of the baby boom and the year prior to the onset of Generation X, I felt in 1995 comfortably and uncomfortably between the generations, a spectator without authentic 'access' to either grouping and, despite my moment of gloom, naively sanguine about the future of feminism's second wave.

While it has become both fashionable and treacherous to imagine second/third wave feminist conflict in terms of a generational clash, I agree with Jane Spencer in her Afterword that the clash seems more to do with the onset of age, or working through the differing stages of womanhood which make no sense until you have inhabited them. When I wrote *Modern Feminist Thought*, I never expected to become a mother and yet now I and my close contemporary and third wave icon Madonna have children, and have crossed what seems from this side the abyss between youth and middle age. The gulf, I now think, is not caused by generational conflict in the sense that daughters must rebel against their mothers, discredit their ambitions and assert their own identity. Rather, it is purely about life stages and the effects of moving from one significant milestone to another. Betty Friedan and Germaine Greer are examples of feminists who have changed perspective as they have moved through such landmarks; it is not that these stages have some intrinsic meaning from a biological point of view or that everyone reaches such stages at the same time, but women who move from singledom to partnership, to motherhood or confirmed childlessness (selective or otherwise) have to deal with massively shifting social perspectives on their life choices. Physiologically, the ageing female body has been well documented as a process of deterioration rather than framed more positively as a growing towards wisdom or full maturity, and the fetishisation of the young (even pre-pubescent) female body maintains its sway over postmodern popular culture. Mothers have rarely had a good press, but ageing women generally find that their views are not entirely welcome.

Whether or not generational shifts or simply age offer the most useful pointers to the gap between second and third wave feminism, the biggest changes to impact upon the possibilities open to third wavers have been technological ones. The use and growing expertise in navigating the internet, producing webpages, electronic zines and blogs has given feminism the global reach it could only dream of in the 1970s and 1980s. Networking equates in 'second wave' speak to consciousness-raising sessions where women gravitated to small groups to speak their pains in a secure environment (and many clearly did not because of a fear of intimidation or because they simply did not know such women). The internet allows for confession to millions in relative safety. It allows for both painful authenticity and inauthenticity; it allows for women to choose and debate their feminist politics with the benefit of a broader perspective than that offered by their local feminist 'chapter.' It allows for a kind of DIY feminism that has become the trademark of the third

wave.⁴ Having said that, I think that Stacy Gillis in this collection is right
to caution against overstating the freedoms of technology for women,
not least because technological freedoms are still the province of the
prosperous in this world; and perhaps playful identity-shifting is itself a
rarefied luxury.

While I was completing my gloomy conclusion to my book, the third
wave was being born in America. Rebecca Walker had used the term in
1992 in an article for *Ms.*, and her anthology *To Be Real: Telling the Truth and
Changing the Face of Feminism* was published in 1995, as was Barbara
Findlen's *Listen Up: Voices from the Next Feminist Generation.* These collections were to dictate the shape of this new feminism for some time to come.
Far from the lament that feminism was locked in the academy, Walker's
anthology gave voice to those outside – in many cases outside the ethnic,
sexual and sociological mainstream – talking about what feminism means
to them today and how it informs even the most mundane aspects of
their identities. The essays in Walker's volume are in many ways a celebration of individuality, a confirmation that there is no single way to 'be'
a feminist in deliberate opposition to her view of the legacy of the second
wave containing 'a host of mystifications, imagistic idealisations, and
ingrained social definitions of what it means to be a feminist' (Walker
1995, xxxii). Youth is held up as one of the uniting factors of the collection and Gloria Steinem, in the role of elder stateswoman writing the
foreword to Walker's volume, is at times sceptical of this new movement.
Yet what is most striking is the number of contributors who wish to stake
their claim as individuals who cross identities, be they bi-racial, multi-
sexual or so forth. The volume's title *To be Real* underscores the high
value placed on authenticity, but might also be read as a plea from the
heart in a postmodern world of simulacra and 'passing'.

Third Wave Feminism is not a collection of third wave feminist
writings. What is most engaging about this collection is how soon you
forget that demarcation of distance and come to recognise that third
wave feminism, for good or ill, can be sceptical of its own agenda. The
different sections remind us that third wavers and their contemporaries are well educated in gender politics – whether it be in their
ability to re-evaluate the legacies of French feminist theory and see the
third wave tendency as itself encompassed there, or in the embracing of
studies in popular culture, ecofeminism and ethnicity. As the introduction claims, the collection brings a critical eye to feminism's third
wave and, in rooting such debates within the academy, none of the
heady excitement of doing feminism (as third wavers would have it)
is lost.

The activism implied by *doing* feminism may not for some herald the long awaited revolution in consciousness. Elaine Showalter, interviewed in this volume, doubts whether there will be another radical movement for feminism; one thing all of the contributors agree on in this phenomenon of third wave feminism is that it differs and moulds to as many identities as there are practitioners and thinkers. The pleasurable and refreshing aspects of third wavers' playfulness are highlighted, most notably their embracing of popular culture – which young women consume, appropriate and reuse to their own purposes. There are so many questions to ask of such a free-ranging and individualist statement of political purpose (and one day I will ask them at length), but it seems right that the expression of a feminist politics should be a joyful thing and that in this participatory interrogation of culture we may see more shifts in women's social roles. Women, feminists in particular, have not been especially adroit at handling the mass media, but are now winning territory in an arena of people's lives which is arguably more meaningful to them than their political identities or any kind of social or civic responsibility. As Showalter implies, any future movement could not draw on a broad collective base; and the role of men in relationship to the third wave is crucial, especially as some suspect – and Heywood and Drake imply in their chapter – that young women share more of their social experiences with men of the same age than they do with women in general.

If the role of the Foreword is in any way to give a flavour of the whole volume I am sure that I will fail dismally. This work gathers together numerous essays which respond to the *idea* of third wave feminism – some from a position 'within' a space they recognise as part of the wave, and some hesitating at the borders (with the second wave horizon fast receding), ever wary of the possibility of falling into postfeminist discourse with all the negative baggage that it has come to carry. Girl power, the rallying cry of the cutting-edge female musician and the manufactured pop idol alike, reminds us that for feminism to be popular (theoretically a concern from second wave days) means engaging with some pretty thorny ambiguities. Essays on female heroes remind us that feminism has not always treated its figureheads that well (something Showalter touches on in her interview), yet third wavers seem to enjoy their *Buffy* despite her manufactured empowerment. Perhaps the lesson here is that feminism needs its champions, fantastical and otherwise, just as it needs to be more relaxed about seemingly irresolvable contradictions (as viewed in our contemporary world order).

Third wave feminism, from my perspective, offers a mixture of the technological and the domestic. For every zine crafted with the best of modern know-how, there is also a knitting pattern or cross stitch template in the pages of such magazines as *BUST*. Such patterns, recipes and advice columns summon the expertise of generations of women's magazines while turning domestic quietism on its head (the pattern for a sampler which reads 'Babies Suck' is a personal favourite of mine, for its mixture of literal statement of fact and iconoclastic anti-maternalism). The disembodiment of the sexed body promised by cyberculture is counterpoised by this provocative yet enchanting flirtation with female-centred certainties, thus accurately reflecting the maze of social contradictions in which a third (or first or second?) wave feminist would find themselves. On reflection what I like about this collection is its historical and cultural mobility rather than what it says about the third wave *per se*. In pondering this new wave (and wondering whether to care if it really can be a 'wave' or a moment or something entirely other)[5] I found myself once again caring that I am a feminist, whatever the era.

Notes

1. 'One of the sad conclusions I have reached in writing this book is that feminists have reinvented the wheel a number of times' (Donovan xii).
2. Gloria Steinem argues the opposite and asserts: 'you may want to make them a different size or color, put them on a different wagon, use them to travel in a different direction, or otherwise make them your own – but many already exist' (xix).
3. Devoney Looser perfectly summarises this view of generational conflict: 'Younger feminists are sometimes said to be undutiful daughters, careerists and theorists who are not political enough – not sufficiently grateful to the past generation for fighting the battles that made today's lives possible. Older feminists are often painted as bad mothers who long to see themselves in their offspring, who resist deviations from their second-wave plan, and who can't properly wield the power they have garnered' (ix).
4. I take DIY feminism to mean the appropriation of popular cultural images of women and culture to new effects, allowing some distance from the intended meanings of the images and artefacts used in this way. Elsewhere I have linked this to early second wave writings, especially in the assertion of youth (Whelehan 2004). For example, see Jo Freeman: 'the younger branch of the movement prides itself on its lack of organisation. Eschewing structure and damning the idea of leadership, it has carried the concept of "everyone doing their own thing" almost to its logical extreme' (par. 11).

5. It is a 'wave' which has fast concretised its own recent history, as demonstrated by the publication of Leslie L. Heywood's *The Women's Movement Today: An Encyclopedia of Third Wave Feminism* (2005).

Works cited

Donovan, Josephine. *Feminist Theory: The Intellectual Traditions of American Feminism*. Exp. ed. New York: Continuum, 1992.

Findlen, Barbara, ed. *Listen Up: Voices from the Next Feminist Generation*. Seattle: Seal, 1995.

Freeman, Jo. 'The Women's Liberation Movement: Its Origins, Structure and Ideas.' 1971. Documents from the Women's Literature Movement: An Online Archival Collection, Duke University. April 1997. Accessed: 1 Sept. 2006. <http://scriptorium.lib.duke.edu/wlm/womlib/>.

Heywood, Leslie, ed. *The Women's Movement Today: An Encyclopedia of Third Wave Feminism*. 2 vols. Westport: Greenwood Press, 2005.

Looser, Devoney. Preface. *Generations: Academic Feminists in Dialogue*. Ed. Devoney Looser and E. Ann Kaplan. Minneapolis: University of Minnesota Press, 1997. ix.

Steinem, Gloria. Foreword. *To Be Real: Telling the Truth and Changing the Face of Feminism*. Ed. Rebecca Walker. New York: Anchor, 1995. xiii–xxviii.

Walker, Rebecca. 'Becoming the Third Wave.' *Ms.39* (Jan.–Feb. 1992): 39–41.

——. Being Real: An Introduction. *To Be Real: Telling the Truth and Changing the Face of Feminism*. Ed. Rebecca Walker. New York: Anchor, 1995. xxix–xl.

Whelehan, Imelda. 'Having it All (Again?).' *New Femininities and Sexual Citizenship*. ESCR seminar series. London School of Economics. 19 Nov. 2004. Accessed: 1 Sept. 2006. <http://www.lse.ac.uk/ collections/newFemininities/ HAVING%20IT%20ALL%20final.pdf>.

——. *Modern Feminist Thought: From Second Wave to 'Post-Feminism'*. Edinburgh: Edinburgh University Press, 1995.

Introduction

Stacy Gillis, Gillian Howie and Rebecca Munford

There have always been women writing about, concerned with and acting in the interests of women. A 'feminist' history, however, is different from a history of both women and/or the women's movement.[1] We have come to understand such a feminist history in terms of three distinct stages or generations. The first generation, those involved in the nineteenth-century women's movement, responded to a common exclusion from political, social, public and economic life. The objective shared by this generation was to extend the social contract so that it included political citizenship for women. Whether all women active in this movement could be described as feminists is a moot point, but by the second stage in feminist history in the 1960s and 1970s, a clear, self-defined and self-identified feminist movement had emerged. Reflecting on the gains of the suffragists, a second generation of feminists emerged, no longer convinced that inclusion into formal universal political structures would solve the problem. Disappointed by the fact that substantive change had not followed on from the modification of political structures, second wave feminists concerned themselves with broader social relations. Situated within a context which already included a programme for legal and political emancipation, this second generation of feminists concentrated on issues which specifically impacted upon women's lives: reproduction, mothering, sexual violence, expressions of sexuality, and domestic labour. Despite – or perhaps because of – the political intensity of peace camps, anti-racist activities, consciousness-raising and 'Reclaim the Night' marches, this concentration on 'woman', as both the object and subject of discourse, resulted in a shift within the movement.

The concept 'woman' seemed *too* fragile to bear the weight of all contents and meanings ascribed to it and, as Naomi Zack points out, the 'foundation of second wave feminism collapsed sometime during the 1980s and feminists did not unite to rebuild it' (1). The elusiveness of this category of 'woman' raised questions about the nature of identity, unity and collectivity. Appearing to undercut the women's movement, fundamental principles of the feminist project were hotly contested in

the aftermath of the second wave of feminism. What we now understand as the third generation of feminism – the 'third wave' – emerges
from these contestations – and the responses to them.[2] To speak about a
'third wave' of feminists is to name a specific moment in feminist theory and practice. To incite others to speak about this wave is, in effect,
to proliferate discourse in such a way as to define 'the wave' as an object
which can be considered and interrogated. We are concerned that the
generational account inherited from Julia Kristeva, which divided feminism into generations,[3] reduces the complexity of each of these three
waves. More profoundly, we are aware that by speaking about any of the
generations or waves in this way, we cannot address or interrogate disparate theories and simplifying differences between social groups. By
gathering together so many diverse strands as a 'wave' in feminist history, and by consequently being able to treat these waves as objects of
academic enquiry, we could impose imperatives driven by an external
discourse. At all times, we are aware that we are speaking about a
moment in feminism which is 'a consequence of a certain feminist history and has consequences itself as a moment of feminist history to
come' (Kavka xvii). However, an overriding concern is how the wave
model – the generational account of feminist history – opens and closes
debates within feminism.

Third wave feminists have been extremely eager to define their feminism as something 'different' from previous feminisms. Identifying
themselves as a wave, the attempt to offer at least a provisional
delineation of the parameters of the third wave – even while acknowledging the difficulties attending such a mapping of the subject – has
been an underlying concern of many of those works making claims
for its existence. For Jennifer Baumgardner and Amy Richards, for
instance, the third wave is 'women who were reared in the wake of the
women's liberation movement of the seventies' (2000, 15); while for
Leslie Heywood and Jennifer Drake it is the generation 'whose birth
dates fall between 1963 and 1974' (4). The elision of meaning between
a delineation of the third wave through birthdate and a definition of
the third wave foregrounds the question of who can claim – or 'own' –
this particular feminist identity. Astrid Henry points out that the
'ways in which historical moment, ideology, and age are frequently
conflated within third-wave discourse complicates any easy separation of the term's meaning' (35). While Rory Dicker and Alison
Piepmeier are keen to resist arbitrary delineations in *Catching a Wave:
Reclaiming Feminist for the 21st Century* (2003) – '[t]hough we often refer
to our feminism as the third wave, we want to render problematic an

easy understanding of what the third wave is' (5) – they assume that 'their' feminism is best described as the third wave.

The third wave impulse to delineate its trends and tendencies is realised most starkly with the recent publication of Leslie Heywood's two-volume *The Women's Movement Today: An Encyclopedia of Third Wave Feminism* (2005) – a text which at once stakes a compelling claim for third wave feminism's historical location as well as provides a canon of third wave con/texts. The teleological impulse of Kristeva's generational account echoes in the memory of feminists who claim this time for their own. While making a persuasive argument for the limitations of the wave model as a way of thinking and knowing feminist histories and communities, Jo Reger nonetheless acknowledges its rhetorical power in the title *Different Wavelengths: Studies of the Contemporary Women's Movement* (2005), the most recent collection in the field.[4] Third wave feminism has seen a definable shift away from the politics of the individual, as evidenced in such early collections as Rebecca Walker's *To Be Real: Telling the Truth and Changing the Face of Feminism* (1995) and Barbara Findlen's *Listen Up: Voices From the Next Feminist Generation* (1995), and the implicit problems contained within the neo-liberal individualist ideology. What have emerged more recently are what could be described as 'cultural analyses of contemporary feminism' (Reger xvii) by self-termed third wavers. Yet the question of who 'owns' third wave feminism remains a contentious one.

The question of ownership informs the constellation of narratives underlying claims of the third wave blurry origins – both as an item of feminist nomenclature and, more broadly, as a generationally defined movement. The first documented mention of the term 'third wave' can be traced back to an anthology by M. Jacqui Alexander, Lisa Albrecht and Mab Segrest, entitled *The Third Wave: Feminist Perspectives on Racism*. Planned in the late 1980s for publication with Kitchen Table: Women of Color Press, the book promised a conceptualisation of the third wave centred around the challenges by women-of-colour feminists to the racial biases of second wave feminism. Ednie Kaeh Garrison wryly points out that 'the desire for it is such that people do speak as though it exists' (249); indeed, the anthology itself did not materialise following the closure of the publishing house. In her charting of other early references to a third wave, Garrison also foregrounds Chela Sandoval's claim, in her frequently cited article on U.S. Third World feminisms published in *Genders* (1991), that the recognition of a 'differential consciousness is vital to the generation of a next "third wave" women's movement and provides grounds for alliance with other decolonizing movements for emancipation' (qtd. in Garrison 250).[5] Over the last fifteen years, however, the feminist consciousness and activity promised by these formulations has given way to an emphasis on generational distinction and distinctiveness. Since the middle of the 1990s, there has been an explosion of popular and academic texts claiming the existence and delineating the contours and complexities of the 'third wave' as a new (and improved) feminist generation. The canonical enunciation of the term as a call for action is attributed to Rebecca Walker, co-founder of the Third Wave Foundation (formerly the Third Wave Direct Action Corporation). In a 1992 article for *Ms.*, entitled 'Becoming the Third Wave', Walker declared 'I am not a postfeminism feminist. I am the Third Wave' (41) – and thus established the double character of third wave feminism as distinct from both a media-endorsed 'after-the-fact' (post)feminism as well as the extant frameworks of second wave feminism.

Although wide-ranging in the positions they adopt in relation to questions of feminist theory and praxis, many third wave texts share a common ground in their eagerness to signal a break from an earlier feminist generation. As is evidenced by only a fleeting examination of their titles, Walker's *To Be Real: Telling the Truth and Changing the Face of Feminism*, Findlen's *Listen Up: Voices from the Next Feminist Generation*, Heywood and Drake's *Third Wave Agenda: Being Feminist, Doing Feminism* (1997), Baumgardner and Richards' *Manifesta: Young Women, Feminism, and the Future* (2000) and Dicker and Piepmeier's *Catching a Wave: Reclaiming Feminism for the 21st Century* all index some degree of departure from second wave feminism – a departure that, in spite of its caveats, inevitably risks positing the second wave 'as a definable phenomenon, as embodying a more or less coherent set of values and ideas which can be recognized and then transcended' (Bailey 1997, 23).[6] One reason for this insistence on generational distinction could be that third wave feminists tend to consider second wave feminism as triangulated in essentialism, universalism and naturalism and as having reaped the political consequences. Having learnt the lessons of history, they prefer contradiction, multiplicity and difference. For the confessional pieces in *To Be Real* and *Listen Up*, this means giving expression to the sometimes messy negotiation of feminist politics in everyday life; or, as Walker puts it, challenging the parameters of a feminist 'identity and way of living that doesn't allow for individuality, complexity, or less than perfect personal histories' (Walker 1995, xxxiii).

Natalie Fixmer and Julia T. Wood find this valorisation of the individual and the personal rather wearying, pointing out that third wavers' 'claim that they are distinct in emphasizing personal politics reveals remarkable gaps in understanding of the first and particularly the second wave of feminism' (249).[7] However, for the contributors to anthologies such as *Third Wave Agenda* and, to some extent, *Catching a Wave*, the notion of contradiction and duality is more often configured as part of a strategic engagement with (loosely understood) postmodern and poststructuralist theorisations of identity and difference – although, in these later collections, a far greater emphasis is placed on mapping continuities in feminist histories. Dicker and Piepmeier, in particular, 'are troubled by the ease with which scholars, writers, and activists lay claim to multiplicity in third wave discourse' at the expense of set of core political beliefs and goals (17). Indeed, the privileging of generational difference implicit in the ideological binarisation of third wave feminist multiplicity versus second wave feminist rigidity risks obfuscating the multiple ways in which, to cite Lisa Maria Hogeland, '[f]eminists are differently situated in relation to what the feminist movement has (and has not) accomplished' (107). Kimberly Springer, for example, points up the way in which, in popular accounts of the third wave, Rebecca Walker's generationally inspired coinage in the *Ms.* article of the term 'third wave' has usurped the anti-racist impetus for a 'third wave' shaping the Kitchen Table anthology. Moreover, in her discussion of the possibilities of a 'third wave black feminism', Springer proposes that the wave model has 'drowned out' the history of black feminism in its disregard for the influence of race-based movements on gender activism (1061), something which the essays in Daisy Hernández and Bushra Rehman's *Colonize This!* (2002) also address.

In allowing 'generational difference to stand in for political difference' (Hogeland 107), dominant understandings of third wave feminism lock feminist debate within a divisive rather than a dialogic framework. Moreover, this framing of feminist histories, through the mother-daughter metaphor, has focused on the implications – and limitations – of second wave theorising for a 'new' generation of young feminists. As Catherine M. Orr reminds us,

> the mother-daughter metaphor has just as many implications for the mother's politics as for the daughter's. ... If the third wave marks a different stage in the contemporary movement, then perhaps it is time for the second wave to identify exactly what its historical legacy is or should be. (42)[8]

What, then, does the emergence of third wave feminism, and its generational account of feminist histories, mean for second wave feminists? For

Jacquelyn N. Zita, in her introduction to the *Hypatia* special issue on *Third Wave Feminism* (1997), the 'cross-generational moment' is one that holds much potential for understanding feminist histories and imagining feminist futures; it is 'a passage of legacy, wisdom, memory and yet unanswered questions and resolved conflicts belonging to political and intellectual struggles that are much larger than life and much too important to leave behind' (1). Nevertheless, privileging generational differences between feminists and reading feminist history solely through the lens of Oedipal conflict submits to a masculinist logic of hierarchised familial structures that forces quarrel and confrontation inwards and reinforces divisions and divisiveness between women. In order to more fully understand feminist histories and *responsibilities*, we need to enable, and allow, a constructive dialogue between feminists that is not mired by mother-daughter conflict – a dialogue that is not owned by any one generation.[9]

The question of ownership is raised, once again, through the conflation of third wave feminism with (post)feminism. Amanda D. Lotz points out that conversations 'about both third-wave feminism and post-feminism remain difficult due to the lack of shared understanding of what the terms delineate' (106). While the essays in this collection do not seek to outline the debates surrounding (post)feminism, it has certainly become impossible to discuss third wave feminism without giving it some mention – as anticipated by Walker's statement in the *Ms.* article. In 1982, the *New York Times Magazine* featured an article by Susan Bolotin entitled 'Voices from the Post-Feminist Generation' and the term has since circulated widely, first in the media and subsequently in academic discussions of contemporary feminism. In its more widespread media form, (post)feminism describes

> a movement when women's movements are, for whatever reasons, no longer moving, no longer vital, no longer relevant; the term suggests that the gains forged by previous generations of women have so completely pervaded all tiers of our social existence that those still 'harping' about women's victim status are embarrassingly out of touch. (Siegel 75)[10]

An increasing awareness of the term, along with the publication of Susan Faludi's *Backlash: The Undeclared War Against American Women* (1991), led to some feminist scholars taking up this label to describe this new 'generation' of feminism. Jane Gerhard notes that 'the question was no longer "are you a cultural or radical feminist?" but "is feminism dead or alive?" Were we going through a backlash against feminism, a markedly new third wave of feminism, or a moment of postfeminism?' (40) There are admittedly differences in the use of (post)feminism.[11] While third wave feminists have been keen to distance themselves from (post)feminism, which is identified by some as referring to the conservative or power feminism of Camille Paglia and Rene Denfeld, Katie Roiphe and Naomi Wolf, other feminist scholars have questioned the distinction between third wave feminism and (post)feminism: 'in spite of the insistence on the absolute difference between these two terms, definitions of and assumptions about both third-wave and post-feminism often overlap in a variety of ways, highlighting a number of similarities and continuities' (Braithwaite 337). The conflation between these two terms is something which third wave feminists are keen to resist, despite the similarities.

Heywood and Drake, for example, open their discussion of third wave feminism by identifying how the third wave is most definitely not (post)feminist: '[i]n the perpetual battle of representation and definitional clout, the slippage from "third wave feminism" to "postfeminism" is important, because many of us working in the "third wave" by no means define our feminism as a groovier alternative to an over-and-done with feminist movement' (1). While Heywood and Drake are adamant that it differs from (post)feminism, the version of third wave feminism proposed in their collection does, at times, veer towards a 'groovier' or at least 'more in touch' alternative to second wave feminism. Ann Braithwaite points out that many third wave feminists – including Heywood and Drake, Baumgardner and Richards, and Walker – share some of the perceptions about the rigidity of second wave feminism which they often ascribe to (post)feminism. Moreover, the emphasis on the personal (and, crucially, the pleasurable) which is articulated in the language of choice which informs third wave feminism also veers closely towards (post)feminism. To cite Braithwaite again: '[t]his insistence on examining one's personal life, on exploring its many contradictions, desires, and pleasures and fun marks one especially salient example of the overlaps and similiarities between third-wave and post-feminism' (339). While she goes on to argue that (post)feminism 'can and does elicit a number of other signifieds besides the end of feminism' (340), we must be careful that we do not succumb to the power of the prefix: 'post-' before feminism impacts on a completely different political realm than, for example, before the terms 'modernism' or 'structuralism'.

In addition to the confusion between (post)feminism and third wave feminism, this new generation of feminism has also been witness to an antagonism by those on the streets to the intellectualising, rather than activising, of feminist discourse (not that the two are necessarily different).[12] Jennifer Purvis seeks to move beyond this impasse, hoping that we can 'approach the generational, or a third-wave political movement, as a theoretical space which incites both awareness and revolt. ... The creation and maintenance of this intergenerational space, or a community as pastiches ... combines all the wisdom and strategies of feminism to date and acts as a moment of rupture and conveyance' (119). However, the activist/theorist divide remains strong. The third wave feminism that emerged in the U.S. from the Third Wave Foundation and its attempts to get young women voting has been repeatedly foregrounded as an example of the work which third wave feminism does in reaching out to the community. Indeed, positioning the activist-feminist as the 'real' feminist has been a keynote of some third wave feminist arguments. The emphasis on activism has been a key component of Baumgardner and Richards's version of third wave feminism, from the appendix in *Manifesta* to their more recent *Grassroots: A Field Guide to Feminist Activism* (2005). They ask 'why don't we have a totally activist, voting, engaged citizenry? Why do so many issues remain unresolved? Why do shelters have to turn away homeless people and why don't more women hold political office? Where is the discontent between these would-be revolutionaries and the pressing issues?' (2005, 13). While the equation of third wave feminism with a neo-liberalist activism has rendered problematic some of the possibilities for feminist political action, Baumgardner and Richards do provide examples of how small-scale action can lead to large-scale change. That said, both *Manifesta* and *Grassroots* largely rely upon a personal, confessional model, with various individuals piping up to reveal their frustration with a specific situation and how they resolved it.[13] Similar accounts are provided in Vivien Labaton and Dawn Lundy Martin's *The Fire This Time: Young Activists and the New Feminism* (2004). These resonate a little too closely with the confessional modes of some of third wave feminist writings such as Marcelle Karp and Debbie Stoller's *The BUST Guide to the New Girl Order* (1999) and Merri Lisa Johnson's *Jane Sexes it Up: True Confessions of Feminist Desire* (2002). Moreover, the emphasis on individual effort over group activism verges dangerously close to the solipsism of (post)feminism.

The essays collected here explore the possibilities, as well as the limitations, of both third wave feminism and the wave metaphor. The historical narrative, underlying the generational account of stages within feminist theory and practice, overly simplifies the range of debates and arguments preceding the stipulated 'era', and appears to be enmeshed in a sororal anxiety relating to inheritance. Treating third wave feminism as an object of enquiry, rather than an established 'fact', the essays in this collection cross this schism, interrogating what it means to be a feminist today, regardless of age, gender, sexual orientation, race and/or ethnicity. This does not mean that the collection subverts the dominance of Anglo-American feminist models but it does gesture towards the situated nature of feminist theory. Heywood and Drake, amongst others, have pointed up how 'U.S. third world feminism changed the second wave of the women's movement for good' (9). Third wave feminist texts have, to date, been quick to point out the whiteness of this academic feminism but have not yet fully articulated possibilities for global feminisms. Our intention is to interrogate the wave metaphor, whilst ensuring that the voices, ideas and arguments of self-termed third wavers are heard. Drawing lines and charting territories is a perilous task; the boundaries drawn between the range of essays in a collection like this will always, to some extent, be provisional.

Although the essays in this revised edition are organised into three parts which reflect areas of key concern for contemporary feminist theory *and* practice, they speak to one another within and across section headings – a dialogue which is carried into the two closing interviews with Luce Irigaray and Elaine Showalter. We begin with Generations and Genealogies, one of the dominant themes of third wave feminist theorising. Exploring feminist (dis)continuities and communities, the essays in this section interrogate the generational model of the waves as a characterisation of the material conditions of feminist history, and pose this in relation to possible futures and ways of thinking about the feminist 'body'. These debates are furthered in Part II, entitled Locales and Locations. Grounding their discussion of third wave feminism within the material conditions of the global economy, these essays both explore and challenge the third wave's Anglo-American hegemony and examine the ways in which conceptualisations of space and place have been and continue to be vital to feminist knowledge production and circulation. Part III, Politics and Popular Culture, deals with one of the most contentious areas of third wave feminist debate. Cultural production has been identified as a key site of analysis and activity for third wave feminism, but to what extent do the versions of feminist agency it claims – from Buffy the Vampire Slayer to pornographic confession – trouble its progressive projections? or do they submit to the seduction of the (post)feminist model?

Despite the tensions identified here, we have been encouraged by the multiplicity and variability of the contemporary feminisms emerging from those working in feminist theory and history. Although the generational paradigm limits the transgressive potential of the wave metaphor, the metaphor can transcend these limits. But what is still not clear is whether the term 'third wave feminism' helps this project. Feminism – as many of the essays here argue – needs to be multiple, be various, be polyphonous and we must encourage this. As Misha Kavka notes, '[f]eminism is not ... the object of a singular history but, rather, a term under which people have in different times and places invested in a more general struggle for social justice and in so doing have participated in and produced multiple histories' (xii). The wave metaphor thus invites the questions: how can we articulate mythical time with historical or linear time? How do we articulate multiple histories with economic history? How do we understand social groups as differentiated with the recognition of the (universal) values of affinity and friendship? Mythic time, as suggested by the wave metaphor, may be the key with which to unlock pathways through feminism and between feminists and to help us to negotiate the drive for knowledge of the past, with the constraints imposed by the past, and with the knowledge of the present that is yielded by the past. The generational impulse is the anxious displacement that blocks our appreciation of the past in the light of the new. We need to fight for feminism, and with it, and through it, and by it – but to do so we must learn to speak and hear one another across the generations.

This book does not seek to provide a uniform theory of feminism – this would go against what feminism is – but seeks to provide ways of thinking about contemporary feminism that move beyond the personal and the confessional, which so often marks contemporary feminist work, both popular and academic. Third wave feminism has been witness to increasing tensions over its 'ownership': 'new' feminism *must* belong to new (for which read: 'young') feminists. Anger between those who regard themselves as excluded and included has – for *too* long – inf(l)ected feminist histories. The essays in this collection consider the ways in which a generational and linear account of social and intellectual history has been woven into the wave metaphor, as adopted by third wave feminists. They also indicate how the generational impulse might lead to a model of conflict, resistance and closure being imposed on a rich and diverse intellectual and cultural terrain. Feminisms should not withdraw behind lines of engagement: we must remember that the activist/academic schism and generational model enables only backlash politics.[14] This collection speaks to second wave feminists, self-identified third wavers as well as those, like ourselves, who are excluded by both of these categories to engage with the notion of a third wave.[15] 'What is feminism? Who is a feminist? Contention rather than accord is what we must explore in answering such questions today' (Segal 4). This collection is not asking so much what *is* the third wave; rather, through an exploration of the versions of the third wave that are circulating in Anglo-American feminist discourses, it is asking how and whether another wave contributes to the future of feminism. Bearing in mind Judith Butler's reminder that laughter, in the face of serious categories, is indispensable for feminism (viii), we indicate a crossroads where the past and present meet in order to mark out trajectories for future feminist praxis.

Notes

1. The third wave has been left out of recent histories of feminism, an indication that it has not yet been received into the canon of feminist history. For example, the only mention of the third wave in Estelle B. Freedman's history of feminism is to the Third Wave Foundation in relation to its voter registration campaign among young women (339). Others have criticised third wave feminism's lack of historical knowledge in terms of continuity with previous waves (Bailey 1997; Orr). Criticising third wave feminism has also become a commonplace among some feminist scholars – see Natalie Fixmer and Julia T. Wood for more on this.
2. See Rosalind Delmar for a clear and concise introduction to the question of 'What is Feminism?'
3. Kristeva's model of the three generations does not map directly onto feminist history. It also articulates the possibility of the '*parallel* existence of all three in the same historical time, or even that they be interwoven one with the other' (209; emphasis in original).
4. Similarly, even those feminists who, like Amber E. Kinser, situate themselves 'between the waves' (125) tend to deploy the wave metaphor as a structuring principle of feminist genealogies.
5. See also Chela Sandoval (4). For another mapping of references to a 'third wave' see Catherine M. Orr and for an account of third wave feminist history see Leslie Heywood (2005).
6. While celebrating the poetic and political value of the wave as a feminist metaphor, Cathryn Bailey nonetheless delineates its problematic appropriation by a new generation of feminists. According to Bailey, while the 'second wave is so named primarily as a means of emphasizing continuity with earlier feminist activities and ideas', the third wave very often deploys the metaphor as a 'means of distancing itself from earlier feminism, as a means of stressing what are perceived as discontinuities with earlier feminist thought and activity' (1997, 17–18).
7. Speaking of third wave feminism, Henry argues that '[w]ithin this "ideology of individualism" feminism has frequently been reduced to one issue: choice' (44). For more on individualism, choice and the conflation of the personal and the political see Munford (2008).
8. For more on this see Bailey (2002).
9. This is rendered problematic by the way in which third wave feminists decry viciously those who critique the movement. Purvis is one of the few to

defend third wave feminism – many see the possibilities but are concerned about the defensive tone of many third wave feminist publications: '[t]o avoid weak feminism, third wavers must come to see dialogue about clarifying the vicissitudes and authenticity of feminism as inviting rather than threatening' (Kinser 146).

10. See Camille Nurka and Mary Hawkesworth for more on the use of autopsy, death and the body in descriptions of contemporary feminism and post-feminism.

11. For more on this see Gillis and Munford (2007).

12. This has been exacerbated by the closure of numerous Women's Studies and Gender Studies programmes on both sides of the Atlantic. As a result, feminist work has had to adapt to the intellectual compartmentalisation promulgated by the modern university. Feminism now 'belongs', in one way or another, to various disciplines – including Philosophy, English, Sociology, Cultural Studies, History and Communications – but, despite the lip-service paid to interdisciplinarity by universities, often these disciplines do not speak to one another.

13. In her review of *Manifesta*, Michele Jensen notes that her students were frustrated by the overwhelmingly personal tone of the writings they were reading on her course on contemporary feminism; they were 'longing for a militant, argumentative feminism – one that would abandon the personal essay with its fetishization of contradiction and get on with elaborating a political program' (par. 2).

14. See Gillis and Munford (2004) for more on the relationship between backlash politics and third wave feminism.

15. This uses the same model as Rebecca Walker's collection *To be Real*, with its foreword by Gloria Steinem and afterword by Angela Y. Davis. However, Walker's collection repudiates the supposed inflexibility of second wave feminist discourses: 'For many of us it seems that to be a feminist in the way that we have seen or understood feminism is to conform to an identity and way of living that doesn't allow for individuality, complexity, or less than perfect personal histories' (xxxiii).

Works cited

Bailey, Cathryn. 'Making Waves and Drawing Lines: The Politics of Defining the Vicissitudes of Feminism.' *Third Wave Feminisms*. Ed. Jacquelyn N. Zita. Spec. issue of *Hypatia: A Journal of Feminist Philosophy* 12.3 (1997): 17–28.

——. 'Unpacking the Mother/Daughter Baggage: Reassessing Second- and Third-Wave Tensions.' *Women's Studies Quarterly* 30.3–4 (2002): 138–54.

Baumgardner, Jennifer, and Amy Richards. *Manifesta: Young Women, Feminism, and the Future.* New York: Farrar, Straus and Giroux, 2000.

——. *Grassroots: A Field Guide for Feminist Activism.* New York: Farrar, Straus and Giroux, 2005.

Bolotin, Susan. 'Voices from the Post-Feminist Generation.' *New York Times Magazine* (17 Oct. 1982): 29–31; 103–16.

Braithwaite, Ann. 'The Personal, the Political, Third-wave and Postfeminisms.' *Feminist Theory* 3.3 (2002): 335–44.

Butler, Judith. *Gender Trouble: Feminism and the Subversion of Identity.* London: Routledge, 1990.

Delmar, Rosalind. 'What is Feminism?' *Theorizing Feminism: Parallel Trends in the Humanities and Social Sciences.* Ed. Ann Herrmann and Abigail Stewart. Boulder: Westview, 1994. 5–25.

Dicker, Rory, and Alison Piepmeier. Introduction. *Catching a Wave: Reclaiming Feminism for the 21st Century.* Boston: Northeastern University Press, 2003. 3–28.

Faludi, Susan. *Backlash: The Undeclared War Against American Women.* New York: Anchor, 1991.

Findlen, Barbara, ed. *Listen Up: Voices From the Next Feminist Generation.* Seattle: Seal, 1995.

Fixmer, Natalie, and Julia T. Wood. 'The Personal is *Still* Political: Embodied Politics in Third Wave Feminism.' *Women's Studies in Communication* 28.2 (2005): 235–57.

Freedman, Estelle B. *No Turning Back: The History of Feminism and the Future of Women.* New York: Ballantine Books, 2002.

Garrison, Ednie Kaeh. 'Are We On a Wavelength Yet? On Feminist Oceanography, Radios, and Third Wave Feminism.' *Different Wavelengths: Studies of the Contemporary Women's Movement.* Ed. Jo Reger. New York: Routledge, 2005. 237–56.

Gerhard, Jane. '*Sex and the City:* Carrie Bradshaw's Queer Postfeminism.' *Feminist Media Studies* 5.1 (2005): 37–49.

Gillis, Stacy, and Rebecca Munford. 'Generations and Genealogies: The Politics and Praxis of Third Wave Feminism.' *Women's History Review* 13.2 (2004): 165–82.

——. *Feminism and Popular Culture: Explorations in Post-Feminism.* London: I.B. Tauris, 2007.

Hawkesworth, Mary. 'The Semiotics of Premature Burial: Feminism in a Postfeminist Age.' *Signs* 29.4 (2004): 961–85.

Henry, Astrid. *Not My Mother's Sister: Generational Conflict and Third-Wave Feminism.* Bloomington: Indiana University Press, 2004.

Hernández, Daisy, and Bushra Rehman, eds. *Colonize This! Young Women of Color on Today's Feminism.* New York: Seal, 2002.

Heywood, Leslie L. 'Introduction: A Fifteen-Year History of Third-Wave Feminism.' *The Women's Movement Today: An Encyclopedia of Third-Wave Feminism.* Vol. 1. Ed. Leslie L. Heywood. Westport: Greenwood, 2005. xv–xxii.

Heywood, Leslie, and Jennifer Drake. Introduction. *Third Wave Agenda: Being Feminist, Doing Feminism.* Minneapolis: Minnesota University Press, 1997. 1–20.

Hogeland, Lisa Maria. 'Against Generational Thinking, or, Some Things that "Third Wave" Feminism Isn't.' *Women's Studies in Communication* 24 (2001): 107–21.

Jensen, Michele. 'Riding the Third Wave.' *The Nation.* 11 Dec. 2000. Accessed: 1 Sept. 2006. <http://www.thenation.com/doc/20001211/jensen>.

Johnson, Merri Lisa. *Jane Sexes it Up: True Confessions of Feminist Desire.* New York: Thunder's Mouth Press, 2002.

Karp, Marcelle, and Debbie Stoller. *The BUST Guide to the New Girl Order.* London: Penguin, 1999.

Kavka, Misha. Introduction. *Feminist Consequences: Theory for the New Century*. Ed. Elisabeth Bronfen and Misha Kavka. New York: Columbia University Press, 2001. ix–xxvi.

Kinser, Amber E. 'Negotiating Spaces For/Through Third-Wave Feminism.' *NWSA Journal* 16.3 (2004): 124–53.

Kristeva, Julia. 'Women's Time.' 1979. Trans. Alice Jardine and Harry Blake. *The Kristeva Reader*. Ed. Toril Moi. Oxford: Basil Blackwell, 1986. 187–213.

Labaton, Vivien, and Dawn Lundy Martin, eds. *The Fire This Time: Young Activists and the New Feminism*. New York: Anchor, 2004.

Lotz, Amanda D. 'Postfeminist Television Criticism: Rehabilitating Critical Terms and Identifying Postfeminist Attitudes.' *Feminist Media Studies* 1.1 (2001): 105–21.

Munford, Rebecca. '*BUST*-ing the Third Wave: Barbies, Blowjobs and Girlie Feminism.' *Mainstreaming Sex: The Sexualisation of Culture*. Ed. Feona Attwood, Rosalind Brunt and Rinella Cere. London: I.B. Tauris, 2008. forthcoming.

Nurka, Camille. 'Postfeminist Autopsies.' *Australian Feminist Studies* 17.38 (2002): 177–89.

Orr, Catherine M. 'Charting the Currents of the Third Wave.' *Third Wave Feminisms*. Ed. Jacquelyn N. Zita. Spec. issue of *Hypatia: A Journal of Feminist Philosophy* 12.3 (1997): 29–45.

Purvis, Jennifer. 'Grrrls and Women Together in the Third Wave: Embracing the Challenges of International Feminism(s).' *NWSA Journal* 16.3 (2004): 93–123.

Reger, Jo. Introduction. *Different Wavelengths: Studies of the Contemporary Women's Movement*. Ed. Jo Reger. New York: Routledge, 2005. xv–xxx.

Sandoval, Chela. 'U.S. Third World Feminism: The Theory and Method of Oppositional Consciousness in the Postmodern World.' *Genders* 10 (1991): 1–24.

Segal, Lynne. *Why Feminism? Gender, Psychology, Politics*. Cambridge: Polity, 1999.

Siegel, Deborah L. 'Reading between the Waves: Feminist Historiography in a "Postfeminist" Moment.' *Third Wave Agenda: Being Feminist, Doing Feminism*. Ed. Leslie Heywood and Jennifer Drake. Minneapolis: Minnesota University Press, 1997. 55–82.

Springer, Kimberly. 'Third Wave Black Feminism?' *Signs: Journal of Women in Culture and Society* 27.4 (2002): 1059–82.

Walker, Rebecca. 'Becoming the Third Wave.' *Ms.* 39 (Jan.–Feb. 1992): 39–41.

——. 'Being Real: An Introduction.' *To Be Real: Telling the Truth and Changing the Face of Feminism*. Ed. Rebecca Walker. New York: Anchor, 1995. xxix–xl.

Zack, Naomi. *Inclusive Feminism: A Third Wave Theory of Women's Commonality*. Lanham: Rowman & Littlefield, 2005.

Zita, Jacqueline N. 'Third Wave Feminism: An Introduction.' *Third Wave Feminisms*. Spec. issue of *Hypatia: A Journal of Feminist Philosophy* 12:3 (1997): 1–6.

——, ed. *Third Wave Feminisms*. Spec. issue of *Hypatia: A Journal of Feminist Philosophy* 12:3 (1997).

Part I
Generations and Genealogies

1

'Feminists Love a Utopia'
Collaboration, Conflict and the Futures of Feminism

Lise Shapiro Sanders

Feminists love a utopia . . . .[u]topias offer hope and fuel the imagination. They present near-perfect feminist worlds and new social contracts based on 'feminine' qualities and achievements. They promise to transform human nature itself through feminist social revolution.

(Kitch 1)

* * *

What is the historical relationship between feminism and utopia? And what relevance does utopia have for feminism today? Despite the pragmatism that has consistently been associated with feminist efforts, the discourse of utopia has deeply informed feminism. In her critique of the place of utopia in American feminist theory, Sally Kitch contends that utopianism – as a thought process and a strategy for envisioning social change – cannot 'accommodate the complexities of feminist concerns – gender difference, differences among women, or the intersection of sex, race, and class with various social domains' (2–3). In her view, 1970s slogans like 'Sisterhood is Global!' and 'Let a Woman Do It!' signal the essentialist, binary and idealising aspects of feminism's past. To advance her argument for a move beyond utopia, Kitch distinguishes between utopianism, which rejects the past in favour of a vision of future perfection, and realism, which in its pragmatic self-reflexivity emphasises the value of contingency and change. This distinction leads her to conclude that '[i]f utopianism maps uncharted territory, then realism functions mostly in the known, pluralistic, confusing, and inevitably imperfect world. It is immersed in history' (9).

3

Although this distinction is an intriguing one, Kitch may be too quick to discard utopianism as a model for feminist thinking, as a way of envisioning alternatives to an oppressive present and as a mode through which ideals may be envisioned. I concur with her suspicion of utopianism as structured through the desire for a static and codified ideal that, through a metonymic fallacy, takes the experiences and desires of a part for those of the whole – in which, as she puts it, 'some women become all women' (5). Yet, on occasion, Kitch herself takes the part for the whole in her analysis, taking *some* utopian visions for *all* utopianism. For Kitch, realism presents an alternative to the dangers of utopian thinking; for me, utopian thinking has value, but only as long as it remains open to the very things feminism must acknowledge and embrace: in Kitch's words, 'contingent truths, inevitable conflicts, and complex motivations and loyalties ... the serendipity and vagaries of human life, identity, relationships, and institutions' (12).

Despite – or perhaps because of – their connotation of ideal or perfect worlds, utopias have long been recognised as suspect for their 'prescriptive rigidity' (Wilson 258) and for their desire to 'freeze time', to 'produce the future on the model of the (limited and usually self-serving) ideals of the present' (Grosz 270). Moreover, the very meaning of the word utopia coined by Thomas More in 1516 – from the Greek *ou* meaning not or *eu* meaning happy, and *topos* meaning place – suggests an impossibility in the term itself: utopia may be the good place or the impossible place; the good place may be no place, or no place may in fact be the good place. Utopia may be beyond place altogether.[1] This may be the only possibility for imagining utopia's relevance to – and promise for – feminism: utopia is only viable if it is left permanently open, contested, in contradiction with itself, if it is never put into practice as a static, cod-ified entity, but remains a shifting landscape of possibility. Utopia's potential lies in its transformative nature, but this transformative quality must be brought to bear on the very meaning of the term for it to be significant in the future.

The desires and frustrations associated with utopia are particularly relevant for feminism today, often viewed as troubled by differences that divide rather than unite its constituencies. Feminism's transformation – from a political struggle emphasising women's shared oppression to an anti-essentialist discourse focusing on the construction of female identity and on the material and cultural differences among women – has resulted in a range of new and often splintering perspectives on what feminism means in the present, even in a rejection of the designation altogether – hence the contentious term postfeminism. Postfeminism should not be confused with third wave feminism, as Leslie Heywood and Jennifer Drake remind us in the introduction to *Third Wave Agenda* (1997): 'many of us working in the "third wave" by no means define our feminism as a groovier alternative to an over-and-done feminist movement. Let us be clear: "postfeminist" characterizes a group of young, conservative feminists who explicitly define themselves against and criticize feminists of the second wave' (1). These 'young' feminists include Katie Roiphe, who wrote *The Morning After: Sex, Fear and Feminism on Campus* (1993) ostensibly to present her encounter with 'victim feminism' at Harvard, and Rene Denfeld, whose *The New Victorians: A Young Woman's Challenge to the Old Feminist Order* (1996) is regarded as a sort of sequel to Roiphe's account. Naomi Wolf's work, particularly *Fire With Fire: The New Female Power and How to Use It* (1994) has been labelled postfeminist by some, including Heywood and Drake and Deborah Siegel; however, her explicit effort to claim and reinterpret feminism beginning with the publication of *The Beauty Myth* (1990) suggests that she holds a more complicated position in contemporary feminism than the label postfeminist implies. Finally, postfeminism should not be solely associated with the writings of younger feminists; in recent years Camille Paglia, Christina Hoff Sommers and Sylvia Ann Hewlett have all been criticised for their postfeminist leanings, even as they purport to advance feminism's goals. Hence the concept of the 'post' in postfeminism must be read not (or not merely) through the logic of generational difference but through the political and social implications of the claims made in these texts, as well as the ways in which they have circulated in the media and the popular imagination.[2]

Third wave feminists, by contrast, see their work as founded on second wave principles, yet distinguished by certain cultural and political differences. The editors and contributors to *Third Wave Agenda* see feminism's second and third waves as 'neither incompatible nor opposed', defining the third wave as 'a movement that contains elements of second wave critique of beauty culture, sexual abuse, and power structures while it also acknowledges and makes use of the pleasure, danger, and defining power of those structures' (Heywood and Drake 3). However, the third wave is not only concerned with cultural and sexual politics, but also with political and social issues, ranging from ongoing wage discrimination, access to education and domestic violence, to eating disorders, globalisation and the effects of racism and classism on the movement – all historically feminist concerns. Third wave feminism, like its predecessors, therefore resists a single definition, as Misha Kavka has noted. In the introduction to *Feminist Consequences*, she observes that

> the problem is not the death or the end of feminism, but, rather, coming to terms with the fact that political, strategic and interpretive power has been so great as to produce innumerable modes of doing – whether activist, practical, theoretical, or just 'quiet' – that have moved well beyond the mother term, already fractured at its origin. (xi)

Even this usage of the maternal metaphor, or as Rebecca Dakin Quinn phrases it, the 'matrophor', is indicative of the simultaneity of feminist efforts to establish connections among women and the resistance to generational logics fraught with hierarchy (179).

This chapter addresses the question of generational and other differences in feminism through recourse to the work of self-identified second and third wave feminists, as well as those uncomfortable with the very notion of waves, generations and other conceptualisations of feminism's history and progression. These reflections take the form of a series of juxtapositions, highlighting contrasts and contradictions, in an effort to explore the possibilities a newly expanded conception of utopia might hold for the future of feminist theory and – and in – practice. In short, I want to question the wholesale rejection of utopianism as a possibility for the future of third wave feminist vision. In contrast to Kitch, I contend that feminisms in general, and the third wave in particular, need the imaginative potential of utopian thinking to counter the anxiety of historical insignificance (particularly in regard to the generational logic that frames third wave feminism purely in reaction to the second wave) and the frustrations of postfeminism (which shuts down ongoing efforts to work towards change on the level of both theory and practice). What animates feminism *is* the productive potential of utopic vision, even when some accounts of feminism disavow this connection; and the definition of utopia may be productively expanded and enriched through its association with feminism's multiple futures.

*   *   *

The characterisation of feminism as occurring in generations or 'waves' has been well documented in recent scholarship in a number of anthologies that strove to articulate the connections and distinctions between 'second' and 'third' wave feminism. The first proposed collection to draw on the term 'third wave' for its title – M. Jacqui Alexander, Lisa Albrecht and Mab Segrest's *The Third Wave: Feminist Perspectives on Racism*[3] – articulated one of the defining features of the third wave in its analysis of the critique by women of colour and third world women of the white, middle-class biases of the second wave. Publications like Barbara Findlen's *Listen Up: Voices from the Next Feminist Generation* (1995) and Rebecca Walker's *To Be Real: Telling the Truth and Changing the Face of Feminism* (1995), the latter containing contributions by such second wave icons as Gloria Steinem and Angela Davis, used autobiographical and personal narratives to provide a perspective on the lives and experiences of feminists of the 'next' generation (sometimes merged in the popular imagination with 'Generation X'). Heywood and Drake's *Third Wave Agenda* aimed to present a more critical perspective on feminism in the late 1990s, one informed by cultural theory and interdisciplinary academic scholarship, but nevertheless with a personal or autobiographical component. This anthology also strove to present 'the voices of young activists struggling to come to terms with the historical specificity of [their] feminisms' (Heywood and Drake 2), defined generationally and through the hybridity and contradiction they viewed as constitutive of the third wave. 'Even as different strains of feminism and activism sometimes directly contradict each other, they are all part of our third wave lives, our thinking, and our praxes: we are products of all the contradictory definitions of and differences within feminism, beasts of such a hybrid that perhaps we need a different name altogether' (Heywood and Drake 3). This sense of a feminism that is constructed by – indeed, animated *through* – contradiction and difference is fundamental to many conceptions of third wave and contemporary feminisms. None of these writers and activists imagine feminism as a monolithic, universalised entity – another legacy of the gains wrought by the transformations of the second wave. Drawing upon the critiques of universalism and essentialism from within and outside the movement, third wave feminists have come to emphasise the diversity of women's experience over the similarities amongst women, often to such a degree that feminism's present and future can seem irretrievably fractured.

The foundational third wave anthologies of the 1990s were followed by Jennifer Baumgardner and Amy Richards's *Manifesta* (2000), written as a response to the perception that feminism had little to no significance for women under thirty-five. In essays on Barbie, the girls' movement, Katie Roiphe and the other 'backlash babes', and accounts of activism throughout feminism's history, Baumgardner and Richards highlighted the tensions between younger women who 'never knew a time before "girls can do anything boys can! " ' and older women who may feel their accomplishments have gone unrecognised (17). As the authors note, the efforts of younger women to 'rebel against their mothers' can result in self-imposed blinders to the ways that feminists of all ages can learn from one another. Instead, they suggest the need to recognise feminism's history: 'Pragmatically, recounting the stories of feminism shows older women that the next generation is aware of their struggles, and shows younger women that their rebellion has a precedent. Having our history might keep feminists from having to reinvent the wheel every fifty years or so' (Baumgardner and Richards 68). *Manifesta* also includes a response to Phyllis Chesler's *Letters to a Young Feminist* (1997), which was perceived by many young feminists as condescending, self-aggrandising and poorly informed; Baumgardner and Richards' 'Letter to an Older Feminist' replies, 'You're not our mothers ... stop treating us like daughters' (233). The questioning of the meanings of the term generation, with its implication of a matriarchal lineage and its associations with the concept of inheritance and the logic of reproduction, characterises *Manifesta*'s effort to carve out a space and identity for third wave feminism that is neither a reaction to the second wave nor a rejection of feminism's past – rather a positive articulation of feminism's future.

Baumgardner and Richards's resistance to being treated as 'daughters' echoes the concerns of other feminists of varying ages. As Gina Dent observes in her contribution to *To Be Real*,

> the fact that everyday feminism doesn't always look like the [capital F] Feminism that appears in books anymore is partly a function of the generational shift that has led to the description of the feminist movement in waves. This generational language hides other differences within it – national trajectories, sexual orientation, professional status [and a myriad of others]. (70)

To speak solely of feminism in waves, in other words, results in another form of universalising tendency, and polarises its practitioners by demanding that they identify with the members of 'their' generation. Judith Roof puts this another way:

> adopting a generational metaphor means espousing more than a convenient way of organizing the relations among women of different ages, experience, class position, and accomplishment. It means privileging a kind of family history that organizes generations where

they don't exist, ignores intragenerational differences and intergenerational commonalities, and thrives on a paradigm of oppositional change. (72)

The polarisation of feminism has a positive as well as a negative side, however, for the introduction and negotiation of conflict can energise a movement and open up new epistemological possibilities. In response to concerns like Roof's, Devoney Looser observes that '[t]oday's generational conflicts seem to me to be about what exactly the reproduction of feminist knowledge (and the reproduction of feminists) will look like. ... How many of us adhere to a naïve expectation of linear history? Do we expect that feminism must have "a" history?' (Looser and Kaplan 5). Looser's implication that feminism does not have a singular, linear past or a unified identity suggests the importance of viewing feminism through multiple lenses and the need to question the desire for commonality that has shaped so much of feminism's history.

Yet for an 'older feminist' like Steinem, the sensitivity of Baumgardner and Richards's *Manifesta* to the significance of history, whether one or many, may not be characteristic of the movement as a whole. Despite her respect and admiration for many of the essays included in Walker's *To Be Real*, Steinem noted in her foreword that

I confess that there are moments in these pages when I – and perhaps other readers over thirty-five – feel like a sitting dog being told to sit. Imagine how frustrating it is to be held responsible for some of the very divisions you've been fighting against, and you'll know how feminists of the 1980s and earlier may feel as they read some of these pages. (xxiii)

Steinem's frustration suggests the impasse that could ensue if generations of feminists were to neglect opportunities to learn from one another's experiences, failures as well as successes. As Baumgardner and Richards note, this impasse may result from a lack of consciousness on the part of some younger women:

The chasm between [the younger generation's] belief in basic feminism (equality) and its feminist consciousness (knowledge of what one is doing and why one is doing it) explains why, according to a 1998 Time/CNN poll, more than 50 percent of women between eighteen and thirty-four say they are simpatico with feminist values but do not necessarily call themselves feminists. Lack of consciousness is one reason that the movement is stalled. (83)

For Baumgardner and Richards as well as for Steinem, then, young women need not only to recognise the history of feminism and to acknowledge the gains of the past, but also to articulate a more conscious and explicit relationship to feminism's present and future. Other writers grappling with the relationship between feminists of different generations locate the impasse in an inability on the part of some older women to 'listen' to and engage with the contributions of younger, 'junior' or less established feminists. This is made evident in several essays in Devoney Looser and E. Ann Kaplan's collection *Generations: Academic Feminists in Dialogue* (1997) that recount tensions at conferences such as the CUNY Graduate School's 1994 symposium on 'Women's Studies for the Year 2000' and the Berkshire Conference on the History of Women. Yet conflict between feminists is nothing new; indeed it is often brought to the centre of conversations about the possibility of solidarity and community. Jane Gallop's dialogues with Marianne Hirsch and Nancy K. Miller in *Conflicts in Feminism* (1990) and with Elizabeth Francis in *Generations* provide some insight into the often 'painful refusal[s] of commonality' that arise within feminism (Gallop and Francis 126). For Gallop, founded in the desire for community and unity against common enemies, 'feminism produces the expectation that it should be different, and so when it isn't different it's much more painful ... feminism makes all of these things that weren't supposed to be seem much worse, more like betrayal' (ibid. 129); whereas for Francis, community has always been suspect: as she observes, '[f]eminism always had this individualistic impulse, so it wasn't just about community ... community was always an impossibility' (ibid. 130). In this context, then, rifts between generations of feminists can signal the challenges of envisioning community as either a conceptual model or a practical organising principle for feminist action. When feminism confronts its own failure to provide common ground in the present, it also confronts a long history of tensions between individual and collective visions for the future.

Indeed, the debate over community can be usefully set alongside the debate over utopia as I have articulated it here. Just as utopia can only be productive for feminism if it resists the impulse towards stasis, so community can only operate successfully if it resists the tendency towards universalism. For Iris Marion Young, notes Judith Newton 'the word *community* itself is problematic in that it "relies on the same desire for social wholeness and identification that underlies racism and ethnic chauvinism on the one hand and political sectarianism on the other" ' (340; emphasis in original). The resistance to community's universalising tendencies results in a move towards coalitional alliances such as those expressed in Nancie Caraway's call for 'multicultural coalitions without domination in which persons live together in relations of mediation among feminists with whom they are not in sisterhood but in solidarity' (201). To this more 'realist' vision Newton, 'a woman of a certain age and a veteran of the sixties', responds: 'I myself might prefer what Sheila Rowbotham once called greater "cosiness" than this, something involving communal dining, socialist volleyball, a sense of humor, wine at twilight, and comforting food' (341). But generational differences are not the only ones distinguishing different visions of solidarity, coalition and alliance for the women whose work is cited here, and indeed it is striking that both Newton and the editors of *Third Wave Agenda* find themselves drawn to yet another formulation of community, that presented by bell hooks as a 'yearning' for an end to domination: 'Rather than thinking we would come together as "women" in an identity-based bonding we might be drawn together rather by a *commonality of feeling*' (217; emphasis in original). The emphasis on feeling instead of identity works to enable such alliances but not to ignore the presence of power and hierarchy in the historic relations among women; it strives to make a place for the articulation of conflict without fraying the various strands of the feminist movement altogether.

hooks's expression of unity in the effort to work for social justice meets up with Caraway's vision of solidarity to destabilise the opposition between realist and utopian approaches to feminist practice. The collaborative tactics involved in these formulations, and in projects ranging from many of the co-edited volumes described here to the pedagogical work that goes on daily in the feminist classroom, help us to conceive of a new approach to the place of utopia in contemporary feminism. And indeed the question of utopia's relevance for feminist pedagogy is another place where my argument both intersects with and departs from Kitch's critique. Kitch argues that

> feminist pedagogy has been especially susceptible to utopian thinking. When students demand a classroom that is a 'safe space' for women, for example, they imply a utopian desire for learning to occur without offense. But can it? If a 'safe space' promotes misinformation or unexamined conclusions, even in the name of protecting feelings, then it interferes with learning and perpetuates ignorance. (102)

Certainly any pedagogical environment that does not both allow and encourage students to critically examine their own and other's assumptions does a disservice to all its members.

But what Kitch's discussion of feminist pedagogy makes clear is that she envisions utopia as a conflict-free zone – something that may be historically supported in actually existing utopic communities and movements of the past and present, but that need not necessarily be the case. Elsewhere she observes,

> [i]ndeed, feminism's varied and contentious history may help explain the attraction of utopianism, which seems to offer harmony among the myriad positions that have characterized feminist thought and theory over the years. But is harmony the highest goal? Doesn't the quest for harmony itself indicate a utopian mind-set in its automatic distrust of conflict, dialectic and debate? How do we know that feminism is better off with a unified rather than a cacophonous voice? How do we know that internal dissension is not feminism's greatest strength? (107)

This notion of utopianism as 'harmony' echoes the desire for feminist community expressed by Gallop and Newton, yet is not identical to the concepts of solidarity, coalitional alliance and commonality of feeling described above. Each of these concepts allows for the establishment of connections to facilitate political and social change, yet emphasises the importance of difference and dissension. In drawing these concepts together I want to underscore the importance of Kitch's call for dialectic and debate, cacophony rather than harmony, in feminist practice. An expanded conception of utopian thinking would allow for the productive expression and negotiation of conflict, and would clarify utopia's potential as a mode of envisioning social change that emphasises the transformative over the perfected vision. As this chapter has shown, the contention and conflict that inevitably arise as individuals and collectives negotiate their visions of alternatives to oppression are an integral component of feminism's future – a future that need not discard entirely its utopian past.[4]

I do not imagine that collaboration provides an idealised answer to the conflicts feminism faces today. Rather, we might envision collaboration, and the larger model of pedagogy inspired by the interrogation and refusal of masterful knowledge as advocated by Barbara Johnson in her essay 'Teaching Ignorance' (1989), as a kind of mutual education that refuses utopia's tendency to freeze potential into mastery, yet resists the desire to discard utopia altogether (72). Johnson's work on the gender politics of pedagogy strives to detach the exchange of knowledge from its association with being 'masterful' (too often aligned in the West with being male), and as Jane Moore suggests, may be useful to feminist efforts to produce other forms of knowledge (72). This would also entail following Judith Butler's call to ask ourselves – as students and teachers, rather than mothers and daughters or even 'sisters' – some exceedingly difficult questions, and to leave those questions 'open, troubling, unresolved, propitious' (432) – questions whose answers only lead to more, and more productive, questions.

Notes

1. These comments have been informed by conversations with Amy Bingaman and Rebecca Zorach, and by Elizabeth Grosz's comments on utopia's relationship to space and time; see especially Grosz 267ff.
2. For a fuller discussion of postfeminism, see Heywood and Drake, Siegel, and Baumgardner and Richards. For a critical analysis of the backlash against feminism following the second wave, see Susan Faludi.
3. Although this collection was first mentioned by Kayann Short in an article in 1994, and was scheduled for publication by Kitchen Table/Women of Color Press in 1998, the book never appeared – even if, as Ednie Kaeh Garrison highlights, 'the desire for it is such that people do speak as though it exists' (249).
4. On this point, see also Lauren Berlant, who argues against the imperative to 'learn the lessons of history' (125) and remains committed to the possibilities of utopian thinking, which she sees as productive even, or especially, in its failures. She also suggests the need to explore more fully the 'transmission of feminist knowledges and support intergenerationally' (154), a project addressed in this chapter.

Works cited

Baumgardner, Jennifer, and Amy Richards. *Manifesta: Young Women, Feminism, and the Future*. New York: Farrar, Straus and Giroux, 2000.

Berlant, Lauren. ' '68, or Something.' *Critical Inquiry* 21 (1994): 124–55.

Butler, Judith. 'The End of Sexual Difference?' *Feminist Consequences: Theory for the New Century*. Ed. Elizabeth Bronfen and Misha Kavka. New York: Columbia University Press, 2001. 414–34.

Caraway, Nancie. *Segregated Sisterhood: Racism and the Politics of American Feminism*. Knoxville: Tennessee University Press, 1991.

Chesler, Phyllis. *Letters to a Young Feminist*. New York: Four Walls Eight Windows, 1997.

Denfeld, Rene. *The New Victorians: A Young Woman's Challenge to the Old Feminist Order*. New York: Warner, 1996.

Dent, Gina. 'Missionary Position.' *To Be Real: Telling the Truth and Changing the Face of Feminism*. Ed. Rebecca Walker. New York: Anchor, 1995. 61–75.

Faludi, Susan. *Backlash: The Undeclared War Against American Women*. New York: Crown, 1991.

Findlen, Barbara, ed. *Listen Up: Voices from the Next Feminist Generation*. Seattle: Seal, 1995.

Gallop, Jane, and Elizabeth Francis. 'Talking Across.' *Generations: Academic Feminists in Dialogue*. Ed. Devoney Looser and E. Ann Kaplan. Minneapolis: Minnesota University Press, 1997. 103–31.

Gallop, Jane, Marianne Hirsch, and Nancy K. Miller. 'Criticizing Feminist Criticism.' *Conflicts in Feminism*. Ed. Marianne Hirsch and Evelyn Fox Keller. New York: Routledge, 1990. 349–69.

Garrison, Ednie Kaeh. 'Are We on a Wavelength Yet? On Feminist Oceanography, Radios, and Third Wave Feminism.' *Different Wavelengths: Studies of the Contemporary Women's Movement*. Ed. Jo Reger. New York: Routledge, 2005. 237–56.

Grosz, Elizabeth. 'The Time of Architecture.' *Embodied Utopias: Gender, Social Change and the Modern Metropolis*. Ed. Amy Bingaman, Lise Sanders and Rebecca Zorach. London: Routledge, 2002. 265–78.

Heywood, Leslie, and Jennifer Drake. Introduction. *Third Wave Agenda: Being Feminist, Doing Feminism*. Ed. Leslie Heywood and Jennifer Drake. Minneapolis: Minnesota University Press, 1997. 1–20.

hooks, bell. *Outlaw Culture: Resisting Representations*. New York: Routledge, 1994.

Johnson, Barbara. 'Teaching Ignorance.' *A World of Difference*. Baltimore: Johns Hopkins University Press, 1989. 68–85.

Kavka, Misha. Introduction. *Feminist Consequences: Theory for the New Century*. Ed. Elisabeth Bronfen and Misha Kavka. New York: Columbia University Press, 2001. ix–xxvi.

Kitch, Sally. *Higher Ground: From Utopianism to Realism in Feminist Thought and Theory*. Chicago: Chicago University Press, 2000.

Looser, Devoney, and E. Ann Kaplan. Introduction 1: An Exchange. *Generations: Academic Feminists in Dialogue*. Ed. Devoney Looser and E. Ann Kaplan. Minneapolis: Minnesota University Press, 1997. 1–12.

Moore, Jane. 'An Other Space: A Future for Feminism?' *New Feminist Discourses: Critical Essays on Theories and Texts*. Ed. Isobel Armstrong. London: Routledge, 1992. 65–79.

Newton, Judith. 'Feminist Family Values; or, Growing Old – and Growing Up – with the Women's Movement.' Ed. Devoney Looser and E. Ann Kaplan. *Generations: Academic Feminists in Dialogue*. Minneapolis: Minnesota University Press, 1997. 327–43.

Quinn, Rebecca Dakin. 'An Open Letter to Institutional Mothers.' *Generations: Academic Feminists in Dialogue*. Ed. Devoney Looser and E. Ann Kaplan. Minneapolis: Minnesota University Press, 1997. 174–82.

Roiphe, Katie. *The Morning After: Sex, Fear and Feminism on Campus*. New York: Little, Brown, 1993.

Roof, Judith. 'Generational Difficulties; or, The Fear of a Barren History.' *Generations: Academic Feminists in Dialogue*. Ed. Devoney Looser and E. Ann Kaplan. Minneapolis: Minnesota University Press, 1997. 69–87.

Short, Kayann. 'Coming to the *Table*: The Differential Politics of *This Bridge Called My Back*.' *Genders* 20 (1994): 3–44.

Siegel, Deborah L. 'Reading between the Waves: Feminist Historiography in a "Postfeminist" Moment.' *Third Wave Agenda: Being Feminist, Doing Feminism.* Ed. Leslie Heywood and Jennifer Drake. Minneapolis: Minnesota University Press, 1997. 55–82.

Steinem, Gloria. Foreword. *To Be Real: Telling the Truth and Changing the Face of Feminism.* Ed. Rebecca Walker. New York: Anchor, 1995. xiii–xxviii.

Walker, Rebecca, ed. *To Be Real: Telling the Truth and Changing the Face of Feminism.* New York: Anchor, 1995.

Wilson, Elizabeth. 'Against Utopia: The Romance of Indeterminate Spaces.' *Embodied Utopias: Gender, Social Change and the Modern Metropolis.* Ed. Amy Bingaman, Lise Sanders and Rebecca Zorach. London: Routledge, 2002. 256–62.

Wolf, Naomi. *The Beauty Myth: How Images of Beauty Are Used Against Women.* 1990. New York: William Morrow, 1991.

——. *Fire with Fire: The New Female Power and How to Use It.* 1993. New York: Fawcett, 1994.

Young, Iris Marion. 'The Ideal of Community and the Politics of Difference.' *Feminism/Postmodernism.* Ed. Linda J. Nicholson. London: Routledge, 1990. 300–23.

2
On the Genealogy of Women
A Defence of Anti-Essentialism

Alison Stone

Within feminist philosophical and theoretical contexts, third wave feminism may be defined as encompassing 'all critical work ... that points ... to the homogenizing or exclusive tendencies of earlier dominant feminisms' (Heyes 1997, 161).[1] Third wave feminists object, in particular, to exclusive tendencies within the dominant feminist theories of the 1970s and 1980s, theories that emerged more or less directly from second wave feminism as a political movement (e.g. Catherine MacKinnon's critique of pornography reflecting feminist activism around the sex industry). Subsequent feminist thinkers, writing in the later 1980s and 1990s, articulated their objections to these exclusive tendencies primarily through critiques of 'essentialism'. The central target of anti-essentialist critique was the belief – arguably widely held amongst second wave feminists – that there are shared characteristics common to all women, which unify them as a group. Anti-essentialists of the third wave repeatedly argued that such universalising claims about women are always false, and function oppressively to normalise particular – socially and culturally privileged – forms of feminine experience.[2] The widespread rejection of essentialism by feminism's third wave generated problems in turn. Ontologically, the critique of essentialism appeared to imply that women do not exist at all as a distinct social group; and, politically, this critique seemed to undercut the possibility of feminist activism, by denying women the shared identity or characteristics that might motivate them to engage in collective action. The central problem of third wave feminist theory, then, is that it risks undermining feminism both as a political practice and as a critique of existing society premised on the ontological claim that women constitute a (disadvantaged) social group.

Confronting this problem, I argue that feminists could fruitfully reconceive women as a social group of a particular type: a *genealogy*. This would allow feminists to oppose essentialism without undermining either political activity or claims about women as a definite social group. I defend a 'genealogical' conception of women in the following stages. I begin by reviewing critiques of essentialism, offering a brief account of the ontological and political worries these critiques have raised. I then assess two notable feminist responses to these worries: strategic essentialism and Iris Marion Young's idea that women form a series. I suggest that neither response satisfactorily resolves the problems generated by anti-essentialist critiques. I then argue that, without sharing any common characteristics, women can still exist as a distinctive social group, susceptible to political mobilisation, insofar as they constitute a genealogy.[3] I derive the project of a feminist appropriation of the concept of genealogy from Judith Butler, whose professed aim in *Gender Trouble* (1990) is to outline a *'feminist genealogy* of the category of women' (5; emphasis in original). Tracing this concept of genealogy back to Friedrich Nietzsche, I suggest that all cultural constructions of femininity re-interpret pre-existing constructions and thereby compose a history of overlapping chains of interpretation, within which all women are situated. Thus, although women share no common understanding or experience of femininity, they are nevertheless assembled into a determinate social group through their location within this complex history. I conclude that a genealogical approach could enable third wave feminist theory to overcome its earlier problems and stimulate, rather than deter, feminist political activism.[4]

Essentialism and its critics

Let us recall what was at issue in the heated controversies over essentialism that dominated much of 1980s and 1990s feminist writing. At first glance, the various critiques of essentialism from this period seem to address quite disparate targets. Elizabeth Spelman's classic critique *Inessential Woman* (1988) castigates recurring tendencies within feminism to take certain privileged women's experiences or situations as the norm. Meanwhile, post-structuralist thinkers such as Judith Butler emphasise the relations of power and exclusion underpinning any general claims about women. The diverse theoretical backgrounds and orientations of these critiques of essentialism has led some commentators, such as Gayatri Spivak, to conclude that 'essentialism is a loose tongue' (1994, 159). Yet, retrospectively, it is possible to identify all these critiques as targeting essentialism in a recognisable philosophical sense. Philosophically, essentialism is the belief that things have essential properties, properties that are necessary to those things being what they are. Applied within feminism, essentialism becomes the view that there are properties essential to women, in that any woman must necessarily have those properties to be a woman at all. So defined, essentialism entails a closely related view, *universalism*: that there are some properties shared by, or common to, all women – since without those properties they could not be women in the first place. Essential properties, then, are also universal. 'Essentialism' as generally debated in feminist circles embraces this composite view: that there are properties essential to women and which all women (therefore) share. Notice that, in this definition, the properties that are universal and essential to all women might be either natural or socially constructed. As this suggests, critics of essentialism from the later 1980s and 1990s typically attacked any view ascribing necessary and common characteristics to all women, even if those characteristics were taken as culturally constructed.[5]

Traditional views of womanhood, prevalent before second wave feminism, are usually essentialist and assume that all women are constituted as women by certain biological features (wombs, breasts or child-bearing capacity) – features that all women are presumed to share. Second wave feminist formulations of the sex/gender distinction problematised this picture, arguing that sexed biology is both different from, and causally inert with respect to, gender (an individual's socially acquired role and sense of identity). So, while being *female* may require certain anatomical features, being a *woman* is something different, dependent on identification with the feminine gender (the social traits, activities and roles that make up femininity). Following this recognition of the gap between gender and sex, many influential second wave feminist theorists tried to identify an invariant set of social characteristics that constitute femininity and that all women, *qua* women, share. Possibilities included women's special responsibility for domestic, affective, or nurturant labour, the views, for example, of Nancy Hartsock; their construction as sexual objects rather than sexual subjects, as suggested by MacKinnon; their comparatively weak ego-boundaries – Nancy Chodorow's version of psychoanalytic theory; or, as famously argued by Carole Gilligan, their relational style of ethical and practical reasoning.[6]

In the 1980s and 1990s, however, numerous feminist thinkers showed repeatedly that such universal claims about women are invariably false. It cannot plausibly be maintained that women's experiences have any common character, or that women share any common location in social and cultural relations, or sense of psychic identity.[7] Essentialism, then, is simply false as a description of social reality. Moreover, critics pointed out that the descriptive falsity of essentialism renders it politically oppressive as well. The (false) universalisation of claims about women in effect casts particular forms of feminine experience as the norm, and, typically, it is historically and culturally privileged forms of femininity that become normalised in this way. Essentialist theoretical moves thereby end up replicating between women the very patterns of oppression and exclusion that feminism should contest.

One might, at this point, object that we can uphold essentialism without postulating any social or cultural characteristics common to all women if we, instead, identify women's essential properties with their biologically female characteristics. This need not entail returning to the traditional, misleadingly anatomical, definition of womanhood: one might hold that femininity is socially constructed in diverse ways, but that all these constructions are united in that they build upon and interact with individuals' biologically female characteristics. However, this option was foreclosed by the feminist philosophies of the body that developed in the 1990s. Judith Butler, Moira Gatens, and Elizabeth Grosz, in particular, argued that bodies are thoroughly acculturated, and so participate in the same diversity as the social field that they reflect. First, social forces continually alter and reconfigure bodies' physical characteristics, not merely superficially but at a deep internal level. Second, our bodies are first and foremost the bodies that we live, phenomenologically, and the way we live our bodies is culturally informed and constrained at every point. Sexed embodiment is therefore not external but internal to the gendered realm of social practices and meanings. Consequently, one cannot appeal to any unity amongst female bodies to fix the definition of women, since the constitution and significance of bodies varies indefinitely according to their socio-cultural location.

The increasing rejection of essentialism within feminist thought posed two well-known, closely interwoven, problems. Ontologically, anti-essentialism 'cast doubt on the project of conceptualising women as a group' (Young 713). In denying women any shared features, anti-essentialism seemed to imply that there is nothing in virtue of which women can rightly be identified as forming a distinct social group. This ontological denial appeared, in turn, to undermine feminist politics: if women share no common social location, they cannot readily be expected to mobilise around any concern at their common predicament, or around any shared political identity or allegiance. Moreover, if essentialism is false, then it becomes unclear how feminists can 'represent' women's interests, since women have no unitary set of interests for the putative representatives to articulate. Thus, the third wave's two-pronged critique of the descriptive falsity and political oppressiveness of essentialism left feminism in a dilemma: 'a specious choice', as Cressida Heyes puts it, 'between difference-denying generalizations and a hopeless fragmentation of gender categories' (2000, 11). Feminists have offered several responses to this dilemma, and I shall now critically assess two of the most significant: strategic essentialism and the idea that women form a series.

Two responses to anti-essentialism

Confronted with the spectre of a dissolution of feminist politics, many feminist theorists in the 1980s and 1990s espoused 'strategic' essentialism, the position that some form of essentialism is necessary as a political strategy. Spivak, for example, argued that one acknowledges that essentialism is descriptively false (it denies the real diversity of women's lives), but, in limited contexts, one continues to act *as if* essentialism were true, so as to encourage a shared identification among women that enables them to engage in collective action (1984–85). Many of the bold statements in Luce Irigaray's later work can be construed as strategically essentialist. In *Thinking the Difference* (1994), she claims that women share certain bodily rhythms that give them a deep attunement to nature (24–26). Rather than attempting to describe women as they really are, Irigaray may well be urging women to *think* of themselves as sharing certain rhythms, as a strategic identification that will galvanise them to collectively resist ecological degradation.

A crucial and largely overlooked difficulty afflicts this strategic essentialist position. Any political strategy will be effective in proportion as it allows agents to gain a grip on the real events and forces that make up the social field, and to intervene materially into this field. But a strategy can be effective, in this sense, only insofar as it embodies an accurate understanding of the character of the social field. Consequently, a strategy of affirming fictitious commonalities amongst women cannot be expected to facilitate effective action in a world where women do not really have any common characteristics or experiences. If strategic essentialism is nonetheless held to be effective, this must be because its proponents continue, tacitly, to presuppose that women do share a common social position into which intervention is required. Unless women share such a position, there is little reason to regard strategic *essentialism* as an effective lever for change.

This suggests that, although strategic essentialists explicitly deny upholding essentialism as a description of social reality, implicitly they must continue to presume the descriptive truth of essentialism just in taking it to be politically efficacious. Consider, for example, Denise Riley's statement that 'it is compatible to suggest that "women" don't exist – while maintaining a politics of "as if they existed" – since the world behaves as if they unambiguously did' (112). For Riley, essentialism is strategic in that it enables us to engage with, and resist, the social practice of treating women as if they constituted a unitary group. Yet in saying that the social world treats women in this way, Riley is implicitly embracing a form of descriptive essentialism after all: she is claiming that all women share a common mode of treatment, a common way of being positioned by social institutions. This confirms that, ultimately, one cannot defend essentialism on merely strategic grounds without first showing it to be descriptively true as well. But since, in fact, essentialism is descriptively false (as we have seen), it cannot be defended as politically effective either.

In 'Gender as Seriality' (1994), Iris Marion Young offers a preferable solution to the onto-political dilemma posed by anti-essentialist critiques. Importantly, she suggests that we can retrieve feminism as a social ontology, while still recognising the descriptive falsity of anti-essentialism, if we rethink the *type* of social group that women are. Specifically, she advocates reconceiving women as a *series*, a specially non-unified kind of group: 'vast, multifaceted, layered, complex and overlapping' (728). Deploying the taxonomy of Jean-Paul Sartre's *Critique of Dialectical Reason* (1960), Young distinguishes series from groups in the strict sense: the latter are collections of individuals who mutually recognise significant areas of shared experience and orientation to common goals.[8] In contrast, membership in a series does not require sharing any attributes, goals or experience with the other members. The members of a series are unified passively through their actions being constrained and organised by particular structures and constellations of material objects. Women, for example, are passively positioned in a series by the particular set of gender rules and codes infusing everyday representations, artefacts and spaces. Young's understanding of women as 'serialised' allows her to deny that women share any common identity or characteristics, by arguing that they take up the constraints of gender structures in variable ways, within the contexts of entirely different projects and experiences. At the same time, she can consistently claim that women retain the broad group status of a series insofar as the same set of 'feminising' structures remains a background constraint for them all (728). Having secured women status as a social group – in this broad, non-unified, sense – Young concludes that women can become conscious of their group status and so become motivated to act together politically.

Young's approach has a drawback: her defence of women's group status tacitly reinstates the essentialism she explicitly repudiates. Although she denies that women share a common experience or identity, she does affirm that all women are 'oriented around the *same* objects or ... structures' (728; emphasis added). Young concedes that the content of these structures varies contextually, but still maintains that, despite their diversity, these structures share certain unifying characteristics – they all embody a central set of expectations about normative heterosexuality and appropriate gender roles (729–30). For Young, it is precisely through these allegedly unifying features that social structures co-operate in constituting women as a single, distinct, gender. Thus, she retains a coherent feminine gender only by invoking a form of essentialism with respect to the constraining structures of the social milieu. Anti-essentialists can plausibly object, though, that no single set of expectations about sexuality or gender roles unifies all the social structures to which women relate. The problem, then, is that ultimately Young continues, like the strategic essentialists, to rely on the tacit invocation of an implausible form of descriptive essentialism.[9]

Young's important insight into the need to reconceive femininity as a non-unified type of social group can be more consistently developed if we rethink femininity as not a series but a specifically genealogical group. This genealogical rethinking of femininity entails a concomitant rethinking of feminist politics as coalitional rather than unified. We should rethink collective feminist activities as predicated not upon any shared set of feminine concerns but, rather, on overlaps and indirect connections within women's historical and cultural experience. I will now outline how a genealogical and coalitional rethinking of feminism could surmount the dilemma generated by critiques of essentialism.

Women as genealogy

Several prominent feminist thinkers have suggested that the concept of genealogy might allow us to reinstate, from an anti-essentialist viewpoint, the idea that women are a distinct social group. In *Gender Trouble*, Butler appropriates this concept to outline a genealogical understanding of what it is to be a woman (5). Similarly, Gatens proposes 'a genealogy of the category "woman" or "women" ... a genealogical approach asks: how has "woman"/"women" functioned as a discursive category throughout history?' (76). These references to genealogy imply that femininity is historically constructed in multiple, shifting, ways, its fluctuations in meaning registering changes in social relations of power. However, Butler and Gatens do not explicate precisely what a genealogical rethinking of femininity consists in. To fill in this gap, we must trace the concept of genealogy back to Nietzsche's *On the Genealogy of Morality* (1887).[10]

One of Nietzsche's principal aims in the *Genealogy of Morality* is to deny that any common characteristics unite all the institutions, practices and beliefs classified under the heading of morality. As such, Nietzsche adopts an anti-essentialist approach to morality. He understands its diverse practices and beliefs as falling under the rubric of morality solely because they belong within a distinctive history. This history is to be studied through a novel form of enquiry – 'genealogy'. The genealogist traces how some contemporary practice has arisen from an indefinitely extended process whereby earlier forms of the practice have become reinterpreted by later ones. Genealogists treat any current phenomenon as arising from a reinterpretation of some pre-existing practice, which it harnesses for a new function, and to which it assigns a new direction (54–56). Thus, a genealogy takes shape when a practice (such as punishment) becomes subjected to repeated reinterpretations that impact upon its meaning and structure. For instance, an early aim of punishment was to secure a yield of pleasure for the punisher, but subsequently the practice became reinterpreted – moralistically – as serving to restore justice in the wake of a criminal infraction (57).

According to Nietzsche, any reinterpretation must install itself by accommodating, as far as possible, the meanings embedded in the pre-existing practice, though necessarily it sheds any irreconcilable elements of those meanings. Reinterpretation is therefore a conflictual process in which present forces strive actively to take over recalcitrant elements of the past.[11] Crucially, for Nietzsche, any practice that succumbs to reinterpretation has itself already taken shape as the sedimentation of earlier layers of interpretation. But these layers of meaning do not just accumulate: because irreconcilable elements of meaning are shed with each instance of reinterpretation, a process of attrition takes place through which earlier layers of meaning gradually get erased altogether. Consequently, no common core of significance endures through all the successive waves of reinterpretation of any practice: for example, no common significance is shared by punishment practices in ancient times and today. Similarly, the earlier meanings of all the other practices making up morality are gradually, but inexorably, scratched out through recurring acts of reinterpretation.

In studying an item genealogically, then, we situate it within a given group – for example, the group 'morality' – not because of any essential characteristics that this item shares with all the other members of this group, but because the item is appropriately historically related to the others in the group. More specifically, a set of such items is grouped together only because each emerges as a reinterpretation of one or more of the others. For Nietzsche, any set of items related in this overlapping way comprises a genealogy. Nietzsche's concept of a genealogy as a chain of historically overlapping phenomena opens up a promising way of reconceiving women as a social group without yielding to essentialism. Genealogically, we can understand women as a social group, yet not as united by common characteristics but, rather, infinitely varying while entangled together historically.

The point of departure for a genealogical analysis of femininity is that femininity is a mutable cultural construction, not something causally determined by biological sex. To identify femininity as cultural is not necessarily to treat it as the attribute of an immaterial mind. Part of what it is to live, think and experience as a woman is to acquire a feminine way of living one's *body*, a way of living physiologically. Moreover, acquiring femininity need not mean being passively moulded by external cultural forces. Femininity is acquired, over time, insofar as one actively takes up and internalises available cultural standards. As Butler puts it, acquiring a gender involves 'an incessant project, a daily act of reconstruction and interpretation ... a subtle and strategic project ... an impulsive yet mindful process of interpreting a cultural reality laden with sanctions, taboos and prescriptions' (1988, 131). However, each appropriation of existing standards concerning femininity effects a more or less subtle *modification* of their meaning with reference to changing contexts, power relationships, and histories. As Butler states, 'gender identity ... [is] a personal/cultural history of received meanings subject to a set of imitative practices' (1990, 138). Received meanings regarding gender are subjected to a continuous process of practical reinterpretation, or 'imitation', with reference to differing histories of personal and cultural experience.

This constant modification makes the meaning of femininity considerably less unified than it might, on superficial acquaintance, appear. There is no unitary meaning of femininity on which all women agree: although all women may identify with femininity, their femininity invariably differs in content. Nonetheless, on a genealogical approach, all women remain identifiable *as* women. Although they do not share any characteristics simply *qua* women, in each case their femininity reworks pre-existing patterns of cultural interpretation. Through this reworking, each woman becomes located within a historical chain comprising of all those (women) who have successively reinterpreted the meaning of femininity. All women are thus located within chains of reinterpretation that bring them into complex filiations with one another.

Following Nietzsche's understanding of a genealogy, any reinterpretation of femininity must overlap in content with the interpretation that it modifies, shedding some elements of that pre-existing interpretation while preserving others. Consequently, each woman finds herself in a series of gradually diminishing connections with women of previous generations. Intra-generationally, too, each woman's reinterpretation of femininity must overlap in content, to varying degrees, with other women's reinterpretations of the same set(s) of pre-existing meanings. Over time, though, successive modifications in meaning necessarily build upon one another so that determinate historical patterns of interpretation of femininity emerge, each pursuing a particular direction. As this branching occurs, the process of attrition whereby earlier elements of meaning get worn away ensures that quite separate cultures of femininity emerge, within which different women become located, who cease to share any common experience of femininity. In these cases, women remain connected only indirectly, via the vast chains of overlapping meaning that span the gap between them. Thus, instead of forming a unitary group, women are connected together in complex and variable ways, through historical chains of overlapping interpretations of femininity.

This seemingly abstruse point about the ontology of women suggests that anti-essentialism can support and stimulate feminist politics. Although women do not form a unitary group, united in possession of shared characteristics, they remain a social group in that they constitute a genealogy. And, as a distinctive social group, women remain in a position to mobilise together in pursuit of distinctive concerns. Nonetheless, since a genealogy is a specially non-unified group, and women's concerns are correspondingly diverse, a non-unitary mode of collective activity is appropriate. Accordingly, those who advocate a genealogical approach generally endorse a coalitional politics. Butler states that her genealogy of woman forms the 'prerequisite' for a 'new sort of feminist politics' that operates 'within the framework of an emergent coalition' (1990, 5, 14). Similarly, Nancy Fraser and Linda Nicholson contend that 'feminist political practice ... is increasingly a matter of alliances rather than one of unity around a universally shared interest or identity. ... This, then, is a practice made up of a patchwork of overlapping alliances, not one circumscribable by an essential definition' (35). Coalitions may be said to arise when different women, or sets of women, decide to act together to achieve some determinate objective, whilst yet acknowledging their differences as irreducible. A genealogical conception of femininity allows us to explain why women might, despite their irreducible differences, reasonably seek to mobilise together on such a coalitional footing. From a genealogical perspective, coalitional alliances are appropriate in several ways. Each woman's historically shaped experience inevitably overlaps in content with that of at least some other women, giving them areas of partial commonality that they might reasonably seek to transform together. Moreover, in each woman's case, there will be many other women with whose experience her own has no direct overlap, yet to whom she remains indirectly connected through the whole web of overlapping relations between women. She might, therefore, seek to act in concert with such women because improvements in either of their situations could be expected, indirectly, to have positive repercussions for the other. Between these types of case, other forms of motivation for feminist coalitions are possible, corresponding to women's different degrees of cultural overlap and connectedness.

Conclusion

In this chapter I have addressed what is arguably the central problem facing third wave feminist theory: that its anti-essentialism risks fragmenting women as a social group, thereby dissolving the possibility of feminist politics. Many feminist thinkers have attempted to resolve this problem while preserving anti-essentialism, but the most promising of these attempts – strategic essentialism and the idea of women as a series – are inadequate: their defences of feminist politics work only by tacitly reinstating essentialism as a descriptive claim about social reality. In contrast, I have sought to develop a more consistently anti-essentialist feminism by outlining a conception of women as a genealogy, inspired, in part, by Judith Butler. According to my argument, every cultural construction of femininity takes over and reinterprets pre-existing constructions, themselves the precipitates of still earlier layers of reinterpretation, so that all these constructions form overlapping chains. These chains of interpretation make up a distinctive (although complex, internally diverse) history within which all women are (differently) situated. Thus, although women do not form a unity, they are nevertheless assembled through their location within this history into a determinate social group, amenable to collective mobilisation on a coalitional basis. This suggests that the idea of women as a genealogy can be fruitful, both in explaining how women can exist as a social group despite their lack of common characteristics, and in facilitating a reinvigorated feminist politics that avoids recourse to spurious grounds of unity. By drawing on the concept of genealogy, third wave feminism can overcome its earlier difficulties and encourage, rather than impede, feminist social critique and political activism.

Notes

1. Thanks to the participants in the 'Essentialism and Difference' panel at the *Third Wave Feminism* conference at the University of Exeter (2002) and the 'Feminist Philosophy' panel at the Pacific American Philosophical Association conference (2003). A revised version of this chapter appeared as 'Essentialism and Anti-Essentialism in Feminist Philosophy' in the *Journal of Moral Philosophy* 1.2 (2004): 135–53.
2. Here I am identifying as 'third wave' those feminist thinkers who criticise essentialist tendencies within dominant second wave theories. I do not mean to suggest that there are firmly demarcated second and third waves: third wave critique depends on close dialogue with second wave theories (Heyes 1997, 142–43), and is animated by the same political opposition to women's exclusion and oppression that galvanised the second wave (Prokhovnik 187–88). Nonetheless, the two 'waves' differ insofar as the third offers a 'more complex theorisation of multiple forms' of oppression that received relatively little attention within the second (Prokhovnik 176).
3. A genealogy is usually understood as a particular type of historical explanation. However, just as a 'history' can be the object of a historian's study as well as the study itself, I use the term 'genealogy' for the already existing historical chains which genealogists reconstruct.
4. Throughout, I assume that feminist activism grows in some way from women's (socially constituted) experiences. I regard this as a key insight of second wave feminism, which a viable third wave approach should preserve even as it attends to the historical and social constitution of experience. For more on this see Joan W. Scott.
5. This may sound odd, since 'essentialism' is often contrasted to 'constructionism'. But social constructionists can readily be essentialists if they believe that a particular pattern of social construction is essential and universal to all women. For a related analysis of the essentialism within constructivism, see Diana Fuss.
6. I am simplifying here, as several of these thinkers – especially Gilligan – have revised their theories to mitigate the exclusive tendencies critics detected in them (e.g. Jill Taylor *et al.*).

7. One could, of course, defend statistical generalisations, such as that women perform most domestic labour. However, the most influential second wave theorists (e.g. Hartsock 231; 237) sought stronger commonalities within women's life-situations and experiences.

8. For Sartre, groups in the strict sense involve shared goals and experience, so that series count as groups only in a broad or, as he says, 'neutral' sense (256).

9. Young inherits this residual essentialism from Sartre, who counts series as groups at all only insofar as they are *self-alienated* versions of groups in the strict (unified) sense. Series are self-alienated groups because their unity is located outside them in objective artefacts or structures (Sartre 258–59). Thus, Sartre still really understands series on the model of unified groups, of which series are a deformation.

10. Gatens (76–77) draws explicitly on Nietzsche as does Butler in *Gender Trouble* – although Butler's view of Nietzsche is mediated through Foucault.

11. Arguably, Nietzsche grounds reinterpretations in the will to power, whereby bodily forces naturally strive to *'overpower, dominate'* the practices confronting them (55; emphasis in original). His anti-essentialist view of morality thus remains subtended by an essentialist account of bodily forces. This problem need not affect feminist appropriations of genealogy, though: they can explain reinterpretations of femininity solely in terms of diverse *cultural* contexts (11–12).

Works cited

Butler, Judith. *Gender Trouble*. New York: Routledge, 1990.

——. 'Variations on Sex and Gender: Beauvoir, Wittig and Foucault.' *Feminism as Critique*. Ed. Seyla Benhabib and Drucilla Cornell. Minneapolis: Minnesota University Press, 1988. 128–42.

Chodorow, Nancy. *The Reproduction of Mothering*. Berkeley: California University Press, 1978.

Fraser, Nancy, and Nicholson, Linda. 'Social Criticism Without Philosophy: An Encounter between Feminism and Postmodernism.' *Feminism/Postmodernism*. Ed. Linda Nicholson. London: Routledge, 1990. 19–38.

Fuss, Diana. *Essentially Speaking: Feminism, Nature, and Difference*. London: Routledge, 1989.

Gatens, Moira. *Imaginary Bodies*. London: Routledge, 1996.

Gilligan, Carole. *In a Different Voice*. Cambridge: Harvard University Press, 1982.

Grosz, Elizabeth. *Volatile Bodies: Toward a Corporeal Feminism*. Bloomington: Indiana University Press, 1994.

Hartsock, Nancy. *Money, Sex, and Power: Toward a Feminist Historical Materialism*. New York: Longman, 1983.

Heyes, Cressida. 'Anti-Essentialism in Practice: Carol Gilligan and Feminist Philosophy.' *Hypatia* 12.3 (1997): 142–63.

——. *Line Drawings: Defining Women Through Feminist Practice*. Ithaca: Cornell University Press, 2000.

Irigaray, Luce. *Thinking the Difference: For a Peaceful Revolution*. 1989. Trans. Karin Montin London: Athlone, 1994.

MacKinnon, Catherine. 'Feminism, Marxism, Method and the State: An Agenda for Theory.' *Signs* 7.3 (1982): 515–44.

Nietzsche, Friedrich. *On the Genealogy of Morality.* 1887. Trans. Carol Diethe. Ed. Keith Ansell-Pearson. Cambridge: Cambridge University Press, 1994.

Prokhovnik, Raia. *Rational Woman: A Feminist Critique of Dichotomy.* Manchester: Manchester University Press, 2002.

Riley, Denise. *'Am I That Name?' Feminism and the Category of Women in History.* London: Macmillan, 1982.

Sartre, Jean-Paul. *Critique of Dialectical Reason, Vol. I: Theory of Practical Ensembles.* 1960. Trans. Alan Sheridan-Smith. London: New Left Books, 1976.

Scott, Joan W. 'Experience.' *Feminists Theorize the Political.* Ed. Joan W. Scott and Judith Butler. London: Routledge, 1992. 22–40.

Spelman, Elizabeth. *Inessential Woman: Problems of Exclusion in Feminist Thought.* London: The Women's Press, 1988.

Spivak, Gayatri Chakravorty. 'Feminism, Criticism and the Institution.' *Thesis Eleven* 10/11 (1984–85): 175–87.

——. 'In a Word: Interview.' By Ellen Rooney. *The Essential Difference.* Ed. Naomi Schor, and Elizabeth Weed. Bloomington: Indiana University Press, 1994. 151–84.

Taylor, Jill, *et al. Between Voice and Silence: Women and Girls, Race and Relationship.* Cambridge: Harvard University Press, 1996.

Young, Iris Marion. 'Gender as Seriality: Thinking about Women as a Social Collective.' *Signs* 19.3 (1994): 713–38.

3
Kristeva and the Trans-Missions of the Intertext
Signs, Mothers and Speaking in Tongues

Mary Orr

> Kristeva's thought is peculiar: it is transparent enough that it tends to be reduced very quickly to a set of bipolar opposites by her critics (and thereby criticized as being everything from ultraanarchistic to ultraconservative); but at the same time, it is opaque enough to be uncritically idealized by her most fervent admirers.
>
> (Jardine 106)

> With respect to feminism, then, Kristeva leaves us oscillating between a regressive version of gynocentric-maternalist essentialism, on the one hand, and a postfeminist antiessentialism, on the other. Neither of these is useful for feminist politics. In Denise Riley's terms, the first *overfeminizes* women by defining us maternally. The second, by contrast, *underfeminizes* us by insisting that 'women' do not exist and by dismissing the feminist movement as a proto-totalitarian fiction.
>
> (Fraser 190; emphasis in original)

*   *   *

Although published in the same year, these two responses to Julia Kristeva's work offer a résumé of the complex, positive-negative reception which her *œuvre* has generated both outside and within specifically feminist circles.

The key to both quotations is their antinomic structure; advances in one area are counterbalanced by regress in another. In the light of Kristeva's own and repeated denial of the label 'feminist' (2001, 117–18) in spite of her iconic status within (French) feminism, it seems timely to ask whether Kristeva still has a part to play in shaping feminist debates of the twenty-first century, especially in the fertile arenas of postcolonial and third wave feminisms. While her contributions to feminist psychoanalysis and the maternal as 'subject-in process' have already been ruled out of court by many feminists, such as Janice Doane and Devon Hodges or Diana Meyers, Kristeva's work on language, including the pre-semiotic, continues to elicit positive support from critics of a no less feminist hue such as Toril Moi and Anne-Marie Smith. Kristeva's example-in-writing thus positions her both 'outside' feminism of whatever wave, yet directly within the *aegis* of feminist concerns about language, writing and power pertinent to all waves. This chapter does not try to settle the question of Kristeva's 'feminist' credentials, but asks how far her 'feminist-postfeminist' position and politics make her work, at the very least, a whetstone to sharpen contemporary third wave feminist theory and practice.

It is worth returning first to some basic tenets of all feminist enquiry: the need to identify and investigate the omissions of women and the woman question in the cultural story. It is this approach which immediately challenges previous feminist accounts of Kristeva in English, since little specific reference is made there to Kristeva's early and groundbreaking *Semeiotikè* (1969), mainly because so little of this text has been translated from the French. Even Kristeva's most prominent advocates, let alone her detractors, have largely ignored it, so that it has been severed from Kristeva's better-known contributions on the abject, the pre-semiotic, the *chora*.[1] Marginalisation of whatever kind is a quintessentially feminist issue, regardless of wave or nationalising identity (such as Anglo-American, French or subaltern feminisms), and for theory and practice. Moreover, given that Kristeva has spoken of herself in terms of 'severing' (2001, 86) by referring to the image she used in her novel *Possessions* (1996) of '*la femme décapitée*' ['the woman beheaded'],[2] some serious feminist work needs to be done to conjoin, not further separate, her thinking into decisive phases. This chapter begins the task of reconnection by recuperating in *Semeiotikè* a number of key constants fundamental to it, but also central to Kristeva's so-called psychoanalytical period from the 1980s onwards. By arguing here for the retrospective significance of the essays which make up *Semeiotikè* before the 1980s, a more holistic feminist reevaluation can be begun of what has often sweepingly been categorised as the era of 'high' French feminist theory (epitomised in the contributions of

Irigaray and Kristeva in the late 1970s–1990s) from which third wave feminism emerged. At the same time, Kristeva's more recent work on revolt and gendering female genius can be resituated as part of a continuum of interests rather than a new departure in her *œuvre*. It is the unsettling, unsettled and polyphonic nature of the essays in *Semeiotikè* that I argue continue to challenge the kind of neat bipolarisations encapsulated in the epigraphs above about Kristeva's work in particular, and about feminist critical discourse more widely. The not always fully formed ideas in *Semeiotikè* therefore arguably continue to be relevant to particular concerns, problems and confusions within current feminism, especially around questions of ethnicity. As a concerted rereading of *Semeiotikè* in its entirety is not possible here, the third essay, 'le texte clos' (the closed text), will serve as a textual model of Kristeva's thinking as symbiosis and open connection, rather than clean disjunction into dialectical thesis, antithesis and synthesis. A suggestive space within a multifaceted collection, 'le texte clos' and its open host, *Semeiotikè*, together alert contemporary feminist rethinking to the necessary translingual and transnational parameters of its interdisciplinary concerns.

'Le texte clos': The Translinguistic, the Lady and the Novel

'Le texte clos' is the third essay in *Semeiotikè* and is fundamental to the wider investigations of language and semiotics in the collection not least because it is here that Kristeva first introduces the concept of 'intertextuality' as permutation of texts, and within a context that acknowledges her indebtedness to Mikhail Bakhtin.[3] Kristeva opens discussion, however, on the importance of the translinguistic as the realm of semiotic practices of various kinds. Quickly moving from oral exchanges to the text as a translinguistic medium which redistributes orders of language, and then to intertextuality, Kristeva firmly places such productivity of translinguistic practices within the *space* of the text. The teeming multiplicity of translinguistic text and its space as model of cultural production is perhaps best encapsulated by the index to *Semeiotikè* (316). Here, translinguistic text is glossed as (1) irreducible to an utterance (*énoncé*) which can be broken into parts; (2) a site where categories of language are redistributed; (3) transgression of the laws of grammar; (4) a 'writing-reading' (that is an active appropriation of the other into total participation);[4] (5) estrangement to language (*étrangeté à la langue*); and (6) theatricality of the text. This translinguistic arena of the text is later qualified in *Semeiotikè* to distinguish the *phenotext* (the signifying structure of the printed (fixed, closed) text from the *genotext* (the signi-fying productivity).[5] The translinguistic (as the genotext and intertext) is therefore infinitely open to signification, irreducible to a singular given or designation as 'other' (i.e. popular or vernacular form) of the text. While a potential totality, it is the dynamic, dialogic and socially bounded operations of the translinguistic that allow ideologemes to become apparent in signifying systems, whether oral discourses or textual language. If the intertext cannot itself be designated 'feminist' (this or other situations outside the text being absent), Kristevan translinguistics has profound significance for current feminist considerations of female agency, imagination and finding voice in not just one but several tongues. *Semeiotikè* is conceptualised and written in French as Kristeva's second, not mother tongue (she is Bulgarian), yet takes full advantage of her fluency at the same time in Russian. It was not Todorov but Kristeva in this text who introduces Bakhtin's ideas about dialogism into France. In other words, core questions about language and power such as Spivak's famous 'Can the subaltern speak?' have always already been replaced by the history of multilingual women's voices negotiating power translingually. Thus, Kristeva's work not only complicates and questions theories of linguistics with 'nationalising' identity tags (such as 'Saussurian', i.e. 'French'), it also practises translingual production. If inter-esting work has begun on translingualism and the literary imagination, as Steven G. Kellman demonstrates, feminists currently unhappy with monolingual oppression in high theory and cultural production need to take fresh stock of the territories which Kristeva's early work opens up.

While the first three pages of Kristeva's essay are extraordinarily dense and allusive, the contextual and conceptual scene is set for two inter-connected and important qualifications. The first is to mark the late medieval period (thirteenth–fifteenth centuries) as the transition from symbol to sign: universals give way to phenomena and the symbol as solution of contradictions was displaced by sign as connector by means of non-disjunction, a term Kristeva later qualifies (1969, 58). In short, for Kristeva this is the moment where hermeneutics (theological or metaphysical) was replaced by semanalysis before it was known as such. Second, late medieval literature, in particular Antoine de La Sale's *Histoire du petit Jehan de Saintré* (1456), is for Kristeva the paradigm or prototype of the polyphonic novel à la Bakhtin. As perhaps the earliest prose text in the vernacular, or at least among the first recorded in written form, *Histoire du petit Jehan de Saintré* combines historical dis-course with a heterogeneous mosaic of prior texts to permit Antoine de La Sale's own narration as the story of Saintré to emerge in a rhetorical representation which also circumscribes the history of the book. Doubles and doubling of discourse constitute the signature of *Histoire du petit Jehan de Saintré*, with non-disjunction (pseudo-oppositions which are revealed as such) as further structural variant. A throwaway line then opens up a second knot of Kristeva's analysis of this medieval text to qualify 'non-disjunction': 'Recent research has proved the analogies between the cult of the Lady in provençale literature and ancient Chinese poetry' (68–69). For Kristeva, these genres are first and foremost a hieroglyphic semiotic practice based on connective disjunction of two sexes which are irreducibly differentiated yet simultaneously alike. If Western literature then made the Dame 'the Other' to distinguish her from 'the Same' (the male author), de La Sale's text for Kristeva sets the Dame on the cusp of same-other textual politics. Not yet and uniquely a divine or idealised Lady, nor merely a human character capable of unfaithfulness and falsehood, neither mother nor mistress, the Dame is both the figure of the non-disjunctive which centres and grounds the work, and the authority (of taste, language) to whom the male protagonist and writer defer. Is Kristeva tacitly pinpointing the critical role (in all senses) of such highly articulate (culturally literate) and often at least trilingual women for artistic renewal at critical periods of cultural history? Does Kristeva's reading, and more important writing, of the Lady speak into her own intellectual trajectories through the pre-semiotic and on to explorations of a female genius? And how far does Kristeva's recuperation and rewriting of the story of Saintré as the story of the writing process reshape the fiction of closure ('le texte clos') within the open (translinguistic) work of a culture for female and male voices outside nationally bounded cultures?

As theory about self-other repositioning, the translinguistic is key to Kristeva's *Semeiotikè* and wider *œuvre*. For current feminist agendas concerning race, ethnicity, identity, multilingualism and self-representation, Kristevan translinguistics offers a rich field for future work whether in high theory, on poetic language or the pre-semiotic. The dynamics of translinguistic transference are, moreover, also visible in 'le texte clos'. On the one hand these will be taken up by Kristeva with reference to the translation and transmission of the sensate (*le sensible*), and to the situation of being in another's language. On the other, they will inform her most recent psychoanalytic work on revolt and its disorders.[6] Perhaps most important of all, the highly 'intellectual' Kristeva of 'le texte clos', an essay marked by its abstract, difficult and convoluted style and structures, confronts and re-envisages from a central-European woman's perspective a central image of Western philosophy, Plato's cave. The open-closed space of forms and the language of representation may be otherwise configured as the genotext or non-disjunctive space of cultural production. If actual maternity (and its figurations in 'Stabat Mater' in *Histories d'amour*) are in the future of 'le texte clos' and *Semeiotikè* as a whole, the latent ideas of 'le texte clos' and analysis of the Dame in particular address dynamic doubling and open closure, the 'yin and yang' of non-disjunction as alternative to mimesis, and the anchoring of (translinguistic) text in individual formations of language which is (and is not) the mother-tongue even for monolingual speakers. The early writing therefore finds in the image of the woman beheaded not some variant of castration in the feminine, but an endowment of the female head as necessary for *her* embodiment of text. How this textual body connects to material incorporation with a gendered identity finds expression as the economy of the Dame, overtly hidden in, yet also the screen of, the whole text. It is in the shuttle passing between them, the lines in language and in the script of experience readable only after the event, that connection occurs. The post-'le texte clos' phase in Kristeva's work might then be seen to envisage such transmissions less as theory but as praxis of this in-between.

Chinese women, the maternal and the in-between ('l'entre-deux')

The issue in Kristeva's *œuvre* which has arguably most provoked feminist critical ire and disconnected her from 'serious' feminist politics remains the maternal. For Doane and Hodges, for example, Kristeva's psychoanalytic work on the maternal and pre-semiotic almost blithely ignores women's socio-political contexts: 'A signifying practice like Kristeva's, a discourse that refuses to discuss the social, political and economic situation of women (except as symptoms or an archaic relation to a maternal object) can offer little insight into the complex sources of female depression and little hope for a cure' (77). For Lisa Lowe, 'the examples of China and Chinese women are cited only in terms of Western debates, are invented as solutions to western political and theoretical problems' (141). Kristeva's vaunting of pre-patriarchal, non-Western matriarchal systems such as that found in ancient China is for Lowe offensively orientalist, a version of maternity which perniciously returns to male-female binaries. Such critical assertions, however, omit to investigate the rather more complex network of socio-political and other material contexts informing Kristeva's thinking directly after *Semeiotikè*. These omissions in the cultural story may not ultimately 'solve' some of the inherent problems and difficulties with Kristeva's figurations of the maternal perceived above, but they do mitigate and therefore reorientate them.

The informed comparison between the cult of the Lady in provençale literature and ancient Chinese poetry already present in 'le texte clos', while of vital importance to Kristeva's later intertextual rereading of Marina Warner's work on the Virgin Mary in 'Stabat Mater', first finds a political rather than a post-theological outlet.[7] The comparison to ancient Chinese poetry also suggests that Kristeva had already become interested in China, including its policies on women, rather earlier (and not necessarily for the same reasons) than the *Tel Quel* group. As Kristeva has stated in a recent interview:

> If we were interested in China, it was because we had the impression that its national tradition – Confucianism, Taoism, the place of writing, the specificities of the Chinese language, the role of women in this culture etc. – could influence socialist ideology which purported to be global, and to lead it in an interesting direction. We thought that from such a springboard, whatever impasses were in existence would then no longer be the same. (2001, 38)

To return to the received account also circulated by feminist critics, *Tel Quel*'s disillusionment with the intellectual left in France, especially adherence to French-style communism, shifted their interest in the early 1970s to Maoism, and was actualised in the visit of a number of its members to China to see Maoist politics in action for themselves. This version fails to distinguish the group 'they', or lumps Kristeva synonymously with 'them'. Kristeva was the only woman of the party – the others were Philippe Sollers, Roland Barthes, François Wahl and Marcelin Pleynet – and the only member to have learned some Chinese prior to departure. Pleynet's travel account – *Le Voyage en Chine* (1980) – is a fascinating record of how different Kristeva's position was on a number of counts, particularly as she is not centre-stage for most of it. In terms of interaction with Chinese people, Pleynet notes for example at the Great Wall that she is mistaken for a Chinese person until she speaks Chinese, and also records how her long skirt was a constant source of fascination for Chinese *women* of all ages as different to their ubiquitous blue trousers (108). However, Pleynet perhaps more significantly recounts her difference within the *Tel Quel* group dynamics: in intellectual and political discussions about the role of intellectuals in galvanising petit bourgeois commitment she is noted as particularly pessimistic (43).

She is often the more persistent on visits in trying to gather information, and is noted as spending free or journey time learning Chinese. While Pleynet arguably corroborates Lowe's view that Kristeva only saw China through a westernised optic – the group as a whole and especially Barthes rarely moved outside tourist space, or if visiting hospitals or other institutions found the official translators a barrier – Kristeva's already non-French and ex-Soviet Block positioning constitute a differently 'Western' stance to theirs regarding China. While she fulfils the role of the 'translinguist' and was the spokesperson of the group about women's affairs, her encounter as intermediary, both as translator and the 'in-between' of cultures, was not new to the visit to China.[8] This foreigner-yet-insider situation constituted Kristeva's position from her earliest interventions in Barthes's seminar in 1965, and her role within *Tel Quel* itself. Indeed, she has described herself as the 'lightning conductor' or go-between of its factions (2001, 35–36), as the doubly-coded *woman* stranger (*étrangère*) within.

While Moi (171–72) has accused Kristeva of an over-romanticised theorisation of the marginal figure as subversive, the interest of the *étrangère* Kristeva pinpoints is precisely her shadowy, ambiguous yet ubiquitous status. The *étrangère* (like the Dame) is not locked into national, temporal, geographical or symbolic essences but evades them even as she is named by them and may be as much inside such boundary definitions as outside them. While it was Mao's then focus on the role of women in China (as a key economic but under-exploited additional workforce) that Kristeva admits first drew her, not least because this chimed with her growing awareness of French women's issues, the main common reference points in fact became for her the particularity of women's sexuality, their writing and their place in society (2001, 42–43). In France, and endorsed by the visit to China, Kristeva discovered that the female body and libido, as well as the maternal or role of the mother, were subjects of 'non-conversation' by women of themselves in ways which had nothing to do with class, education or ethnicity.[9] In terms of reconnecting the metaphorical decapitated head to the disembodied body of the Kristevan *œuvre* in all its parts, then, the visit to China was strategic on several counts. It triggered Kristeva's entry into more creatively 'political' as opposed to 'high' academic language which purports to be gender neutral. Kristeva cannot then be accused of not being aware of the socio-political contexts of 'real' women or only of white, Western middle-class ones. Her 'French' *étrangère* persona and position-in-writing thus found more expressive outlets, perhaps facilitated precisely by her disappointment and rupture with Maoism (as system) and, as a close reading of Pleynet indicates, by a separation from *Tel Quel* group identity, even mentality. Whether *about* Chinese or French women, *Tel Quel's* collectively unarticulated issues and agendas meshed intimately with Kristeva's own revolution of poetic language and embodied experience in both China and France.

Kristeva's disappointment with Maoism is thus much more directly striking in her writing as compared with that of either Sollers or Barthes. Both her fictional and political voices began to emerge more clearly after this visit alongside her 'abstract' French to form parts of her own 'translinguistics' of expression, including psychoanalytic investigation of the pre-semiotic, with its tacit but no less gendered agenda. While the focus remains on the areas of lack in Jacques Lacan's (rather than Sigmund Freud's) theorising of woman, Kristeva's transmissions and translations of her discovery of the missing elements in Mao's policy for Chinese women into discussion of the maternal and female psycho-erotic relationships, from the female and *étrangère* viewpoint, need to be made more prominent in feminist critiques of Kristeva's 'maternal'.[10] Too much emphasis has been placed on reading the primordial (essentialising, mythologising, archaic Chinese, *etc.*) and pivotal roles of the mother in Kristeva's theories of the pre-semiotic, including the importance of the mother for a child's (rather than as feminists would like, a daughter's) successful entry into language. Her work on the maternal, then, needs to be understood in the much broader terms of the translingual since this includes material, and specific cultural frames, as well as a search for feminocentric conceptualisations of maternal erotics. To find a voice for such terrains, Kristeva has paradoxically never used her mother tongue, and undertaken her own psychoanalysis through French to try to access the pre-linguistic and pre-semiotic. Everywhere, her focus on being an outsider-to-language (*l'entre-deux*, or perhaps *une personne décapitée*) chimes with her own experiential and intellectual developments in the main as a voluntary exile (severed in body) from her mother tongue/land, yet reconnected in head and body otherwise through her adoptive position in French.

Kristeva's comparison in 'le texte clos' between the Dame in provençale literature and ancient Chinese poetry, however, offers further illumination and reorientation if the terms of the comparison are reversed. Taking as primary such female configurations of oral-textual sophistication in ancient matriarchal cultures such as China's, it is not so much the Western Virgin-mother (in *Stabat Mater*) who is the site of the non-disjunction of the real, the sign and the symbolic, but her translinguistic, transnational cousin the Dame. As acme of oral and written expression, this significantly childless maternal but matriarchal construction facilitates cultural production in ways that have similarly been recorded in ancient China. And this cultural production is not grounded in any one culture as superior to the others; it is a motor within all known cultures, albeit in different forms.

That key throwaway line in 'le texte clos' is then a double return of the expressed in Kristeva's post 1970s writings. The open disclosure in this essay is that the Kristevan intertext is as much an inter-cultural as an intra-cultural site of cultural production. Moving beyond any sense of 'French-ness' inherent in the label *'écriture féminine'*, Kristeva's reconsideration of revolutions in poetic language and of poetic 'translation' of the sensible world beyond language in Marcel Proust moves in tandem with her fictional transcriptions of China in her novel *Les Samouraïs* (1990), her theorisations of the child's pre-linguistic and linguistic developments or with the abject and child psychoses. Productivity stems from a translinguistic 'yin and yang' of the host text and its new guest (analogous with the relation of mother and foetus/child). *Semeiotikè* thus lets slip the constants of Kristeva's work, especially its junctures, but also the high occidental, French theory context of its inception, the *Tel Quel* group and Barthes's seminar. Her many disjunctions from these key groups, even before their joint visit to China, are however also already visible through careful rereading of the position of the 'Dame' in Kristeva's early work. As *étrangère* and (m)other, Kristeva's subsequent marginalisation in the 1980s from high theory in France (because its philosophers cannot be women), yet repositioning within psychoanalytic theory with a particularly feminist and feminising orientation, must not then be further disconnected in third wave feminist re-evaluation. Kristeva's *travail* ('going into labour' and 'work') or 'mothership' of the term intertextuality as translinguistic *productivity* is the first step of her wider feminocentric work within French psychoanalytic theory, which makes the maternal pivotal as *process* not role. It seems striking that Kristeva finds 'mothership' of her own critical French 'voice' precisely through her trans-missions within *Tel Quel* about Chinese women. The double-voiced discourse (*entre-deux*) of her critical writing from the earliest to the most recent will, post-1974, be further combined in her creative writing and actual maternity. The 'beheaded' and 'incorporated' aspects of her 'mothership' are therefore not separate stages, but a process. It is Kristeva's cross-cultural labour, the physical-emotional *and* intellectual-intuitive work of the creative maternal body (whether it gives birth literally or not) on the productivities of the translinguistic that third wave feminist daughters need to adopt, but beyond the demarcations of their own subalternity.

Speaking *with* Tongues: A Feminist Language or language of the Dame?

I've had a lot of difficulty with the feminist movement for I don't feel comfortable with movements and militant groups. It happened that the huge explosion of French feminism coincided with the institutional and personal criticism that I was leveling at the Left (I was just back from China) and my disengagement concerning these ideologies. Feminism quickly seemed to me like another form of dogmatism. I won't go into details about my discussion with various feminist groups – it's all past history – but I was struck by the fact that these groups often repeated the ossifications and dogmatism of 'macho' groups to which they were opposed. ... In contrast, the basic questions that the movement posed – the particularity of female sexuality, the role of the mother for the autonomy of the child, dependence *vis-à-vis* the mother, the place of the mother in language and symbolic apprenticeship, the particularities of 'écriture féminine' and woman's art, and other themes have always interested me. ... I was trying to pursue them in my own way. (Kristeva 2001, 117–18)

In the light of this statement, Kristeva's recoil from feminist groups cannot neatly be labelled 'postfeminist' while the constants of her work – the translinguistic, the *étrangère*, the maternal – remain clearly key issues for third wave feminist agendas. As against the 'high' language of her early work, Kristeva's recent interviews and essays clearly frame the speaker in tongues within the knotty realm of the everyday and 'ordinary' language, including its psychological dimensions, which are much harder to grasp cognitively or assimilate linguistically. Language, as Kristeva has known from the outset, is vital to women's empowerment and their articulation of counter-representations. To inhabit the dominant other's tongue has always been both a subversive and survival strategy, as postcolonial writers and critics, male and female, have recognised. It is this speaking in and *with* tongues that connects Kristeva more with the outsiders to, and precursors of, feminist movements *per se*. For visible and vocal pre-modern women, education was key to their command of several languages and particularly writing. Such women polyglots as successful transmitters and cultural negotiators inhabited space thanks to powerful male protectors and because of their own awareness of how to circumnavigate the local ideological exigencies of their time and space in a particular cultural history. Kristeva's 'politics' fits such a lineage of linguistic adoption, adaptation and male group patronage rather than that of direct confrontation or separatism within feminist groupings. As for Simone de Beauvoir before her, Kristeva's rapid prominence within intellectual circles in France which are largely modelled on (male) classical philosophy would have been much more difficult otherwise. This course has also directly informed Kristeva's recent exploration of female genius – Hannah Arendt, Colette and Melanie Klein – outside such classical models to showcase the situation of women's insider-outsider status to major Western patriarchal frameworks. Such a standpoint and situation is exactly that of the Dame in 'le texte clos'. Feminists – whether third wave or not – need to take stock of their mutual heritage with women 'fellow-travellers' in male circles who ground gender agendas in the longer histories or different geographies of feminocentric endeavour. It is also arguable that some of the most lasting 'feminist' work has taken place outside overtly feminist organisations, groups or generational metaphors. Kristeva's concept of the *entre-deux* might then also be an apt description of her own being-in-writing position between feminism and direct action on women's issues, the constellation of parts she herself played in her visit to China.

The polyglot position of the *étrangère*, whether mediating between discourses or languages, also serves as a model of retrospective and proleptic vision. In spite of strides within such areas as feminist linguistics, psychoanalysis, politics or *écriture féminine*, the *travail* of women of/in other tongues needs more overt recognition. Such recuperation would do much to disinvest translation (as text and process) as 'lesser' work to theory, as well as to promote insights on a range of women's issues from non-Western and non-postmodern vantage points. While Woman as single essence or construct does not exist, the ability of the *étrangère* to speak in several tongues has a timely relevance to counter the cultural monologism of certain brands of globalisation or its theories. At the same time, the woman speaker in tongues of today, as formerly, conjoins interdisciplinary and intellectual pursuits with political and religious interests so that neither head nor maternal body and incorporated spirit is excluded, severed or necessarily hierarchised. How such women negotiate this potential non-disconjunction depends as much on their multiple situated-ness in a given time and place, as on their transnational heritages.

If the 'difficult' *Semeiotikè* as paradigmatic of Kristeva's early work would seem irrelevant both in its contents and opaque formulations to real women of different cultures, the semanalytic search and outcome Kristeva overtly proposed for it is perhaps of abiding pertinence. This was not envisaged as some further abstracting of language or theory, but a bid to find a 'materialist gnoseology', that is, embodied ways of knowing. Admittedly Kristeva has not clarified what forms such an epistemology would adopt, especially for women, but the many facets of *Semeiotikè* as demonstrated in her later works do push towards the issues of real women and in a variety of transnational (as opposed to universalising) contexts. Perhaps both the Dame and the translingual *étrangère* incorporate aspects of such a materialist gnoseology whereby the needs and voices of women outsiders to social inclusion – intellectual outcasts and pariahs or literal victims of mental, physical or religious violence, torture and persecution – can begin to be heard?

Doing such maternal work (*travail*), whether understood as actual birthing or other cultural and gnoseological labour, certainly provides a common point for feminist and women's agendas within first and non-first world cultures. Kristeva's theories of the maternal, in spite of re-qualification, may ultimately fail to satisfy feminists of various hues and waves in their bid to renegotiate female sexuality and reproduction let alone articulate it in their own words. But perhaps this has less to do with the insufficiencies in Kristeva's theories of the pre-semiotic and maternal body *per se*, than with the founding premises or theories by which she recasts them. The 'mother question' for feminist politics, thinking and action is, more strategically than before, the daughter question. Especially as third wave feminists renegotiate the work of their foremothers, how important and strategic is being a 'Daddy's girl' or 'Mummy's girl' for women intellectuals? Can feminist psychoanalysis return the repressed of a daughter's entry into language and sexuality? These questions are no less pertinent to Kristeva's intellectual trajectories as to her œuvre which is arguably modelled too closely on the tenets of male high theories, whether Freud, Lacan or *Tel Quel*, even if she later works against their grain. Her own suggestive connection of the Dame, the yin and yang, and a materialist gnoseology it seems to me all point to the disconjunctions that Carl Jung has always explored as alienation and coniunctio, with psychosis as the place where psychic work can begin to integrate and rebalance previously 'abjected' parts of the self. Jungian psychic work of reintegration is then a way to understand the antinomy as regards Kristeva's reception by feminists with which this essay began.[11]

Throughout, this chapter has argued strongly for the non-suturing of Kristeva's work into periods by recuperating something of the plethora and constants of Kristeva's early *Semeiotikè* in 'le texte clos'. By doing so, it refuses the major injunction of deconstruction to divorce text and writer whereby the works of high critical theorists are examined in the light of other texts in intellectual movements, not the personal evolutions, emotions or experiences of their writers. Where much high postmodern feminist work clones this rupture of text and writer, many non-first world feminists have taken up earlier feminist paths, to recuperate forgotten women's lives and their works in order to uncover and critique patriarchal structures, texts and language. If Kristeva's early writing can be accused of blind adherence to male critical modes of high theorising, it is precisely *her* linguistic cloak in the other's tongue which begins to divulge the subversive force of translingualism as her 'biosemanalysis'.

By looking again at the nodal points of 'le texte clos' for their importance as connectors rather than severings, this essay also highlights the running threads and dynamics of Kristeva's ensuing works. *Via* the Dame as stranger-in-the-feminine to his language, Kristeva exposes a place where male-bounded territories may begin to be confronted. It is then by means of a translinguistic, interdisciplinary form of thinking that Kristeva's particular contributions open up the spaces of the cultural, the daughterly and the polyglot to twenty-first-century thinking women aware more than ever of the gendered and sexed natures of their existence. In the entirety of her work, Kristeva's *travail* on and through language as a psycho-politically circumscribed space, recuperates places where women have been kept outsiders to cultural, let alone cross-cultural definition. Thinking feminism in terms of waves, then, may not actually do justice to the interdisciplinary concerns or the nexus of contemporary women's issues. Perhaps this is the lesson for current feminisms to take forward from Kristeva's early work as *travail*, both process and expression, ever in dialogue as the *entre-deux* for the onward transmission of feminocentric understanding, and for understanding our longer translingual and transnational feminist histories.

Notes

1. See my *Intertextuality* (2003) for a discussion of the manifold reasons for such marginalisation of the early Kristeva on both sides of the Atlantic. These include the lack of a female, let alone feminist, philosophical tradition in France and the lack of translations into English until 1980. Even today, anthologies contain only selected essays (and not 'le texte clos'), so that the concept of 'intertextuality' cannot be properly situated within *Semeiotikè* more widely.

44 *Mary Orr*

2. Unless otherwise stated all translations are mine.
3. For further discussion of this as the core definition of Kristeva's intertextuality, see Orr (25–32).
4. This is developed in the fifth essay of *Semeiotikè*, 'Pour une sémiologie des paragrammes' (120).
5. This is further developed in the eighth essay, 'L'engendrement de la formule' (219–21).
6. The essay 'L'autre langue ou traduire le sensible' picks up the ideas of being a stranger to language addressed in *Étrangers à nous-mêmes* (1986), both taking forward the ideas in the first essay of *Semeiotikè*.
7. See also Kristeva's co-authored work with Catherine Clément (42–43).
8. Kristeva was commissioned by the feminist press *des Femmes* to write *Des Chinoises* (1974) [*About Chinese Women*] on her return.
9. See her initial rectifications of this in *La Révolution du langage poétique* (1974) and *Histoires d'amour* (1983).
10. This continued downplaying and side-stepping of the importance of the question of the maternal body in Kristeva is encapsulated in Maria Margaroni's recent analysis and term 'uncomfortable remainders' (24–26).
11. In alchemical terms, which were a fascination and ground for Jung's work, antimony was the simple element of the alchemists and the word 'antimonium's first usage is recorded by the *OED* in 1477, the time frame of *Histoire du petit Jehan de Saintré* and the Dame.

Works cited

Barthes, Roland. *Essais critiques*. Paris: Points Seuil, 1971.

Doane, Janice, and Devon Hodges. *From Klein to Kristeva: Psychoanalytic Feminism and the Search for the 'good enough' Mother*. Ann Arbor: Michigan University Press, 1992.

Fraser, Nancy. 'The Uses and Abuses of French Discourse Theories for Feminist Politics.' *Revaluing French Feminism: Critical Essays on Difference, Agency, and Culture*. Ed. Nancy Fraser and Sandra Lee Bartky. Bloomington: Indiana University Press, 1992. 177–94.

Jardine, Alice. 'Opaque Texts and Transparent Contexts: The Political Difference of Julia Kristeva.' *The Poetics of Gender*. Ed. Nancy K. Miller. New York: Columbia University Press, 1986. 96–116.

Kellman, Steven G. *The Translingual Imagination*. Lincoln: Nebraska University Press, 2000.

Kristeva, Julia. *Au risque de la pensée*. La Tour d'Aigues: Éditions de l'aube, 2001.

——. 'L'autre langue ou traduire le sensible.' *French Studies* 52.4 (1998): 386–96.

——. *Des Chinoises*. Paris: Éditions des Femmes, 1974.

——. *Étrangers à nous-mêmes*. Paris: Fayard, 1986.

——. *Histoires d'amour*. Paris: Denoël, 1983.

——. *Possessions*. Paris: Fayard, 1996.

——. *La Révolution du langage poétique: l'avant-garde à la fin du xixe siècle*. Paris: Seuil, 1974.

——. *Les Samouraïs*. Paris: Fayard, 1990.

——. *Semeiotikè*. Paris: Seuil, 1969.

Kristeva, Julia, and Catherine Clément. *Le féminin et le sacré*. Paris: Stock, 1998.

La Sale, Antoine de. *Histoire du petit Jehan de Saintré*. 1456. Geneva: Droz, 1965.

Lowe, Lisa. *Critical Terrains: French and British Orientalisms*. Ithaca: Cornell University Press, 1991.

Margaroni, Maria. 'The Semiotic Revolution: Lost Causes, Uncomfortable Remainders, Binding Futures.' *Julia Kristeva: Live Theory*. Ed. John Lechte and Maria Margaroni. London: Continuum, 2004. 6–33.

Meyers, Diana T. 'The Subversion of Women's Agency in Psychoanalytic Feminism: Chodorow, Flax, Kristeva.' *Revaluing French Feminism: Critical Essays on Difference, Agency, and Culture*. Ed. Nancy Fraser and Sandra Lee Bartky. Bloomington: Indiana University Press, 1992. 137–61.

Moi, Toril. *Sexual/Textual Politics*. London: Methuen, 1985.

Orr, Mary. *Intertextuality: Debates and Contexts*. Cambridge: Polity, 2003.

Pleynet, Marcelin. *Le Voyage en Chine*. Paris: Hachette, 1980.

Smith, Anne-Marie. *Julia Kristeva: Speaking the Unspeakable*. London: Pluto, 1998.

4
Feminist Dissonance
The Logic of Late Feminism

Gillian Howie and Ashley Tauchert

Since Julia Kristeva penned 'Women's Time' (1979), the metaphor of waves has become a trope for understanding and describing what seem to be breaks in the history of feminist thought. These breaks – if breaks at all – are, for Kristeva, three different and successively held attitudes to linear temporality, or historical progression. It has become common-place to refer to 'first', 'second', and, more recently, 'third' attitudes or generations as if they were waves in the feminist critical tradition, denoting historically bracketed phases of thought – from the suffragist movement of the late nineteenth century, through the Women's Movement of the 1960s and 1970s, and into the newest recognisable phase of feminist thought commonly understood as poststructuralist and/or postmodernist. Yet the metaphor of the wave is more suggestive than its common use implies and, paradoxically, runs the risk of simpli-fying the tradition it is called upon to describe. For instance, whether or not the first wave was '[u]niversalist in its approach' and '*globalise[d]* the problems of women of different milieux, ages, civilisations' and 'varying psychic structures' (Kristeva 197; emphasis added), it also followed on from (and continued) a long history of critical thinking, writing, and political activism by and on behalf of women. This history is formed through the voices of women as diverse as Elizabeth Stanton, Sojourner Truth, Mary Astell and Mary Wollstonecraft, among many others.

Waves are characteristically complex phenomena, and this complexity is registered by the word's operation as verb *or* noun: both the occur-rence of rhythmic or undulating movement, and one of a sequence of perceivable peaks in rhythmic motion as manifested at (usually) the sur-face of a material body (most often the sea). To perceive a wave at all, we artificially arrest the movement by which it is constituted, and separate out *one* of *myriad* manifestations of that movement. At the most abstract level the wave is understood as an energy-carrying disturbance propagated through displacement of the medium without any overall movement of matter. A wave is also a gesture, a sign, an attempt at non-verbal communication, and associated with the perpetuation of movement (waving someone on). If the metaphor has any lasting purchase in the tradition of feminist consciousness, it might indicate shifting constellations of relations within the abstract medium constituted by thinking women at any moment of time. This sense is apparent in Kristeva's delineation of women's time as at once attitudinal and generational, and she maintains that the third attitude can endorse the parallel existence of all three phases in the same historical moment. But coexistence would be impossible if the generational feature were to be identified as phasic, so that only those born after a specific historic moment could be described as third wave; or if the term identified a movement *beyond* something; or if the contradictions shaping female identity were analysed as merely cultural phenomena. The presentation of recent shifts in feminist self-consciousness and practice as a third wave presents historical and theoretical problems in a way that risks a new mode of 'false consciousness' for women. These risks are illuminated by Fredric Jameson's account of postmodernism as the cultural logic of late capitalism.

In this chapter we propose that some strands of third wave feminism seem at least indirectly committed to an anti-realism in epistemology, at odds with the second wave materialist analysis of social and economic conditions, and that such theoretical strands cannot run parallel, or coexist, in any meaningful sense. Instead, we argue that third wave cultural insights into the aesthetic and affective manifestations of subject identity, can be *woven into* an account of constituted identity, and that this in turn facilitates a critique of the politics of representation; without relegating the feminist dream to the acting out of parodic surface manifestations. As a working alternative to the nomenclature 'third wave', we propose a return to, and revision of, 'materialist' feminism. This is because we believe that materialist feminism, updated in the light of global capital, is the most appropriate theoretical device for grasping and explaining the contradictions that structure female identity. This tension, between constituted identity and the presentation of that identity, produces contradictions between experience, representation and aspiration, which engender the affect of dissonance that is characteristic of contemporary feminist thought. We qualify the term 'dissonance' by 'feminist' to indicate both muted truth claims concerning the nature of the conditions of the experience, and the belief that critical positions are still available to 'late' feminism, and indeed necessary to its survival of 'developed' patriarchy. Moreover, in our search for strands that can be woven together, we have attempted to avoid simplifying events, theories and personalities, collectively referred to as second wave, in order to generate a historical genealogy of the third wave.[1] The symbolic beginning of the second wave is assumed to be 1968, but a change in emphasis can be detected throughout the 1970s from the earlier liberal agenda of equal pay and opportunities to a broader set of political goals. Within the Women's Movement in the 1970s, liberal, socialist and radical politics seem to have coexisted with ecofeminism, peace campaigns and anarchism. Underlying the diverse commitments, and acting as a driver for the change in emphasis, was a concurrence of opinion that women have never been simply *excluded from* the social contract. Modern social structures, it was recognised, managed to *include* women *within* the political order, in such a way that formal demands for equal treatment could be seen to be met, without producing the more substantial transformation of the social structures it had been thought would necessarily follow. Theories of patriarchy seemed to offer the most convincing explanation for this phenomenon.[2]

Never simply essentialist, second wave feminists set the terms of the current equality and difference debates, agreeing that the liberal political slogan 'equal *but* different' mystified the fundamental fact that masculinity is 'always already' valued over femininity, and men are guaranteed a form of sanctioned domination over women. Claims that the appropriate values to replace those present in, and perpetuating, the system were those associated with femininity, clashed with arguments by Mary Daly, Shulamith Firestone and Stevi Jackson that characteristics associated with femininity were themselves a by-product of the very system to be replaced. Although any description of second wave feminism as simply essentialist betrays the complexity of the principal arguments, underpinning almost all arguments was a real belief in the moral equality and value of men and women. This belief in metaphysical equality existed alongside beliefs that the two sexes are biologically different, and that, because social systems change over time, the *type* of human subject also changes. Significantly, the idea of a changing human subject inaugurated a break from 'abstract individualism', typical of the first wave, but it was this which was carried over to give substance to the second wave notion of emancipation. A number of questions concerning the nature of emancipation, and the causal origins of oppression, perplexed second wave feminists. To give direction to the discussion, socialist and Marxist feminists analysed the material structures of patriarchy and capitalism, but had first to decide whether or not patriarchy should be analysed as a social institution distinct from capitalism,with its own history and its own causal origins. Dual systems theorists argued that patriarchy and capitalism were two distinct systems that may, or may not, intersect. Unified systems theorists argued that capitalism and patriarchy can be seen as a single, unified set of social relations, and that therefore one conceptual scheme ought to be adequate (Nicholson 39–42). In a nutshell, the problem was how to explain the relation of production to reproduction: whether women's subordination to men is an effect of economic dependency, a dependency that is the result of women's role in sexual reproduction, a role that is required by capitalism; or whether economic dependency is just another facet of a more general system of male power, which might or might not coincide with the specific organisation of labour defined as capitalism.

Prefiguring third wave concerns about the apparent benefits of (global) capital to some women, Marxist feminists argued that there is a tension within liberal capitalism because it both requires a reserve pool of labour and extends its labour market, so that the potential consumer market can be increased. This discussion came to a head in the domestic labour debate of the 1970s. As pointed out by Shelia Rowbotham and Veronica Beechey, dual systems theorists (often referred to as socialist feminists) had a tendency to be softer on Marxism. This was because they could accommodate gender analysis within an exposition of patriarchy, rather than forcing the economic analysis of Marxism to answer the questions outlined above. In *Women's Estate* (1971), Juliet Mitchell contended that the two systems were theoretically irreducible, and argued that there had been a tendency in Marxism towards reductionism, which meant that the economic base was taken to determine the function and role of reproduction, sexuality and socialisation. The merits of this particular interpretation of Marxism aside, we can see emerging here a genealogy of a number of 'third wave' questions, concerning the acquisition of mature subject identity. If we accept that an adult subject will desire things that will, in effect, maintain the current social organisation, and if we believe that the congruence of sex, gender and sexual orientation is the result of various processes that secure desires, and that our sense of who we are depends on these beliefs, desires and behaviours – then it makes sense to look for a theory which describes ways in which the individual is *assigned a place* in the social order. By extending and developing Marx' account of ideology it seemed possible to make some sense of women's false consciousness, as Michèle Barrett argues throughout *Women's Oppression Today* (1988). For this reason, dual systems theorists, such as Mary McIntosh, turned to Althusserian Marxism, seeking in his theory of interpellation an account of ideology that would be able to explain the exigencies and force of patriarchal ideology. Often consciously working outside of academic or institutional constraints, radical feminists developed a plethora of views about the complex nature of subject identity, and the ways in which heterosexuality functions to maintain social stability; views which influenced the above arguments between dual and unified systems theorists. 'Grass roots' issues relating to sexuality were brought to bear on the political agenda, mainly through work arising from women's refuges, rape crisis centres and around pornography. This culminated in the separatist and political lesbianism debates, a feature of the middle 1970s to early 1980s (Evans 54–74). These arguments, centring on embodied identity and sexuality, occurred as the British left, most notably the *New Left Review*, moved onto a philosophical terrain that could accommodate psychoanalysis and theories concerning the cultural significance of various forms of representation. According to Kristeva, interest in semiotics and psycho-analysis was fuelled by a perceived 'saturation of socialist ideology' and the assumed exhaustion of its potential as a programme for a new social contract (200). Whatever the reasons for the Left's hospitality, from a critical incorporation of Lacanian psychoanalysis – exemplified by Luce Irigaray, Juliet Mitchell, Jacqueline Rose and Jane Gallop – arose a curi-ous and powerful hybrid of literary and cultural studies. Terry Lovell suggests that the convergence of textual with socio-historical analysis made the rather eclectic Cultural Studies a natural environment for developing feminist theory. Within Cultural Studies, humanist and economist readings of Marx were replaced by an interest in marxian the-orists such as Antonio Gramsci, Louis Althusser, Roland Barthes and Michel Foucault. The critique of the subject, the idea that our experience of, and belief in, unified subject identity is actually a consequence of antecedent linguistic and psycho-sexual processes, led to a series of argu-ments about the nature of psychoanalysis, the historical character of the human subject, its tendency to define and represent the other, and about the exclusionary quality of the socio-symbolic contract. Although Marxism and psychoanalysis are concerned with processes of change, conflict and resolution, there is fundamental disagreement as to the nature of the processes in question. In effect, Marxists could argue that psychoanalysis was an individualised response to the misery of alien-ation and that the abstraction of the *experience* of alienation, from its material context, resulted in a means to reconcile the individual to the status quo. 'Freudian Marxism' is not an oxymoron, but the distinct theories cannot occupy the same symbolic space without a fair amount of groundwork. This is still as true for any psychoanalytic – Freudian, Lacanian or Kleinian – reading of cultural texts.

In Britain, identity theory made its appearance in the 1980s, as 'identity politics' emerged on the national political stage. The 1980s saw a tremendous change in the political culture, and there is an intricate relationship between the rise of Thatcherism, 'free market' fiscal policy, Left disunity, and the demise of feminism as a political force. During the 1980s, with a number of important exceptions, including the Miner's Strike and anti-Section 28 demonstrations, there was a general decline in British trade union and labour activity, with a resulting diminishment of collective spaces for feminist debates. A further factor in the demise of feminism as a political force over the 1980s can be located in tensions emerging within the Women's Movement that had already been brewing for over a decade. Conflicts between radical and socialist feminists, between middle-class and working-class feminists, between black feminists and white feminists, heterosexual and lesbian feminists, were played out in local organisations, at conferences and through the editorial boards of *Spare Rib, Trouble and Strife* and the *Feminist Review*. These conflicts forced feminists into recognising their own 'specific location', and acknowledging the universalising tendencies within feminist thought. It was no longer feasible to argue that just because an individual had a certain sexed body s/he naturally would, or ought to, align with a particular political movement. As a consequence, the goals of feminism as a political movement became harder to identify and justify with any confidence. This recognition occurred as divisions concerning the appropriate place for feminist activity became entrenched.

The metaphysical argument over the principle of identity, reflected in 'identity politics', came down to the claim that the belief in subject identity (the autonomous rational agent of liberalism, the proletariat of Marxism or the individual of radical feminism) was premised on a prior commitment either to an ontology of natural kinds, underlying certain forms of materialism, or to principles of rational, logical, identity underlying certain forms of rationalism. Poststructuralist feminists argued that radical and Marxist feminists deployed this problematic principle of identity and this explained the elision of experiences and exclusion of women not conforming to this cognitive framework: particularly black women, lesbian and transsexual women, and working class women.[3] The critique of the subject led to an investigation of the differences *between* men and women, differences *within* the group 'women', and differences embodied in 'one' woman. Feminist theory became aligned with a method of reading: a mode of interpretation aiming to uncover the hidden or suppressed Other in texts. This, in turn, produced a focus on the ways in which meaning is constructed, and how values percolate through language and texts. Consequently, questions concerning representation became questions about 'reality' itself. The demise of feminism as a coherent political force occurred simultaneously with the consolidation of academic feminism with, for example, the publication of Ann Oakley and Juliet Mitchell's collection *What is Feminism?* (1986). Academic feminism has, in turn, been described as a de-radicalisation of feminist theory and this has been linked by us (2002) as well as by Joni Lovenduski and Vicky Randall to the rise of 'municipal feminism', the filtering through of women and feminist theory into public institutions, including, but not exclusively, those of higher education. There are two main reasons why an increase in the mass of women in higher education institutions might be causally related to a de-radicalisation of feminist theory. The first refers us to the ways in which the institutional body manages to exert a determining influence on the type of work done. The second refers us to the type of academic theory prevalent under those conditions.

An institution can be defined as a form of physical organisation, which includes sedimented relations of power and lines of funding management. A certain 'norm' of academic practice and an image of an 'ideal' academic practitioner filter through. The rules of academic practice produce normative principles in the material and questions appropriate to study and research.[4] This is endemic to all forms of academic enquiry, but was exacerbated, specifically in relation to feminist research, by the impact of vicious budget cuts and related casualisation dating from the 1980s just as Women's Studies courses had been gaining ground. This coincidence offers a case for claiming that the type of academic work sustainable under these conditions is of a form and content that could be safely funded and published. A further explanation for the de-radicalisation of feminist theory concerns the nature of the theory itself. Identity politics and theory have provided strategic and theoretical problems. Kate Soper has argued that feminist discourses of difference have effectively pulled the rug from under feminism as a politics. Once the *diversity* of women is recognised and privileged over *community*, any sort of collective and goal-directed action becomes harder to justify. Furthermore, the focus of feminist theory rapidly became *itself*, and the purpose of theory became the reflection upon – and the interrogation of – internal divisions and conflicting subject positions *within* feminist theory. This type of autogenetic feminist theory is directly influenced by psychoanalytic literary theory and poststructuralist linguistics, which in effect amounts to a rejection of realism: the reflection of the (Continental) linguistic turn. If feminist theory *can* be reduced to a mode of reading, then there is no privileged female standpoint and men can justifiably call themselves 'feminist', a claim made in several collections, most notably Alice Jardine and Paul Smith's collection *Men and Feminism* (1987). Under these conditions political goals had to be reassessed. Owing to its rejection of the values of modernity and to its anti-realism in ethics, post-1980s feminist strategy became constrained within an increasingly sophisticated demonstration of the ambivalence or ambiguity of conceptual discrimination. The only aim left was to experience, or perhaps to desire, outside the parameters of 'Western logic'.

Kristeva heralds the challenge to the principle and logic of identity as inaugurating the third feminist stage (214–15). But such a challenge reverberates within epistemology, and, in consequence, it becomes increasingly difficult to argue about the causal origins, effects and even nature of material practices – the very issues central to 'second wavers'. Against the grain, some theorists – such as Liz Stanley, Michèle Barrett and Alison Assiter – have attempted to revise traditional epistemology in the light of feminist criticisms, and to take subjectivity into account, whilst retaining a form of realism. The work by Margrit Shildrick and by Lois McNay aims both to maintain an idea of material social conditions and to stress the located, partial and social nature of knowledge. Feminism is a fundamentally modern project, with the general political goal to end the oppression of morally valuable human subjects: women. Without wishing to collapse the third wave into the poststructuralist, and the poststructuralist into the postmodern, this problem of substantive goal remains a common feature. Throughout the diverse strands we can identify a few consistent solutions offered to the problem: a critical return to the body; queer theory; cyberfeminism, cultural or popular feminism; and postfeminism. The first replaces the concept of the moral agent with the concept of the (unnatural) body, and attempts to give content to the term 'oppression' by referring to negative and positive physical effects. The second is a revision of identity politics as queer theory, where images and representations are deployed in a way which is supposed to force a renegotiation of basic political categories and a reappraisal of the purposes of political action. The third strand, perhaps more honestly, tends towards the elimination of the problems of a human subject, moral agency and consciousness by reducing 'mind' to 'brain', and 'brain' to a computational data processing organ.

As discussed by Stacy Gillis elsewhere in this volume, the idea of 'cyber-feminism', however appealing, is revealed as a contradiction when physicalists eliminate the very gender categories on which feminism bases its politics, and then reduce subjectivity to causally determined physical laws. Some subtle strands of third wave feminism bypass the cloistered space of textual exchange, restating the second wave commitment to grass-root activism, and, by foregrounding the medium of culture, intervene directly in popular struggles. Our abiding concern is with the intended outcome of these modes of activism. Finally we should note that some feminists, such as Naomi Wolf, argue that liberal aspirations really have been met and that the social conditions, that made feminism a pertinent analysis of the failings of formal structures, have now been superseded.

The critical question is whether or not feminism can claim to *be* postmodern if the actual conditions of modernity remain. So far we have suggested that the 'third wave' was prefigured by a recognition that feminist theory had to be able to recognise not only location, but also multiple locations, acknowledge the universalising tendencies within feminist thought, and account for the fact that it subsumed individuals under general concepts. Yet if, in this context, we retain a commitment to the material objects and processes of scientific investigation, we can prise apart the real and its representation, and rescue epistemology. The powerful second wave argument, that processes, systems and structures distribute tasks and roles to the detriment of an identifiable group of individuals (women), can be secured and give direction to a reinvigorated idea of praxis: critical theory and practice. We maintain that the problem is not *only* one of representation, but emerges at an intersecting point, where the particularities of representation coincide with systems of distribution. We might describe this in terms of a feminisation of labour within global, multinational, and very modern, capitalism. This analysis seems to return us to the second wave intersection of radical and Marxist feminism, but with an assurance that the 'new' feminist agent needs to be aware of her own conditions, to restrain any enthusiastic generalisations and to be sceptical about the determination of possibilities. However, if the subject *is* a consequence of antecedent processes, structures, engagements and relationships then that, in one sense, is precisely what she *is*. As Rosi Braidotti has persuasively argued in 'The Politics of Ontological Difference' (1993), our being women, just as our being mortal and our being in language, is one of the constitutive elements of our subjectivity. One is both born *and* constructed a woman, but the consequences of the construction are real. If we concede to

Judith Butler the claim that no identity can exist before or outside or beyond the gendered acts that perform it, it does not follow that gender is itself a performance: the performance of a performance or the sediment of various performances. This would be, in effect, to presume either the spectre of a transcendent subject, or a libidinal scene, behind or before such acts, or result in the despairing cry that identity is no more than the sedimentation of prior acts.

Some specific theoretical strands are incommensurable and cannot coexist within a newly sublated 'third' stage. The phasic account of these analytical stages obscures this incommensurability by conflating various arguments within general trends. Indeed, some arguments concerning the philosophy of history would endorse a 'logic' of historical change; others would question the reliability of the construction of historical narrative and, without begging the question, these arguments cannot be assumed to be successive historical moments. The generational account of feminist phases seems to express anxiety and disappointment, with each stage or generation responding by rejecting its predecessor; a fairly common trend identified by Harold Bloom as the anxiety of influence. Unfortunately, because patriarchy is built upon the symbolic and real severance of productive matrilinear relations, the generational transitions within the feminist tradition are inherently fraught, and conflict is aggravated by increasingly competitive conditions within, and without, the academy. The disappointment, however, indicates more than infantile and sororal conflict, or a dream of the perpetually new, because it is a gesture towards the structural conditions of unfulfilled aspirations. Cultural, or populist, third wave feminists might revalorise constituted female identity and its representation, whilst incorporating both a radical analysis of the signifying chain and a belief that the agent can somehow manipulate that which is signified. The point that marks third wave feminism as the pivotal moment of late (developed) patriarchal capitalism, is whether or not it can grasp both the agency within self-representation and the appropriation of that agency.[5] Thus, the argument about the commodification of the feminine aesthetic becomes an argument about whether or not valorisation is identical to reification. As Rebecca Munford argues elsewhere in this volume, the *real* argument is whether the recent reification of 'difference', its fetishisation as intensity, self-affirmation and even grrrl power, is a precise response to particular social conditions. What appears to be the creative harnessing of 'archaic' power might instead turn out to be the subordination of the aesthetic itself to modern commercial logic; the repetitive sameness of the exchange commodity form that must appear always to be new (Lunn 157).

We can align the fetish of exaggerated femininity, camp exchange, with the relatively recent myth of an iconic and free female individual struggling to find her own destiny. This myth fairly grooves along in the rut of a bourgeois society, which perpetually threatens to eclipse the subjectivity in question (Jacoby 41). There are fragments of truth discernible in camp exaggeration of the feminine: glimpses of the contingency of the general. A sense of this contingent relationship, between individual and universal, can help to make explicit the contradictory governing principles shaping identity. It would be dangerous, however, to rest in feelings of well-being brought about through the conscious play of cultural form. These may offer no more than a substitute gratification, cheating subjects out of the same happiness that it deceitfully projects. Dissonance, for Rosi Braidotti in *Patterns of Dissonance* (1991), is the effect of the lack of symmetry between the discourse of the crisis of modernity and the impossible elaboration of theories of subjectivity. Rather than conceiving the crisis in this way, it seems more effective to define the *true* crisis in terms of the fragile attempts of the subject to express her conflicting and dissonant experiences of modernity as a struggle against the very forces that incorporate her (constituted) subjectivity. The notion of dissonance itself presents this uncomfortable and almost unintelligible experience of contradiction, and gestures towards the social antimonies structuring it.

The question remaining is two-fold: Is there an appropriate theoretical tool for analysing the contradictions of modernity? And how might we think an attitude towards, and a movement through, these contradictions? Ascribing logic to feminist theory is a consequence of our primary commitment to a materialist analysis of linear historical sequence, and a parallel belief that theoretical labour has, at most, quasi-autonomy. The description of feminism as 'late' indicates the risk of the incorporation, and consequent de-politicisation, of critical thought under the conditions of global gendered capital. Whether or not any form of critical thought can withstand the onslaught of bureaucratic procedures within the academy is a moot point. It may turn out to be the case that self-defined third wavers are right to be suspicious of the inherent neo-conservatism of academic feminism.

Notes

1. See Gillian Howie for a discussion of feminism, materialism and postmodernism.
2. For variations upon this see the collections edited by Olivia Harris and Kate Young, Zillah Eisenstein, and Annette Kuhn and AnneMarie Wolpe.

3. For an elaboration of these debates see Barrett (1987), Chris Weedon and Linda Alcoff.
4. For more on this see the chapters in 'Part I: Methodology' in Ann Garry and Marilyn Pearsall's *Women, Knowledge and Reality* (1989).
5. For more on agency and representation in third wave feminism see Stacy Gillis and Rebecca Munford.

Works cited

Alcoff, Linda. 'Cultural Feminism versus Post-structuralism: The Identity Crisis in Feminist Theory.' *Signs* 13.3 (1988): 405–36.

Assiter, Alison. *Enlightened Women: Modernist Feminism in a Postmodern Age.* London: Routledge, 1996.

Barrett, Michèle. 'The Concept of Difference.' *Feminist Review* 26 (1987): 29–41.

——. *Women's Oppression Today: The Marxist/Feminist Encounter.* Verso: London, 1988.

Beechey, Veronica. 'Some Notes on Female Wage Labour in Capitalist Production.' *Capital and Class* 3 (1977): 45–66.

Bloom, Harold. *The Anxiety of Influence: A Theory of Poetry.* Oxford: Oxford University Press, 1973.

Braidotti, Rosi. *Patterns of Dissonance: A Study of Women and Contemporary Philosophy.* Cambridge: Polity, 1991.

——. 'The Politics of Ontological Difference.' *Between Feminism and Psychoanalysis.* Ed. Teresa Brennan. London: Routledge, 1993. 89–105.

Butler, Judith. *Gender Trouble: Feminism and the Subversion of Identity.* London: Routledge, 1990.

Daly, Mary. *Gyn/Ecology: The Metaethics of Radical Feminism.* Boston: Beacon, 1978.

Eisenstein, Zillah, ed. *Capitalist Patriarchy and the Case for Socialist Feminism.* New York: Monthly Review, 1978.

Evans, Judith. *Feminist Theory Today: An Introduction to Second-Wave Feminism.* London: Sage, 1995.

Firestone, Shulamith. *The Dialectic of Sex: The Case for Feminist Revolution.* New York: Bantam, 1970.

Gallop, Jane. *Feminism and Psychoanalysis: The Daughter's Seduction.* Ithaca: Cornell University Press, 1982.

Garry, Ann, and Marilyn Pearsall, eds. *Women, Knowledge and Reality: Explorations in Feminist Philosophy.* London: Routledge, 1989.

Gillis, Stacy, and Rebecca Munford. 'Generations and Genealogies: The Politics and Praxis of Third Wave Feminism.' *Women's History Review* 13.2 (2004): 165–82.

Harris, Olivia, and Kate Young, eds. *Patriarchy Papers.* London: Women's Publishing Collective, 1976.

Howie, Gillian. 'Feminism, Materialism and the Debate on Postmodernism in British Universities.' *The Edinburgh Encyclopaedia of Modern Criticism and Theory.* Ed. Julian Wolfreys. Edinburgh: Edinburgh University Press, 2002. 818–27.

Howie, Gillian, and Ashley Tauchert. 'Institutional Discrimination and the "Cloistered" Academic Ideal.' *Gender, Teaching and Research in Higher Education: Challenges for the 21st Century.* Ed. Gillian Howie and Ashley Tauchert. Aldershot: Ashgate, 2002. 59–72.

Irigaray, Luce. *Speculum of the Other Woman.* Trans. Gillian C. Gill. Ithaca: Cornell University Press, 1985.

Jackson, Stevi. *On the Social Construction of Female Sexuality.* London: Women's Research and Resources Centre, 1978.

Jacoby, Russell. 'The Politics of Subjectivity: Slogans of the American New Left.' *New Left Review* 79 (1973): 37–49.

Jameson, Fredric. *Postmodernism, or The Cultural Logic of Late Capitalism.* London: Verso, 1991.

Jardine, Alice, and Paul Smith, eds. *Men in Feminism.* London: Methuen, 1987.

Kristeva, Julia. 'Women's Time.' Trans. Alice Jardine and Harry Blake. 1979. *The Feminist Reader: Essays in Gender and the Politics of Literary Criticism.* Ed. Catherine Belsey and Jane Moore. Basingstoke: Macmillan, 1989. 197–217.

Kuhn, Annette, and AnneMarie Wolpe, eds. *Feminism and Materialism: Women and Modes of Production.* London: Routledge, 1978.

Lovell, Terry, ed. *British Feminist Thought: A Reader.* Oxford: Blackwell, 1990.

Lovenduski, Joni, and Vicky Randall. *Contemporary Feminist Politics: Women and Power in Britain.* Oxford: Oxford University Press, 1993.

Lunn, Eugene. *Marxism and Modernism: A Historical Study of Lukács, Brecht, Benjamin, and Adorno.* Berkeley: California University Press, 1982.

McIntosh, Mary. 'The State and the Oppression of Women.' *Feminism and Materialism: Women and Modes of Production.* Ed. Annette Kuhn and AnneMarie Wolpe. London: Routledge and Kegan Paul, 1978. 254–89.

McNay, Lois. *Foucault and Feminism: Power, Gender and the Self.* Cambridge: Polity, 1992.

Mitchell, Juliet. *Woman's Estate.* Harmondsworth: Penguin, 1971.

Nicholson, Linda. *The Play of Reason: From the Modern to the Postmodern.* Buckingham: Open University Press, 1999.

Oakley, Ann, and Juliet Mitchell, eds. *What is Feminism?* Blackwell: Oxford, 1986.

Rose, Jacqueline. *Sexuality in the Field of Vision.* Verso: London, 1986.

Rowbotham, Sheila. 'The Trouble with "Patriarchy".' *The Woman Question: Readings on the Subordination of Women.* Ed. Mary Evans. London: Fontana, 1982. 73–79.

Shildrick, Margrit. *Leaky Bodies and Boundaries: Feminism, Postmodernism and (Bio)Ethics.* London: Routledge, 1997.

Soper, Kate. *Troubled Pleasures: Writings on Politics, Gender and Hedonism.* London: Verso, 1990.

Stanley, Liz, ed. *Feminist Praxis: Research, Theory and Epistemology in Feminist Sociology.* London: Routledge, 1990.

Weedon, Chris. *Feminist Practice and Poststructuralist Theory.* Oxford: Blackwell, 1987.

Wolf, Naomi. *Fire with Fire: the New Female Power and How it will Change the Twenty-First Century.* London: Chatto & Windus, 1993.

5

Transgender Feminism
Queering the Woman Question

Susan Stryker

Many years ago, I paid a visit to my son's kindergarten room for parent-teacher night. Among the treats in store for us parents that evening was a chance to look at the *My Favorite Things* book that each child had prepared over the first few weeks of classes. Each page was blank except for a pre-printed line that said 'My favorite color is (blank)' or 'My favorite food is (blank),' or 'My favorite story is (blank)'; students were supposed to fill in the blanks with their favourite things and draw an accompanying picture. My son had filled the blanks and empty spaces of his book with many such things as 'green', 'pizza' and *'Goodnight Moon'*, but I was unprepared for his response to 'My favorite animal is (blank)'. His favourite animal was 'yeast'. I looked up at the teacher, who had been watching me in anticipation of this moment. 'Yeast?' I said, and she, barely suppressing her glee, said, 'Yeah. And when I asked why yeast was his favorite animal, he said, "It just makes the category animal seem more interesting." '

At the risk of suggesting that the category 'woman' is somehow not interesting *enough* without a transgender supplement, which is certainly not my intent, I have to confess that there is a sense in which 'woman', as a category of human personhood, is indeed, for me, *more* interesting when we include transgender phenomena within its rubric. The work required to encompass transgender within the bounds of womanhood takes women's studies, and queer feminist theorising, in important and necessary directions. It takes us directly into the basic questions of the sex/gender distinction, and of the concept of a sex/gender system, that lie at the heart of Anglophone feminism. Once there, transgender phenomena ask us to follow basic feminist insights to their logical conclusion (biology is not destiny, and one is not born a woman, right?) And yet, transgender phenomena simultaneously threaten to refigure the basic conceptual and representational framework within which the category 'woman' has been conventionally understood, deployed, embraced and resisted.

Perhaps 'gender', transgender tells us, is not related to 'sex' in quite the same way that an apple is related to the reflection of a red fruit in the mirror; it is not a mimetic relationship. Perhaps 'sex' is a category that, like citizenship, can be attained by the non-native residents of a particular location by following certain procedures. Perhaps gender has a more complex genealogy, at the level of individual psychobiography as well as collective socio-historical process, than can be grasped or accounted for by the currently dominant binary sex/gender model of Eurocentric modernity. And perhaps what is to be learned by grappling with transgender concerns is relevant to a great many people, including nontransgendered women and men. Perhaps transgender discourses help us think in terms of embodied specificities, as *women's* studies has traditionally tried to do, while also giving us a way to think about gender as a system with multiple nodes and positions, as *gender* studies increasingly requires us to do. Perhaps transgender studies, which emerged in the academy at the intersection of feminism and queer theory over the course of the last decade or so, can be thought of as one productive way to 'queer the woman question'.[1] If we define 'transgender phenomena' broadly as anything that disrupts or denaturalises normative gender, and which calls our attention to the processes through which normativity is produced and atypicality achieves visibility, 'transgender' becomes an incredibly useful analytical concept. What might 'transgender feminism' – a feminism that focuses on marginalised gender expressions as well as normative ones – look like?

As an historian of the United States, my training encourages me to approach currently salient questions by looking at the past through new eyes. Questions that matter now, historians are taught to think, are always framed by enabling conditions that precede them. Thus, when I want to know what transgender feminism might be, I try to learn what it has already been. When I learned, for example, that the first publication of the post-WWII transgender movement, a short-lived early 1950s magazine called *Transvestia*, was produced by a group calling itself The Society for Equality in Dress (Meyerowitz 2002, 179), I not only saw that a group of male transvestites in Southern California had embraced the rhetoric of first wave feminism and applied the concept of gender equality to the marginalised topic of cross-dressing; I also came to think differently about Amelia Bloomer and the antebellum clothing reform movement. To the extent that breaking out of the conventional constrictions of womanhood is both a feminist and transgender practice, what we might conceivably call transgender feminism arguably has been around since the first half of the nineteenth century.

Looking back, it is increasingly obvious that transgender phenomena are not limited to individuals who have 'transgendered' personal identities. Rather, they are signposts that point to many different kinds of bodies and subjects, and they can help us see how gender can function as part of a more extensive apparatus of social domination and control. Gender as a form of social control is not limited to the control of bodies defined as 'women's bodies', or the control of female reproductive capacities. Because genders are categories through which we recognise the personhood of others (as well as ourselves), because they are categories without which we have great difficulty in recognising personhood at all, gender also functions as a mechanism of control when some loss of gender status is threatened, or when claims of membership in a gender are denied. Why is it considered a heterosexist put-down to call some lesbians mannish? Why, if a working-class woman does certain kinds of physically demanding labour, or if a middle-class woman surpasses a certain level of professional accomplishment, is their feminine respectability called into question? Stripping away gender, and misattributing gender, are practices of social domination, regulation and control that threaten social abjection; they operate by attaching transgender stigma to various unruly bodies and subject positions, not just to 'transgendered' ones.[2]

There is also, however, a lost history of feminist activism by selfidentified transgender people waiting to be recovered. My own historical research into twentieth-century transgender communities and identities teaches me that activists on transgender issues were involved in multiissue political movements in the 1960s and 1970s, including radical feminism. The ascendancy of cultural feminism and lesbian separatism by the mid-1970s – both of which cast transgender practices, particularly transsexuality, as reactionary patriarchal anachronisms – largely erased knowledge of this early transgender activism from feminist consciousness. Janice Raymond, in her outrageously transphobic book, *The Transsexual Empire* (1979), went so far as to suggest that 'the problem of transsexualism would best be served by morally mandating it out of existence' (178).[3] Even in this period, however, when identity politics effectively disconnected transgender feminism from the broader women's movement and before the queer cultural politics of the 1990s revitalised and expanded the transgender movement, it is possible to find startling historical episodes that compel us to re-examine what we think we know about the feminist history of the recent past. The Radical Queens drag collective in Philadelphia, for example, had a 'sister house' relationship with a lesbian separatist commune during the early 1970s, and participated in mainstream feminist activism through involvement with the local chapter of N.O.W. In the later 1970s in Washington, DC, secretive clubs for married heterosexual male cross-dressers began holding consciousness-raising sessions; they argued that to identify as feminine meant they were politically obligated to come out as feminists, speak out as transvestites, and work publicly for passage of the Equal Rights Amendment.[4]

In addition to offering a revisionist history of feminist activism, transgender issues also engage many of the foundational questions in the social sciences and life sciences as they pertain to feminist inquiry. The biological body, which is typically assumed to be a single organically unified natural object characterised by one and only one of two available sex statuses, is demonstrably no such thing. The so-called 'sex of the body' is an interpretive fiction that narrates a complex amalgamation of gland secretions and reproductive organs, chromosomes and genes, morphological characteristics and physiognomic features. There are far more than two viable aggregations of sexed bodily being. At what cost, for what purposes, and through what means do we collapse this diversity of embodiment into the social categories 'woman' and 'man'? How does the psychical subject who forms in this material context become aware of itself, of its embodied situation, of its position in language, family or society? How does it learn to answer to one or the other of the two personal pronouns 'he' or 'she', and to recognise 'it' as a disavowed option that forecloses personhood? How do these processes vary from individual to individual, from place to place, and from time to time? These are questions of importance to feminism, usually relegated to the domains of biology and psychology, that transgender phenomena can help us think through. Transgender feminism gives us another axis, along with critical race studies or disability studies, to learn more about the ways in which bodily difference becomes the basis for socially constructed hierarchies, and helps us see in new ways how we are all inextricably situated, through the inescapable necessity of our own bodies, in terms of race, sex, gender or ability.

When we look cross-culturally and trans-historically at societies, as anthropologists and sociologists tend to do, we readily see patterns of variations in the social organisation of biological reproduction, labour, economic exchange and kinship; we see a variety of culturally specific configurations of embodiment, identity, desire, social status, and social role. Which of these patterns do we call 'gender', and which do we call 'transgender'? The question makes sense only in reference to an unstated norm that allows us to distinguish between the two. To examine 'transgender' cross-culturally and trans-historically is to articulate the masked assumptions that produce gender normativity in any given (time-bound and geographically constrained) context. To examine 'transgender' is thus to risk decentring the privileged standpoint of white Eurocentric modernity. It is to denaturise and dereify the terms through which we ground our own genders, in order to confront the possibility of radically different ways of being in the world. This, too, is a feminist project.[5]

A third set of concerns that make transgender feminism interesting for women's studies is the extent to which 'transgender', for more than a decade now, has served as a laboratory and proving ground for the various postmodern and poststructuralist critical theories that have transformed humanities scholarship in general over the past half century, and which have played a role in structuring the generational debates about 'second wave' and 'third wave' feminism. This is a debate in which I take an explicitly partisan position, largely in response to the utterly inexcusable level of overt transphobia in second wave feminism. An unfortunate consequence of the second wave feminist turn to an untheorised female body as the ultimate ground for feminist practice (which has to be understood historically in the context of reactionary political pressures that fragmented all sorts of movements posing radical threats to the established order and required them to find new, often ontological, bases for political resistance) was that it steered feminist analysis in directions that ill equipped it to engage theoretically with the emerging material conditions of social life within advanced capitalism that collectively have come to be called, more or less usefully, 'postmodernity'. The overarching tendency of second wave feminism to couch its political analyses within moral narratives that link 'woman' with 'natural', 'natural' with 'good', 'good' with 'true' and 'true' with 'right' has been predicated on an increasingly non-utilitarian modernist epistemology. Within the representational framework of Eurocentric modernity, which posits gender as the superstructural sign of the material referent of sex, transgender practices have been morally condemned as unnatural, bad, false and wrong, in that they fundamentally misalign the proper relationship between sex and gender. The people who engage in such misrepresentations can be understood only as duped or duplicitous, fools or enemies to be pitied or scorned. The failure of second wave feminism to do justice to transgender issues in the 1970s, 1980s and afterward is rooted in its more fundamental theoretical failure to recognise the conceptual limits of modernist epistemology.[6] Transgender theorising in third wave feminism begins from a different – postmodern – epistemological standpoint which imagines new ways for sexed bodies to signify gender. Within the feminist third wave, and within humanities scholarship in general, transgender phenomena have come to constitute important evidence in recent arguments about essentialism and social construction, performativity and citationality, hybridity and fluidity, anti-foundationalist ontologies and non-referential epistemologies, the proliferation of perversities, the collapse of difference, the triumph of technology, the advent of posthumanism and the end of the world as we know it. While it is easy to parody the specialised and sometimes alienating jargon of these debates, the issues at stake are quite large, involving as they do the actual as well as theoretical dismantling of power relations that sustain various privileges associated with normativity and injustices directed at minorities. Because these debates are irreducibly political, because they constitute an ideological landscape upon which material struggles are waged within the academy for research funds and promotions, for tenure and teaching loads, transgender phenomena have come to occupy a curiously strategic location in the working lives of humanities professionals, whether they like it or not. This brings me at last to the crux of my remarks.

For all the reasons I have suggested, transgender phenomena are *interesting* for feminism, women's studies, gender studies, sexuality studies, and so forth. But *interesting*, by itself, is not enough, when hard decisions about budgets and staffing have to be made in academic departments, priorities and commitments actualised through classroom allocations and affirmative action hiring. *Interesting* also has to be *important*, and transgender is rarely considered important. All too often transgender is thought to name only a largely irrelevant class of phenomena that occupy the marginal fringe of the hegemonic gender categories man and woman, or else it is seen as one of the later, minor accretions to the gay and lesbian movement, along with bisexual and intersexed. At best, transgender is considered a portent of a future that seems to await us, for good or ill. But it remains a canary in the cultural coal mine, not an analytical workhorse for pulling down the patriarchy and other associated social ills. As long as transgender is conceived as the fraction of a fraction of a fraction of a movement, as long as it is thought to represent only some inconsequential outliers in a bigger and more important set of data, there is very little reason to support transgender concerns at the institutional level. Transgender will always lose by the numbers. The transgender community is tiny. In (so-called) liberal democracies that measure political strength by the number of votes or the number of dollars, transgender does not count for much, or add up to a lot. But there is another way to think about the importance of transgender concerns at this moment in our history.

One measure of an issue's potential is not how many people directly identify with it but, rather, how many other issues it can be linked with in a productive fashion. How, in other words, can an issue be *articulated*, in the double sense of 'articulation,' meaning both 'to bring into language', and 'the act of flexibly conjoining.'[7] Articulating a transgender politics is part of the specialised work that I do as an activist transgender intellectual. How many issues can I link together through my experience of the category transgender?

To the extent that I am perceived as a woman (which is most of the time), I experience the same misogyny as other women, and to the extent that I am perceived as a man (which happens every now and then), I experience the homophobia directed toward gay men – both forms of oppression, in my experience, being rooted in a cultural devaluation of the feminine. My transgender status, to the extent that it is apparent to others, manifests itself through the appearance of my bodily surface and my shape, in much the same way that race is constructed, in part, through visuality and skin, and in much the same way that the beauty system operates by privileging certain modes of appearance. My transsexual body is different from most other bodies, and while this difference does not impair me, it has been medicalised, and I am sometimes disabled by the social oppression that takes aim at the specific form of my difference. Because I am formally classified as a person with a psychopathology known as Gender Identity Disorder, I am subject to the social stigma attached to mental illness, and I am more vulnerable to unwanted medical-psychiatric interventions. Because changing personal identification documents is an expensive and drawn-out affair, I have spent part of my life as an undocumented worker. Because identification documents such as drivers licenses and passports are coded with multiple levels of information, including previous names and 'AKAs', my privacy, and perhaps my personal safety, is at risk every time I drive too fast or cross a border. When I travel I always have to ask myself whether some aspect of my appearance, some bit of data buried in the magnetic strip on some piece of plastic with my picture on it, will create suspicion and result in my detention? In this era of terror and security, we are all surveyed, we are all profiled, but some of us have more to fear from the state than others. Staying home, however, does not make me safer. If I risk arrest by engaging in non-violent demonstrations, or violent political protest, the incarceration complex would not readily accommodate my needs; even though I am a post-operative male-to-female transsexual, I could wind up in a men's prison where I would be at extreme risk of rape and sexual assault. Because I am transgendered, I am more likely to experience discrimination in housing, employment and access to health care, and more likely to experience violence. These are not abstract issues: I have lost jobs, and not been offered jobs, because I am transgendered. I have had doctors walk out of exam rooms in disgust; I have had more trouble finding and retaining housing because I am transgendered; I have had my home burglarised and my property vandalised, and I have been assaulted, because I am transgendered.

Let me recapitulate what I can personally articulate through transgender: misogyny, homophobia, racism, looksism, disability, medical colonisation, coercive psychiatrisation, undocumented labour, border control, state surveillance, population profiling, the prison-industrial complex, employment discrimination, housing discrimination, lack of health care, denial of access to social services, and violent hate crimes. These issues are my issues, not because I think it is chic to be politically progressive. These issues are my issues, not because I feel guilty about being white, highly educated or a citizen of the United States. These issues are my issues because my bodily being lives the space where these issues intersect. I articulate these issues when my mouth speaks the words that my mind puts together from what my body knows. It is by winning the struggles over these issues that my body as it is lived for me survives – or by losing them, that it will die. If these issues are your issues as well, then transgender needs to be part of your intellectual and political agenda. It is one of your issues.

I conclude now with some thoughts on yet another aspect of transgender articulation, the one mentioned in my title, which is how transgender issues articulate, or join together, feminist and queer projects. 'Trans-' is troublesome for both LGBT communities and feminism, but the kind of knowledge that emerges from this linkage is precisely the kind of knowledge that we desperately need in the larger social arena. Trans is not a 'sexual identity', and therefore fits awkwardly in the LGBT rubric. That is, 'transgender' does not describe a sexual orientation (like homosexual, bisexual, heterosexual or asexual), nor are transgender people typically attracted to other transgender people in the same way that lesbians are attracted to other lesbians, or gay men to other gay men. Transgender status is more like race or class, in that it cuts across the categories of sexual identity.[8] Neither is transgender (at least currently, in Eurocentric modernity) an identity term like 'woman' or 'man' that names a gender category within a social system. It is a way of being a man or a woman, or a way of marking resistance to those terms.

Transgender analyses of gender oppression and hierarchy, unlike more normative feminist analyses, are not primarily concerned with the differential operations of power upon particular identity categories that create inequalities within gender systems, but rather with how the system itself produces a multitude of possible positions that it then works to centre or to marginalise.

Transgender practices and identities are a form of gender trouble, in that they call attention to contradictions in how we tend to think about gender, sex and sexuality. But the transgender knowledges that emerge from these troubling contradictions, I want to argue, can yoke together queer and feminist projects in a way that helps break the impasse of identity politics that has so crippled progressive movements in the United States. Since the early 1970s, progressive politics have fragmented along identity lines practically to the point of absurdity. While it undoubtedly has been vital over the past few decades of movement history to enunciate the particularities of all our manifold forms of bodily being in the world, it is equally important that we now find new ways of articulating our commonalities without falling into the equally dead-end logic of totalising philosophies and programmes.

Transgender studies offers us one critical methodology for thinking through the diverse particularities of our embodied lives, as well for thinking through the commonalities we share through our mutual enmeshment in more global systems. Reactionary political movements have been very effective in telling stories about shared values – family, religion, tradition. We who work at the intersection of queer and feminist movements, we who have a different vision of our collective future, need to become equally adept in telling stories that link us in ways that advance the cause of justice, and that hold forth the promise of happy endings for all our strivings. Bringing transgender issues into women's studies, and into feminist movement building, is one concrete way to be engaged in that important work.

While it is politically necessary to include transgender issues in feminist theorising and organising, it is not intellectually responsible, nor ethically defensible, to teach transgender studies in academic women's studies without being engaged in peer-to-peer conversations with various sorts of trans- and genderqueer people. Something crucial is lost when academically based feminists fail to support transgender inclusion in the academic workplace. Genderqueer youth who have come of age after the 'queer' 90s' are now passing through the higher education system, and they increasingly fail to recognise the applicability of prevailing modes of feminist discourse for their own lives and experiences. How we each live our bodies in the world is a vital source of knowledge for us all, and to teach trans studies without being in dialogue with trans people is akin to teaching race studies only from a position of whiteness, or gender studies only from a position of masculinity. Why is transgender not a category targeted for affirmative action in hiring, and valued the same way that racial diversity is valued? It is past time for feminists who have imagined that transgender issues have not been part of their own concerns to take a long, hard look in the mirror. What in their own constructions of self, their own experiences of gender, prevents their recognition of transgender people as being somehow like themselves – as people engaged in parallel, intersecting, and overlapping struggles, who are not fundamentally Other?

Transgender phenomena now present queer figures on the horizon of feminist visibility. Their calls for attention are too often received, however, as an uncomfortable solicitation from an alien and unthinkable monstrosity best left somewhere outside the village gates. But justice, when we first feel its claims upon us, typically points us toward a future we can scarcely imagine. At the historical moment when racial slavery in the United States. at long last became morally indefensible, and the nation plunged into civil war, what did the future of the nation look like? When greenhouse gas emissions finally become equally morally indefensible, what shape will a post-oil world take? Transgender issues make similar claims of justice upon us all, and promise equally unthinkable transformations.[9] Recognising the legitimacy of these claims will change the world, and feminism along with it, in ways we can now hardly fathom. It is about time.

Notes

1. This essay was first delivered as a keynote address at the *Third Wave Feminism* conference at the University of Exeter, UK (25 July 2002); and in revised form at the Presidential Session plenary on 'Transgender Theory' at the *National Women's Studies Association* Annual Meeting, Oakland California (17 June 2006). Many of the ideas I present here have been worked out in greater detail elsewhere in my work (see Stryker 1994, 1998, 2004, and 2006); see also my conversation with Marysia Zalewski. For another account of the relationship between recent feminist scholarship and transgender issues see Cressida Heyes.

2. My thoughts on the role of transgender phenomena for understanding US history in general are significantly indebted to Joanne Meyerowitz (2006).
3. See also Bernice Hausman (9–14) for an overview of cultural feminist critiques of transsexuality, and Dwight B. Billings and Thomas Urban for a particularly cogent exposition and application of this approach.
4. See also Victor Silverman and Members of the Gay and Lesbian Historical Society, for transgender involvement in progressive grassroots political activism in the San Francisco Bay Area in the 1960s.
5. See Evelyn Blackwood and Saskia Wieringa, and Lynn M. Morgan and Evan B. Towle, on cross-cultural studies of transgender phenomena.
6. For a poststructuralist, anti-foundationalist critique of second wave feminism, see Judith Butler.
7. The concept of 'articulation' is taken from Ernesto Laclau and Chantal Mouffe (93–194).
8. See Joshua Gamson on the trouble transgender presents to identity movements.
9. On monstrosity and justice see Nikki Sullivan.

Works cited

Billings, Dwight B., and Thomas Urban. 'The Sociomedical Construction of Transsexualism: An Interpretation and Critique.' *Social Problems* 29 (1981): 266–82.

Blackwood, Evelyn, and Saskia Wieringa, eds. *Female Desires: Same Sex Relations and Transgender Practices Across Cultures*. New York: Columbia University Press, 1999.

Butler, Judith. 'Contingent Foundations: Feminism and the Question of "Postmodernism".' *Feminists Theorize the Political*. Ed. Judith Butler and Joan W. Scott. New York: Routledge, 1992. 3–21.

Gamson, Joshua. 'Must Identity Movements Self-Destruct? A Queer Dilemma.' *Social Problems* 42.3 (1995): 390–406.

Hausman, Bernice. *Changing Sex: Transsexualism, Technology, and the Idea of Gender*. Durham: Duke University Press, 1995.

Heyes, Cressida. 'Feminist Solidarity after Queer Theory: The Case of Transgender.' *Signs* 28.4 (2003): 1093–120.

Laclau, Ernesto, and Chantal Mouffe. *Hegemony and Socialist Strategy: Towards a Radical Democratic Politics*. 2nd ed. London: Verso. 2001.

Members of the Gay and Lesbian Historical Society. 'MTF Transgender Activism in San Francisco's Tenderloin: Commentary and Interview with Elliot Blackstone.' *GLQ: A Journal of Lesbian and Gay Studies* 4.2 (1998): 349–72.

Meyerowitz, Joanne. *How Sex Changed: A History of Transsexuality in the United States*. Cambridge: Harvard University Press, 2002.

——. 'A New History of Gender.' *Trans/Forming Knowledge: The Implications of Transgender Studies for Women's, Gender, and Sexuality Studies*. University of Chicago, 17 Feb. 2006. Accessed: 27 June 2006. <http:// humanities.uchicago.edu/ orgs/cgs/Trans%20Conference%20Audio%20Files/Session%202_Intro_Meyerowitz.mp3>.

Morgan, Lynn M., and Evan B. Towle. 'Romancing the Transgender Native: Rethinking the Use of the "Third Gender" Concept.' *GLQ: A Journal of Lesbian and Gay Studies* 8.4 (2002): 469–97.

Raymond, Janice. *The Transsexual Empire: The Making of the She-Male.* 1979. New York: Teachers College Press, 1994.

Silverman, Victor, and Susan Stryker, dirs. *Screaming Queens: The Riot at Compton's Cafeteria.* Documentary Film. Frameline, 2005.

Stryker, Susan. '(De)Subjugated Knowledges: An Introduction to Transgender Studies.' *The Transgender Studies Reader.* Ed. Susan Stryker and Stephen Whittle. New York: Routledge, 2006. 1–18.

——. 'Introduction: The Transgender Issue.' *GLQ: A Journal of Lesbian and Gay Studies* 4.2 (1998): 145–58.

——. 'My Words to Victor Frankenstein Above the Village of Chamounix: Performing Transgender Rage.' *GLQ: A Journal of Lesbian and Gay Studies* 1.3 (1994): 237–54.

——. 'Transgender Studies: Queer Theory's Evil Twin.' *GLQ: A Journal of Lesbian and Gay Studies* 10.2 (2004): 212–15.

Sullivan, Nikki. 'Transmogrification: (Un)Becoming Others.' *The Transgender Studies Reader.* Ed. Susan Stryker and Stephen Whittle. New York: Routledge. 2006. 552–64.

Zalewski, Marysia. 'A Conversation with Susan Stryker.' *International Feminist Journal of Politics* 5.1 (2003): 118–25.

6
Theorising the Intermezzo
The Contributions of Postfeminism and Third Wave Feminism
Amanda D. Lotz

At first glance, observing the scene on 24 April 2004 in the streets of Washington, DC felt like falling through a feminist looking glass. Hundreds of thousands of protesters filled the streets – a million according to some reports – to create what organisers estimated to be the city's largest protest in a *March for Women's Rights*. It was not the slogans on the signs that seemed so oddly out of place as we had seen the words on these placards before: Stand Up for Choice; Keep Abortion Safe and Legal; Our Bodies, Our Choice; Reproductive Justice for All. It was their rose-colored hue that made this image of protest filled streets so different. Planned Parenthood, the Feminist Majority and the American Civil Liberties Union (ACLU) had all contributed placards with various slogans that were taken up by the feminists who marched that day, and the signs used the same color scheme so that a raging tide of hot pink moved through the streets of Washington. Two weeks earlier, I attended the *Interrogating Post-feminism: Gender and the Politics of Popular Culture* conference at the University of East Anglia, UK and had received my materials in a pastel pink binder. The conference program was also printed in two tones of pink. If I was uncertain at the conference that feminism had reclaimed pink – so long the gendered signifier of femaleness, emblematic of the difference assigned to women moments after birth, and borne as oppression, discrimination and harassment throughout their lives – the streets of Washington made it very clear that the feminist color scheme had changed. Could this shift in the meaning of pink be considered postfeminist? Is it characteristic of third wave feminism? Given the broad range of meanings attributed to third wave feminism and postfeminism, it is easy to answer 'yes', although such distinctions offer little insight into the significance or cultural meaning of this development. Feminist theory and cultural criticism at the turn of the twenty-first-century struggle to explain shifts in signification because I propose that we currently exist in a period of intermezzo. We have entered a new era in feminism: one between the overwhelming structural impediments to gender justice that existed before the activist efforts of second wave feminism yet a world in which complete equity has not been achieved. There is nothing new about this particular intermezzo: for example, one could easily suggest an intermezzo began after suffragettes won the vote. The scope of the gains which feminism has endeavoured to achieve could not be immediately accomplished and the duration required for change necessitates such in-between periods. However, binary paradigms of thinking insistent upon identifying that which is feminist and that which is anti-feminist, that which is 'before' and 'after' feminism, complicate the task of understanding the gender politics of cultural texts and practices. Thinking in terms of an intermezzo is helpful for disrupting binaries that have been imposed upon feminism since the second wave. We are always simultaneously before and after: after sweeping adjustments with regards to women and the public sphere and yet before access to the same rights for all.

But what if we possessed terminology and theory through which we could frame this *both/and* intermediacy? What if feminist theorists and cultural critics shared terms that acknowledged the substantial gains achieved by second wave feminism while simultaneously denoting the unfinished status of this revolution? What if feminists could indicate both their awareness of feminist history and their concern with exclusions contained within past strategies with a single key word which enabled us to connect with and build upon feminist legacies instead of emphasizing disidentification and disavowal? Feminists need a language to negotiate the complexity of the intermezzo, a language that places them relative to feminist histories, contemporaneous issues and possible futures, but this language must be established and shared before it can be meaningfully used. Such a language might provide a way through which we could discuss the shifting meaning of such signifiers as the colour pink, make-up, domesticity and motherhood. This language could also enable us to understand how the practices, representations and artefacts that exist now might mean something differently than they did before. It would also allow for the evolution of feminist theory and the embracing of strategies previously less feasible, such as a greater attention to differences among women rather than appeals to commonality. Most importantly, this language could acknowledge the changing nature of social power, indicating that not all the goals of feminism have been achieved. Postfeminism and third wave feminism emerged and persist because of a perceptible need for conceptual frameworks that assist in theorising and analysing the complicated post-second wave feminist milieu in which some feminist gains have been achieved, while, for the most part, the patriarchy remains hegemonic.

Variations of third wave feminism and postfeminism emerged as a result of uncertainty about the relationship between contemporary and pre-second wave feminist culture and have been tentatively linked and confusingly interchanged since they first emerged in the 1990s.[1] Although the thought and scholarship identified as third wave and/or postfeminist are exceptionally varied, some versions might provide valuable tools for maintaining feminism during this intermezzo. Feminists have used both terms to distinguish new theoretical and activist formations that advance feminist projects. Such work began with experiential anthologies such as Rebecca Walker's *To Be Real: Telling the Truth and Changing the Face of Feminism* (1995) and Barbara Findlen's *Listen Up: Voices from the Next Feminist Generation* (1995) which used third wave or a 'next generation of feminism' as an explicitly feminist alternative to the use of postfeminism in the popular press. Walker had made her understanding of the terms clear in an oft-cited *Ms.* article three years earlier when she noted, 'I am not a postfeminism feminist. I am the third wave' (Walker 1992, 41). Findlen and the authors in her collection avoid either term, but as editor of *Ms.*, Findlen must have been aware of Walker's use of these terms. These earlier publications, along with Jennifer Baumgardner and Amy Richard's *Manifesta: Young Women, Feminism, and the Future* (2000), often emphasised metaphors of generation and the experience(s) of being a woman after the gains of second wave feminism (15–18). The development of a coherent theoretical distinction that indicated how third wave feminism differed or why it was necessary to modify 'feminism' emerged slowly. Leslie Heywood and Jennifer Drake's collection *Third Wave Agenda: Being Feminism, Doing Feminism* (1997) began this endeavour by including some elaborately footnoted chapters more engaged with feminist theory and an introduction that began to clearly situate third wave feminism as a distinction of more than generation (3–9). Heywood and Drake's collection was the first academic book to take up third wave feminism, even though the previous more popular market publications were also used in academic settings because little else existed. Yet *Third Wave Agenda* was still a preliminary work that only began a necessary sustained critical examination of the need for and contribution of third wave feminism. Many of its chapters were similar to those found in *Listen Up* and *To Be Real* – emphasising experience rather than carrying through the consideration of third wave feminism as a theoretically distinct entity with a particularly characteristic activist formation as Heywood and Drake suggest in their introduction (2–3).

A more sustained theoretical examination emerged the same year in Ann Brooks' *Postfeminisms: Feminism, Cultural Theory and Cultural Forms* (1997). Brooks, writing in New Zealand, constructs the distinction of postfeminism in a manner very similar to that of the third wave suggested by Americans Heywood and Drake, but she does not indicate any awareness of the 'third wave' discourse occurring in the preceding years. Within the US, postfeminism had primarily been used in the popular press to suggest the current era was 'after feminism' in a manner that at least implicitly suggested that feminism's goals had been achieved and activism was no longer necessary. Brooks grounded the need to delineate a new distinctive feminism based upon 'a conceptual shift within feminism from debates around equality to a focus on debates around difference' (4). She denied the apolitical use of postfeminism common in the popular press and instead described postfeminism as 'fundamentally ... a political shift in feminism's conceptual and theoretical agenda' (4). Yet Brooks' intervention avoids assessment of how this theoretical difference might yield a shift in activism and its organization. Few theorists have followed Brooks' use of postfeminism or offered a sustained theoretical development. Some have, however, subsequently offered increasingly detailed arguments for the theoretical distinctiveness of third wave feminism that closely align with her effort. Elsewhere in this volume, Ednie Kaeh Garrison invokes a pattern of activism and vision of social movements offered by Chela Sandoval. Garrison's theoretical distinction of third wave feminism is similar to Brooks' postfeminism, while her argument that third wave feminism is differentiated by a shift in the strategic consciousness of feminist ideology and praxis advances thinking about how the operation of a feminist movement might differ after the second wave. Alternatively, in the introduction to their third wave feminist collection *Catching a Wave* (2003), Rory Dicker and Alison Piepmeier have argued that third wave feminists are 'concerned not simply with "women's issues" but with a broad range of interlocking topics' (10). One way to interpret this parallels Garrison's assertion that third wave feminism functions as a 'new social movement', an argument that I have also made (5–7). Dicker and

Piepmeier's claim also might be read to suggest that attention to interlocking issues differs from the case of second wave feminism in a manner that problematically reduces the activism of that era to a single-issue agenda. Like Brooks, Garrison and Heywood and Drake also particularly attend to the emphasis of differences among women as a characteristic of third wave feminism (Garrison 2000, 145; Heywood and Drake 3). The political connotations of both third wave feminism and postfeminism remain contested and uncertain, although postfeminism has been more widely deployed in popular publications and vernacular, particularly in the U.S.[2] Both terms are shifting signifiers that are inconsistently defined, contradictorily invoked and burdened by complicated rhetoric too easily seized and retrofitted to advance anti-feminist goals. Yet the near-simultaneous emergence of these terms and their persistence in popular and academic writing is unsurprising. Certain national contexts have produced a generation of women that have come of age since the height of second wave feminism and live in societies that have adopted enough feminist reform to make their experience substantially different than those who came before. The achievement of some feminist gains has realigned power relationships and redefined feminist strategies and signifiers; however, we lack a language through which we might talk about these changes and communicate the ongoing nature of feminist endeavour amidst a tendency in the popular press to locate feminism within the second wave. This chapter explores what postfeminism and third wave feminism contribute to explaining and exploring the contemporary feminist intermezzo. Elsewhere I have suggested that postfeminism is one version of third wave feminism (4); while I maintain the utility of that distinction I have now adapted my position relative to the shifts in these highly uncertain concepts. I continue to believe that a theorised postfeminism can be of great value to feminism, but have grown less convinced that this term can overcome the anti-feminist connotation that also has come about. The development of third wave feminism as a theoretically distinctive way of thinking about and practicing feminism may make third wave feminism a more viable term than postfeminism. My concern in this chapter is less with advocating either postfeminism or third wave feminism as a theorised distinction capable of rethinking the particularities of discrepant access to power characteristic of this era, but with asserting that feminism needs to theorise one or another of these terms in order to explore gender politics in the post-second wave feminist period and to move beyond counterproductive disavowals of previous feminisms and shell-shocked presumptions of backlash. It is, however, difficult to address meaningfully the relationship of third wave and postfeminism because both terms continue to be used inconsistently; in some cases they are effectively synonymous, while other uses make them much more distinct.

Considering postfeminism

The use of 'postfeminist' as a modifier has consistently appeared in the popular press, although with inconsistent meaning. In some cases, postfeminist marks a historical period after the height of second wave feminism such as in the *Boston Globe* article 'The Postfeminist Mommy Track' which stated that 'Still, not everything is right with this postfeminist world' (Young A13). Sometimes postfeminism is used to denote this historical period and is also used to describe backlash perspectives that developed to contain feminism's gains, as with Ruth Shalit's critique of Ally McBeal: 'Yet these feminine virtues are accompanied by feminine weaknesses – by the painstaking vulnerability that has become the trademark of television's postfeminists' (32). In other places, postfeminism acknowledges a historical specificity while engaging and incorporating feminist ideas: writing of musician Laurie Anderson, Karen Schoemer notes that the 'sardonic postfeminism of 'Babydoll,' off her *Strange Angels* album (1989), outlined the tenets of the riot grrrl movement back when Courtney Love was still hurling demo tapes around punk clubs' (24). In the last decade, postfeminism also has become increasingly common in scholarship examining contemporary media, although its intended signification is rarely stated and its use varies appreciably in this work as well. Most date the first academic use of postfeminism to Judith Stacey's discussion of the term in 1987. In using postfeminism, Stacey reclaimed it from use in popular journalism at the time, explaining that she viewed 'the term as analogous to "postrevolutionary" ', and used 'it not to indicate the death of the women's movement but to describe the simultaneous incorporation, revision, and depoliticization of many of the central goals of second-wave feminism' (8). Importantly, she argues that postfeminism is distinct from anti-feminism and sexism. Rayna Rapp added to this definition, indicating that 'depoliticization often takes the form of the reduction of feminist *social* goals to individual "lifestyle" ' (358; emphasis in original). Despite this more negative delimitation of postfeminism, Rapp is unconcerned about the disidentification which Stacey recognises in postfeminism and accepts this as an inevitable part of historical and generational distancing.

Nearly two decades later, discrepant uses of postfeminism hinge on these same nuances. Most subsequent citations of Stacey have emphasized the aspect of depoliticisation as characteristic of postfeminism, yet the situation she explored in her article seems less a case of depoliticisation than an instance of shifting strategies of activist organisation and feminist identification. The informants she studied, who are the daughters of second wave feminist women, identified less readily as feminists, yet internalised many of its assumptions so that they embodied the changed social, political and cultural environment clearly resultant from second wave feminist activism. Stacey drew her insight from fieldwork done in the mid-1980s, a time during which the stability of second wave feminist achievements seemed much more tenuous and uncertain than was the case in the early years of the twenty-first century. Her definition does not wholly preclude the possibility of using postfeminism as a term describing a politicised incorporation and continuation of many of the goals of second wave feminism – an endeavour with significant potential for feminist advance that emerged in Brooks' use of the term.[3] Brooks presented a detailed and extensive theorisation of postfeminism that considered it as a feminist endeavour, although she primarily applied it to the realms of cultural theory and popular culture. She defines postfeminism as

> not a depoliticisation of feminism ... about a critical engagement with earlier feminist political and theoretical concepts and strategies as a result of its engagement with other social movements for change. Postfeminism expresses the intersection of feminism with postmodernism, poststructuralism and post-colonialism, and as such represents a dynamic movement capable of challenging modernist, patriarchal and imperialist frameworks. (4)

The vision of postfeminism Brooks presents is unyieldingly feminist and focused on perpetuating feminist thinking in response to some of the theoretical challenges such as postmodernism and poststructuralism that emerged after the second wave.

Subsequent to this scholarship, a variety of somewhat contradictory uses of postfeminism emerged in feminist media studies. Two general versions emerged, although neither is particularly theoretically informed. One line of scholarship draws from the brief consideration and use of postfeminism by Charlotte Brunsdon in *Screen Tastes: Soap Opera to Satellite Tastes* (1997) in which she used postfeminism to mark the historical specificity of discourses emerging after the intervention of second wave feminism. Brunsdon argues that because of the interventions of second wave feminism, the postfeminist woman has a different relationship to femininity than pre-feminist and feminist women in the use of the term consistent with the notion of intermezzo.

This leads Brunsdon to a more redemptive reading of *Pretty Women* (1990) than commonly argued by feminist critics in which she indicates that postfeminist is a helpful classification for acknowledging the film's historical specificity as following depictions of sex-work in *Klute* (1971) and *McCabe and Mrs. Miller* (1971). She notes that '*Pretty Woman* is very knowing about its retrenchments, simultaneously informed by feminism and disavowing this formation' (95). Likewise, she acknowledges that the postfeminist woman might *appear* trapped in a pre-feminist femininity or driven by pre-feminist constructs of performance, style and desire. The changed context allows Brunsdon to derive a different analysis than Suzanna Danuta Walters, who first brings Stacey's use of postfeminism to popular culture critique and argues that the film 'offers a backlash dystopia', that in its 'assumed mutuality between the rich man and the prostitute undercuts and avoids the power relations inherent in the situation of prostitute and john' (127–28). Brunsdon subsequently critiqued her own analysis of *Pretty Woman* as characteristic of the 'Ur feminist article' that problematically disavows the assessments of second wave feminism by periodizing feminism (2005, 112–13). Despite her uncertainty regarding the feminist deployment of postfeminism, much subsequent media scholarship draws from her 1997 use as a critical model: Rachel Moseley and Jacinda Read argue that Brunsdon's writing is 'crucial ... to debates about feminism and television' and 'British debates about postfeminism' even though she does not offer an elaborate theorisation of postfeminism and uses the word sparingly in her writing (233).

Alternatively, 'postfeminist' has been used to describe cultural discourses and media texts in a manner that indicates a regressive slant to this historic specificity. In this use, 'postfeminist' sometimes suggests an era after second wave feminism in which feminism's gains have been uniformly achieved and feminism is consequently no longer needed. This is the definition used, for example, by L. S. Kim in her examination of 'single girl' television narratives (321). In this connotation, postfeminist is effectively synonymous with anti-feminist, as here 'postfeminist' suggests the dismantling of the imperative of any further feminist activism. Bonnie J. Dow also determines postfeminism to be 'a hegemonic negotiation of second-wave ideals, in which the presumption of equality for women in the public sphere has been retained,' while 'the most radical aspects of feminism, those centered in sexual politics and a profound awareness of power differences between the sexes at all levels and in all arenas, have been discarded as irrelevant or threatening' (88). Some of the scholarship employing understandings of postfeminism in accord with Kim and Dow uses the term to indicate an emphasis on individualism that results from a misallocation of the feminist endeavour for choice. Such writers label 'postfeminist' situations in which women behave in accordance with a 'logic' which Stacy Gillis has explained as: 'I want to do this, I do it, therefore it is a good thing to do. And, because I am a woman living in the early twenty-first century, in the aftermath of second wave feminism, this activity is enlightened, and one more step in the progressive myth that is women's liberation.' In this use, 'postfeminism' is obviously a very negative development because of its depoliticisation and reduction of 'feminism' to a justification for lifestyle and commodification. Critics such as Brunsdon and Brooks would also object to the outlook, although they would not view this as an articulation of postfeminism. These more negative definitions that understand postfeminism as clearly counter-feminist dominate much American scholarship, particularly that emerging from U.S.-focused communication scholarship, as opposed to more internationally conversant forms of media studies that are more likely to draw from the work of Brunsdon and Brooks. Still other uses of postfeminism can be found in the work of Laurie Ouellette, Diane Negra and Angela McRobbie that both bear similarity to and deviate from the definitions noted here.

As these few cases suggest, academic uses of postfeminism are wide-ranging. Sarah Projansky offers five categories of postfeminism – all with some internal variation in her detailed chronicle of popular and academic references to postfeminism prior to 2000 (66–89). The differences just amongst those noted here suggest some coherence among definitions of postfeminism based on discipline and national context, although these distinctions are hardly absolute. Clear bifurcation in developing postfeminist intellectual histories exists, but it also has become possible to seek out a narrow and specific group who use the term similarly. Unfortunately there is little engagement of oppositional understandings or consideration of how more coherence in use might better advance the feminist purposes supported by all feminist scholars using postfeminism, despite the different ways that they use the term. And so great uncertainty develops when critics and theorists – both academic and popular – use terms such as 'postfeminist culture', 'postfeminist era', 'postfeminist media studies', 'postfeminist age', 'postfeminist drama', 'postfeminist icon' or just plain 'postfeminism'. The meaning of postfeminism seems to have become more muddled in recent years throughout the academy at large, while some coherence has developed within subfields. Little scholarship takes up the subject of postfeminism on its own, rather than in relation to a media text, which has prevented the development of shared theory that might then lead to the use of postfeminism as a consistent framework for criticism. The lack of a more widely shared vocabulary of postfeminism and more expansive theory building prevents postfeminism from developing as a critical tool able to explain the complicated cultural constructions that emerge in the period of intermezzo.

What feminism does (not) in distinctions of post and third wave feminism

Feminists need a way to advance our conversations at this complicated and contradictory point in gender politics. We need a language that indicates an understanding of the complexity of interconnected and sometimes oppositional interests of women who have discrepantly enjoyed second wave feminism's gains. We need a way of distinguishing the resulting shifts in strategy, organisation and issue conception in a manner that is not antagonistic to second wave feminism and moves beyond the trope of disavowal that separates the current and future foci of feminism from the past. We need a language that makes sense of this space between the pre-second wave feminist world and the eradication of patriarchy that supersedes 'the defensive posture of the 1980s and 1990s to a collective assertiveness much more characteristic of the feminist movement during the 1960s and 1970s', as Lynn Chancer argued in an expansion of what had previously been one of the earliest feminist uses of third wave feminism (265). But our need for language is not only a need for words, but a need for theorised concepts rooted in shared meaning and shared understanding. The delineation of a theoretical distinction for postfeminism and/or third wave feminism is an important antecedent to their use in cultural criticism and popular discourse. Both postfeminism and third wave feminism can provide a distinction that acknowledges important theoretical shifts broader than the popular realm; yet this theoretical engagement must be balanced with the exploration of spaces of popular culture that have articulated important sites of crisis about feminism and gender roles. As in the case of theory in general, postfeminist/third wave feminist theory should provide a lens that offers a way of understanding a phenomenon or set of relationships, and as such, should serve as a tool that aids the continuation of the feminist project. Such a theorised distinction enables critics to mark the process of changing gender politics without the expectation that cultural artefacts only evince binary extremes such as feminist/antifeminist or before/after feminism.

A language for feminism that contextualises second wave feminism better enables activist formations such as that of differential consciousness suggested by Sandoval in which feminists adapt their activist strategy to the situation or issue at hand – a flexibility she explains as comparable to the shifting of gears in a car (15). Such mutability and adaptation are necessary for the intermezzo, while this conceptual framing also allows us to view the construction of binary gender distinctions as a strategy particular to the early second wave feminist era. At that time, feminists particularly needed to defy hegemonic gender roles and power structures that appeared naturalised and as 'common sense'. After years of critique and deconstruction, many of the constructs once confining women have been denaturalised to an extent decreasing the utility of emphasising their commonality. Likewise, language and theory particular to the intermezzo yields understanding of the relationships between dominant, emergent and residual ideologies during periods of change and the variant ways they might be contested or advanced. Feminism does not need for third wave feminism or postfeminism to indicate only generational distinctions as some have emphasised, particularly in early third wave feminist writing as in Baumgardner and Richards's *Manifesta* (15). Many have written detailed examinations of the unproductive tensions such a distinction creates in breaking from second wave feminism and the complexity of continuing the 'wave' metaphor despite the uncertain emergence of an activist corps comparable to those who fought for suffrage in the first wave and equal access to public spaces in the second wave. Cathryn Bailey has argued that it is problematic to speak of the third wave because of the way it has been used to distance itself from previous feminisms (17), while Deborah Siegel has noted the manner in which young women are an 'always shifting constituency' and of the poststructuralist dilemma of the existence of a category called 'women' (55). Garrison has recently defied the dominant use of the ocean wave metaphor and instead explores how the metaphor of radio waves better indicates the simultaneity of different feminisms in a manner consistent with Sandoval's oppositional consciousness (2005, passim). Indeed, women of a certain age in certain societies do have outlooks that seem to reflect generational positioning, but emphasis on characteristics such as birth year too often elide the more meaningful nature of such a distinction. Large socio-cultural changes have contributed to the fundamental differences in the worldview of women born after the gains of second wave feminism, but these developments are inconsistent and more complicated than just generational distinction. The gains achieved by second wave feminist activism leave women with discrepant access to power that differentiates them in a manner that attention to their generational commonality does not address. The use of these terms as solely chronological distinctions consequently underutilises their potential. This functions more acutely for postfeminism, such as in terming something 'postfeminist' because it occurred in the 1990s or twenty-first century – in which case 'post-second wave feminist' provides a more precise distinction. A theorised post or third wave feminism could provide useful tools for analysing aspects of gender and culture subsequent to second wave feminist intervention, but derives its value from being theoretically as well as historically determined. As Astrid Henry notes, '[a]rticulating this new wave primarily in generational terms, however, has hindered the development of third wave feminism as a political movement or as a critical perspective, particularly because such a movement or perspective requires solidarity premised on more than just generational location' (82). Many of the discourses and representations emerging in or after the 1990s that are casually identified as 'postfeminist' are theoretically linked to second wave feminism, such as empowered women in the role of violent predator/defender characters who are able to be simultaneously musclebound, sweaty and glamorous. Indiscriminately labelling contemporary cultural forms as postfeminist or third wave feminist erodes the likelihood of developing a more precise use of the terms and dilutes any limited shared understanding by increasing the breadth of meaning. Despite the uncertainty such a period of intermezzo might produce, everything that is different from what has come before cannot and should not be named postfeminist or characteristic of third wave feminism. Using postfeminism and third wave feminism as signifiers of too many disparate ideas diminishes their utility and further exacerbates existing confusion about the terms. The frequent use of postfeminism to demarcate arguably 'feminist' developments raises questions about whether these terms can be used interchangeably in certain contexts or what a distinction of third wave is meant to signal. Sparing and deliberate use of these terms and continued discussions aimed at establishing their theoretical and political distinction will be most valuable to thinking through this period of intermezzo and reasserting feminist activist agendas.

Some of the more common uses of postfeminism, particularly in critical media studies, are at odds with the argument for the theoretically based distinction advocated for here. Much of this scholarship is very good and provides valuable analysis; however, decontextualised and unexplained 'term dropping' of postfeminism, particularly in cases where feminism or feminist (or anti-feminism/ist) provides a more accurate theoretical identification, works contrary to the establishment of a theoretically informed delimitation of these terms. Neither post nor third wave feminism has yet become an organised (or even disorganised) political movement of any significance. Postfeminism has not won women any freedoms and in rare cases does the term third wave feminism denote the organisation of a distinct activist formation. An exception may be the U.S.-based Third Wave Foundation. Here too, although emphasising diversity among women seems central to the organisation, the distinction from second wave feminism remains unclear and the group problematically identifies its distinctiveness as its focus on 'young women and transgendered youth'. What happens when these youth age beyond the 15 to 30-year-old focus of the organisation? Are they too old for third wave feminism? In an interview with Stacy Gillis and Rebecca Munford in this book, Elaine Showalter noted the sense among many of her generation that feminism was in the midst of 'a very bad patch' and expressed doubt that another women's movement would exist. The absence of a 'women's movement' should not suggest the end of feminism or activism, but the complexity of the diverse goals women and men now seek in gender politics and social justice, as well as the emergence of new social movements, take different formations and use different strategies. Distinctions such as postfeminism and third wave are most beneficial when they aid us in making sense of the historical, cultural and economic norms feminists now encounter. These words can be powerful tools for continuing feminist legacies but should not serve as soundbites or as a way to make those of us who have enjoyed the most privileges feel special and as though we have a feminism of our own. The uncertainty of intermezzo and complexity of generational transition are not media constructions, but challenges that feminism faces alongside many remaining goals in its pursuit of equitable and just societies.

Notes

1. Susan Faludi traces the use of postfeminism to the 1920s following the feminist victory in the right to vote. Until the mid-1990s, postfeminism was more uniformly used to denote something 'after' feminism (Faludi 50). The word begins appearing more frequently in the popular press coterminously with Faludi's influential book.
2. A query in April 2006 searching uses of each term in the full-text of major international newspapers in the past five years in the Lexis-Nexis database

yielded 143 entries for postfeminism and 48 for third wave feminism. Both hyphenated and unhyphenated uses of both terms are included in the tallies.
3. Brooks mistakenly confuses the work of the sociologist Judith Stacey and the film scholar Jackie Stacey in her bibliography in a manner that may confuse some.

Works cited

Bailey, Cathryn. 'Making Waves and Drawing Lines: The Politics of Defining the Vicissitudes of Feminism.' *Hypatia* 12.3 (1997): 17–29.

Baumgardner, Jennifer and Amy Richards. *Manifesta: Young Women, Feminism and the Future*. New York: Farrar, Straus and Giroux, 2000.

Brooks, Ann. *Postfeminisms: Feminism, Cultural Theory, and Cultural Forms*. New York: Routledge, 1997.

Brunsdon, Charlotte. 'Feminism, Post-feminism, Martha, Martha, and Nigella.' *Cinema Journal* 44.2 (2005): 110–16.

——. *Screen Tastes: Soap Opera to Satellite Dishes*. London: Routledge, 1997.

Chancer, Lynn S. *Reconcilable Differences: Confronting Beauty, Pornography and the Future of Feminism*. Berkeley: California University Press, 1998.

Dicker, Rory and Alison Piepmeier. Introduction. *Catching a Wave: Reclaiming Feminism of the 21st Century*. Ed. Rory Dicker and Alison Piepmeier. Boston: Northeastern University Press, 2003. 3–28.

——, eds. *Catching a Wave: Reclaiming Feminism of the 21st Century*. Boston: Northeastern University Press, 2003.

Dow, Bonnie J. *Prime-time Feminism: Television, Media Culture, and the Women's Movement Since 1970*. Philadelphia: Pennsylvania University Press, 1996.

Faludi, Susan. *Backlash: The Undeclared War Against American Women*. New York: Crown, 1991.

Findlen, Barbara, ed. *Listen Up: Voices from the Next Feminist Generation*. Seattle: Seal, 1995.

Garrison, Ednie Kaeh. 'Are We On a Wavelength Yet? On Feminist Oceanography, Radios, and Third Wave Feminism.' *Different Wavelengths: Studies of the Contemporary Women's Movement*. Ed. Jo Reger. New York: Routledge, 2005. 237–56.

——. 'U.S. Feminism-GRRRL Style! Youth (Sub)Cultures and the Technologics of the Third Wave.' *Feminist Studies* 26.1 (2000): 141–70.

Gillis, Stacy. ' "Which Domestic Goddess Are You?": (Post)feminism and the Fetishisation of the Domestic.' *Society for Cinema and Media Studies* Conference. London, April 2005.

Henry, Astrid. 'Solitary Sisterhood: Individualism Meets Collectivity in Feminism's Third Wave.' *Different Wavelengths: Studies of the Contemporary Women's Movement*. Ed. Jo Reger. New York: Routledge, 2005. 81–96.

Heywood, Leslie, and Jennifer Drake. Introduction. *Third Wave Agenda: Being Feminist, Doing Feminism*. Minneapolis: Minnesota University Press, 1997. 1–20.

——, eds. *Third Wave Agenda: Being Feminist, Doing Feminism*. Minneapolis: Minnesota University Press, 1997.

Kim, L. S. 'Sex and the Single Girl in Postfeminism: The F Word on Television.' *Television & New Media* 2.4 (2001): 319–34.

Lotz, Amanda D. 'Communicating Third-Wave Feminism and New Social Movements: Challenges for the Next Century of Feminist Endeavor.' *Women and Language* 26.1 (2003): 2–9.

McRobbie, Angela. 'Post-feminism and Popular Culture.' *Feminist Media Studies* 4.3 (2004): 255–64.

Moseley, Rachael and Jacinda Read. 'Having it *Ally*: Popular Television (Post-)feminism.' *Feminist Media Studies* 2.2 (2002): 231–49.

Negra, Diane. ' "Quality Postfeminism?": Sex and the Single Girl on HBO.' *Genders* 39 (2004). <www.genders.org/g39/g39_negra.html>. Accessed 7 July 2004.

Ouellette, Laurie. 'Victims No More: Postfeminism, Television, and *Ally McBeal*.' *The Communication Review* 5 (2002): 315–35.

Projansky, Sarah. *Watching Rape: Film and Television in Postfeminist Culture*. New York: New York University Press, 2001.

Rapp, Rayna. 'Is the Legacy of Second-Wave Feminism Postfeminism?' 1988. *Women, Class, and the Feminist Imagination*. Ed. Karen Hansen and Ilene J. Philipson. Philadelphia: Temple University Press, 1990. 357–62.

Sandoval, Chela. 'U.S. Third World Feminism: The Theory and Method of Oppositional Consciousness in the Postmodern World.' *Genders* 10 (1991): 1–24.

Schoemer, Karen. 'A High-Culture Aristocrat who's Tops in Pop, Too.' *New York Times* 19 Aug. 2001, B24.

Shalit, Ruth. 'Canny and Lacy.' *The New Republic* 6 Apr.(1998): 32.

Siegel, Deborah L. 'The Legacy of the Personal: Generating Theory in Feminism's Third Wave.' *Hypatia* 12.3 (1997): 46–75.

Stacey, Judith. 'Sexism by a Subtler Name?: Postindustrial Conditions and Postfeminist Consciousness in Silicon Valley.' *Socialist Review* 96 (1987): 7–28.

Walker, Rebecca. 'Becoming the Third Wave.' *Ms.* January (1992): 39–41.

Walker, Rebecca, ed. *To Be Real: Telling the Truth and Changing the Face of Feminism*. New York: Doubleday, 1995.

Walters, Suzanna Danuta. *Material Girls: Making Sense of Feminist Cultural Theory*. Berkeley: California University Press, 1995.

Young, Cathy. 'The Postfeminist Mommy Track.' *The Boston Globe* 26 Sept. 2005, A13.

7

'You're Not One of Those Boring Masculinists, Are You?'

The Question of Male-Embodied Feminism

Andrew Shail*

> [T]his is akin to saying that a non-white view is desirable because it would help to fill in a hole to lessen the critical pressure and to give the illusion of a certain incompleteness that needs the native's input to be more complete, but is ultimately dependent on white authority to attain any form of 'real' completion. ... Indigenous anthropology allows white anthropology to further anthropologize Man.
>
> (Minh-Ha 72)

* * *

Can men be feminists? Is 'male feminism' even viable? Is it at all politically requisite? If the progression central to the development of anti-patriarchal cultural consciousness is 'Feminine, Feminist, and Female' (Showalter 1977, 13), can men have any business in the sisterhood? If women 'need to need men less in order to enjoy them more' (Greer), then 'male feminism' may be equivalent to ignorant sabotage. But every third wave feminist must have asked whether social and sexual change requires men to be more than pro-feminists. In this chapter I discuss problems with existing models of male-embodied feminism as well as the two potential validations of male-embodied feminism offered by masculinity studies and transgender studies, and go on to posit a way out of the male-embodied feminist impasse.

From *in* feminism to *doing* feminism

The question of men and feminism was raised in the earliest Women's Liberation Movement demonstrations and conferences, and academia has been both the forum and the subject of discussion on male-embodied feminism.[1] In 1976, Annette Kolodny claimed that men in the academy were hijacking feminist achievements when the label of feminist gave them the privilege of teaching areas that others had made possible, often by risking their entire professional careers (831). In 1983, Elaine Showalter suggested that feminist criticism was being co-opted by academic men who found in it 'the mixture of theoretical sophistication with the sort of effective political engagement they have been calling for in their own critical spheres' (131). Newly 'feminist' scholars Jonathan Culler and Terry Eagleton, she argued, typified a broader cultural attempt to silence feminism by speaking 'for' it. The following year Stephen Heath concurred:

> The effects of feminism in academic institutions with the development of women's studies and an awareness generally of the need to consider women and their representation have led to a situation where 'things to do with women' are tolerated ... if not accepted, as an area of interest, of possible study, with men thus able to make radical gestures at little cost. (18)

Male-embodied feminism appeared as the latest repetition of 'an age-old rapine, colonizing, and finally silencing gesture' (Smith 1994, par. 2), a symptom of (distinctly non-feminist) competitive professional anxiety.

Worse, Heath wrote, as men are 'agents of the structure to be transformed' (1), male-embodied desire to be 'in' feminism was just the last feint in a long history of patriarchal colonisations. Alice Jardine argued in 1987 that 'men are jumping on the feminist theory bandwagon at a time when it is experiencing a certain success in the academy and – paradoxically – at a time when the larger political context in which we are living gets more reactionary for women' (57). The male-embodied impulse to 'enter' feminism was identified, at worst, as confidence that feminism posed no practical danger to male hegemony and, at best, as fuelled by a desire to lessen a sense of guilt. This first phase of scholarship on male feminism read the phenomenon as both signalling the demise of feminist activity in Western culture at large and as an echo of a familiar historical reduction of women to the stakes in a homo-erotic struggle. Male feminism implied both that women must be taught by men how to win their rights, and an approach expressible as 'thanks for bringing this patriarchy stuff to our attention ladies, we'll take it from here' (Kimmel 1998, 62). Rowena Fowler pointed out that women were beginning to warn of the dangers of wholesale male engagement with feminist criticism 'at the same time that men are using the complaint of exclusion to launch a counterattack on it' (51). Even those later revising Showalter and Heath could not deny that it was all too easy for a 'male feminist' voice to become entangled with patriarchal rhetoric, a common conclusion being that the men-feminism relationship could not therefore confidently extend beyond 'conscientious hearing' (Smith 1994, par. 6).

At the end of the 1980s a second phase of thought on male feminism, which included Michael Cadden, Andrew Ross, Joseph Boone and Paul Smith, pointed to male academics with no pre-feminist career, men who 'have no choice but to work with feminism because its discourses are preeminently instructive in relation to issues which are simultaneously men's problems and feminism's cause' (Smith 1987, 39), as the *bona fide* male feminists. Boone and Cadden cited Showalter's part in bringing about their collection when arguing that the targets of her rejoinder were in fact not identical with the whole phenomenon of 'men and feminism'. The real male feminists, they argued, were not the big names that, as she had pointed out, had been attempting to hijack the theoretical fruits of feminist struggle, but a generation of men who, they wrote, had been ' "engendered" by feminism' (Boone and Cadden 2). While the emergence of this generation did not in itself allay the problem of appropriation, it suggested 'a scenario qualitatively *different* from ... "Bandwagoning" or "Divide and Conquer" theories of male feminism' (Boone 11; emphasis in original). Boone, and most of the contributors to Boone and Cadden's *Engendering Men* (1990), also suggested that labelling male feminism as rapine was based on an unsubstantiated belief that male interest was driven by heterosexual desire (23). The subsequent collections on men and feminism – David Porter's *Between Men and Feminism* (1992), Tom Digby's *Men Doing Feminism* (1998) and Steven Schacht P. and Doris W. Ewing's *Feminism and Men* (1998) – indicated a widespread academic acceptance of at least the possibility, if not the necessity, of something like male-embodied feminism.

It could be argued that male gender scholars are disadvantaged because of a tendency amongst critics to ascribe bad feminist scholarship by women to phallogocentric normativity and bad feminist scholarship by men to willing collusion. But there seems little possibility of such qualitative equivalence: introducing their collection, Steven Schacht and Doris Ewing justify claims for the necessity of male feminism with reference to feminism's supposed errors in properly theorising gender, claims which betray their own failure to understand feminist theory. 'Much of contemporary feminism', they write, 'has demonised men as the oppressive other, refusing to give its energy to men's issues and concerns' (1998, 8). Their recent work *Feminism with Men* (2004) perceives feminism as an identity movement based on 'simply and categorically defining men as the enemy' (7). This accusation of feminist failing lacks awareness of feminist theory. Such slight theoretical dexterity in the thinking of many 'male feminists' is used to answer the question of 'can men be feminists?' affirmatively while simultaneously displaying a vast insufficiency in the kinds of theorising seen by the male-embodied as 'adequately' feminist. It seems that even if there are sincere reasons why men can be feminists, there is no question of needing them to be feminists if this is the limit of their feminist ability.

Blind alleys

As most of the impossibilities of male-embodied feminism bemoaned in the first phase of thinking about male feminism related to descriptions of the male-embodied 'penetrating' a women-only subject, these might seem obsolete with masculinity qualifying as both a gender and an object of critical attention. Michael Kimmel claims that it is through studies of masculinity that feminism can become intelligible to men (1998, *passim*). That roughly half of the contributions to Schacht and Ewing's *Feminism and Men* were studies of masculinity or are contributed by established masculinity scholars signals the assumption that feminism by the male-embodied should compensate for their perceived feminist refusal 'to give its energy to men's issues and concerns' (Schact and Ewing 1998, 8) by concentrating on masculinity. Lynne Segal notes, however, that after having exposed 'the institutional space women fought so hard to create just over two decades ago' (232) to the possibility of neutralisation in helping promote the shift from women's studies to gender studies, she was then faced with the appalling spectre of an emerging masculinity studies that claimed equivalence with feminism: 'What men found when finally, in the wake of feminism, they turned to survey themselves ... provided an analogue of women's adversities: evidence of constraint, unease, misery' (237). The ethos of the contemporary men's movement – paralleling a 'men's struggle' alongside 'women's struggle', rewriting oppression histories of feminism, and putting feminism down as either an unsuccessful or over-successful venture – has inflected masculinity studies.[2] Because the formation of the discipline of masculinity studies owed so much to the transformations in thinking about masculinity effected by feminism, masculinity scholars have something of an alibi in calling masculinity studies 'a feminism of its own' (Bristow 60), but this frequently repeats backlash assessments of feminism. Schacht and Ewing point to fractures and differences within feminism, describing it as exclusive and arguing that it should be inclusive of men (2004, 7): in doing so they ascribe its lack of success to feminism itself rather than to opposition to it. Occurring within an ostensibly pro-feminist work, this is precisely the cultural logic of the backlash. This suggests that the acceptance of male feminism is intimately linked to the deradicalisation of feminist theory in the 1980s as described by Gillian Howie and Ashley Tauchert elsewhere in this collection.[3]

Other recent claims to male-embodied feminism have asserted that '[h]aving a woman's experience and perceiving as a woman isn't what makes a woman feminist – plenty of them aren't' (Hopkins 50) and that 'women's experience' is a phenomenon not specific to the female body; available to men because of a radical discontinuity between sex and culturally constructed genders. Is 'male feminism' tenable on the basis of claims to possess a transgendered self? Given that separate-sphere ideology perceives women as 'more gifted than men in the realms of authenticity – in arenas that involve emotion, care-taking, relational ethics' (Voskuil 612) – it would seem that the association of femaleness with authenticity in the incantation 'women's experience' is unable to read the historical text of gender. Transgender theory could be used to point out that supposing men to be merely clones of feminism's nemesis is to severely oversimplify the mechanisms of gender. Judith Halberstam, Eve Sedgwick and others have helped dissolve the critical assumption that everything that can be said about masculinity pertains in the first place to men, Sedgwick writing that 'I as a woman am also a producer of masculinities, and a performer of them' (13). While female masculinities appear pathological in order that male masculinity may emerge as the 'real thing', masculinity has always been produced by and across both male and female bodies, and the identification of men with oppression is one of the myths that have hampered a thoroughgoing theorisation of gender and 'ensured that masculinity and maleness are profoundly difficult to pry apart' (Halberstam 2). The feminist argument for the importance of recognising the danger and arbitrariness of the myth that is the phallus would seem to risk turning history back into nature if it subscribes to the identification of masculinity with biological maleness produced by such statements as 'the problem of feminism was and remains men' (N. Segal 36). Halberstam poses female masculinity as the requisite device for opposing 'a more generalized discussion of masculinity within cultural studies that seems intent on insisting that masculinity remain the property of male bodies' (15). Likewise, feminism performed by 'men' could be, and has been, claimed as an essential counterpart (Schacht and Ewing 2004, 97–98).

Could feminism practised by non-masculine male-embodied subjects be therefore not just possible but helpful or even necessary for the successful dissemination of a radical critique of gender? No. Christine Battersby points out that claims to mental androgyny do not entail any special sympathy with women: for example, 'when a writer like Coleridge insisted that the mind of the great artist is androgynous, he certainly did not mean that such a mind has any special empathy with woman' (7–8). Such valorisations of femininity disguise the fact that it is not femininity but femaleness that has been persistently downgraded in the production of knowledge and in patriarchal culture at large. Indeed, the supposed anti-normativity of transgender theory is dependent, in part, on erroneously selling feminism short as normative and essentialist.

Body

The notion of the sexed being underlying these discussions has bypassed a major stream of feminist theory which has major implications for the identity 'feminist'. As Judith Butler, Rosalyn Diprose, Moira Gatens and Elizabeth Grosz approach in various lexicons, sex is the primary product of the 'intextuating' (Grosz 34) of bodies. Often thought of as an argument that ontological sex differences do not exist, this stream of thought points out that their being held as constitutive of 'sex' is the result of the operation of gender on bodies, and that sex is the result of the discursive 'production of intelligibility' of all physical variations in reference to genitalia/reproduction. The (only) two taxonomic terms – 'male' and 'female' – consequently created are then specified as primary states of being. When looking at a body, certainty of its membership in one or another part of a two-sex system is derived from this operation of gender on the form of ontological knowledge available for use in classification. Bodies that present as neither entirely male nor entirely female expose the complex operation of multiple levels of body-sexing (hormonal sex, gonadal sex, chromosomal sex, internal morphologic sex, external morphologic sex or procreative sex), and hint at the morphological similarity elided in the penis/vagina 'distinction'. Accounts of surgical 'corrections' provide a glimpse of the effect of gender on the production of knowledges about (and of) 'sex' in the first place. Following the early Enlightenment progression from sex understood as variation (with men being simply women with a greater 'vital heat') to sex-as-difference (with maleness and femaleness engineered as distinct and 'opposite' in every physical degree), any diversity of characteristics discovered – where the vast majority of similarities discovered are simply not reported – in bones, flesh organs and chemicals is generated into 'sex' by pre-existing convictions of dualism (Laqueur 5–14; Stolberg 285–89). Gender, therefore, 'ought not to be conceived merely as the cultural inscription of meaning on a pregiven sex'. Rather, 'gender is the discursive cultural means by which "sexed nature" is produced and established as "prediscursive" ' (Butler 1990, 7), a productive apparatus for the establishment of sex.

This is not to base an argument for male-embodied feminism on the supposed 'absence' of 'femaleness.' After writing in 1983 that '[t]he "feminine male" may have experiences that are socially coded as "feminised" but these experiences must be qualitatively different from female experience of the feminine' (150), in 1996 Moira Gatens *maintained* that

> to say that 'woman' has no essence, that she is a constructed fiction, a product of social narratives and practices is not to say that she does not exist ... it calls for a commitment to a historical, or genealogical, approach to understanding the specificity of social, political and ethical relations *as they are embodied* in this or that community or culture. (104–05; emphasis in original)

In her later discussion of the uses of the term 'experience' by Australian judges in rape trials, central to her argument is the idea that while some men have experience of being raped, very few – if any – have experience of being female-embodied and being raped (138–41). Even if the female-embodied do not experience uniform subjugation, they do experience the consequences of their sexing female in a qualitatively specific way and so have a commonality independent of their subordination. To acknowledge that 'sex' and 'naturalness' itself is constituted through discursively constrained performative acts is not to argue either that embodied history is not a prime determinant of experience, or that a political imbalance between male embodiment and female embodiment does not delimit comprehensions within the capacity of the body politic.[4] In the words of Diprose, 'the moral, legal, industrial and inter-personal evaluation of sexual difference is productive: it produces the modes of sexed embodiment it regulates ... any injustice experienced by women begins from this mode of production and maintenance of sexual difference' (viii). Diprose acknowledges that while the idea of the generating of sex through the apparatus of gender is a necessary addition to feminist thought, 'the value and status enjoyed by men in patriarchal social relations is generated through the constitution of women's modes of embodied existence as other to the norm ... sexed bodies are constituted within an economy of representation of sexual difference which limits possibilities for women' (ix). Female sexed identity is both constituted *and* excluded by social relations. The typical pro-'male feminist' argument that '[t]o categorically denounce the possibility that men could become feminists ... is an essentialist argument that treats the categories of male and female as absolute states of being' (Schacht and Ewing 2004, 97) perpetuates ignorance of the constitutedness of sex.[5]

If, as Naomi Schor pointed out in 1987, 'no feminist theoretician *who is not also a woman*' ever espoused claims to a female specificity (109; emphasis in original), ideas of sexual indifferentiation could very well be the latest ruse of phallocentrism, the radical negation of female-embodiment repeating one of the gestures on which male-embodiment is founded: '[m]en take on the roles of neutral knowers only because they have evacuated their own specific forms of corporeality and repressed all its traces from the knowledge they produce' (Grosz 38). Butler advocates *displacement* of the term 'women' (1990, 4) rather than dismissal because she is aware, first, of the danger (and male-embodied tradition) of marking 'the female' as non-existent/false consciousness/ 'make-up' and, second, that the contemporaneity of sexed embodiment does not make it any less of a reality.[6] Because gender designates the operation of power on bodies productive of dichotomous sex, claims to a viable male-embodied feminist space on the basis of a transgendered self not only oversimplify the functions of the term 'experience' but leave a gender ontology essentially intact in sex.[7] On the other hand, while Germaine Greer's comment that a colloquium on men and feminism might as well be entitled 'Men and Menstrual Pain' (qtd. Digby 1) is a keen observation of embodied experience, and referring to menstruality as a touchstone rehearses the establishment of sex as prediscursive. Although, as Valérie Fournier writes, 'the flesh of the wounded body has a vivid and compelling reality (the presence, certainty, immediacy and totality of pain) that can be drafted into the substantiation of ideas' (69), pain is one of the discourses by which a specific body is constituted female. This is not to say that the female-embodied do not feel a disproportionate amount of pain in their life-span, but that pain is generative of, rather than derived from, dichotomous sex. The act of signifying the body as prior to signification, so easily rehearsed by anyone invoking menstruality, demarcates a body that it then claims to find prior to all signification (Butler 1993, 30). Works on the sex of feminists likewise exemplify notions of ontological being-as-dichotomously-sexed, contributing to the internal stability of the terms 'men' and 'women' and relying on gender ('sex' being a result of the productive apparatus of gender) while claiming to relinquish gender altogether. Female-embodied feminists have long been unsettled with a distinction between sex and gender that sees the former as prediscursive (Gatens 1983 passim; Delphy 144).

Feminism

It is very easy to be pro-feminist when difference establishes as prediscursive a range of gendered political operations. As long as male-embodied feminism falls back on beliefs of dichotomous sex, masculinity will continue to be the preserve of maleness, and maleness will always exist on which to rebuild masculinity, allowing crisis – maleness itself being a product/result of the operation of gender upon a set of bodies – to be masculinity's enjoyed condition in perpetuity. With the UK Men's Movement still substantiating Richard Doyle's 1986 statement that feminists are 'would be [sic] castrators with a knee-jerk, obsessive aversion to anything male' (qtd. Kimmel 1996, 305) it is not 'men being feminists' but the radical problematisation of maleness that would successfully dissolve such male-embodied thinking.[8] If the unity of the subject of feminism is effectively undermined by the representational discourse ('women') in which it functions, feminism constituting a single ground which is invariably contested by the (anti-)identity positions it thereby excludes (e.g. anomalous bodies that are not covered by markers of impregnability, XX chromosomes, ovaries, unambiguous genitalia, regular periods, etc.), it does not follow that the subject of feminism should include men. Maleness is one of the primary mechanisms by which 'women' as the other half of a dichotomously sexed production is constituted and maintained. To be anywhere near feminist, the male-embodied cannot continue consolidating the mechanism 'sex' whereby discourse produces the effects that it names. The steady dissemination of the second wave account of the constructedness of gender will continue to be undermined if the subterranean half of the sex-gender loop (that gender epistemologies materialise bodies as sexed) is not mapped onto this model by the third wave of feminism. The critique of the sex/ gender distinction 'is a critique without which feminism loses its democratizing potential' (Butler 1993, 29). Indeed, sociologists are acknowledging that 'the cutting edge' of contemporary social theorising around the body may be located within feminism (Williams and Bendelow 130).

If the third wave of feminism cannot orient its critical practice in the sexed specificity of 'femaleness', the contingencies of female-embodiment *can* continue to provide grounds for feminist politics.[9] Injuries and violations can be verified without reference to sex. Butler writes that the category of women, through deconstruction, 'becomes one whose uses are no longer reified as "referents", and which stand a chance of ... coming to signify in ways that none of us can predict in advance' (1993, 29). Where maleness is both a myth of its own non-existence and a result of the constant repetition of the metaphysics of heterosexism and phallogocentrism, the genealogy/relinquishing of maleness would be a major mobilisation.[10] If uncertainty remains as to whether there is any possibility of effective subversion from within the terms of a discursive identity, possibilities of recirculation for the sites from which gender is produced do always exist. Any invocation of maleness, of which discourse surrounding 'male feminism' is a thorough example, denies the possibility of both disrupting the regulatory fiction of the sex/gender distinction and of dissolving sex as the primary intextuant of bodies. Feminism must not remain reducible in the popular imagination to 'another' articulation of sex-as-difference. It could be argued that the feminist project needs 'women' as much, or as little, as it needs 'men', but the point is not to argue for the practicability of male-embodied spokespeople, rather that the dissolution of the operations of power constitutive of sex needs to be capably imagined. It is time – in this third wave of feminism – to acknowledge not that 'men' can be feminists but that the critique of the category of sex can and must exist beyond the historically contingent sexed ontology that is femaleness.

Notes

* Title quotation: Arlene Rimmer to Arnold Rimmer, in the *Red Dwarf* episode 'Parallel Universe.' (1988).

1. See Amanda Goldrick-Jones for an account of men's pro-feminist organisations and publications in the US, UK and Canada since the 1970s.

2. 'Me-tooism' also substantiates such supposedly feminist works on 'men' as Rebecca Walker's collection *What Makes a Man* (2004), a 'suffocating in their suits of armour' model that likewise underpins Schacht and Ewing's work: feminism inclusive of men is justified for them by the need for men to 'realise that their pain, both physical and mental, is the result of patriarchal values' (1998, 14).

3. In a revival of the 'we'll take it from here' approach mentioned above, Schacht and Ewing use as the second of their three arguments for male feminism that '[s]ince men often have more access to power and money, categorically opposing their participation in the struggle dooms feminism to remain a stalled social movement and an unfinished revolution. Quite simply it is unreasonable to believe that women alone will be able to construct a nonoppressive future' (2004, 97).

4. It is as crucial to note the Spinoza/Nietzsche/Freud/Lacan/Foucault contribution to the genealogy of bodies as it is to note that even Foucault does not address the question of the body-as-dichotomously-sexed (Butler 1993, 69). For a genealogy of the notion of 'experience' aimed at removing the concept from feminist epistemology, see Patrick Hopkins.

5. This is the first of their three arguments for 'male feminism'.

6. As Ashley Tauchert points out, male-embodied 'feminists' have a great excuse for failing to engage with the specific oppressions focused on the female-embodied: 'the ideological dominance of Enlightenment philosophy means that refusing the gender-neutral approach becomes interchangeable with arguing that you shouldn't treat people as individuals' (50).

7. An example of this is Schacht and Ewing's radical sameness agenda (disguised as a case for total relativity), which envisions both 'men's' and 'women's' experiences as contributions to "the advancement of a feminist agenda", since, they argue, the assumption that women have more access to the truth subscribes to the illusion that one perspective on the world can be accurate (2004, 97–98). Placing equal value on male-embodied and female-embodied experience (their third of three arguments for 'male feminism') ignores the fact that these differences are themselves the product of social relations.

8. Schacht and Ewing argue that a paradigm shift from the feminism theory they (reductively) describe to one that conceives of its object as the operations of gender in bodies in general was necessary (2004, 8). That they do so in ignorance of precisely such a shift having already occurred in the work put forward by Butler, Grosz, Gatens and Diprose suggests the kind of theoretical sophistication and awareness with which the arguments for male feminism are content.

9. Grosz argues that feminism must successfully make female embodiment the object of knowledge through a structural reorganisation of (covertly male-embodied) positions of knowing and their effects on the kinds of object known (40) and that the abandonment of knowledges and reversion to intuition or experience is no solution. If experience provides the ground for feminist activism, therefore, it cannot provide the basis for the corpus of feminist politics.

10. This is not to advocate the same 'forgetting' of maleness that informs the perspectives and enunciative positions constitutive of *knowledges*, the isomorphism of theory with male-embodiment already extant.

Works cited

Battersby, Christine. *Gender and Genius: Towards a Feminist Aesthetics*. London: Women's Press, 1989.

Boone, Joseph. 'Of Me(n) and Feminism: Whose is the Sex That Writes?' *Engendering Men: The Question of Male Feminist Criticism*. Ed. Joseph Boone and Michael Cadden. London: Routledge, 1990. 11–25.

Boone, Joseph, and Michael Cadden. Introduction. *Engendering Men: The Question of Male Feminist Criticism.* Ed. Joseph Boone and Michael Cadden. London: Routledge, 1990. 1–7.

Bristow, Joseph. 'Men After Feminism: Sexual Politics Twenty Years On.' *Between Men and Feminism.* Ed. David Porter. London: Routledge, 1992. 57–79.

Butler, Judith. *Bodies That Matter: On the Discursive Limits of 'Sex.'* London: Routledge, 1993.

——. *Gender Trouble: Feminism and the Subversion of Identity.* London: Routledge, 1990.

Delphy, Christine. *Close to Home: A Materialist Analysis of Women's Oppression.* Trans. Diana Leonard. London: Hutchinson, 1984.

Digby, Tom. Introduction. *Men Doing Feminism.* Ed. Tom Digby. London: Routledge, 1998. 1–14.

——, ed. *Men Doing Feminism.* London: Routledge, 1998.

Diprose, Rosalyn. *The Bodies of Women: Ethics, Embodiment and Sexual Difference.* London: Routledge, 1994.

Fournier, Valérie. 'Fleshing out Gender: Crafting Gender Identity on Women's Bodies.' *Body and Society* 8.2 (2002): 55–77.

Fowler, Rowena. 'Feminist Criticism: The Common Pursuit.' *New Literary History* 19.1 (1987): 51–62.

Gatens, Moira. 'A Critique of the Sex/Gender Distinction.' *Beyond Marxism?: Interventions after Marx.* Eds. J. Allen and Paul Patten. Sydney: Intervention, 1983. 143–160.

——. *Imaginary Bodies: Ethics, Power and Corporeality.* London: Routledge, 1996.

Goldrick-Jones, Amanda. 'Men in Feminism: Relationships and Differences.' *Gender, Race and Nation: A Global Perspective.* Ed. Vanaja Dhruvarajan and Jill Vickers. Toronto: Toronto University Press, 2002. 184–204.

Greer, Germaine. 'Do We Really Need Men?' Keynote Address. *Third Wave Feminism* Conference. University of Exeter, UK. 23 July 2002.

Grosz, Elizabeth. *Space, Time and Perversion.* London: Routledge, 1995.

Halberstam, Judith. *Female Masculinity.* Durham: Duke University Press, 1998.

Heath, Stephen. 'Men in Feminism.' 1984. *Men in Feminism.* Ed. Alice Jardine and Paul Smith. London: Routledge, 1987. 1–32.

Hopkins, Patrick. 'How Feminism Made a Man Out of Me: The Proper Subject of Feminism and the Problem of Men.' *Men Doing Feminism.* Ed. Tom Digby. London: Routledge, 1998. 33–56.

Jardine, Alice. 'Men in Feminism: Odor di Uomo or Compagnons de Route?' *Men in Feminism.* Ed. Alice Jardine and Paul Smith. London: Routledge, 1987. 54–61.

Kimmel, Michael. *Manhood in America: A Cultural History.* London: The Free Press, 1996.

——. 'Who's Afraid of Men Doing Feminism?' *Men Doing Feminism.* Ed. Tom Digby. London: Routledge, 1998. 57–68.

Kolodny, Annette. 'The Feminist as Literary Critic.' *Critical Inquiry* 2 (1976): 830–31.

Laqueur, Thomas. *Making Sex: Body and Gender from the Greeks to Freud.* Cambridge: Harvard University Press, 1990.

Minh-Ha, Trin T. *When the Moon Waxes Red.* London: Routledge, 1991.

'Parallel Universe.' *Red Dwarf.* By Robert Grant and Douglas Naylor. BBC2. 11 Oct 1988.

Porter, David, ed. *Between Men and Feminism.* London: Routledge, 1992.

Schacht, Steven P. and Doris W. Ewing. *Feminism With Men: Bridging the Gender Gap*. Toronto: Rowman & Littlefield, 2004.
——. Introduction. *Feminism and Men: Reconstructing Gender Relations*. Ed. Steven P. Schacht and Doris W. Ewing. New York: New York University Press, 1998. 1–17.
——, eds. *Feminism and Men: Reconstructing Gender Relations*. New York: New York University Press, 1998.
Schor, Naomi. 'Dreaming Dissymetry.' *Men in Feminism*. Ed. Alice Jardine and Paul Smith. London: Routledge, 1987. 98–110.
Sedgwick, Eve. 'Gosh Boy George, You Must be Awfully Secure in your Masculinity!' *Constructing Masculinity*. Ed. Maurice Berger, Brian Wallis and Simon Watson. London: Routledge, 1995. 11–20.
Segal, Lynne. 'Back to the Boys? Temptations of the Good Gender Theorist.' *Textual Practice* 15.2 (2001): 231–50.
Segal, Naomi. 'Why Can't a Good Man be Sexy? Why Can't a Sexy Man be Good?' *Between Men and Feminism*. Ed. David Porter. London: Routledge, 1992. 35–47.
Showalter, Elaine. 'Critical Cross-Dressing: Male Feminists and the Woman of the Year.' 1983. *Men in Feminism*. Ed. Alice Jardine and Paul Smith. London: Routledge, 1987. 116–32.
——. *A Literature of Their Own: British Women Novelists from Brontë to Doris Lessing*. Princeton: Princeton University Press, 1977.
Smith, Paul. 'Good Boys: Afterword to *Men in Feminism*.' *Cultronix* 2 (1994). Accessed: 1 Sept. 2006. <http://eserver.org/cultronix/smith/>.
——. 'Men in Feminism: Men and Feminist Theory.' *Men in Feminism*. Ed. Alice Jardine and Paul Smith. London: Routledge, 1987. 33–40.
Stolberg, Michael. 'A Woman Down to her Bones: The Anatomy of Sexual Difference in Early Modern Europe.' *Isis* 94 (2003): 274–99.
Tauchert, Ashley. 'Writing Like a Girl: Revisiting Women's Literary History.' *Critical Quarterly* 44.1 (2002): 49–76.
UK Men's Movement. Barry Worrall. N. pub. Accessed: 1 Sept. 2006. <http:// www. ukmm.org.uk/>.
Voskuil, Lynn. 'Acts of Madness: Lady Audley and the Meanings of Victorian Femininity.' *Feminist Studies* 27.3 (2001): 611–39.
Walker, Rebecca, ed. *What Makes a Man: 22 Writers Imagine the Future*. New York: Riverhead, 2004.
Williams, Simon, and Gillian Bendelow. *The Lived Body: Sociological Themes, Embodied Issues*. London: Routledge, 1998.

Part II
Locales and Locations

8
Wa(i)ving It All Away
Producing Subject and Knowledge in Feminisms of Colours

*Mridula Nath Chakraborty**

This chapter is an intervention into post-identity and post-second wave feminist debates about essentialism and difference. Hegemonic feminism has obviated the possibilities of coalitions with differential feminisms through abandoning essentialism as a necessary tool by which to theorise identity politics. Hegemonic feminism's prioritisation of sex over race has been characterised by – and is symptomatic of – its anxiety over race, racial identity politics and racialised essentialism. This anxiety, in turn, marks itself as white, neutral and normative. Wendy Brown, in arguing for 'the impossibility of women's studies', notes this anxiety as the 'compensatory cycle of guilt and blame' which is 'structured by women's studies' original, nominalist, and conceptual subordination of race (and all other forms of social stratification) to gender' (93). Robyn Wiegman 'interprets this anxiety as indicating that women's studies – perhaps Western feminism as a whole – cannot *not* be inhabited by the powerful pain of racial wounds (1999, 125; emphasis in original). But since the 'specificity of sexual difference cannot be taken as a singular constant, but is ... linked to explicit political questions of rights and equality' (Price and Shildrick 18) it is become imperative that hegemonic feminism reinterrogates its Eurocentric agenda. Instead of perpetuating the wave metaphor, in which each successive wave signifies a further 'evolution' in the progressive narrative of feminist history, hegemonic feminism needs to attend to its wake-up call the 'differential consciousness' of other feminisms present through their 'oppositional ideology' (Sandoval 43). Feminists of colour argue that the very idea of a phase/stage/wave-based consciousness is an ideological construct of the Eurocentric subject that seeks to subsume and consume the challenges posed to it through notions of 'inclusion' and 'solidarity'. Chandra Talpade Mohanty insists on 'a shared frame of reference among Western, postcolonial, Third World feminists in order to decide ... the specificity of difference based on a vision of equality' (2002, 502). Since this vision is located within a paradigm of decolonisation, debates in twenty-first-century feminism are imbricated in 'race' as a relational as well as an essential category. This chapter makes the case for an embodied essentialism that is imagined within the locus of race in all its nominal and constructed force, and that acknowledges woman as an *essentially* racialised category within configurations of the contemporary nation state.

Hegemonic feminism is a useful way of historicising what has been variously (and troublingly) called white or Western feminism. Chela Sandoval reminds us that this feminism 'transcodes political practice to reproduce exclusionary forms of knowledge' (47). The Eurocentric teleological narrative of a 'unified female subject' is a 'fictional landscape' which can only lead to the 'intellectual exhaustion that characterised the discussion of identity throughout the 1990s' (Wiegman 2000, 805). Judith Butler also points out how the 'contemporary feminist debates over the meaning of gender lead time and again to a certain sense of trouble, as if the indeterminacy of gender might eventually culminate in the failure of feminism' (ix). Indeed, this fear colours the dominant tenor of anti-essentialism that shifted from debates of gender to those around race in second wave feminism. Where once hegemonic feminism – complicit in the project of Enlightenment – could confidently represent a unified subject, it can no longer purport to speak on behalf of an increasingly fragmented constituency. When its singular identity was threatened by the 'communities of resistance' and 'imagined communities' of colour, dominant feminism had to insist that these racialised categories were neither politically contingent nor valid; rather they were essentialist ways of imagining the female body (Mohanty 1991, 5).

Just as the Western canon announced the death of the author at the moment in which female and feminist subjectivities claimed their place in literature, hegemonic feminism deployed what Naomi Schor calls 'the shock troops of anti-essentialism' (vii) against the tensions posed by feminists of colour who mobilised around common racial and cultural grounds. The insistence on the category of anecdotal and historical experience and the uses of cultural memory and non-academic intellectual scholarship in the process of identity formation, conjured up the bogeyman of essentialism. Essentialism became the ugly four-letter word of feminism, and was held responsible for, as Diana Fuss puts it, the 'impasse predicated on the difficulty of theorizing the social in relation to the natural, or the theoretical in relation to the political' (1). Even more of an entrenched word now than when Fuss urged feminists to take 'the risk of essence' in 1989, an 'essentialist' identity is the most contentious issue in contemporary cultural politics. At a time when hegemonic feminism is fighting a desperate battle of hermeneutics to hold on to its preferred identity and constituency of 'woman', it is not surprising that it wants to remove essentialism from the battlefield. Whether the challenge is real or nominal, hegemonic feminism demands that race-based essentialism be written out of its parlance.

A(nother) history of oppositional consciousness

With reference to why hegemonic feminism finds the prospect of an essentially racialised identity so troublesome, Wiegman contends that theory constantly hotfoots between feminism as a subjective formation and feminism as a knowledge formation (2000, 819). Because the notion of subject formation is crucial to the feminist academy, a host of theoretical, identitarian, and seemingly generational differences have come to interrupt feminism's on-time arrival in a post-patriarchal future. In order to perpetuate its self-narration of continuity and unity, hegemonic feminism has to make invisible its culpability in the project of racial homogeneity and insist upon 'woman' as its proper and natural object of study. However, despite being challenged and interrogated relentlessly on the foundational premise that hegemonic feminism serves the entire identitarian constituency of 'neutral' womankind, white privilege remains intact while the arguments used to defuse the tension that difference produces have become much more sophisticated and insidious. When women of colour have argued that feminist politics need to be professed from different locations within specific histories of oppression, hegemonic feminism has broadened the very idea of difference to argue that its own project comes from a different place and is thus equally valid. Because mainstream feminism is so suspectible to selective amnesia, it forgets all too readily its role in the creation of the explicitly racialised woman. Furthermore, because feminists are also citizens of nations, and because the Western nation-state has become even more powerful post-9/11, members of the dominant majority respond to their national narratives and make Others of those who they have always claimed to include in 'the sisterhood'. Governments in Western nations operate on a code of racial logic, reflected in myriad social practices. In the feminist nation, the response is effected through parallel constitutions, codes of conduct and other regulatory bodies in the shape of academic hirings, publishing practices, conference circuits and keynote speaker allocations.

Hegemonic feminism derives the very definition and understanding of its subjectivity from the idea of difference. Whether it is the New Woman engaged in its imperial mission of civilising the heathen woman, or the neo-colonial feminist invested in bringing liberty and freedom to the veiled Islamic one, hegemonic feminism imagines itself only by creating its Other. Arising 'out of the matrix of the very discourse denying, permitting and producing difference' (Sandoval 41), this Other, however, is not just a test-subject for consciousness raising: it articulates an entire '*history of oppositional consciousness*' (ibid. 53; emphasis in original). The spectre of embodied Otherness, which takes the form of racialised Black and coloured women, makes explicit the colonising underpinnings of a self-serving white narrative. In its attention to histories of slavery, imperialism, colonisation, global capitalism, migration movements and other displacements of violence, this differential consciousness centralises racialised gender and is thus able to provide a textured reading of the race relations that haunts the body of hegemonic feminist knowledge. On the one hand, it diagnoses the processes whereby narratives of race and racialised bodies are willfully produced and perpetuated through sanctioned ignorance and deliberate malevolence; on the other hand, it deploys the constantly shifting terrain of the experiencing subject in its identitarian trajectory from Gayatri Chakravorty Spivak's 'strategic essentialism' to Judith Butler's 'performance'.

Concomitant with the debate on essentialism is the notion of difference posited in the biological and cultural essence of womanhood. According to the *Encyclopedia of Feminist Literary Theory*, difference is a 'tool for analyzing literature or cultural practice' and a concept that has been traditionally understood as 'organized into hierarchical pairs, into binary oppositions (such as male/female) in which one term is seen as the dominant original, and against which the other is seen as derivative, inferior, secondary' (116–17). Feminists of colour have repeatedly argued, raved and ranted against the discursive production of racialised women as the 'they' versus the 'us' of Eurocentric women. Racially constructed women are either seen as 'traditional' and trapped in social mores that position them as 'fragmented, inarticulate voices in (and from) the dark' (Mohanty 1990, 180) or exotic hothouse flowers who represent special interest groups. Western women, meanwhile, are free to pursue their legitimate goals in feminism, unconstrained by any of the racial 'chips on the shoulder' that paralyse their coloured sisters. So the issue of 'universal' daycare for women can be argued *ad nauseum* without taking the time to 'see' for whom the service caters and who the service providers are. Another example is the Palestinian female suicide bomber who perceived as a traitor to the feminist cause, without any questioning of the Eurocentric stake in 'international' feminist politics. Differences can only provide exotic variety at the feminist table so long as they attest to the culinary positional superiority of the dominant majority. The continuing ghettoisation of African and other Third World feminisms in 'separate sessions at conferences, separate chapters in anthologies, separate and unequal political agendas and activist efforts' (Woodhull 80) is a symptom of the management politics of white feminism, as it struggles to keep its 'normal' place in the hierarchy. Essentialism, no longer understood in terms of gender alone, has been reinterpreted and reinforced in racialised forms, with difference as the pivot upon which universalism and internationalism now spin. Embodiment is invoked both as a racial absolute as well as a relational concept in service of the cultural artefact of identity. This means that the oppositional feminist is both validated and erased, at the same moment, by virtue of her difference and difference alone. This has repercussions for the feminist of colour who comes to occupy a tenured space within the feminist academy and has power to speak – indeed is invited to speak – on behalf of difference *but* against essentialism.

The transatlantic debate between essentialism and difference is tied to the establishment and consolidation of multicultural white settler states. White settler states arrange themselves politically, institutionally and socially within the binaries of insider and outsider, resident and alien, citizen and subject, home and exile, settler and immigrant, while the 'native' and the 'aborigine' is violently and systematically erased from the map. The national narrative in such states is based on 'an assimilationist universalism, deployed through a language of liberal pluralism and citizenship' (Bannerji 17). The Others in such states are necessarily categorised and pathologised in opposition to the normative Eurocentric subject. Racialised subjects have the double burden of proving that they are equally valid candidates for citizenship at the same time as having their difference marked and fetishised. While the Canadian and Australian models of state-sponsored official multi/biculturalism differ from the popular and populist communitarian versions of the same in the U.S. and the U.K., the point needs to be reiterated that the racial logic underpinning these social and government policies has been particularly disingenuous. The feminist nation acts in much the same way.

> [N]on-white, non-Western women in 'white/Western' societies can only begin to speak with a hesitating 'I'm a feminist, but' ... in which the meaning and substance of feminism itself becomes problematised. Where does this leave feminism? Feminism must stop conceiving itself as a nation, a 'natural' political destination for all women, no matter how multicultural. Rather than adopting a politics of inclusion (which is always ultimately based on a notion of commonality and community), it will have to develop a self-conscious politics of partiality, and imagine itself as a *limited* political home, which does not absorb difference within pre-given and predefined space but leaves room for ambivalence and ambiguity. In the uneven, conjectural terrain so created, white/Western feminists too will have to detotalise their feminist identities and be compelled to say: 'I'm a feminist, but'. (Ang 57–58; emphasis in original)

Ien Ang contends that mainstream Western feminism operates like a nation with boundaries defined through the binaries of inclusion and exclusion, insider and outsider, citizenship and alien residentship. Just as the border patrol of white settler colonies use markers such as race, religion, language and culture – which are based on the three-worlds theory – to regulate entry into their lands of opportunity, dominant white feminism uses the binary categories of theory and experience to gatekeep its hallowed portals. Thus the racially experiencing subject can only be an 'icon' of difference.

To continue with the metaphor of nation-under-seige, the moment a matter of internal security and/or solidarity crops up, the feminist of colour is regarded with the suspicion reserved for non-citizens and aliens. This is exemplified in a particular kind of post-9/11 rhetoric E. Ann Kaplan adumbrates:

> While in the 1990s, US women were appropriately taken up with different projects to do with continuing to improve gender equality and organizing around women's needs, *women in the rest of the world were* in different situations, with different needs and agendas. ...
> To put the question perhaps too strongly for the sake of argument: *have at least some feminists achieved enough regarding gender equality that we can set aside such issues* [of diversity] and deal with terrorism? ... problems have not been solved for euro-centric women,

let alone for diasporic women or women living in cultures that repress women and their bodies. Do *we need to reorganize our priorities so that we focus on what women can do to help with the battle of our times, namely terrorism,* moving on from thinking about what can be done for women, to *what women can do for the world ...* ? (51; 53; emphases added)

Kaplan's 'we' cannot underscore more concretely the militant Christian propaganda that targeted and signaled out people of colour, demanding that they prove their nationalistic affiliations following the destruction of the Twin Towers in New York City in 2001. It is depressing indeed to envision a 'common' future of feminism that is so totally implicated in the machinations of modern rogue nations. Sara Ahmed uses the trope of 'strange encounters' to describe this kind of 'stranger fetishisation' and 'stranger danger' that, on the one hand, celebrates otherness and difference in the name of plurality, and, on the other, sets off alarms in the neighbourhood watch scheme of feminism at the slightest questioning of its limits (4).

Essentialism's great text: The body

How do the marginalised and disenfranchised voices in first world feminisms conduct dialogue as they weave in and out of the ayes and nayes of their racially essentialised identities? The central metaphor for this chapter is hotfooting, referring to the constant dance, from one foot to another, of the feminist of colour, as she inhabits the hotspot reserved for her in the postcolonial academy. Chicana feminist Norma Alarcon diagnoses this phenomenon as the constantly shifting 'space of *la differand,* the site of a conflict, collision or contest' (67) whereby the feminist of colour hotfoots between being and not being the native informant, between being and not being the race-maid in the academic kitchen, between trying to negotiate her newly acquired job profile and, at the same time, self-reflexively, interrogating the conditions of possibilities that make her presence viable. Walking the razor's edge between desire and rejection, agency and abjection, token subaltern and empowered migrant intellectual, the feminist of colour masters the game of hotfooting. She learns to speak of, for, and from a position of privilege in the margins, but becomes, in the process, the voice of the margin within the centre. As Gargi Bhattacharya testifies, the 'most risky disguise is taking the centre – by yourself, on the enemy's terms. The least elegant passing, the walking-on-daggers bargain which never stops cutting'

(251). In the nation of feminism, the feminist of colour comes to occupy the transnational borderland, earns frequent flyer points for 'world-travelling' (Lugones 390) and constantly negotiates an insider-outsider position.

It would not even be an understatement to declare that at the feminist table not everyone is equal. An unfortunate development in the past two decades has been the way in which hegemonic feminist projects have followed the example of their respective multiculturalist narratives and national imaginaries, refusing to insist on a cogent and embodied critique of the discourse of difference. There are two ways in which this has happened. First, difference has been ghettoised into 'area studies' of global feminism, for example, African, Chinese, Caribbean, First Nations, Indian, Iranian, Kenyan, Middle-Eastern, Somalian, and so on; and then relegated to items in poorly-funded women's studies departments. Secondly, difference has branched out into broader postcolonial categories such as U.S. third world feminism, postcolonial feminisms, immigrant feminisms, feminisms of colour, and other such. These categories would not have such nomenclatural power and meaning in contexts outside of white-dominated multicultural nations. Most informed analyses of the first kind (i.e. global feminist models) take into account the political economy of their socio-cultural milieu and are contingent upon broad-based approaches to questions of equity rather than a simple gender divide. They offer sustained critiques of rising fundamentalism and other patriarchal forms of oppression in their own nations, of the effect of the developmental model of World Bank funded projects, environmental degradation, structural adjustment programmes, globalisation, sweat-shops and other kinds of North-initiated neo-colonial modes of exploitation. Models of US third world feminisms, on the other hand, have been linked to the phenomenally successful rise of postcolonial studies in the Anglo-American academy in the past two decades. They constitute what Sandoval insists is a 'new typology' (53) that engages with multiculturalism, racialised class formations, immigration and naturalisation laws, street-level and institutionalised racism, social sector responsibility, reproductive health, affirmative action and constructions of whiteness. They have enjoyed great success, as the postcolonial academy falls over itself in the scramble for the Other on its own home grounds, but have also been trapped in the Scylla and Charybdis of their 'matter' and 'essence'. Questions of silence, voice, appropriation, agency, experience and identity have reigned paramount in such debates, leading to feminism's 'melancholy' (Wiegman 2000, 805).

The challenge to hegemonic feminism has thus been great, both in terms of the articulations of feminists of colour and the material positions they have come to acquire within institutions. The institutional presence of feminists of colour is both a symptom of the desire in the academy for epistemologies of the Other, and subsequent attempts to contain and consume the Other. Paying attention to issues at stake would require that white feminists depart from their positions as the neutral subjects and referential points of feminism and stop posing a divisive resistance to the Other in order to retain the status quo. This entails challenging the motives behind the qualifications of class, sexuality and age which intersect with any and every analysis of race. As theorists of colour work through these motives and qualifications, they are quite aware of the enormity of the task ahead of them. But attention-deflecting challenges like this are not only a denial of the deeply entrenched racial grooves of feminism, but actually leave all of us in a cul-de-sac of sanctioned ignorance, willful inertia and inevitable stasis. The discourses of 'all of us are Others' and 'all of us are Different' that have become alarmingly prominent in feminist phraseology, negates the experiential and essential fact of being racialised and embodied entities. When difference is thus deployed to render all forms of gender oppression theoretically equal, it brings into play a historically amnesiac and politically crippling model of feminism, without allowing for a recognition of the incommensurability of the difference involved and the impossibility of reaching a 'home' in feminism. Of course, feminists of colour have questioned the very motives for trying to arrive at a congenial and convivial model of home. After all, we arrive, literally as well as conceptually, from other homes to create new and multiple homes. Ang argues that the ubiquity of the difference factor can allow a white feminist to 'become a "politically correct" anti-racist by disavowing the specificity of the experience of being a racialised "other", reducing it to an instance of oppression essentially the same as her own, gender-based oppression' (61).

Departures and arrivals

The Spivakian concept of strategic essentialism has, in the past, offered feminists of colour many grounds for the negotiation and performance of identity politics. It allows for an assessment of the implications as well as the complicities of feminists of colour in what Inderpal Grewal calls the transnational flow of capital, labour and bodies (53). But it has also complicated the role of the feminist of colour as the 'self-marginalising or self-consolidating migrant or postcolonial masquerading as a "native informant" ' (Spivak 1999, 6). In order to work through the machinations of this schizophrenia, I advocate a head-on collision with essentialism as it speaks to us and on the terms it is practised and enacted socially. I no longer want to side-step, slide and elide, or surreptitiously slip in the issue of the situated knowledges, special 'affects' and investments we as coloured bodies bring into feminism. The first step is to name this way of knowing the world as an *embodied epistemological essentialism*. This has resonances with what Evelyn M. Hammonds calls our 'invisible, visible (exposed), hypervisible and pathologized' bodies (170) and what Spivak calls 'women marked by origins' (1999, 262). This essentialism is the heritage/baggage we carry on our backs as Cree/First Nations, Indian/South Asian, Egyptian/Middle-Eastern, Hispanic/Chicana, Korean/Asian-American. We know our worlds both through our origins and through social and political nomenclature. This essentialism is that which gets talked about whenever we congregate, break bread, eat each other's salt, wash lentils together, speak in our tongues and speak-bitter. This essentialism contains the perks and privileges, pains and pitfalls that accrue to us all as racialised entities. It is an essentialism that I no longer wish to disavow or apologise for. I want to claim back the essentialism that makes me a woman of colour in the first place, however mediated that place and location is. What it means to be a woman of colour is embedded and linguistically expressed in the experience of the body, and I want to recuperate the validity of this in-body experience so as to make its 'deep contextual knowledges' available and relevant to a third wave of feminism (Alexander and Mohanty xx).

M. Jacqui Alexander and Chandra Talpade Mohanty persuasively argue that what feminism remembers is 'contingent, yet grounded and strategic' (xxii). If this third wave is to be possessed of any lasting significance then it must remember and document the lessons of the second wave. We have to create the genealogies and histories of its counter-hegemonic moments. The only way of not forgetting these lessons is constant repetition and representation. Whether hegemonic feminism is tired, or whether feminists of colour want identity to be a beginning rather than an ending, we have to keep on talking about identity without mincing our words. This means not embracing the idea of a transnational feminist praxis without doing our homework. A horizontal comradeship of women is possible but we need to change the very manner in which we conduct our feminist democracies. This may mean a turn to the literary, and using the 'information retrieval' model that Spivak warns against, so that we know *who* we are talking about (1990, 77). We need to learn our enemies well, something imperialists, colonists and the minions of transnational globalisation know all too well. But we need to know our friends as well, as Maria Lugones advises (401). The company we keep conceives of our identities in essential terms, notwithstanding the important work done in the borderlands on hybridity and metisage. The 'not here, not now' of migrant identities can be grounded and employed well in the service of feminism through the essential lessons of embodiment we have learnt.

How does one come to the feminist table with a 'flesh and blood' understanding of specific, specialised experiences which have become so entrenched in the past two decades so as to be essential to us? If identity politics continue to be organised around the tropes of racial hegemony and oppositions to it (no matter how hybrid or deconstructed those binaries might be) how do we continue to talk about selfhood as both foundational and relational? One becomes a woman of colour not only through what Himani Bannerji calls an 'agentic' process of 'anti-imperialist political conscientization' (25), but also through an accident of history and the experience of the body as political. When colour becomes the 'cognate of race' in multiculturalised corporatised language, we cannot but be essential. All essentialism is strategic. Whether it is the normative invisible category of so-called white women or the nomenclature of choice for their visible non-white counterparts, essentialism has always been a way of standardising acceptability and gauging inclusion. The current trend of anti-essentialism merely reinscribes the racist and ethnocentric assumptions of hegemonic feminist theorising. This chapter has argued for essentialism to be urgently revalued as a political tool for epistemological feminist transformation because even when we speak of the hybrid and the heterogeneous, the standard is an imagined entity. If we are to understand communities of feminist affinity, we have to begin with the definitional. The desire for a feminist unity which is transnational and global is utopic – unless we start with this premise, there can be no third wave.

Note

* I am indebted to Heather Zwicker for a preliminary reading of this paper and to the editors for their exemplary support.

Works cited

Ahmed, Sara. ' "It's a sun-tan, isn't it?" Auto-biography as an Identificatory Practice.' *Black British Feminism: A Reader*. Ed. Heidi Safia Mirza. New York: Routledge, 1997. 153–67.

Alarcon, Norma. 'Cognitive Desires: An Allegory of/for Chicana Critics.' *Las Formas de Nuestras Voces: Chicana and Mexicana Writers in Mexico*. Ed. Claira Joysmith. Mexico: Universidad Nacional Autonoma de Mexico, 1995. 65–85.

Alexander, M. Jacqui, and Chandra Talpade Mohanty. 'Introduction: Genealogies, Legacies, Movements.' *Feminist Genealogies, Colonial Legacies, Democratic Futures*. Ed. M. Jacqui Alexander and Chandra Talpade Mohanty. New York: Routledge, 1997. xiii–xlii.

Ang, Ien. 'I'm a Feminist but ... "Other" Women and Postnational Feminism.' *Transitions: New Australian Feminisms*. Ed. Barbara Caine and Rosemary Pringle. New York: St. Martin's, 1995. 57–73.

Bannerji, Himani. *The Dark Side of the Nation: Essays on Multiculturalism, Nationalism and Gender*. Toronto: Canadian Scholars, 2000.

Bhattacharya, Gargi. 'The Fabulous Adventures of the Mahogany Princess.' *Black British Feminism: A Reader*. Ed. Heidi Safia Mirza. New York: Routledge, 1997. 240–52.

Brown, Wendy. 'The Impossibility of Women's Studies.' *Women's Studies on the Edge*. Ed. Joan Wallach Scott. Spec. Issue of *differences: A Journal of Feminist Cultural Studies* 9. 3 (1997): 79–101.

Butler, Judith. *Gender Trouble: Feminism and the Subversion of Identity*. New York: Routledge, 1990.

Encyclopedia of Feminist Literary Theory. Ed. Elizabeth Kowaleski-Wallace. New York: Garland, 1997.

Fuss, Diana. *Essentially Speaking: Feminism, Nature and Difference*. New York: Routledge, 1989.

Grewal, Inderpal. 'The Postcolonial, Ethnic Studies, and the Diaspora.' *Socialist Review: The Traveling Nation* 24.4 (1994): 45–74.

Hammonds, Evelyn M. 'Toward a Genealogy of Black Female Sexuality: The Problematic of Silence.' *Feminist Genealogies, Colonial Legacies, Democratic Futures*. Ed. M. Jacqui Alexander and Chandra Talpade Mohanty. New York: Routledge, 1997. 170–82.

Lugones, Maria. 'Playfulness, "World"-Travelling, and Loving Perception.' *Making Face, Making Soul / Haciendo Caras: Creative and Critical Perspectives by Feminists of Color*. Ed. Gloria Anzaldua. San Francisco: Aunt Lute Foundation, 1990. 390–402.

Kaplan, E. Ann. 'Feminist Futures: Trauma, the Post-9/11 World and a Fourth Feminism?' *Third Wave Feminism and Women's Studies*. Ed. Stacy Gillis and Rebecca Munford. Spec. issue of *Journal of International Women's Studies* 4.2 (2003): 46–59. Accessed: 1 Sept. 2006. <http:// www.bridgew.edu/ SoAS/ jiws/ April03/kaplan.pdf>.

Mohanty, Chandra Talpade. 'Cartographies of Struggle: Third World Women and the Politics of Feminism.' *Third World Women and the Politics of Feminism*. Ed. Chandra Talpade Mohanty, Ann Russo and Lourdes Torres. Bloomington: Indiana University Press, 1991. 1–47.

——. 'On Race and Voice: Challenges for Liberal Education in the 1990s.' *Cultural Critique* 14 (1990): 179–208.

——. ' "Under Western Eyes" Revisited: Feminist Solidarity through Anticapitalist Struggles.' *Signs: Journal of Women in Culture and Society* 28.2 (2002): 499–535.

Price, Janet and Margrit Shildrick. 'Openings on the Body: A Critical Introduction.' *Feminist Theory and the Body: A Reader.* Ed. Janet Price and Margrit Shildrick. New York: Routledge, 1999. 1–20.

Sandoval, Chela. *Methodology of the Oppressed.* Minneapolis: Minnesota University Press, 2000.

Schor, Naomi. Introduction. *The Essential Difference.* Ed. Naomi Schor and Elizabeth Weed. Bloomington: Indiana University Press, 1994. vii–xix.

Spivak, Gayatri Chakravorty. *A Critique of Postcolonial Reason: Toward a History of the Vanishing Present.* Cambridge: Harvard University Press, 1999.

——. 'Postmarked Calcutta, India.' Interview with Angela Ingram. *The Postcolonial Critic: Interviews, Strategies, Dialogues.* Ed. Sarah Harasym. New York: Routledge, 1990. 75–94.

Wiegman, Robyn. 'Feminism's Apocalyptic Futures.' *New Literary History* 31.4 (2000): 805–25.

——. 'Feminism, Institutionalism, and the Idiom of Failure.' *differences: A Journal of Feminist Cultural Studies* 11.3 (1999): 107–36.

Woodhull, Winifred. 'Global Feminisms, Transnational Political Economies, Third World Cultural Production.' *Third Wave Feminism and Women's Studies.* Ed. Stacy Gillis and Rebecca Munford. Spec. issue of *Journal of International Women's Studies* 4.2 (2003): 76–90. Accessed: 1 Sept. 2006. <http://www.bridgew.edu/SoAS/jiws/April03/woodhull.pdf>.

9

'It's All About the Benjamins'
Economic Determinants of Third Wave Feminism in the United States

Leslie Heywood and Jennifer Drake

Although conversation and debates about third wave feminism have been ongoing since the 1990s, there has been a lack of theory that delineates and contextualises third wave feminist perspectives, especially in the U.S. This chapter provides a partial redress of this through illustrating how third wave feminist perspectives are shaped by the material conditions created by economic globalisation and technoculture, and by bodies of thought such as postmodernism and postcolonialism. Since writers usually identified as the 'third wave' are most likely to be part of a generation that has come of age in these contexts, the chapter outlines some of the economic variables that have heavily impacted the current generation in the U.S., and demonstrates how they have resulted in a feminist movement that is not focused on narrowly defined 'women's issues', but rather an interrelated set of topics including environmentalism, human rights and anti-corporate activism. While discussions of third wave feminism have tended to limit themselves to the context of North American consumer culture – and have thus largely been identified with writers living in the U.S. – these discussions can only have theoretical and practical value if they are set within the larger frames of globalisation and technoculture.

We must identify definitional criteria that delineate the economic and demographic determinants of a generational perspective, a perspective that influences critical strategies employed by women and men who identify as third wave feminists in the United States. This perspective is not monolithic and does not exclude persons of other generations, but most third wave feminists (although not all who identify as such) were born after the baby boom.[1] Transnational capital, downsizing, privatisation, and a shift to a service economy have had a drastic impact on the world these generations have inherited. The shift away from the public works philosophy of the Roosevelt years to the free market fundamentalism of the Reagan/Thatcher years clearly contextualises the third wave tendency to focus on individual narratives and to think of feminism as a form of individual empowerment. In collections such as Barbara Findlen's *Listen Up* (1995), Rebecca Walker's *To Be Real* (1995), Ophira Edut's *Adios, Barbie* (1998) and Marcelle Karp and Debbie Stoller's *The BUST Guide to the New Girl Order* (1999), third wave feminist writers took the second wave feminist mantra of 'the personal is political' seriously, using their own experiences to help name and situate their own feminist views. This valuation of the personal as a theoretical mode has led to charges that third wave feminism is 'a youthful continuation of individualist, middle-class liberal feminism', and that its preoccupation with popular culture and media images is 'not serious enough' (Messner 204). These charges misunderstand third wave feminist work, which can be understood through an examination of how the lives of post-boomer women and men in the U.S. have been impacted by economic globalisation and technoculture.

The economics and demographics of post-boomer generations in the U.S.

Gender-based wage and education gaps are closing, especially in younger age groups, and this relative gender equality has shaped third wave perspectives. The 1994 USA census provides evidence that the wage gap has closed to within five percent for women and men aged 20–24, and that more women now earn bachelors and master's degrees than do men. The U.S. Department of Labor's report *Highlights of Women's Earnings in 2001* states that

> [t]he women's-to-men's earnings ration varies significantly by demographic group. Among blacks and Hispanics, for example, the ratios were about 87 and 88 percent, respectively, in 2001; for whites, the ratio was about 75 percent. Young women and men had fairly similar earnings; however, in the older age groups, women's earnings were much lower than men's. (1)

While overall women only make 78 cents for every dollar that men make, this varies widely depending on the group of women. Moreover, gender inequality persists on the highest levels of the economic ladder. This reveals the feminisation of poverty and a blind spot in standard feminist analysis of women's wages. According to the United States Congress Joint Committee on Taxation, 90 per cent of American families make less than $100,000 a year, and, according to Bernie Sander, the annual income per person in the U.S. is $28,553. This makes the $25,000–$30,000 category – in which women's and men's wages are largely equal – very close to the national average. However, the feminist analysis of these numbers often emphasises the fact that men comprise the vast majority of top wage earners, despite the fact that the majority of women are not 'topped' in this particular manner. For example, Rory Dicker and Alison Piepmeier refer to the data that '97.3 percent of top earners are men' to help make their valid point that there is still very much a need for feminism today (6). Yet, as is characteristic of much feminist work on the gender wage gap, they fail to mention the situation of men who are not 'top earners', and the relatively equal wages of men and women at lower income levels. If feminist analysis is truly differentiated for class, it becomes clear that for the majority of American women, especially in post-boomer generations, there is more gender parity in terms of wages except for the richest ten per cent of the population.

Peg Tyre and Daniel McGinn point up that women who make more money than men is 'a trend we had better get used to' (45). In 2001, in 30.7 per cent of married households with a working wife, the wife's earnings exceeded the husband's (ibid. 45). A 2002 report from the US Department of Labor indicated that women now make up 46.5 per cent of the labour force. However, the highest debt-to-income ratio in history undermines real wages and the progress that many women have made (Casper 4).[2] People coming of age after the baby-boom generation have attained middle-class status only with both women and men in the labour market working longer hours; setting up dual or multiple income homes; going into debt; postponing marriage and children; and/or having fewer children (Casper 3–5). In *Nickel and Dimed: On (Not) Getting By in America* (2001), Barbara Ehrenreich pointed out that, according to the Economic Policy Institute, the living wage for one adult and two children is $30,000 a year (213). But 60 percent of American workers earn less than the $14 hourly wage that this standard of living requires. The economic situation may look better in terms of gender equality, but in terms of overall economic well-being, the situation is worse for both women and men with the exception, again, of the very top wage-earners.

Third wave feminist thinking, then, is informed by the fact that the majority of young Americans have experienced relative gender equality in the context of economic downward mobility. It has also been shaped by the racial and ethnic diversity of post-boomer generations. According to the 2000 US census, non-Hispanic whites account for 73 per cent of baby boomers and an even larger proportion of older Americans, but they account for only 64 per cent of Generation Xers and 62 per cent of the Millennial Generation (United States Census Bureau 1). These post-civil-rights generations were raised on a multicultural diet and their attitudes about racial, cultural and sexual diversity have continued to be shaped by the increasing globalisation of entertainment and image-based industries, including the import of Asian cultural products such as anime and kung-fu films, the national dissemination of grassroots cultural practices like grunge, hip hop, and car culture, the increasing visibility of gays and lesbians in the media and the normalisation of porn imagery.

The economic and demographic determinants of third wave feminist thinking can be catalogued as follows. First, women are *as* likely or *more* likely to identify with their generation as with their gender. Because post-boomer men and women have substantially narrowed the wage gap, because they are likely to occupy similar entry-level to mid-level positions in workplace power structures, and because these realities mean economic struggle, women now often have more in common with men of their own age group than they do with women of previous generations.[3] Second, codes for 'good' and 'bad' as well as gender ideals are no longer polarised. This shapes third wave feminism's simultaneous endorsement and critique of media representations, particularly sexual imagery.[4] It also shapes third wave feminist cultural production. For example, various aspects of Girlie culture use the humorous re-appropriation of traditions and symbols to craft identities in the context of structural disempowerment, such as reclaiming words like girl, bitch and cunt. This playful re-appropriation of stereotypes is often interpreted as marking a lack of seriousness, but such play is a serious part of third wave feminism's critical negotiations with the culture industries. Third, women and men of the third wave tend not to locate meaning and identity in one place, particularly not in a job or profession. Owing to corporate downsizing and the shift to the service sector that occurred just as the oldest post-boomers reached their full-time employment years, these generations cannot expect to spend their entire lives in one workplace accruing benefits and advancing over time. While women in this demographic expect to work, the satisfaction that work offers is most often diminished. As is necessary in a global economy and workforce, workers' identities tend to be flexible and multifaceted, even contradictory. Finally, worldwide globalisation has contributed to a further concentration of wealth at the very top of the pyramid, shifting venues of political struggle from patriarchy to the World Trade Organization. The 'enemy' has been decentralised. While feminist perspectives are still valuable in what Peggy Orenstein calls 'this era of half-change', an economic and demographic analysis has shown that these perspectives cannot fully describe the lived conditions experienced by post-boomer generations (11).

Thus, it is clear that third wave feminists are not simply daughters rebelling for rebellion's sake.[5] Third wave feminist lives have been and will continue to be profoundly shaped by globalisation and the new economy it fosters. What is common to the diversity of third wave feminist thinking is a complicated legacy: this wave of feminism is torn between the hope bequeathed by the successes of the civil rights movement and second wave feminism, and the hopelessness born of generational downward mobility and seemingly insurmountable social and political problems worldwide. Of necessity, third wave feminism locates activism in a broad field that includes the kinds of issues often called 'women's issues', but that also encompasses environmentalism, anti-corporate activism, human rights issues, cultural production and the connections between these. In this era of half-change, when it is clear how global events intersect local lives, here is what third wave feminism knows: women's issues – and women activists – cannot and do not stand in isolation.

Technoculture and third wave feminism

Although third wave feminist thinking can be understood in the context of post-boomer economics and demographics, it must be acknowledged that many women and men choose to identify with third wave feminist perspectives whether or not they are part of a post-boomer generation. Third wave feminism, then, *both* refers to a feminist generation *and* to emerging forms of feminist activism. These uses of the term overlap but are not the same. They both, however, emphasise that feminism takes shape in relation to its time and place. As feminists of all generations craft responses to our current context of technoculture, new forms of activism are emerging. Jodi Dean describes technoculture as an economic-political-cultural formation characterised

> by the rise of networked communication [such as] the Internet, satel-
> lite broadcasting, and the global production and dissemination

of motion pictures; by the consolidation of wealth in the hands of transnational corporations and the migration and immigration of people, technologies, and capital; [and] by the rise of a consumerist entertainment culture and the corresponding production of sites of impoverishment, violence, starvation, and death. (1)

This is a familiar litany of the changes wrought by globalisation. However, Dean raises the question of individual rights, a concept that marks a fundamental contradiction in feminisms generally. Dean argues that 'technoculture is marked by the end of patriarchalism', since the conditions of women's lives changed substantially in the last half of the twentieth century (1). Women now make up a substantial percentage of the paid global workforce, and although working conditions are often appalling, as major wage earners for their families they have increasingly had some modicum of control in relation to sexual partners, marriage and childbearing. For many women, Dean suggests, the patriarchal family has become 'one option among an increasingly diversified set of living and working relations' (2).

This is also increasingly true of women in developing countries. According to Perdita Huston, the concept of individual rights contained within globalisation breaks down traditional notions of male superiority and privilege, thereby improving women's status (4). Further, globalisation has made it necessary for women to work as providers for their families, which improves women's status since the provider function is seen as most valuable (Huston 13). This, however, sets up a difficult dilemma. According to John Cavanaugh *et al.* in *Alternatives to Economic Globalization* (2002), globalisation has radically contributed to the concentration of wealth and inequality in terms of income distribution to the extent that 475 people now have half the world's wealth, which impacts upon women, who are disproportionately poor (30). But globalisation has also brought about an erosion of the gendered division of labour that traditionally denied women opportunities for education and independence. This is a question that feminism must face: if individual rights come at the price of the negative aspects of globalisation, to what extent should that concept of rights define feminist praxis? This is complicated by the fact that, according to Dean, the twin tiers of globalisation and the end of the patriarchy are linked with a 'decline of symbolic efficiency' (1). This means that 'arguments and authorities that might be persuasive in one context may have no weight in another one, [and] the identity we perform in one setting might have little to do with the one we perform in another' (Dean 2). There are three distinctions to be made here. First, the de-authorisation of patriarchy might be claimed as one of the victories of second wave feminism, but because that de-authorisation is part of a larger breakdown of master narratives, second wave feminism itself is understood by third wave feminism as offering perspectives that are persuasive or useful only in some contexts. Second, third wave feminism must negotiate the profound contradiction that the collapse of central authority in postmodern global capitalism, which has given women greater authority, visibility and cultural importance, is the same collapse that reinforces 'the vigor of global capital' (Dean 7). There has been a shift from a top-down, hierarchical culture of power to a power focused in multinational corporations and dependent upon global flows. In this context, power understood as possessed by individuals has become inaccessible to almost everybody, so second wave feminism's promise to obtain more power for women is impossible. Third, the decentralisation that has enabled some women in the first world to access education and better jobs, that has helped to narrow the wage gap, and that has facilitated the construction of empowered women as a consumer demographic, is the same decentralisation that supports globalisation and the inequities it creates between nations, as well as the environmental destruction it perpetuates. Consequently, women's increasing visibility within American culture may have given women greater cultural capital, but at the expense of developing countries and the environment as well as in a contracting national economy. Women have made gains at great cost, and may not have gained much at all – bitter realities that can be glossed over through a narrow (and much more pleasurable) focus on the expanded possibilities for racial and sexual minorities in consumer culture – a focus that has tended to characterise third wave writing until recently. But neither is this focus irrelevant. As Michael Hardt and Antonio Negri note, a strictly economic analysis 'fails to recognize the *profound economic power of the cultural movements*, or really the increasing indistinguishability of economic and cultural phenomena' (275; emphasis in original). That is, both cultural and economic dimensions must be taken into consideration simultaneously.

Through its celebratory and critical engagement with consumer culture, third wave feminism attempts to navigate the fact that there are few alternatives for the construction of subjectivity outside the production/consumption cycle of global commodification. Cornel West asks how we can speak to the 'profound sense of psychological depression, personal worthlessness and social despair so widespread' in black America, a question worth considering in relation to the situation of post-boomer generations more generally (38). Because the nihilism that West invokes has been particularly attributed to 'the hip hop generation', rap music and hip hop culture can be read as providing a powerful perspective on the economic and demographic determinants shaping post-boomer lives, and as expressing the complex emotions created by struggling to survive. In this view, it is also significant that second wave feminists and members of the civil rights generation – all baby boomers – share a sometimes patronising concern over the state of the next generation. We must remember that generational difference shapes worldviews as well as artistic and activist strategies. The attraction of large segments of the contemporary youth market to rap music and hip hop culture cannot be merely understood as a pathological interest in violence or a 'White Negro' appropriation of black male cultural expression. It also indicates a strong post-boomer identification with rap's harsh representation of economic struggle and its obsessive fantasies of economic success.[6] These identifications occur because young women and men of all races have come of age in a contracting economy. It is interesting, then, that the primary third wave feminist texts have tended to avoid the kinds of harsh economic truths found in rap, instead favouring stories of successful sex-gender rebellion and emphasising the pleasures of girl-culture consumption enroute to cultural critique.

However, as third wave feminists grow up and out of youth culture, having come of age through claiming power, the problems created and perpetuated by technoculture must be addressed. As Dean puts it, 'if this is post-patriarchy, something is definitely missing' (3). A paradox for third wave feminism is that this 'something' is missing when it seems like alternative images are part of dominant culture like never before. Multicultural fashion models, images of female athletes like Mia Hamm and Marion Jones, the commodified male body, lesbian chic – as corporate America searched for new markets in the 1990s, difference was glorified and on display. But in this brave new world of niche marketing, everyone is valued as a potential consumer, and no one is valued intrinsically. What looked like progress was a fundamental incorporation into the global machine. As Naomi Klein points out in *No Logo* (1999), a documentation of the rise of anti-corporate activism, 'for the media activists who had, at one point not so long ago, believed that better media representation would make for a more just world, one thing had become abundantly clear: identity politics weren't fighting the system, or even subverting it. When it came to the vast new industry of corporate branding, they were feeding it' (113). Third wave feminism's approaches to activism, and its suspicion of traditional forms of activism, have been forged in this crucible of empowerment and exploitation. Anita Harris argues that young women's alternative ways of conducting political organisation, protest, debate and agitation have been shaped in response to

> the perceived co-optation of left politics as merely a marketable style ... The trend towards an increased surveillance of youth, the re-discovery of young women in particular as the new consumers, and the cultural fascination with girlhood, have all resulted in a deep suspicion of overt activism as the best method for protest and the creation of social change. (par. 21)

As such, third wave feminism is a movement committed to local action and characterised by dispersal and diversity, as opposed to a single-leader and single-issue movement, a strategy that resists cooptation and supports survival in global technoculture.[7] Committed to cultural production as activism, and cognizant that is impossible for most Americans to wholly exit consumer culture, third wave feminists both use and resist the mainstream media and create their own media sites and networks, both of which are key components of successful activism in technoculture.

As socialist feminists have long argued, feminism is an integral part of larger social justice struggles that are framed by global capitalism. The hip-hop phrase 'It's all about the Benjamins' titles this chapter because it signals that the global markets that have made difference visible only value difference for its carriers' ability to consume. This has necessitated the reconceptualisation of 'feminism as a movement to end all forms of oppression' (Warren 328).[8] Therefore, anti-corporate activism like the 1999 Seattle protests has, of necessity, become part of feminism's focus, which makes feminism as a movement less visible than it once was – less visible and more widely dispersed simultaneously, part of multiple social struggles. To think about third wave feminism globally is to understand that 'young feminist membership is much larger than may be initially imagined, and further, is concerned with a feminism beyond merely claiming girls' power' (Harris par. 17). Feminism has become part of a global struggle for human rights that incorporates women's and gender issues. Third wave feminist theory must be a theory broad enough to account for various axes of difference, and to recognise multiple forms of feminist work, including environmentalism, anti-corporate activism and struggles for human rights. While gender play and cultural production are important parts of a third feminist wave approach to action and activism, they are only one part of third wave feminism and they take place in only one site. Third wave feminist perspectives recognise these forms of activism, and place them alongside many other kinds of work.

Notes

1. Generational designations – usually developed for marketers and workplace executives – are always somewhat arbitrary. The 'baby boomer' generation is commonly designated as those born between 1943 and 1960, Generation X as 1961 and 1981, and the Millennial Generation as those born between 1982 and 1998.
2. For more on this see Stephanie Coontz (126–28).
3. This situation parallels that of African Americans and Hispanics, who have also seen a drastic decline in real wages during the past thirty years, who have continued to identify primarily with their communities, and who have had an enormous impact on post-boomer generations in terms of both demographic numbers and cultural influence.
4. For examples of third wave perspectives on sexual imagery, see the magazines *Bitch*, *BUST*, and *Fierce*.
5. For more on this view of the third wave see Phyllis Chesler's *Letters to a Young Feminist* (1997) or Anna Bondoc and Meg Daly's collection *Letters of Intent* (1999).
6. For more on this see Mark Anthony Neal.
7. On the question of leaders in the third wave of feminism, see Jennifer Baumgardner and Amy Richards.
8. While Karen Warren, who is known for her work on ecofeminism, is not identified as a third wave feminist, her insistence that 'at a conceptual level the eradication of sexist oppression requires the eradication of the other forms of oppression' (327) is a concept that has been thoroughly internalised in the third wave.

Works cited

Baumgardner, Jennifer, and Amy Richards. 'Who's the Next Gloria? The Quest for the Third Wave Superleader.' *Catching a Wave: Reclaiming Feminism for the 21st Century*. Ed. Rory Dicker and Amy Piepmeier. Boston: Northeastern University Press, 2003. 159–170.

Bondoc, Anna, and Meg Daly, eds. *Letters of Intent: Women Cross the Generations to Talk about Family, Work, Sex, Love and the Future of Feminism*. New York: Free Press, 1999.

Casper, Lynne M. 'My Daddy Takes Care of Me! Fathers as Care Providers.' *Current Population Reports*. U.S. Census Bureau, 1997. 1–9.

Cavanaugh, John *et al. Alternatives to Economic Globalization: A Better World is Possible*. San Francisco: Berrett-Kohler, 2002.

Chesler, Phyllis. *Letters to a Young Feminist*. New York: Four Walls Eight Windows, 1997.

Coontz, Stephanie. *The Way We Really Are: Coming to Terms With Changing American Families*. New York: Basic, 1997.

Dean, Jodi. 'Feminism in Technoculture.' *The Review of Education, Pedagogy and Cultural Studies* 23.1 (2001): 1–25.

Dicker, Rory, and Alison Piepmeier. Introduction. *Catching a Wave: Reclaiming Feminism for the 21st Century*. Ed. Rory Dicker and Alison Piepmeier. Boston: Northeastern University Press, 2003. 3–28.

Edut, Ophira, ed. *Adios, Barbie: Young Women Write About Body Image and Identity*. Seattle: Seal, 1998.

Ehrenreich, Barbara. *Nickel and Dimed: On (Not) Getting By In America*. New York: Henry Holt, 2001.

Findlen, Barbara, ed. *Listen Up: Voices from the Next Feminist Generation*. Seattle: Seal, 1995.

Hardt, Michael, and Antonio Negri. *Empire*. Cambridge: Harvard University Press, 2000.

Harris, Anita. 'Not Waving or Drowning: Young Women, Feminism, and the Limits of Third Wave Debate.' *Outskirts: Feminism Along the Edge* 8 (2001). Accessed: 1 Sept. 2006. < http:// www.chloe.uwa.edu.au/ outskirts/ archive/ volume8/harris>.

Huston, Perdita. *Families as We Are: Conversations from Around the World*. New York: The Feminist Press, 2001.

Karp, Marcelle, and Debbie Stoller, eds. *The BUST Guide to the New Girl Order*. New York: Penguin, 1999.

Klein, Naomi. *No Logo: Money, Marketing, and the Growing Anti-Corporate Movement*. New York: Picador, 1999.

Messner, Michael. *Taking the Field: Women, Men and Sports*. Minneapolis: Minnesota University Press, 2002.

Neal, Mark Anthony. *Soul Babies: Black Popular Culture and the Post-Soul Aesthetic*. New York: Routledge, 2002.

Orenstein, Peggy. *Flux: Women on Sex, Work, Love, Kids, and Life in a Half-Changed World*. New York: Doubleday, 2000.

Sanders, Bernie. Homepage. 'Working Families in the Global Economy.' N. pub. Accessed: 1 Sept. 2006. <http://bernie.house.gov/economy/today.asp>.

Tyre, Peg, and Daniel McGinn. 'She Works, He Doesn't.' *Newsweek* 12 May 2003: 44–52.

United States Congress Joint Committee on Taxation. 108th Congress, 1st Session. Issue 52–03. 2003. Accessed: 1 Sept. 2006. <http://www.house.gov/jct/>.

United States Census Bureau. 'Census 2000 Summary File 1.' 3 Oct. 2001. Accessed: 1 Sept. 2006. <http://www.census.gov/population/cen2000/phc-t9/tab01.xls>.

United States Department of Labor. *Highlights of Women's Earnings in 2001*. Report 960. Washington: GPO, May 2002.

Walker, Rebecca, ed. *To Be Real: Telling the Truth and Changing the Face of Feminism*. New York: Anchor, 1995.

Warren, Karen J. 'The Power and Promise of Ecological Feminism.' *Environmental Philosophy: From Animal Rights to Radical Ecology*. Ed. Michael Zimmerman *et al*. New Jersey: Prentice-Hall, 2000. 322–42.

West, Cornel. 'Nihilism in Black America.' *Black Popular Culture*. Ed. Gina Dent and Michelle Wallace. Seattle: Bay Press, 1992. 37–47.

10
Imagining Feminist Futures
The Third Wave, Postfeminism and Eco/feminism

*Niamh Moore**

> From my vantage point, the project of ecofeminism is understanding, interpreting, describing and envisioning a past, present and a future, all with an intentional consciousness of the ways in which the oppression of women and the exploitation of nature are intertwined. Without an appreciation of the past, we don't know where we have come from. Without knowledge of the present, we can't know where we are. And, more importantly, without a vision of the future, we can't move forward.
>
> (Vance 126)

*   *   *

The debates around the contentious categories of third wave feminism, postfeminism and eco/feminism should be understood as manifestations of a broader anxiety about the current state of feminism. This anxiety plays out through contestations over versions of feminist histories and the possibilities and desirabilities of imagining feminist futures. These three terms, these 'kinds' of feminism appear to sit in uneasy relation with each other, suggesting very different accounts of these issues: eco/feminism is commonly critiqued for an assumed return to second wave essentialisms; postfeminism seen as a manifestation of the end of feminism, and third wave feminism regarded as suggesting a defiant insistence on the continuity of feminist politics, though in part produced through a suggested rupture with the second wave and the emergence of a new 'younger' generation of feminist activists.

125

The third wave and postfeminism are commonly brought into conversation with each other; this chapter explores the benefits of bringing eco/feminism into these discussions, making a more expansive argument about imagining feminist futures. These three categories all came into wider usage in the early to mid-1990s, at a time of crisis for feminism. This sense of crisis manifested in a variety of ways, with the most notable of these being criticisms from Black feminists and Third World women, and the growing influence of post-structuralism in the academy. These powerful critiques produced a sense of fracture and fragmentation in the project of feminism, and a sense of political paralysis. The combined weight of these critiques raised far-reaching questions about the possibility of feminist politics when the very subject of feminism was being called into question. Foundational tenets of feminism, such as the reliance on women's experiences for theory-building were revealed as implicated in exclusionary practices. These mutually reinforcing criticisms called into question attempts to ground feminist politics in the category of 'woman', and attempts to link women's experiences of oppression, or of activism and resistance, through any simplistic notion of global sisterhood. These criticisms of feminism cohered around a critique of 'essentialism' in second wave feminism. The centrality of essentialism in critiques of the second wave suggests an interesting role in using eco/feminism to think through third wave feminism and postfeminism. While third wave feminism and postfeminism can be understood – in different ways – as efforts to distance themselves from the essentialism of the second wave, critiques of essentialism continue to adhere to much eco/feminism, which is often understood as positing a return to 'women and nature'. Yet those eco/feminists offering a reworking of the categories of women and nature, and how each has been invoked to figure the other, offer some useful insights on questions of essentialism, and on thinking through future feminisms.

This chapter focuses on tensions between eco/feminism and (other) feminisms, questioning whether eco/feminism reproduces essentialist accounts of 'women' and 'nature' which reify both, or whether it provides a more challenging reconfiguration of these categories. Embedded in conflicts over essentialism are crucial subtexts, particularly over the importance and status of theory and activism. Attention to these subtexts is vital, not least because there is little explicit consideration of these in eco/feminist literature (with the notable exception of Noël Sturgeon). Furthermore, debates about theory/activism map onto debates about the distinctions between the second and third waves of feminism, and accounts of being in a postfeminist era. The shift from second to third wave has been marked by the institutionalisation of women's studies and feminism in the academy, and a concomitant anxiety about the effects and meanings of this development. This has raised questions over whether feminism has 'retreated' from the streets to the academy, and remains an academic phenomenon only or, in the case of postfeminism, whether the site of feminism is the media, or, indeed, whether feminist activism continues in any form.[1] Drawing on work by academic eco/feminists, and research on an instance of women's environmental activism in Canada in the 1990s, this chapter articulates the significance of the emergence of eco/feminism at a time of crisis in feminism, and the implications for feminists of taking 'nature' seriously. These questions are intimately related, because arguments about the 'nature of woman' have underpinned their exclusion from the (public) sphere of politics, from rationality, and from the process of knowledge-building.

Eco/feminism

Like much of feminism, eco/feminism remains an internally diverse body of theory and practice. Nonetheless, despite this diversity, eco/feminists cohere around an interest in the relationship between the feminisation of nature, and the naturalisation of women's lives. Trenchant critics see eco/feminism as merely reproducing normative connections between women and nature, such as it being women's nature to nurture, which feminists have long been working hard to challenge. Lynne Segal, for example, has written, sceptical of eco/feminist claims to be a *new* wave, that '[t]he ecofeminism of the eighties, which overlaps with "cultural" feminism and has been called a "new wave" in feminism, suggests that women must and will liberate the earth because they live more in harmony with "nature" ' (6–7). Segal implies that there is little new about eco/feminism as it seems decidedly familiar, resonant both with cultural feminism, and with patriarchal accounts of femininity. Advocates of eco/feminism see a more thoughtful engagement with nature, which they view as crucial for the development of feminism. Cate Sandilands asserts that, '[i]n inhabiting a theoretical space which is critical of other feminism, ecofeminism suggests that liberal, radical, and socialist positions have inadequately addressed the ways in which the domination of Nature lies alongside the domination of women' (90). These controversies over eco/feminism, and over the place of nature in feminism, map onto already existing tensions in feminism over essentialism. Arguments about women's 'nature' have underpinned many of the rationales for women's exclusion from the public sphere, from politics, education and employment, and confinement to the private realm, to domesticity and child-bearing and rearing. For second wave feminists, challenging assumptions about the nature of women, and insisting that women's oppression was a *political* issue rather than an inevitable fact of women's biology, were crucial feminist steps. The concepts of essentialism and social constructionism emerged out of such challenges. Thus gender emerged as a category of analysis that explicitly rejected biological, or natural, explanations of women's lives, and women's oppression was posited as a social construction. Challenging biological determinism and other essentialisms has subsequently been a crucial political strategy for feminists. Rejecting essentialist associations between women and nature has been vital for feminists in suggesting the possibility of bringing about social and political change.

Heated discussions, and accusations, of essentialism, have continued to echo through any number of feminist controversies through the 1980s and 1990s, from the supposed maternalism of the Greenham Common Peace Camp women, to the debates over pornography and sado-masochism of the sex wars. Naomi Schor, in the introduction to *The Essential Difference* (1994), notes that 'the essentialism-anti-essentialism debates define 1980s feminism' (vii). The growing dominance of post-structuralist feminism in the academy – and the related commitment to anti-essentialism – has contributed to the abjection and repudiation of essentialist positions, often identified with radical feminism, spiritual feminisms and eco/feminism. So dominant has anti-essentialism become in feminist theory that accusations of essentialism have become akin to accusations of not being a 'proper' feminist. In this context then, eco/feminist activists and theorists, who seek to re-open the apparently closed question of 'women and nature' have had difficulty in convincing (other) feminists of their feminism. From certain feminist perspectives, eco/feminism appears almost anachronistic, and claims that eco/feminism might be part of a third wave of feminism, appear incongruous. Critics consider concerns about the perceived essentialist, and hence retrograde, feminist politics of eco/feminism to be well founded, given, for example, the maternalist rhetoric which supposedly pervades eco/feminism.

This threatened, or perceived, expulsion from the academic feminist sisterhood because of alleged essentialism, appears to have confused some academic eco/feminists who have been somewhat shaken by the realisation that their feminist credentials have not been so obvious to others. Academic ecofeminists have responded to criticisms of essentialism in two significant ways. First, they have distanced themselves from any purported essentialist manifestations of ecofeminism, and produced accounts which stress eco/feminism as anti-essentialist or at least only strategically essentialist. Second, many academic eco/feminists are beginning to distance themselves from eco/feminism, often through resorting to different terminology – such as ecological feminism. Cate Sandilands writes that 'I craved a language that would describe my growing sense that nature must be an important consideration in any feminist political vision; [...] But the exhilaration I felt as a new convert was over quite soon, and I have never felt so strongly that I belonged in ecofeminism, despite my increasing commitment *to feminist ecological politics* and theory (3; emphasis added). Similarly, Chris Cuomo reflects that

[a]lthough I've been attracted to thinking at the intersections of feminism and environmentalism for years, I hesitate to call myself an ecofeminist. Indeed, I prefer to think of my work as *ecological feminism*, in an effort to keep the emphasis on feminism, and also to distance my approach somewhat from other work done by self-titled ecofeminists. (5–6; emphasis added)

Noël Sturgeon struggles with the label of eco/feminist as a result of '[d]ealing with my own objections to the essentialism of some ecofeminist arguments, and the effects on my work of a widespread assumption by academic feminist peers that such essentialism permanently and thoroughly tarnishes ecofeminism as a political position' (168). These reflections suggest that a simple shift in terminology will solve the dilemma of essentialism. Significantly, while there is now a substantial literature which questions the role that accusations of essentialism have come to play in feminism, eco/feminists have rarely drawn on this literature to support a more nuanced approach to questions of women and nature. Rather, eco/feminists' arguably defensive responses to criticisms of essentialism suggest that some are more concerned with theoretical adequacy and institutional status, than with understanding political activism, or women's everyday experiences of nature. In this process the project of eco/feminist theory-building has become increasingly abstracted from movement politics and women's everyday lives, caught up in an impasse over theories of essentialism which have little meaning for activists. Through their quiescent acceptances of criticisms of essentialism, eco/feminists risk ceding the radical potential of eco/feminism to interrogate the lack of attention given to the politics of nature within feminism.

Third wave feminism, postfeminism and eco/feminism

In the context of these divergences over essentialism, it is interesting to note that a number of eco/feminist writers have explicitly linked eco/feminism with a third wave of feminism.[2] Eco/feminists' investments in linking their project with the supposed cutting edge of feminist theory and/or activism, could be understood as a further defensive response to being linked with essentialism and the second wave. But the project of delineating different waves of feminism is not just one of simple chronology. Efforts to separate the waves of feminism are of interest for their theoretical and political project of naming and boundary creation. Giving specific characteristics to one wave, and not to another, involves an attempt to make some links and to disavow others. Some versions of feminist history would see an implicit teleological progress in feminism from first to second to third waves. Noël Sturgeon, drawing on an interview with Ynestra King, a key figure in the emergence of US eco/feminism, notes that King calls eco/feminism 'the "third wave of the women's movement" '(23), indicating that this most recent manifestation of feminist activity was large and vital enough to parallel the first wave nineteenth-century women's movement and the second wave women's liberation movement of the 1960s and 1970s. Sturgeon concurs, but then qualifies her support for this account of eco/feminism, regarding it as a 'potentiality rather than an actuality' and claims her own work to be 'an attempt to analyze what prevents the closing of that gap between the vision and the practice' (23).

Val Plumwood provides a different focus for her argument for eco/feminism as a third wave of feminism. She argues that it is eco/feminism's critique of dualisms that 'gives it a claim to be a third wave or stage of feminist theory'. She qualifies this, drawing explicitly on the wave metaphor:

> The programme of a critical ecological feminism orientated to the critique of dualism is a highly integrative one, and gives it a claim to be a third wave or stage of feminism moving beyond the conventional divisions in feminist theory. It is not a tsunami, a freak tidal wave which has appeared out of nowhere sweeping all before it. Rather it is prefigured in and builds on work not only in ecofeminism but in radical feminism, cultural feminism and socialist feminism over the last decade and a half. At the same time, this critical ecological feminism conflicts with various other feminisms, by taking account of the

connection to nature central in its understanding of feminism. It rejects especially those aspects or approaches to women's liberation which endorse or fail to challenge the dualistic definitions of women and nature and/or the inferior status of nature. (39)

Plumwood makes a number of related points here. She emphasises eco/feminism's critique of the gendered character of nature/culture dualisms, and its critique of feminisms which ignore nature. In addition she traces eco/feminism's emergence from other feminisms, even as it also draws on the critical resources and insights these feminisms have produced to further the transformatory project of eco/feminism. Whereas Plumwood emphasises eco/feminism's conceptual contributions to feminist theorising, King and Sturgeon focus on eco/feminism as a movement of activists. They regard eco/feminism as a third wave of activism, which is analogous to the first and second waves, but which implicitly goes beyond these waves. Plumwood, however, stresses the links between the waves, understanding eco/feminism as emergent from the second wave. These accounts have in common an insistence that eco/feminism cannot just be understood as a return to what might be seen as the limitations of the essentialism of the second wave and that it represents a way of working through some of the issues which the second wave has thrown up.

Yet while a number of ecofeminist writers have invoked the idea of a third wave of feminism to varying ends, the notion of postfeminism has been much less invoked. Popular understandings of postfeminism as a manifestation of the end of feminism have meant that postfeminism has had less appeal for eco/feminists in furthering anything that might be termed an eco/feminist agenda. Rather eco/feminism has been invoked as evidence of, or as an example of, a manifestation of post-feminism. Ann Brooks, in her book, *Postfeminisms: Feminism, Cultural Theory and Cultural Forms* (1997), reads postfeminism alongside other 'posts' such as postcolonialism and postmodernism. Arguing that just as the 'post' of postcolonialism does not necessarily imply that colonial relations have been overturned, she suggests that postfeminism should not be read as suggesting that patriarchy has been superseded. Instead Brooks thinks of postfeminism as feminism that has been dispersed into other areas of debate, such as cyberfeminism, postmodernism, and eco/feminism. This version of postfeminism then retains feminism as an important site of political mobilisation and debate, and recasts narratives of the fragmentation and dissipation of feminist activism as in fact the very opposite, understanding postfeminism as offering a more creative imagining of feminist futures. In this sense, postfeminism can be seen as allied with an eco/feminist project.[3]

Women's environmental activism

As the early 1990s was a key moment in the nexus of debates over the future of feminism, this chapter will focus on an instance of eco/feminist activism at this period in order to provide a resounding rebuttal to pessimistic rhetoric about the dea(r)th of feminist activism, and the dismissal of activism as essentialist. My research reveals the limitations of those accounts of eco/feminism which are framed by abstract theories of essentialism – and also of academic eco/feminist accounts of activists as essentialist or strategically essentialist. The Friends of Clayoquot Sound, a radical, grassroots environmental organisation, formed in the late 1970s to protest clear-cut logging of temperate rainforest in Clayoquot Sound, on the west coast of Vancouver Island in Canada.[4] Frustrated with the limitations of conventional politics, the Friends turned to non-violent civil disobedience, and to the blockading of logging roads. The Clayoquot Sound Peace Camp was set up to provide a place for people to stay the night before the early morning blockades of logging roads, and to provide a space for learning about non-violence, and for practising the creation of alternative community. Over the course of the summer of 1993 over 800 people were arrested for blockading a logging road into Clayoquot Sound, in one of the largest acts of non-violent civil disobedience in Canadian history. Consensus decision-making with 'eco/feminist principles' was explicitly introduced in meetings by the Friends of Clayoquot Sound. Moreover, eco/feminist principles were manifested, as exemplified by the *Welcome Handout* given to people arriving at the Peace Camp. These instances of eco/feminism at the Camp offer a challenge to notions of activists as inherently essentialist.

In the late 1980s the Friends committed itself to consensus decision-making processes, non-violent philosophy and practice, and feminist principles. However, this significant shift from a more *ad hoc* approach to organisation was not uncontentious. Valerie Langer described the meeting which led to these changes:

> VL: We had a meeting – like we're always having meetings – and two of the men at the meeting just dominated the whole time and after, finally after an hour – both of whom, you know, are men that I admire, and I am still friends with – they just dominated the meeting and finally B—— said, 'you know I'm just tired of

listening to you two have your private conversation. I've had something to say for the last half hour and don't get a chance to get a word in edgeways, and I think it's time regardless of whether you have more [to say]', – 'cos they kept on saying we have another thing to add – 'regardless of whether you have something more to say, I think you should give somebody else a chance to talk', and this created a furore and you know there was this, 'whenever I have something to say I shouldn't be shut up, that's creativity'. What came out of it, was that the meeting kinda blew up, and these two – one guy said 'oh, I didn't realise' and the other just said, 'ah, I can't stand this "feminist stuff", I'm getting out of here' and left.

NM: Had anybody mentioned feminism at this stage?

VL: He did. Because the people who were saying they thought it was time they stopped talking and somebody else get a chance too, were all the women in the group. So, we decided at that meeting that we should begin consensus model decision-making and have a process for running our meetings. You know anarchy was fine until you didn't get to speak, until somebody else always got a chance to speak so ... and you couldn't get a word in edgewise. So we started at that time organising ourselves as a consensus decision-making organisation with feminist principles and it happened to be the feminists in the group who were willing to stick it out, and, I shouldn't say, yeah, the feminists in the group, some of whom were men. Yeah, who said, 'yeah, I agree totally ... let's start looking at how we do it'. So the organisation shifted again there towards having a structure and a process. (Langer)

This exchange illustrates how feminist discourses about gendered communication styles have so permeated contemporary culture as to become almost commonsensical, however much they are also resisted in practice. Although feminism was not initially mentioned when the challenge was to the 'right' to dominate discussion space, this was identified as 'feminist stuff' and subsequently rejected by one man and accepted by the other. In Langer's account, feminism was not tied specifically to women; on consideration, she included men in her understanding of the 'feminists in the group'. This version of feminism can be situated historically in the context of a politics in which (white, privileged) feminists can no longer define feminism as being only about women or gender. This feminism takes for granted the explanatory and analytical power of second wave feminism in its understanding of social and political relations. In the wake of criticisms, specifically from women of colour, feminists have had to rethink the subject of feminism, and the process of doing feminist politics. Langer's account of feminism in the Friends is not defined around any particular subject or identity as 'women', but rather as a way of understanding power relations as a matrix of interlocking systems of dominance and subordination, and a politics which demands attention to process and practice.

Eco/feminism was further contested at the Peace Camp of 1993. In deciding to set up a Peace Camp, the campaign drew explicitly on histories of women's activism, such as the Greenham Common. Despite, or perhaps because of, this legacy of second wave feminism, there were a number of significant differences between Greenham and Clayoquot. Unlike the encampment at Greenham, Clayoquot was not a women-only camp, though there were many women there, and women were actively involved in the construction and organisation of the Camp. Furthermore, maternalist discourses of caring for the earth much invoked at Greenham were not generally appealed to publicly or collectively by women at Clayoquot. The Camp was said to be based on 'feminist principles', and some even articulated these as 'eco/feminist principles'. However the meaning of eco/feminism in the context of the Camp was not always clear; and eco/feminism was contested vigorously at times by feminists and eco/feminists, men and women.[5] The non-violent philosophy and practice of consensus decision-making at the Camp were more widely and more visibly enacted while links between non-violence, consensus and feminism were not transparent. *The Code of Non-Violent Action* was very visibly displayed on the notice board near the kitchen where people queued for meals:

1. Our attitude is one of openness, friendliness and respect towards all beings we encounter.
2. We will not use violence, either verbal or physical, towards any being.
3. We will not damage any property, and will discourage others from doing so.
4. We will strive for an atmosphere of calm and dignity.
5. We will carry no weapons.
6. We will not bring or use alcohol or drugs.

That these ideals might be linked with 'feminist principles' was perhaps less obvious to those who might understand feminism as solely about 'women's issues' as there was no explicit textual mention of feminism or gender issues here.

Perhaps the most visible place where feminist politics were made explicit was on the *Welcome Handout* that people received on arriving at the Camp.[6] Under the sub-heading of 'Intent of Clayoquot Peace Camp', it read:

This is an action base-camp. We are here to bear witness to the destruction, to peacefully resist that destruction, and to educate ourselves and the public about these issues.

You are welcome to participate in the day-to-day running of the Camp, and planning of actions – everyone is a participant. We ask that you volunteer each day to help the Camp run smoothly.

We use a consensus process based on feminist principles. We believe that sexism, racism, and homophobia are forms of oppression which are linked to the oppression of Nature. We strive to make Camp a safe space, free of oppression. (McLaren 76)

Here is some indication of the meanings of feminism for the Camp organisers. Notably, feminist principles were not just specified in terms of gender, or sexuality, but feminist principles were defined in terms of linking sexism, racism, and homophobia with the 'oppression of Nature'. Links with other -isms and oppressions can also be inferred. Feminism was here defined as not just being about women, but about challenging all oppressions, including the oppression of nature, and indicating that these oppressions might be linked. This feminism, with its emphasis on the oppression of nature, might be more overtly understood as eco/feminist.

Explicit in this feminist approach to politics and organisation is the recognition that feminism cannot be about women only, but must address all oppressions. Furthermore, feminism is defined through processes – consensus and non-violence – rather than through the construction of any identity politics. The category of woman as the basis of feminist politics has been shattered and not only for deconstructive feminist theorists. For activists, the question of sustaining activism across differences has been crucial. In a small community, where the politics of race, class, gender and nature – to point only to the most salient material conditions of people's lives in Clayoquot Sound – are everywhere visible, to understand feminism as only about women, and then as only about certain women, remains impossible. This manifestation of eco/feminism is not a reification of 'women and nature', but rather a critical perspective on hegemonic constructions of women and nature. Additionally the group identified themselves in a relationship to a place, as *friends* of Clayoquot Sound, rather than through an identity politics. Eco/feminist politics involved a commitment to non-violence, and to the construction of an alternative community. Campaigning was not only about blockades, but also about envisioning different ways of living. At the Peace Camp, eco/feminism was rather invoked as a particular understanding of power and politics, embodying an alternative system of values, and a decision-making process which sought to challenge hierarchical power relations embedded in more conventional decision-making processes, including the decision-making processes which led ultimately to the Peace Camp, and to the blockades. This late twentieth-century-peace camp should be understood not as a throwback to the disavowed activism of the 1970s and 1980s, but as a place in which the future of eco/feminist politics can be re-articulated.

Essentialism, activism and the academy in the third wave

> It is a confused pattern that waves make in the open sea – a mixture of countless different wave trains, intermingling, over-taking, passing, or sometimes engulfing one another; each group differing from the others in the place and manner of its origin, in its speed, its direction of movement; some doomed never to reach any shore, others destined to roll across half an ocean before they dissolve in thunder on a distant beach.
>
> (Carson 114)

* * *

Reflecting on this cluster of feminisms – the third wave, postfeminism and eco/feminism – through events in Clayoquot Sound, yields a number of fruitful insights about issues which are of ongoing concern for feminists: the changing face of feminism since the 1970s; the Gordian Knot of theory, academia and activism; and specifically how nature figures in accounts of feminist politics and what it means to be a 'woman'. Debates about feminism are also debates about the status and extent of feminist activism, about tension between nostalgia for the 1970s, and the 'end of feminism' narrative of postfeminism, and the future orientation of the third wave. Anxiety that feminist activism is on the wane and that the Women's Movement was a phenomena of second wave feminism, has been intimately bound up with the expansion of women's studies in the academy. However, throughout the 1980s and 1990s, while many academic feminists were bemoaning the decline of the women's movement and feminist activism, those in the newly emerging field of eco/feminism were pointing to the growth of women's grassroots environmental activism around the world: the Chipko movement in India, Greenham Common in the U.K. and the Kenyan Greenbelt movement, to name just a few. Eco/feminist activism also continues with the work of Vandana Shiva, Julia Butterfly Hill and Starhawk. This activism belies academic concerns about the decline of activism. This activism suggests another perspective on concerns about the supposed fading away of the women's movement. As Irene Diamond and Lisa Kuppler have argued:

> Scorned, trivialized, or ignored by many in the academy, the strength of ecofeminism is in the streets. [...] Many critics have claimed that ecofeminism is hopelessly mired in essentialism, reifying the female body and the essential femaleness of nature. While not denying the presence of essentialism within this complex constellation, we also believe that close attention to the practices of ecofeminism recovers what much academic discourse loses. (176)

The activist practices of those campaigning in Clayoquot Sound demonstrate that eco/feminist activism does not inherently involve the reification of the female body, and the essential femaleness of nature. Activists in Clayoquot have been engaged in a radical reconfiguration of the meaning and practice of feminist politics, through their reworking of how 'nature' figures in our understandings of (feminist) politics. This ought to be heartening to academics concerned about essentialism and an apparent wane in activism.

Despite declarations of the end of feminism, women continue to be involved in political activism, in peace activism, anti-immigration and anti-racist work, environmentalism, anti-globalisation movements, in the protests in Seattle, Prague, Genoa and beyond. While there may be a decline in women-only activism, nonetheless many women involved in these protests are feminists, and/or have been inspired by other feminist actions. Elsewhere in this volume, Leslie Heywood and Jennifer Drake suggest third wave feminism is not exclusively focused on women's issues, but on such interrelated topics as environmentalism, human rights and anti-corporate activism. They suggest that anti-corporate activism like the 1999 Seattle protests have become part of what feminism does; making feminism simultaneously less visible and more active in multiple social struggles. Similarly, Jodi Dean argues that feminism cannot focus on sex and gender but speak to other power relations:

Consequently, individual contributions to feminist theory may in fact not speak of sex, gender or women at all. What makes them feminist, then, is always a complex combination of their author's interests and intentions, their ability to provide insights and solutions to feminist problems and issues and their potential for improving women's lives. What makes them feminist depends on how they connect to feminist discourses. The new democracy, then, means that feminism is part of differing constellations of issues and concerns rather than a single aspect of, approach to or interpretation of these issues and concerns. (3)

I suggest that it may not, after all, be the case that feminism or the Women's Movement has lost its way, just that academic feminism thought they had. Feminist activism has changed shape and is no longer identifiable, visible, in the same way. Eco/feminist activism can remind us that feminism is no longer – if, indeed, it ever was – only about women or gender. Careful attention to eco/feminist and other activisms can highlight how activists are engaging in a process of refiguring the project of feminism, providing a useful rebuttal to angst about the demise of feminist activism, and to nostalgia for the second wave activism of the 1970s.

Controversies over nature, particularly the 'nature of women' have been central to all waves of feminism: the need to resist reductive accounts of women and nature persists. An eco/feminist analysis, through its attention to the gendered politics of nature, has the potential to radically destabilise the wave metaphor as a way of constructing and telling histories of feminism. As Rachel Carson notes, waves make a confused pattern: it is difficult to tell where one wave might begin and another end. While the wave metaphor is used to gesture towards different historical periods in feminism, and the (supposed) definitive features of these periods, nonetheless it is the case that 'the second wave doesn't suddenly cease to exist so that the third wave can come of age. Rather the latter brings to the fore features of the former that have been hidden, marginalised, subordinated and considered secondary' (Shaw 45). This understanding of the relationship between second and third waves, which is analogous to Plumwood's account mentioned earlier, resists reducing the relationship between waves to one of chronology or generation. This account of waves is more properly understood as genealogical rather than straightforwardly chronological or generational (Foucault 76ff), and as Alison Stone demonstrates elsewhere in this volume, a genealogical approach too can provide an important counter to essentialism. Thus an eco/feminist destabilisation of the metaphor of waves points to the ongoing and continuing need for eco/feminists to work to challenge particular configurations of women and nature. Theories of essentialism are not always adequately able to convey the myriad complex and changing relationships between women and nature. The development of adventurous methodologies and theories for exploring the transformations in meanings of women and nature has been a challenge through all waves, and remains a necessary and ongoing project for eco/feminists, one in which activists are engaged, just as much as academics.

Notes

* With thanks to: participants in the *Third Wave Feminism* conference at the University of Exeter (July 2002) for comments on the oral version of this chapter; to Margaretta Jolly for ongoing conversations about Greenham, feminism and activism; to the editors for their comments; to Maxine Badger, Bridget Byrne, Rebecca Duffy, Andrea Hammel, Joan Haran, Tee Rogers-Hayden and Anne Rudolph for comments and conversations on earlier drafts.

Throughout I use 'eco/feminism' to gesture towards sometimes fruitful, sometimes unproductive tensions between ecofeminism and feminism. Eco/feminism is both 'of ' feminism and critiques it: this is not unusual as such tensions define feminism. There has been a proliferation of feminisms as critiques have been made by lesbian feminists, black feminists, and from the disability movement, to name just some of the most salient critiques. I still hold on to this label of eco/feminism as productive at this juncture in feminism, to signal a specific constellation of interests which cannot be assumed under the rubric of 'feminism' alone.

1. For some, such as Hokulani Aikau, Karla Erickson and Wendy Leo Moore, the third wave denotes a cohort of women who have come to feminism through academia rather than through activism in the second wave women's movement. Others, such as Ednie Kaeh Garrison and Rhoda Shaw, use the term 'third wave' to denote a cohort of women who have come to feminism through popular culture, particularly music, and phenomena such as Riot Grrrl and through the use of new media technologies and the Internet, and relatedly through environmental and anti-globalisation activism.
2. See Colleen Mack-Canty for more on the relationship between third wave feminism, eco/feminism and postcolonial feminism. Very few have explicitly addressed eco/feminism's relationship with first or second waves of feminism, although do see Barbara T. Gates on the former.
3. I am aware that postfeminism is a contentious term which is used differently in media studies, film and television studies, in women's studies and in the

popular press. I am here arguing for a reclamation of the positive aspects of postfeminism which Brooks identifies.

4. It is beyond the scope of this chapter to provide a detailed account of this campaign. For more information on this campaign, see Warren Magnusson and Karena Shaw, Tzeporah Berman or the Clayoquot Sound Research Group.

5. For further detail on the contestation of eco/feminism at the Camp, see Moore (2003).

6. Not everyone received a copy of the *Welcome Handout* on arrival. Moreover, in a very explicit contestation of the meanings of eco/feminism, one woman spent an evening crossing out the word feminism on a large bundle of the handouts.

Works cited

Aikau, Hokulani, Karla Erickson, and Wendy Leo Moore. 'Three Women Writing/Riding Feminism's Third Wave.' *Qualitative Sociology* 26.3 (2003): 397–425.

Berman, Tzeporah *et al. Clayoquot and Dissent*. Vancouver: Ronsdale, 1994.

Brooks, Ann. *Postfeminisms: Feminism, Cultural Theory and Cultural Forms*. New York: Routledge, 1997.

Carson, Rachel. *The Sea Around Us*. 1951. Oxford: Oxford University Press, 1991.

Clayoquot Sound Research Group. *A Political Space: Reading the Global through Clayoquot Sound*. 2002. Accessed: 1 Sept. 2006. <http://web.uvic.ca/clayoquot>.

Cuomo, Chris. *Feminism and Ecological Communities: An Ethic of Flourishing*. London: Routledge, 1998.

Dean, Jodi. *Feminism and the New Democracy: Resisting the Political*. London: Sage, 1997.

Diamond, Irene, and Lisa Kuppler. 'Frontiers of the Imagination: Women, History and Nature.' *Journal of Women's History* 1.3 (1990): 160–80.

Foucault, Michel. 'Nietzsche, Genealogy, History.' 1971. *The Foucault Reader*. Ed. Paul Rabinow. Harmondsworth: Penguin, 1984. 76–100.

Friends of Clayoquot Sound. The Friends of Clayoquot Sound (FOCS). N. pub. Accessed: 1 Sept. 2006. <http://www.focs.ca>.

Garrison, Ednie Kaeh. 'US Feminism-Grrrl Style! Youth (Sub)cultures and the Technologics of the Third Wave.' *Feminist Studies* 26.1 (2000): 141–70.

Gates, Barbara T. *Kindred Natures: Victorian and Edwardian Women Embrace the Living World*. Chicago: Chicago University Press, 1998.

Langer, Valerie. Personal Interview. By Niamh Moore. 14 Aug. 1996.

Mack-Canty, Colleen. 'Third-Wave Feminism and the Need to Reweave the Nature/Culture Duality.' *NWSA Journal* 16.3 (2004): 154–79.

Magnusson, Warren, and Karena Shaw, eds. *A Political Space: Reading the Global through Clayoquot Sound*. Minneapolis: Minnesota University Press, 2003.

McLaren, Jean. *Spirits Rising: The Story of the Clayoquot Sound Peace Camp 1993*. Gabriola Island, BC: Pacific Edge Publishing, 1994.

Moore, Niamh. 'Ecocitizens or Ecoterrorists? Learning from Environmental Activism in Clayoquot Sound.' *Adult Learning, Citizenship and Community Voices: Exploring Community-Based Practice*. Ed. Pam Coare and Rennie Johnston. Leicester: NIACE, 2003. 92–107.

Plumwood, Val. *Feminism and the Mastery of Nature*. London: Routledge, 1993.

Sandilands, Catriona. *The Good Natured Feminist: Ecofeminism and the Quest for Democracy*. Minneapolis: Minnesota University Press, 1999.

Schor, Naomi. Introduction. *The Essential Difference*. Ed. Naomi Schor and Elizabeth Weed. Bloomington: Indiana University Press, 1994. vii–xvii.

Segal, Lynne. *Is the Future Female? Troubled Thoughts on Contemporary Feminism*. London: Virago, 1987.

Shaw, Rhoda. ' "Our Bodies, Ourselves," Technology, and Questions of Ethics: Cyberfeminism and the Lived Body.' *Australian Feminist Studies* 18.40 (2003): 45–55.

Sturgeon, Noël. *Ecofeminist Natures: Race, Gender, Feminist Theory and Political Action*. London: Routledge, 1997.

Vance, Linda. 'Ecofeminism and the Politics of Reality.' *Ecofeminism: Women, Animals, Nature*. Ed. Greta Gaard. Philadelphia: Temple University Press, 1993. 118–45.

11
A Different Chronology
Reflections on Feminism in Contemporary Poland

Agnieszka Graff

Admit it: Poland makes you think of Pope John Paul II and the millions of people gathered in the streets to mourn his death in the spring of 2005. Remember the singing, the candles, the way cameras lingered on young women's tear-smudged faces? Admittedly, Poland's women's movement is no mass phenomenon compared with the adoration of the last pope, now transformed into the cult of a beloved saint. Still, feminism does exist in Poland: some would even claim we have the most vibrant women's movement in the region. But it does not exist in a vacuum. It is shaped, to a large extent, by the need to resist the overwhelming presence of Catholicism in all spheres of life. Three years ago I titled an earlier version of this essay 'Lost Between the Waves? The Paradoxes of Feminist Chronology and Activism in Contemporary Poland.'[1] Today I drop the question altogether. Polish gender politics do not fit the Anglo-American chronology with the wave metaphor at its centre – our chronology is different, and not paradoxical. Inevitably, feminism is part of a broader context, and ours is dominated by the experience of post-1989 political, economic and ideological transformations – by changes in collective identity and memory that followed four decades of Soviet domination in Poland. Nonetheless, I hesitate to discard the wave metaphor entirely. Despite the specificity of our context, we are hardly isolated from the debates of international feminism. We, too, refer to waves and talk about backlash, post-feminism, as well as feminist generations and hybrid identities. We may not have lived through the Western chronologies, but our feminism – as well as the anti-feminism in our culture – is partly conditioned by Western influences.

This chapter examines Polish feminism from a dual perspective: taking into account the framework implicit in the wave metaphor, but insisting on the crucial importance of Poland's national history and mythology, as well as its political present. What does make the Polish women's movement paradoxical from the point of view of feminist history as it is written in the West is its peculiar mixture of second wave feminist goals and third wave feminist themes and tactics. Our demands concern basic reproductive rights, domestic violence, equal pay for equal work and our street performances show the drudgery behind the domestic ideal and the exploitation of women employees. But this content – redolent of American second wave feminist manifestos such as the street actions of WITCH, or classic essays such as Pat Mainardi's 'The Politics of Housework' (1970) – is dressed in a campy form very much in tune with third wave feminist aesthetics. We speak of 'clicks' and 'awakenings', as did authors of essays in early issues of *Ms*. Yet, we also share a penchant for pink with the third wave Girlie culture and with Code Pink activists. Above all, we partake in third wave feminism's preoccupation with pop culture: when tired with such local questions as to whether or not abortion ought to be legalised within our lifetimes, we turn to discussing *Ally McBeal* (1997–2002), *Buffy the Vampire Slayer* (1997–2003) and *Desperate Housewives* (2004–), all of which have been broadcast by Polish TV channels.

A backlash before feminism?

In her foreword to Rebecca Walker's third wave feminist anthology *To Be Real: Telling the Truth and Changing the Face of Feminism* (1995), Gloria Steinem complains that, after reading the contributors' grievances against her own generation, she feels 'like a sitting dog being told to sit' (xxii). No such exchange would be possible in Poland, for there is no Polish equivalent of Steinem: no generation of feminist 'mothers' exists for self-proclaimed third wavers to 'rebel' against. In other words, if we define third wave feminism in terms of its generational divide from the second wave, as many participants of the debate have done, such as Jennifer Baumgardner and Amy Richards in *Manifesta* (2000) and Astrid Henry in *Not My Mother's Sister* (2004), then the present 'wave' of feminism in Poland cannot be the third wave. No second wave of feminism in the 1960s and 1970s preceded this feminist movement; rather, it is the generation of today's young women that have introduced their own mothers to feminism. If, however, we focus our definition on a shift towards cultural production as a site of struggle – that is, if we understand third wave feminism as primarily an effort to counter the media construct of postfeminism or the widespread notion of the failure of feminism, as Stacy Gillis and Rebecca Munford do (2004) – then the Polish contribution might well be relevant. For despite not having had much of a second wave of feminism, we did experience a backlash. In fact, many of us internalised its message before discovering feminism.

In the fall of 1996, *Pelnym Glosem* [*In Full Voice*], the sole feminist periodical published in Poland at the time,[2] featured a lively debate on the nonexistence of feminism in Poland. Its tone was in turns cynical, resigned and mournful. Only two contributors thought feminism did in fact exist, but even they agreed it could hardly be called a movement (Walczewska 1996, 25; Kozak 29). My own contribution to this argument relied on a liberal account of the absence of feminism: I viewed resistance to women's rights as an extension of Polish culture's profound distrust of individualism (1996, 21).[3] Today such a debate would be unthinkable: *Pelnym Glosem* has been replaced by the more popular *Zadra* [*Splinter*], and feminism is far too visible in the mainstream media to contemplate its own nonexistence. Nonetheless, feminist identity still begins for many women with challenging the basic assumption that 'Polish feminism' is an oxymoron and that we have no women's history of which to speak. Anti-feminist discourse on women's rights in Poland also resists Western chronologies: it is an odd mixture of backlash rhetoric, post-feminist rambling and good old misogyny. The message is wrought with contradictions: feminism never existed; feminism is dead; it is a dirty joke; it threatens family values and the national tradition. At the centre of all this presides a version of Polish history which denies the very possibility of a women's movement. Feminists are hardly immune to their cultures' mythologies, so it was not until the late 1990s that many of us realised there was a heritage we could turn to for a sense of continuity. A spate of books on our political and cultural history have since emerged, with Slawomira Walczewska (1999), Maria Janion and Shana Penn each contributing to this history of feminism in Poland.

American feminists have long been aware of a peculiar correlation between the intensity of negative press coverage and the actual strength of the women's movement. Between 1969 and 1998 *Time* announced the death of feminism at least 119 times, as Baumgardner and Richards note (93). According to third wave feminist authors, a whole new generation of women's rights activists came on the scene between the *Newsweek* article 'The Failure of Feminism' in 1990 and the *Time* cover story 'Is Feminism Dead?' in 1998.[4] In a chapter that extends Susan Faludi's analysis of backlash into the 1990s, Baumgardner and Richards describe the strategies used by mainstream media to denigrate and misrepresent women's issues (87–125). Their point is that this is happening in a culture profoundly affected by the women's movement – a fact arrogantly ignored or trivialised in backlash rhetoric. Polish media employ most of the strategies described in *Backlash* and *Manifesta*, but the logic of anti-feminism is complicated by the relatively young age of both our democracy and our women's movement, and by a political context in which women's rights are constantly held hostage to national pride. Our culture is regarded as unique for two mutually exclusive reasons (often invoked in one breath): (1) women's rights are a luxury we cannot afford; and (2) there is no need for women's rights, because we live in a matriarchy. To grasp the appeal of this latter notion, it must be recalled that the Virgin Mary, repeatedly titled 'Queen of Poland', holds a central place in our religious tradition and collective imagination. Polish women are supposed to emulate the 'Polish Mother' ideal which dates back to the eighteenth century, the heroic precursor of the model of femininity which has been described by sociologists as the 'brave victim' (Marody and Poleszczuk 163). Where women are concerned, suffering is readily equated with strength and sacrifice is regarded as a kind of victory.

The beginnings of backlash-as-cultural-import reach back to the mid-1980s, when Eastern Europe began opening up to the West. Today, most backlash products marketed in Poland are still translations and borrowings: familiar images of man-hating hairy-legged feminists, American self-help books and women's magazines telling their readers how to win back the men who feminism recklessly scared away. Enormous popularity is enjoyed by pop versions of evolutionary psychology, such as John Gray's *Men are from Mars, Women are from Venus* (1992), which prove beyond doubt that men and women are an entirely different species. Nationalist rhetoric overlaps with backlash stereotypes in a circular manner, creating an apparently seamless identity of worthiness, strength and endurance for women who conform to traditional norms. The backlash has found powerful political support: the Church and ultra-conservative parties serve as our version of the New Right and, in fact, maintain close links with their American counterparts. This brings us to some interesting questions concerning feminist chronology. Is some knowledge of feminism necessary for backlash messages to be effective? What is the meaning of *Ally McBeal* in a culture that skipped *Murphy Brown* (1988–98)? How do texts such as John Gray's or Anne Moir and David Jessel's *Brain Sex: The Real Difference between Men and Women* (1991) speak to a context untouched by second wave feminism?

To be fair, Poland did not always remain on the receiving end of cultural transmission. Some of our contributions to backlash are really quite impressive. The popular film comedy *Seksmisja* [*Sexmission*] (1984) offers a vision of feminism as a bleak totalitarian system. This state – with an entirely female population as men are extinct – finally topples thanks to two hapless men who get stuck in the women's world by accident. The film, also a success in the former USSR and East Germany, helped to embed the association between communism and feminism in our collective imagination well before the watershed of 1989. Another comedy, *Tato* [*Daddy*] (1995), is a variation on the backlash classic *Fatal Attraction*, as discussed so thoroughly by Faludi (145–51). In the Polish version, the evil woman yielding sharp objects who later drowns is not the lover but the mentally disturbed wife of the protagonist, who gangs up with other women to deprive her helpless husband of his beloved daughter. What the two films share is an association between feminism and violence, and the visual pleasure drawn from the brutal punishment of the 'liberated woman'.

Elayne Rapping views the chronology of the 1960s to the 1990s in the U.S. in terms of a sudden shift from 'the personal' to 'the political' and then a gradual turn back again (49–63). The feminism of the 1960s called for a rethinking of the entire gender arrangement in terms of politics, power relations and inequality. Despite the impressive gains of this movement, argues Rapping, 'the generation of women that made up the second wave ... met with increasing political disillusionment in the years between 1982 and 1992' (59). The self-help culture which emerged in the late 1970s incorporated the techniques, but abandoned the politics, of feminist consciousness-raising. Paradoxically, it offered solace to women by placing the burden of change once again on their shoulders, redefining inequality in emotional terms. Readers of self-help books do not believe in social change; instead, they attribute their troubles to personal failings and call these failings 'addictions' and hope for 'recovery'. Rapping locates the roots of this cultural shift in the great hopes which feminism awakened, but failed to fulfill: 'What we have, I would argue, is a social and cultural evolution in the making, halfway home, getting tired and doubtful, confused and scared ... The recovery movement comes on the scene at just this critical point in our development, as a community and culture' (63). Rapping's diagnosis takes on an interesting resonance in the Eastern European context. Under totalitarian rule, people learned to distrust anything that came with the label 'politics': self-defence against the intrusiveness of the authoritarian state took the form of building secure and deeply conservative family structures.

In such a context, the very idea of feminism, with its claim that the personal is political, seemed like a form of madness. The message of backlash, on the other hand, though coming from a vastly different cultural context, seemed to make sense. Backlash discourse offered a recipe for happiness that consisted in rejecting the political in favor of the personal – precisely what Eastern Europeans had been doing for decades. The Eastern European story is, indeed, a different chronology. Backlash discourse moved into societies that had vaguely watched feminism from behind the iron curtain, viewing it as an exotic symptom of rich Westerners' boredom and dissipation. Anti-feminism was consumed by women who experience inequality daily, as a fact of life, but had never heard of 'sexism', 'discrimination' or even 'gender'. Faludi insists that we keep the reactive nature of backlash clearly in sight (15). Clearly, the same should be said for postfeminism. In Britain, France and the U.S., postfeminism is just what it says it is: a reaction and a postscript to feminism and a way for popular culture to appropriate and de-politicise the feminist agenda. But in a conservative culture that missed the great wave of modern feminism, the prefix 'post' has a very different sort of resonance. Broadly speaking, I would define the cultural impact of modern feminism as a challenge to the cultural construction of 'nature' – that is, the seeming immutability of gender arrangements as we know them (or as Western societies knew them in the 1960s). Feminism popularised the view that gender roles could be renegotiated. The Polish public is still being told that patriarchal gender roles are firmly grounded in Mother Nature's plan, without having been exposed to the opposite claim. To conclude, we seem to be dealing with selective, and somewhat delayed, cultural borrowing. The backlash works in Poland as the result of an entirely different set of reasons than those that drive it in the West – but it is still recognisable as backlash. One can say that the mainstream of Polish culture was made feminism-proof due to a historical coincidence. While Eastern Europe was living through the final decades of totalitarian rule, Western societies covered a lot of ground in terms of women's rights and shifting gender roles, and by the time communism was crumbling, the message coming from the West was deeply conservative. To put it bluntly, we skipped the radical 1960s and got a double dose of the conservative 1980s.

Feminism as anti-nationalism

Peggy Watson has argued that 'the rise of masculinism and the appearance of masculinist nationalism – mobilised by democratisation – do not prevent feminism in Eastern Europe, but are rather (ultimately) constitutive of it' (161). This is especially true for Poland. For all its diversity, Polish feminism since 1989 has had a solid core: resistance to the image of woman as national property and as symbol of national identity, the bearer of Polish 'difference' in Europe. This has led to a sustained focus on a single issue: abortion rights. This struggle is tied to the (re)construction of Polish national identity after 1989, especially in the context of Poland's accession to the European Union in 2004. Opposition to women's rights in Poland comes, above all, from nationalist quarters and is argued in terms of Poland's national identity and interest. As Floya Anthias and Nira Yuval-Davis argue, women are expected to 'participate in the ethnic and national process' as 'biological reproducers' and 'transmitters of culture' (313). According to nationalists everywhere, a woman is primarily a mother. Polish nationalism relies on a vision of 'our women' as different from, and superior to, the 'un-motherly' women of Western Europe: rather than think of emancipation, we fulfill ourselves in giving birth to and transmitting patriotic and religious values to the next generation of Poles. In short, if resistance to nationalism is key to the self-definition of Polish feminists, it is because gender plays such a central role in our country's collective imagination. Since the late eighteenth century, these values have been consistently allegorised in the figure of Polonia as an enchained and dying (or dead) woman, her pain a constant sacrifice.[5] Polishness is constructed in visual and literary traditions as an identity filled with suffering and loss, demanding constant sacrifice.

While negotiating the terms of Poland's membership in the European Union, Polish politicians repeatedly announced to various EU bodies that 'our women' do not 'need' reproductive rights. Lack of access to family planning was to become the marker of Poland's cultural difference within the European family of nations – motherhood, voluntary or not, was to function as the signifier of Polishness. This arrangement was the effect of the increasing influence of the Catholic Church after 1989. The clergy capitalised on its contributions to national independence and on the reverence Poles had for John Paul II, and demanded influence within the public sphere. Next to the re-introduction of religion into public schools, women's reproductive rights became a key concern. How did this process begin? And when did proponents of reproductive rights realise what game was being played? As early as 1989, it became clear that reproductive freedom would become contested ground, but few were aware of the determination and clout of the Church-sponsored anti-choice groups. The first cold shower came in March 1990, when

Solidarity – the movement that had won freedom for Poland – endorsed a total ban on abortion. This decree triggered dissention within the seemingly monolithic anti-communist camp. The Women's Section of Solidarity announced its commitment to women's reproductive freedom and several months later it opposed the Senate's draft bill proposing severe restrictions and penalties for both doctors and women. In the spring of 1991, after a series of warnings, the Women's Section was dissolved – an event that caused anger and bitter disappointment. In consequence, a feminist movement began to develop with an agenda that cut across political and historical divisions. In April 1991 the Parliamentary Women's Circle was formed, with members from several parties including former communists and the Solidarity movement, in what was a shocking alliance at the time. The Circle was instrumental in blocking the extremely restrictive anti-abortion bill in May 1991. The threat to reproductive freedom also led people into the streets. Demonstrators chanted: 'My uterus belongs to me'; 'Fewer Churches – More Nurseries' and 'God save us from the Church'.

Fifteen years have gone by. Since 1993, abortion has been banned except in cases of rape, incest, grave danger to the woman's health and/or deformation of the foetus. The abortion underground is largely ignored by the authorities and performs an estimated 70,000 to 200,000 abortions a year with prices close to the average monthly salary of around 500 Euros.[6] Not surprisingly, reproductive freedom remains the basic demand of the Polish women's movement. It is an issue that, to a large extent, defines our identity and our image in the public realm. It may seem like a lost cause, because, in a Catholic country, abortion is bound to be illegal. But matters are not quite so simple, since over half of the Polish population supports legal abortion. In 2005, 57 per cent believed that during the early weeks of pregnancy a woman should have the right to decide if she wants to give birth to a child ('Aborcja, edukacja seksualna' 1). Nonetheless, the demand that abortion be made legal is perceived as aberrant and a view that should not be voiced in the public realm. Anyone who raises the forbidden topic is immediately admonished. Politicians on both right and left – though for different reasons – have helped keep the taboo firmly in place. Watson has argued convincingly that what we see here is a certain pattern: new democratic governments of Eastern Europe all began using their power by limiting women's reproductive rights, so that power was gendered male from the outset: 'The democratization of Eastern Europe has been tantamount to a selective political empowerment of (some) men' (148). The abortion debates of the early 1990s carved out a landscape of public debate in which men asserted their political agency by deciding about fates of women, their political identities becoming distinct from one another in the process.[7] The issue of abortion also helped solidify the influence of the Church. The 1993 'compromise bill' – in fact, one of Europe's strictest anti-abortion laws – was introduced by a democratically elected government, which, owing to the pressure of the Church, chose to ignore the will of the majority of voters, as well as a 1.2 million signatures on the petition demanding a national referendum on abortion.

According to Wanda Nowicka, the effort of collecting these signatures should be viewed as a huge civil movement for democracy. Vast numbers of men and women were mobilised in defence of women's reproductive freedom against the pressure of the Church: 'people understood that the struggle for legal abortion was a struggle for real democracy' (1997, 45). Since 1993, many Polish feminists have continued efforts to bring the issue of reproductive freedom back into the public sphere. A key document of this struggle was a protest letter addressed by Polish women to the EU Parliament in March 2002. The 'Open Letter' was widely discussed in Polish media – it could hardly be ignored, given the signatures of some of Poland's most accomplished women, including Nobel Prize-winning poet Wislawa Szymborska, and film director Agnieszka Holland. The 'Letter' stated that:

> [A] peculiar agreement has been reached by the Catholic Church and the government concerning Poland's admission into the European Union. Namely, the Church will support integration with Europe in return for the government's closing the debate on the revision of the anti-abortion law ... [W]omen's rights are bought and sold behind the scenes of Poland's integration with the European Union. This is accompanied by a characteristically biased way of speaking. Protection of unborn life is treated as an objective dogma, while abortion on social grounds is spoken of in quotation marks and treated as an 'ideological' claim made by feminists, who attempt to legalize murder. ('Open Letter')

Responses were largely contemptuous. Right-wing commentators called the letter a disgrace and a call to murder while more moderate voices suggested that it was a grave strategic mistake as abortion rights should wait until Poland's place in the EU is secure. The answer that came from the EU Parliament was evasive: reproductive rights remain outside the scope of interest of EU legislators. The fact that women have no right to control their fertility has come to bear tremendous symbolic weight in

Poland. Needless to say, it is invested with symbolic importance by both sides: Catholic fundamentalists view restrictions on reproductive freedom as a cornerstone of what the Pope called 'the culture of life', as opposed to the 'culture of death' supposedly thriving in Western liberal democracies.

In a document issued on 21 March 2002, two years before Poland's accession to the EU, the Polish Episcopate explained how it viewed the division of labour concerning Polish presence in Europe: the government was to focus on economic and political issues, negotiating the best possible conditions for accession, while the Church would take care of spiritual and ethical aspects of integration. 'The essential calling of the Church is to bring salvation. Its wish is that EU enlargement should go hand in hand with a deepening awareness that what lies at the centre of all our efforts towards integration is Man, and his inalienable dignity, bestowed upon him in the act of creation' (qtd. in Dunin 32; author's translation). The references to 'Man' and 'his dignity' should be understood as code for banning abortion and euthanasia, relegating sexual education from schools, discrimination of gays and lesbians, and making divorce extremely difficult. Other rhetorical elisions include 'human life' for the foetus, 'human rights' for the rights of the foetus and 'murder of Polish citizens' for abortion. This peculiar language, with its mixture of mythical, melodramatic and nationalistic semantics, has managed to colonise public debate in Poland, making feminist claims for women's autonomy sound aberrant, deeply anti-patriotic and evil. According to Kinga Dunin, we are facing a communicative deadlock which the Church deliberately prepared, and has since then capitalised upon (32–34). There can be no real dialogue between a liberal discourse which emphasises freedom and human rights, and a religious discourse, the bottom of line of which is the 'will of God', 'absolute truth' and 'natural law'. Over the years, the liberal camp has simply backed out of the debate about values, leaving the scene to Catholic fundamentalists. The right to define national identity has since been usurped by conservatives, whose rhetoric abounds with references to 'true womanhood'. This puts feminism in the position of nationalism's natural opponent. While there are many themes in feminist activism and theory in Poland, I would argue that the critique of neo-nationalism is at the heart of the movement's identity. To quote from Elżbieta Matynia's study of Polish feminist art, '[de]nationalization also means de-matrionization' (2006, 137). Feminist attitudes towards national identity in Poland are distinct from those held by young feminists in the West. Particularly in the U.S., many activists and writers seem committed to reinforcing their

national, religious or cultural identities, while demanding that feminism give up universalising claims and 'celebrate' these differences.[8]
This trend may be ahead of us, but for the present we are in no position
to affirm national or ethnic identity. Rather, we consider ourselves – as
women who happen to be Polish citizens – to be nationalism's
hostages.[9]

Poland has been in the EU since May 2004 and the Union has largely
tolerated infringements on women's reproductive rights. After all, abortion
is not part of the EU's common policy. With ultra-right wing politicians
in power since the fall of 2005, women's rights are off the political
agenda. In response, feminists seem to have become increasingly political beings. Some have left academia to work for non-governmental
organisations, some are building political careers within existing left-wing
parties, still others participate in building a new political party – Greens
2004. Some of our most intense debates of the last two years have concerned attitudes towards national politics. Should party banners be
allowed at our demonstrations? If we exclude them, we run the risk of
marginalisation; if we admit them, there is danger of appropriation.
Whichever option we choose, we cannot ignore the fact that our role in
Poland is political, rather than merely cultural or intellectual.

* * *

Ruled by local historical forces, Polish feminism clearly resists the
Anglo-American wave chronology. What has caused our recent shift
towards politics, for example, was not a political component of third
wave feminism, but Poland's dramatic turn to the right, towards an
aggressive nationalism which identifies 'Polishness' with Catholicism,
excluding those who do not fit the mould, especially in terms of gender
and sexuality. Nonetheless, I believe there is some explanatory value in
the claim that Polish feminism uses third wave feminist tactics to
achieve second wave feminist goals, and in the argument that Eastern
Europe was exposed to the backlash before it encountered feminism. In
both cases the wave chronology is helpful – although as a convenient
departure point rather than a reliable framework. What is unique to the
Polish scene is the enormous influence of the Church and the resulting
centrality of abortion as the object of struggle. Whether we like it or not,
the rise of nationalism has largely defined the feminist agenda. In the
same period, third wave feminist discourse in the West tended to marginalise reproductive issues, focusing instead on feminist responses to
media icons, on sexuality and body image, on the complex, deeply

ambivalent, relationship between third wave 'daughters' and second wave 'mothers,' and more recently, on feminism's internal ethnic, racial and cultural diversities.

My point in enumerating these themes is that third wave feminist publications – both the popular ones and the academic ones – seem preoccupied with feminism's identity as a cultural movement. If both activists and scholars are so self-reflexive, it is largely because women's basic rights in their countries are secure thanks to an earlier generation of feminists. However, given the rise of religious conservatism and aggressive nationalism around the globe – including in the U.S. – this focus may be up for revision. It was with both awe and satisfaction that Polish feminists read reports of the March for Women's Lives held in Washington, DC in April 2004 and which gathered over a million people in support of women's reproductive rights. Though not quite sure to which wave the event belongs, I would certainly like to be counted as part thereof.

Notes

1. An earlier version appeared in the special issue on *Third Wave Feminism and Women's Studies* of the *Journal of International Women's Studies* 4.2 (April 2003): 100–16.
2. Five issues of *Pelnym Glosem* were published by the eFKa women's foundation in Cracow between 1993 and 1997. In 1999 eFKa introduced the feminist journal *Zadra*, which is aimed at a broader audience and appears more regularly.
3. This is not an argument I would make today. For a nuanced account of both recent and historical debates concerning liberalism in Eastern Europe in relation to feminist critiques of liberalism see Nanette Funk.
4. See Ginia Bellafante and Kay Ebeling respectively.
5. Not surprisingly, some of the most exciting feminist scholarship has consisted in re-interpreting and deconstructing this national imagery. For more on this see Walczewska (1999) and Janion.
6. For more on this see Nowicka (2000).
7. For more on this see Malgorzata Fuszara.
8. For an example of this see Daisy Hernandez and Bushra Rehman's collection.
9. For an extended discussion of these dilemmas see Matynia (2003).

Works cited

'Aborcja, edukacja seksualna, zaplodnienie pozaustrojowe.' *CBOS (Centrum Badania Opinii Spolecznej)*. 2005. Accessed: 1 Sept. 2006. <http://www.cbos. pl/SPISKOM.POL/2005/K_037_05.PDF>.

Anthias, Floya, and Nira Yuval-Davis. 'Women and the Nation State.' *Nationalism*. Ed. John Hutchinson and Anthony D. Smith. Oxford: Oxford University Press, 1994. 312–16.

Baumgardner, Jennifer, and Amy Richards. *Manifesta. Young Women Feminism and the Future*. New York: Farrar, Straus and Giroux, 2000.

Bellafante, Ginia. 'Feminism: It's All About Me.' *Time* 29 June 1998: 54–62.

Dunin, Kinga. 'Czarny ford i dwuglowe ciele, czyli Polak idzie do Unii.' *ResPublica Nowa* 165: XV (June 2002): 29–36.

Ebeling, Kay. 'The Failure of Feminism.' *Newsweek* 19 Nov. 1990: 9.

Faludi, Susan. *Backlash. The Undeclared War against Women*. London: Vintage, 1992.

Fatal Attraction. Dir. Adrian Lyne. Prod. Paramount Pictures, 1987.

Funk, Nanette. 'Feminist Critiques of Liberalism: Can They Travel East? Their Relevance in Eastern and Central Europe and the Former Soviet Union.' *Signs* 29 (2004): 695–726.

Fuszara, Malgorzata. 'Abortion and the Formation of the Public Sphere in Poland.' *Gender Politics and Post-Communism: Reflections from Eastern Europe and the Former Soviet Union*. Ed. Nanette Funk and Magda Mueller. New York: Routledge, 1994. 241–52.

Gillis, Stacy, and Rebecca Munford. 'Generations and Genealogies: The Politics and Praxis of Third Wave Feminism.' *Women's History Review* 13.2 (2004): 165–82.

Graff, Agnieszka. 'Feminizm ryzyka – i dlaczego w Polsce go nie ma.' *Pelnym Glosem* 4 (Fall 1996): 19–24.

——. 'Lost Between the Waves? The Paradoxes of Feminist Chronology and Activism in Contemporary Poland.' *Third Wave Feminism and Women's Studies*. Ed. Stacy Gillis and Rebecca Munford. Spec. issue of *Journal of International Women's Studies* 4.2 (2003): 100–16. <http:// www.bridgew.edu/ SoAS/ jiws/ April03/graff.pdf>.

Gray, John. *Men are from Mars, Women are from Venus*. New York: HarperCollins, 1992.

Henry, Astrid. *Not My Mother's Sister: Generational Conflict and Third-Wave Feminism*. Bloomington: Indiana University Press, 2004.

Hernandez, Daisy and Bushra Rehman, eds. *Colonize This! Young Women of Color on Today's Feminism*. New York: Seal, 2002.

Janion, Maria. *Kobiety i Duch Inności*. Warszawa: Sic!, 1996.

Kozak, Beata. 'O wróbelku.' *Pelnym Glosem* 4 (Fall 1996): 28–31.

Mainardi, Pat. 'The Politics of Housework.' *Sisterhood is Powerful: An Anthology of Writings from the Women's Liberation Movement*. Ed. Robin Morgan. New York: Vintage, 1970. 501–10.

Marody, Mira and Anna Giza Poleszczuk. 'Changing Images of Identity in Poland: From Self-Sacrificing to Self-Investing Woman?' *Reproducing Gender: Politics, Publics and Everyday Life after Socialism*. Ed. Susan Gal and Gail Kligman. Princeton: Princeton University Press, 2000. 151–75.

Matynia, Elzbieta. 'Poland Provoked: How Women Artists En-Gender Democracy.' *Current History. A Journal of Contemporary World Affairs* 105.689 (March 2006): 132–138.

——. 'Provincializing Global Feminism: The Polish Case.' *Social Research* 70.2 (2003): 499–530.

Moir, Anne, and David Jessel. *Brain Sex: The Real Difference between Men and Women*. New York: Dell, 1991.

Nowicka, Wanda, ed. *The Anti-Abortion Law In Poland. The Functioning, Social Effects, Attitudes and Behaviors. The Report*. Warsaw: The Federation for Women and Family Planning, 2000.

———. 'Ban on Abortion in Poland. Why?' *Ana's Land: Sisterhood in Eastern Europe.* Ed. Tanya Renne. Boulder: Westview, 1997. 42–46.

'Open Letter of Polish Women to European Parliament.' 5 Feb. 2002. [Text available upon request: <agraff@poczta.onet.pl>].

Penn, Shana. *Solidarity's Secret: The Women Who Defeated Communism in Poland.* Ann Arbor: University of Michigan Press, 2005.

Rapping, Elayne. *The Culture of Recovery. Making Sense of the Self-Help Movement in Women's Lives.* Boston: Beacon, 1996.

Seksmisja [Sexmission]. Dir. Juliusz Machulski. Prod. Zespol Filmowy, 1984.

Steinem, Gloria. Foreword. *To Be Real: Telling the Truth and Changing the Face of Feminism.* Ed. Rebecca Walker. New York: Anchor Books, 1995. xiii–xxi.

Tato [Daddy]. Dir. Maciej Slesicki. Prod. Syrena Entertainment Group, 1995.

Walczewska, Slawomira. *Damy, rycerze, feministki: Kobiecy dyskurs emancypacyjny w Polsce.* Kraków: efKa, 1999.

———. 'Feminizm? – jest!' *Pelnym Glosem* 4 (Fall 1996): 25–27.

Watson, Peggy. '(Anti)feminism after Communism.' *Who's Afraid of Feminism? Seeing through the Backlash.* Ed. Ann Oakley and Juliet Mitchell. New York: New Press, 1997. 144–61.

12
Global Feminisms, Transnational Political Economies, Third World Cultural Production

*Winifred Woodhull**

Third wave feminism claims – rightly so – that new modalities of feminism must be invented for the new millennium. But is it enough to generate new conceptions of feminism and new forms of activism that pertain almost exclusively to people in wealthy countries, as the third wave has generally done so far? This chapter will argue that in an increasingly globalised context, it is crucial that feminism be conceived and enacted in global terms, and that Western feminists engage with women's movements the world over. Feminism's third wave emerged in the late 1980s and early 1990s, when information technology and transnational finance became the most powerful economic forces in the postindustrial Western countries, enabling those nations to dominate the rest of the world more effectively than ever before. Two aspects of this development fundamentally shaped Western feminism of the 1990s: the erosion of the Left's longstanding bases for political solidarity with the third world and the growing importance of information technologies in mobilising feminist political constituencies, as well as linking women with common interests and concerns, and thus creating new forms of community. Owing to the de-industrialisation in the 1980s, this period was characterised by corporate downsizing, under-employment, and high unemployment, especially in Europe. Western democracies were failing to fulfil their post-Second World War promise to provide a decent life to all members of their societies. Economic recession intensified racial strife and fuelled xenophobia directed at two groups of third world peoples: labourers who 'accepted' grossly exploitative wages and working conditions in the industrial plants that relocated overseas, and non-European immigrants in Europe and the U.S. who were employed mainly in low-wage itinerant positions ('stealing our jobs'). Immigrants and 'foreign' labour, however, were not the only scapegoats in an economic shift that resulted in the collapse of the relatively stable and favourable terms of employment that had prevailed in the West since the Second World War. Women, too, became targets, for as employment prospects disappeared along with a living wage, angry white men in the 'Moral Majority' charged women not only with 'stealing our jobs' but also with abandoning their husbands and children in their selfish pursuit of their own goals, and thus undermining the bedrock of social stability: the patriarchal nuclear family. A powerful anti-feminist backlash eventually prompted both mainstream and extreme right-wing media pundits to declare the demise of feminism.

In the face of these developments, a key mandate of third wave feminism was to prove that feminism was alive and well. The most comprehensive reflections on third wave feminism that appeared in the U.S. – Leslie Heywood and Jennifer Drake's *Third Wave Agenda* (1997), Jacquelyn N. Zita's special issue of *Hypatia* (1997) and Rory Dicker and Alison Piepmeier's *Catching a Wave* (2003) – attest to feminism's capacity to adapt to historical change and to confront the issues currently affecting women and others subject to sexual domination and harassment. Other modes of expression by third wave feminists showed that feminism was not only adapting in the 1990s but was assuming vibrant new forms, not least by renewing its efforts to move beyond the walls of the academy into arenas of everyday life. In the overlapping realms of culture and activism, there was a particularly striking manifestation of the third wave's determination and inventiveness in the concerts of the Riot Grrrl musicians. The Riot Grrrls tied their 'in-your-face feminism' to assertions of their own desires and pleasures as well as to grassroots political movements against racism and class exploitation. They railed against the corporate power that was invading every realm of experience in order to commodify it and capitalise on it. Corporations, they said, were co-opting expressions of opposition to the status quo in order to neutralise their subversive potential and, at the same time, to profit financially from their popular appeal, as with the Spice Girls.

The Riot Grrrls continue to attract huge audiences and to generate a broad base of fans not only in North America and Europe but in venues such as Jakarta. Their activism is one of the most potent expressions of third wave feminism. Yet despite their engagement in real-world conflicts and their international appeal, the Riot Grrrls' politics focus is on the situation of women in the global North. In this respect, they are typical of third wave feminists, who appear to have forgotten second wave feminism's roots not only in the U.S. Civil Rights Movement but also in third world liberation movements as well, in which radical feminists of the 1960s and 1970s considered their own struggles to be inextricably implicated. In those decades, there was an acute consciousness of radical feminism's links to Gandhi's non-violent resistance to British domination, Vietnam's anti-imperialist struggle against the U.S., and Algeria's anti-colonial war against France, whose sexual torture of female freedom fighters like Djamila Boupacha was publicly denounced by Simone de Beauvoir and other French feminists. The awareness of these links seems to have faded, despite the third wave's emergence in tandem with the processes of globalisation. Globalisation involves the globally binding technologies of satellite communications and the Internet as well as other *potentially* democratising technologies such as video and CDs, fax machines and cell phones, alternative radio and cable television. Given the global arena in which third wave feminism emerged, it is disappointing that new feminist debates arising in first world contexts mainly address issues that pertain only to women *in* those contexts, as if the parochialism and xenophobia of the economically depressed 1980s were still hanging over feminism like a dark cloud.

At their best, third wave feminists attend to issues of race and class as they shape the politics of gender and sexuality in the global North – hence the myriad community groups, websites, zines and scholarly publications devoted to economic inequality and the gender struggles of minority women in North America and Europe.[1] Not surprisingly, many third wave feminist websites promote women's empowerment in and through computer technologies. The latter include sites such as DigitalEve which celebrate women's involvement in the field of information technology and encourage all women to make use of it in any way that may be helpful to them and to feminist causes. Symptomatically, however, most of these sites either unabashedly promote capitalist self-advancement in the name of feminism, or else mistakenly assume that their sincere appeal to feminist action, self-help and solidarity really addresses a worldwide audience. For example, Girl Incorporated, which 'designs Web sites and online marketing strategies that make sense', passes itself off as feminist simply by virtue of being a women's business that markets to women in business. Some sites, however, are feminist in a more meaningful sense insofar as they aim to broaden women's access to a masculinist domain and to put information technology in the service of feminism: see, for example, Digital Eve's local chapters such as the one in Seattle. Digital Eve characterises itself as a 'global' organisation – by which it means that it has chapters in the U.S., Canada, the U.K., and

Japan. Thus it seems that in third wave (cyber)feminism, the first world, perhaps unwittingly, is synedochally the whole world. At their worst, third wavers use new technologies, as well as more traditional ones such as the print media, to proffer glib commentaries about the supposed 'elitism' of second wave feminism. Throwing out the baby with the bath water, they summarily dismiss intellectuals' hard-to-read reflections on the politics of feminism, ostensibly with a view towards making feminism less intimidating and more widely accessible. In the process, many of the most audible third wavers depoliticise feminism altogether. In a web interview, the co-author of the well-known third wave feminist text *Manifesta* (2000), Jennifer Baumgardner, opines, for instance: 'Name an issue, if that's what you're interested in, then it's the most important, whether it's eating disorders, sexual harrassment, child care, etc. ... Feminism is something individual to each feminist' (Straus, par. 19). This is consumerism, not politics.

My analysis of this dynamic might risk the charge of elitism from those third wave feminists who applaud the accessibility of pleasure-affirming work and who see established feminist academics and their theories as oppressive and exclusionary. Nevertheless, it must be acknowledged that political theory plays a crucial role in feminist politics: that it plays as crucial a role in the analysis of popular cultural forms as it does in the analysis of elite ones and that it is unhelpful to oppose theory to activism (or to personal needs and interests), as if the one were ethereal and the other real. Only theory can enable us to distinguish, for example, between meaningful modes of participatory democracy made possible by mass communication. Similarly, only theory can allow us to grasp, for example, the political implications of mass-mediated representations of gender, sexuality and power or the new sexualities, pleasures and forms of embodiment that are coming into being through human interaction in the new media, as Stacy Gillis does in her exploration of desire and bodies in 'Cybersex' (2004). Pleasure is an issue for the third wave of feminism, but it is certainly not a simple one: theory can cast light on the subjective processes, bodily experiences and social bonds that generate pleasures and assign value to them. It can also promote an understanding of the links between Western women's pleasurable play with affordable fashions in clothing and make-up, and the sweatshops in which third world women and immigrants labour to produce those sources of middle class (and largely white) enjoyment. Finally, only theory can enable us to grasp how the relation between elite and popular culture has been radically reconfigured in recent decades by global media networks. As Peter Waterman points out, the publishing industry that disseminates elite literature and scholarship 'can hardly be isolated from the more general electronic information, media, and advertising conglomerates into which publishing is increasingly integrated' (52). Theories of the political economy of global media are especially important for third wave feminism, since it is so heavily invested in mass-mediated forms of political affiliation, feminist solidarity and pleasurable, politically engaged subjectivity. The crucial role of theory *in* and *as* politics, as well as the importance of thinking through the mutually constitutive relations between Western feminisms and feminisms in other parts of the world, should be key issues for twenty-first-century feminists of this new 'wave'.

For more than a decade, scholars in the humanities and social sciences have been investigating the globalisation process with the purpose of determining the extent to which it fosters the development of a transnational public sphere and global forms of citizenship.[2] A transnational public sphere is considered to be important because it is rooted in civil society, that is, a social space that is controlled neither by the market nor by national governments, and that promotes a sense of involvement with the affairs of other, unknown, nonkin citizens (Sreberny-Mohammadi 19). As flows of capital and labour alter national and ethnic landscapes worldwide, and as global media networks facilitate new forms of rapid communication, it becomes conceivable that a transnational public sphere could be expanded to include parts of the third world (and, for that matter, the first world) that have so far been excluded, resulting in new freedoms for many people. Of course, fundamental questions remain regarding the possibility that the mere existence of electronic linkages could guarantee meaningful political participation for ordinary citizens, and that new public 'spaces' would work to the benefit of women, ethnic and religious minorities, and others who have traditionally been excluded from effective involvement in the public sphere: '[i]n situations in which there is (as yet?) no civil society, can transnational news media, exile publishing, and the internet really help in the creation of such a space?' (Sreberny-Mohammadi 10). Despite these basic questions, the possibility of a transnational public sphere that empowers the disenfranchised is an enticing prospect. The counterpart of a transnational public sphere is global citizenship, which involves both deepening democracy and expanding it on a global scale, so that 'issues such as peace, development, the environment, and human rights assume a global character' (Sreberny-Mohammadi 11). Indispensable elements in global citizenship include intergovernmental politics (as in the UN), international solidarity movements, independent media and grassroots democracy. In addition, cultural expression is crucial since it alone encourages sensuous and affective investment in social arrangements, both real and imagined. As such, it has greater power to generate progressive change and sustain egalitarian relationships than do rational calculations of shared interest.

For example, given the scattering of African writers and intellectuals across the globe, as well as new modes of political and cultural expression that bear witness to the sweeping economic and social changes of the past twenty years, it is important to consider the political activism and cultural production of African feminists in a global frame. To adopt a global frame surely means taking into account, as all Third World feminists are obliged to do, the neo-liberal economic forces driving globalisation, a process characterised by cross-border flows of finance capital and commodities, as well as by unprecedented migrations of cultures, ideas and people, the majority of them poor labourers or refugees. It means taking seriously the repressive effects of that process, which stem from the operations of exploitative multinational corporations and transnational institutions such as the World Bank and the International Monetary Fund (IMF), as well as the power plays of the world's wealthiest nation states, the U.S. being at the top of the pyramid of those that call the political shots on the international stage at the same time as exercising daunting control over flows of information and culture through vast media networks spanning the entire planet. Finally, adopting a global frame suggests examining the ways in which feminist projects the world over are inevitably being shaped by the growing disparities of wealth, power and well-being not only between the North and the South, but between the rich and the poor in both those arenas.

Yet while it acknowledges the harm inflicted by globalisation, the interpretive frame I propose considers its potentially liberatory dimensions as well. David Rodowick defines the media state as 'a virtual information territory' which, in conjunction with the 'deterritorialized transnational communities' spawned by hegemonic forces, produces a 'cosmopolitan public sphere' (13) – another term for the transnational public sphere. This new public sphere is said to be capable of fostering innovative forms of political activism despite its genesis by the very communication technologies and migratory flows that make possible state-of-the-art modes of domination. A transnational space fraught with contradiction, it is noticeably eroding the traditional functions of the state, sometimes in progressive ways. Echoing many earlier theorists of globalisation, Rodowick argues that one dimension of this space concerns the transnational concept of human rights, which is increasingly being defended on the ground by interstate and non-governmental organisations (NGOs) in situations where states fail to protect the rights of their citizens. He demonstrates that, like human rights, citizenship is now a concept that is meaningful and effective beyond the frontiers of individual nation states. Owing in part to the communication networks linking individuals and communities in different parts of the world, growing numbers of citizens are in a position to put direct democracy into practice with respect to 'issues that are increasingly global and local at the same time' (Rodowick 14).

The other dimension of the cosmopolitan public sphere is 'defined by the global reach of electronic communication and entertainment networks' (Rodowick 14). While global media forms may themselves elude state regulation and restrict both the content and the dissemination of information in ways that undermine democracy the world over, they are not monolithic: rather 'they are heterogeneous and contradictory with respect to their source (print, film, television, video, radio, and the varieties of computer-mediated communication) and to modes of reception' (Rodowick 14). Media conglomerates create networks (e.g. satellite communications, cellular phones and the Internet), the velocity and global range of which offer myriad possibilities for political intervention on the part of activists operating independently of repressive states. They provide technological resources that can be taken up by alternative media and channelled into new circuits. Once they have been 'recontextualised in *immigré* and activist communities' (Rodowick 14), they can help to generate new modes of identification and forms of collective action that are consonant with democratic politics – world-wide.

So, for example, how is the concept of human rights being defended by the most democratic, independent African non-governmental organisations in the transnational public sphere that is being created by progressive users of global media networks? How do these efforts affect African women? There are multiple examples: in Algeria, which has been in a violent civil war since 1991, feminists of the older generation – notably Khalida Messaoudi – continue to defend women's rights, legitimising and strengthening local grass roots movements through reference to the UN Convention to Eliminate Discrimination Against Women.[3] Messaoudi's democratic activism on the world stage works for oppressed citizens in the name of human rights, independently of control by any state; as such it implicitly contests the presumption of wealthy countries to embody democracy and to define it for the rest of the world, even as the U.S. and other first world powers impose economic policies that undermine democratic forces in countless venues across the globe.

Another example of a genuinely progressive African NGO defending human rights as a transnational concept is the group Women in Nigeria (WIN). The WIN collective is a grassroots African feminist organisation, one that sees women's liberation as inextricably linked to the liberation of poor urban workers and peasants in Nigeria, and that aims to 'merge the concern for gender equality into popular democratic struggles' (Imam 292). WIN works actively, through direct democracy in its own activities and through 'conscientisation,' to overcome hierarchies and conflicts not only of gender and class but also of language, region, ethnicity and religion in its promotion of all Nigerian women's interests.

Women in Nigeria necessarily focuses much of its effort on dealing with the socioeconomic fallout of IMF- and World Bank-inspired structural adjustment policies (SAPs) imposed in Nigeria, as well as in much of the rest of sub-Saharan Africa since the late 1970s. These policies, which are intended to stabilise economies in order to make them attractive to lenders and foreign investors, require governments of poor nations to ensure that their people produce mainly for export, which often has the effect of requiring that most consumer goods be imported and purchased at inflated prices. Moreover, in the name of an 'open economy', price controls and protective tariffs are abolished, with the result that local small- and medium-sized businesses are forced to fight a losing battle against multinational giants. Finally, in order to direct all possible elements in a nation's economy towards servicing the debt, the SAPs also impose radical reductions in public spending, which may cover everything from roads and transportation that do not directly serve foreign investors, to civil service jobs and pensions, as well as education, health and other social services.

Ayesha M. Imam demonstrates that since the SAPs have been in place in Nigeria, the macroeconomic effects have been devastating. The rate of growth of the GDP has fallen precipitously (7.9 per cent in 1990 to 4.3 per cent in 1991); the value of the local currency, the Naira, has fallen dramatically against the U.S. dollar, and the external debt has increased exponentially. At the social level, the effects of SAPs have been almost uniformly negative, with a general decrease in the standard of living and in purchasing power. Contributing factors are growing unemployment, wage freezes and delays of several months in payment of wages and/or benefits, if payments are made at all. As employment shrinks in the public sector, there is increasing pressure on the informal economy, which translates into greater competition and lower returns on labour there. Other factors include staggering levels of inflation and the effects of the cuts in social services, which disproportionately affect women and children. There have been marked decreases in the number of girls attending school at all levels, marked increases in infant mortality and alarming increases in the numbers of people infected with HIV and AIDS. For feminist groups like WIN, a key concern in all of this is the dramatic increase in rape and domestic violence that has resulted from the combination of rising economic hardship, declining opportunities for meaningful political action, a burgeoning of misogynist fundamentalisms of all kinds and the fact that in many African cultures, woman-beating is seen as the right of husbands and male relatives.

Unfortunately, the situation in Nigeria – the terrible effects of the SAPs, the repressive government, official and unofficial violence against women – exists, in various forms, all over sub-Saharan Africa. And while democratic and feminist NGOs *are* doing invaluable work in the defence of human rights in both national and international arenas, I am sceptical, not so much about the liberatory *potential* of the transnational public sphere and grassroots democratic politics in Africa, but about their liberatory effectiveness in the here and now. As Imam points out, already in the mid-1990s, the SAPs had taken such a toll that it was almost impossible for WIN to raise funds for its operations by selling books and T-shirts, as it had done in the past, as a means of resisting state control and state appropriation. It could no longer even rely on donated meeting space, because the economic crisis was so acute. In order to support its 'projects, campaigns, research, meetings, and publishing activities' (Imam 305), it was increasingly relying on grants from external sources. And while its policy in the mid-1990s was to accept outside funding only for projects that WIN had designed independently, it is hard to imagine that the organisation has been able to remain as autonomous as it once was.

Nigerian feminists have, since the late 1990s, expanded their means of political organising to include email networks and websites.[4] Yet even as we take seriously the possibilities opened up by the newest forms of mass communication, we would do well to explore the ways in which groups like WIN might benefit, or do benefit, from more established media networks, such as the forms of piracy that enable Africans to circulate videos outside official channels, with row after row of subtitles in Wolof, Arabic and other African languages. WIN has reported some success in using popular theatre for consciousness raising; could it also make use of mass-circulated popular cultural forms such as romance novels, as writers and publishers are doing in Nigeria and Ivory Coast?[5] Could other African feminist organisations adjust the romance formulas to appeal to particular ethnic or national audiences, drawing on local traditions that provide a point of entry for raising questions about the gender politics of intimate relationships, work and cosmopolitan modes of identification? Could they do so in a critical way that does more than to market print commodities profitably? We must also continue to give due attention to the ways in which older forms of cultural production, such as 'elite' literature, enjoy considerable prestige and power to shape people's thinking in many parts of the world, including Africa.

However 'elite' it may be, a good deal of the literature published by well-known African writers since the mid-1990s takes up many of the same issues that concern activist groups, such as the WIN collective. That is, the writings of Buchi Emecheta (Nigeria/U.K.), Lília Momplé (Mozambique), Nuruddin Farah (Somalia/U.K.), Nadine Gordimer (South Africa) and many others address the ways in which today's global economies adversely affect Africa. They promote feminist and other grassroots democratic struggles, while at the same time enjoining readers to imagine and embrace new forms of political subjectivity. The questions concerning the accessibility and political effectiveness of these different modes of communication, within the transnational public sphere, are pressing ones: not just for Africans and Africanists, but for everyone if indeed we live in a globalised world. The larger issue is that reflections on the emancipatory possibilities of both the new and traditional media need to incorporate a serious consideration of the parts of the world that are not wealthy, that is, most of the world. This issue is especially acute for third wave feminism, since the latter is defined by the historical moment of its emergence, a moment of unprecedented interrelation between the local and the global, between the West and 'the rest'.

Notes

* An earlier version of this piece appeared in the special issue on *Third Wave Feminism and Women's Studies* of the *Journal of International Women's Studies* 4.2 (April 2003).

1. See Abby Wilkerson for more on sexuality and race and Michelle Sidler for more on class inequities.

2. For an introduction to globalisation from a social science perspective see Sandra Braman and Annabelle Sreberny-Mohammadi, Georgette Wang, Jan Servaes and Anura Goonasekera's or Nigel Dower and John Williams.

3. For more on Khalida Messaoudi see Ronnie Scharfman.

4. Thanks to Omofolabo Ajayi-Soyinka for pointing this out in response to a version of this paper presented at the 'Cultures in Motion: The Africa Connection' conference at the University of Tennessee (6–9 Feb. 2003). For an example of innovative uses to which the Internet is being put in the

African/diasporic cultural arena see Daniela Merolla on Couscousnet, which links members of scattered Berber communities.
5. See Brian Larkin for more on the circulation of films and Moradewun Adejunmobi for more on the uses of romance fiction.

Works cited

Adejunmobi, Moradewun. 'Romance without Borders: Connecting Foreign and Local Fiction of Love in West Africa.' African Literature Association Conference. San Diego, California. 3–7 April 2002.
Baumgardner, Jennifer, and Amy Richards. *Manifesta: Young Women, Feminism, and the Future.* New York: Farrar, Straus and Giroux, 2000.
Braman, Sandra, and Annabelle Sreberny-Mohammadi, eds. *Globalization, Communication and Transnational Civil Society.* Cresskill: Hampton, 1996.
Dicker, Rory, and Alison Piepmeier, eds. *Catching a Wave: Reclaiming Feminism for the 21st Century.* Boston: Northeastern University Press, 2003.
DigitalEve Seattle. N. pub. 1 Sept. 2006. <http://www.digitaleveseattle.org/>.
Dower, Nigel, and John Williams, eds. *Global Citizenship: A Critical Introduction.* New York: Routledge, 2002.
Gillis, Stacy. 'Cybersex.' *More Dirty Looks: Gender, Pornography and Power.* Ed. Pamela Church Gibson. London: British Film Institute, 2004. 92–101.
Girl Incorporated. 2003. Accessed: 1 Sept. 2006. <http://www.girlincorporated.com/>.
Heywood, Leslie, and Jennifer Drake, eds. *Third Wave Agenda: Being Feminist, Doing Feminism.* Minneapolis: Minnesota University Press, 1997.
Imam, Ayesha M. 'The Dynamics of WINning: An Analysis of Women in Nigeria (WIN).' *Feminist Genealogies, Colonial Legacies, Democratic Futures.* Ed. M. Jacqui Alexander and Chandra Talpade Mohanty. New York: Routledge, 1997. 280–307.
Larkin, Brian. 'African Video Films under the Sign of Neo-Liberalism.' Society for Cinema Studies Conference. Washington, DC. 24–27, May 2001.
Merolla, Daniella. 'Digital Imagination and the "Landscape of Group Identities": Berber Diasporas and the Flourishing of Theater, Home Videos, and CouscousNet.' African Literature Association Conference. San Diego, California. 3–7 April 2002.
Rodowick, David. 'Introduction: Mobile Citizens, Media States.' *Publications of the Modern Language Association* 1 (2002): 13–23.
Scharfman, Ronnie. 'Upright and Out There: The Political Trajectory of Khalida Messaoudi.' *Parallax* 7 (1998): 185–88.
Sidler, Michelle. 'Living in McJobdom: Third Wave Feminism and Class Inequity.' *Third Wave Agenda: Being Feminist, Doing Feminism.* Ed. Leslie Heywood and Jennifer Drake. Minneapolis: Minnesota University Press, 1997. 25–39.
Sreberny-Mohammadi, Annabelle. Introduction. *Globalization, Communication and Transnational Civil Society.* Ed. Sandra Braman and Annabelle Sreberny-Mohammadi. Cresskill: Hampton, 1996. 1–19.
Straus, Tamara. 'A Manifesto for Third Wave Women.' *AlterNet.org.* 24 Oct. 2000. Accessed: 1 Sept. 2006. <http://www.alternet.org/story.html?StoryID = 9986 >.
Wang, Georgette, Jan Servaes, and Anura Goonasekera, eds. *The New Communication Landscape: Demystifying Media Globalization.* New York: Routledge, 2000.

Waterman, Peter. 'A New World View: Globalization, Civil Society, and Solidarity.' *Globalization, Communication and Transnational Civil Society.* Ed. Sandra Braman and Annabelle Sreberny-Mohammadi. Cresskill: Hampton, 1996: 37–61.

Wilkerson, Abby. 'Ending at the Skin: Sexuality and Race in Feminist Theorizing.' *Third Wave Feminisms.* Ed. Jacquelyn N. Zita. Spec. issue of *Hypatia: A Journal of Feminist Philosophy* 12.3 (1997): 164–73.

Zita, Jacquelyn N., ed. *Third Wave Feminisms.* Spec. issue of *Hypatia: A Journal of Feminist Philosophy* 12.3 (1997).

13

Neither Cyborg Nor Goddess
The (Im)Possibilities of Cyberfeminism

Stacy Gillis

The generational model of feminism requires that each new feminism is understood as better or more engaged with real, lived experiences than the previous versions. One of the differences between the second and third waves of feminism has been the need to negotiate and engage with the new technologies that have emerged since the personal computing revolution of the early 1980s. Cyberfeminism emerged in the 1990s, positioned as an example of what feminism could be and could do in the supposedly disembodied spaces of the Internet. New communication technologies and cyberspace have been widely regarded as providing the opportunities needed to bring about the global feminist movements of the new millennium – this third wave of feminism – and the Internet has been vaunted as the global consciousness-raising tool which the first and second waves lacked: '[cyberfeminism is a] woman-centred perspective that advocates women's use of new information and communication technologies for empowerment' (Miller 200). Susan Hawthorne and Renate Klein claim that cyberfeminism is 'a philosophy which acknowledges, first, that there is a difference in power between men and women specifically in the digital discourse' and, crucially, that 'CyberFeminists want to change that situation' (2). While it is undeniable that the changes in the material conditions of technology have wrought new kinds of relationships and new ways of theorising bodies and identities, my question here is whether or not cyberfeminism is an adequate term to describe these changes. It is arguable that the myth of cyberfeminism – that women are using cyberspace in powerful and transgressive ways and that cyberspace is providing women with a disembodied space in which to move beyond gender – is far removed from online experiences. This chapter identifies how cyberfeminism's transgressive potential is limited by the specificities of embodied online experiences. While feminist theory should not be uniform, and this chapter takes its inspiration from Rosi Braidotti's argument that 'it would be more beneficial to all concerned if the tensions that are built into the end-of-century crisis of values were allowed to explode inside feminism, bringing its paradoxes to a fore' (2002, 210), I am here concerned with the ways in which, like third wave feminism and (post)feminism, ways of defining and managing cyberfeminism are difficult and contentious.

Future cunt

For a movement which celebrates the potential for moving beyond the confines of the (gendered) body, cyberfeminism remains remarkably concerned with the corporeal. This is, in part, the result of many of the tenets of cyberfeminism emerging from the work of Donna Haraway and Sadie Plant. Haraway posits a cyborg feminism, arguing that the metaphor of the cyborg breaks down the binary oppositions of meat/metal and offers the possibility of a post-gender identity: the cyborg is a 'myth about transgressed boundaries, potent fusions, and dangerous possibilities' (154). Haraway has provided what is acknowledged to be a key text in the widespread work on body theory which occurred in the aftermath of second wave feminism. Her metaphor of the cyborg has been widely discussed and referenced, largely because of its promise of resistance which is disruptive of patriarchal models of gender, the body and identity: 'rendering ambiguous the distinction between machines and organisms, the cyborg demonstrates that technology does not exist "outside" ourselves and that we are not mere users of it' (Castricano par. 15). For Haraway, the cyborg disrupts because it 'lapses into boundless difference' (161) and can thereby resist hegemonic readings: 'cyborg politics insist on noise and advocate pollution, rejoicing in the illegitimate effusions of animal and machine' (176) and resisting 'models of unity' (181). The cyborg's apparent potential for transgression – with its visual evidence of the hybridisation of meat and metal, body and technology – has meant that it has become one of the most pervasive and persuasive symbols of postmodernity. Haraway's post-gender cyborg has become representative of the embodied artifice of the gendered body as Jenny Sundén argues: '[t]he politics of cyborgs are not to be found in collective, social movements, but are inextricably linked to their constantly moving borderland bodies' (219). Cyborg feminism has fed into cyberfeminism, with its promise of agency through monstrosity and transgression.

Unlike Haraway, who has distanced herself from cyberfeminist debates, Plant has embraced them. She has been lauded by cyberfeminism because of her articulation of women's relationship with cybernetic technologies. Embedded within essentialism, she points up women's supposed affinity with the new freedoms of cyberspace as the Internet promises women 'a network of lines on which to chatter, natter, work and play; virtuality brings a fluidity to identities which once had to be fixed; and multi-media provides a tactile environment in which women artists can find their space' (2000, 265). Like Haraway, she stresses the transgressive potential of these new exchanges although also arguing that women have always been linked with cybernetic technologies. For her, the computer

> was always a simulation of weaving: threads of ones and zeros riding the carpets and simulating silk screens in the perpetual motions of cyberspace. It joins women on and as the interface between man and matter, identity and difference, one and zero, the actual and the virtual. An interface which is taking off on its own: no longer the voice, the gap, or the absence, the veils are already cybernetic. (1995, 63)

The weaving metaphors which were frequently used of the World Wide Web in the mid-1990s offered Plant the opportunity to identify women as the common factor to both: weaving, women, the Web. Plant's argument that women will find a natural 'home' in cyberspace remains, however, locked into an account of cyberspace as a body-less space. While she references the post-human, which brings to mind Haraway's post-gender cyborg, Plant is unable to articulate precisely what this post-humanity involves. That said, her understanding of women in cyberspace as cyber-goddesses has proven powerfully seductive for cyberfeminism.

Cyborgic monsters and cyber-goddesses, then, make up much of the utopic cyberfeminist landscape. Bearing these symbols in mind, it is perhaps not surprising that cyberfeminism first appeared in feminist art groups in the 1990s and it is amongst artists that cyberfeminism has retained much currency. VNS Matrix were among the first to use the term, placing their 'Cyberfeminist Manifesto' on a billboard in Sydney, Australia in 1991:

> we are the virus of the new world disorder
> rupturing the symbolic from within
> saboteurs of big daddy mainframe
> the clitoris is a direct line to the matrix. ...
> infiltrating disrupting disseminating

corrupting the discourse
we are the future cunt (VNS Matrix)

While this group does have a website (which regularly changes servers) the actual cyber-activities remain oblique. More recent examples of cyberfeminist artists include subRosa, a 'reproducible cell of cultural researchers committed to combining art, activism, and politics to explore and critique the effects of the intersections of the new information and biotechnologies on women's bodies, lives and works' (par. 2). With regular exhibitions and publications, subRosa uses the monstrosity of the cyborg to explore various themes, including the politics of biotechnology. However, subRosa produce IRL ('in real life'), rather than web-based, exhibitions (although some pictures of their exhibitions are available on their website). This is not to say that exhibitions on, for example, biotechnology are not contributing to gender and technology debates, but the cyberfeminist element remains difficult to assign. Another self-termed cyberfeminist artist is Karen Keifer-Boyd, whose *The Cyberfeminist House* is a web-based art game intended to teach 'how to investigate the complex ways that power, oppression, and resistance work in our media-saturated visual culture' (par. 1). The project seeks to explore embodied experiences, drawing upon such texts as Charlotte Perkins Gilman's 'The Yellow Wallpaper' (1892). Again, the relationship with cyberfeminism is oblique: is this cyberfeminist because it is concerned with feminism and is on the Web? This is not to question these forms of cyber-activity, but rather to question the usefulness of the term 'cyberfeminist' in connecting these activities.

Although it first appeared in reference to the work of some feminist artists, by the mid-1990s cyberfeminist had become a term used to refer to the phenomenon of the activist cybergrrrl or webgrrrl. These new 'kinds' of feminists claimed to manipulate technology in order to resist patriarchal subject positions. Carla Sinclair defines a grrrl site as 'created by a woman who addresses issues without acting like women are victims. Grrrls take responsibility for themselves – we don't blame men for anything, but instead focus on ways to improve and strengthen ourselves. Grrrls enjoy their femininity and kick ass at the same time' (qtd. in Deloach, par. 1). This is revealing about the gender fantasies which the Internet – rather than the Internet itself – permits thinking about drawing simultaneously upon Riot Grrrl and girlie ideologies. That is, thought about the Internet is mediated through various technologically inspired gender fantasies, something which Sinclair picks up in her power-feminist claim that grrrl sites are for those who engage in grrrl-power 'without acting like women are victims' (par. 1). In addition to the grrrls and their ubiquitous zines (now largely replaced by blogs and online communities like LiveJournal), there are those IRL off-line women's groups which use the web as an organisational tool for larger activities off-line so as to 'seek through networking and through their different experiences with technology to create special women's spaces of resistance' (Sundén 215). Not only has cyberspace been identified as a space in which new alliances and actions can take place, but it has also been argued that there is something unique about cyberspace which marks it as a space ideal for female-female communication. Scarlet Pollock and Jo Sutton identify the Internet as an extension of the modes of networking supposedly common to women – '[d]ialogue, encouraging others, listening, sharing, dealing with conflict' (33) – and Dale Spender argues that 'the medium is more attuned to women's way of working in the world than to men's ... [and] has the capacity to create community; to provide untold opportunities for communication, exchange, and keeping in touch' (229). While the Internet does offer information and communication opportunities which far surpass what had been available before, it is naïve to assume that this (inter)networking is unique to women – the Internet facilitates communication for all sorts of interest groups, from Riot Grrrls to JonBenet Ramsey fantasists.[1]

While the Internet clearly offers opportunities for transparency and dialogue for feminist activists and theorists, cyberfeminism has been unwilling to examine under what conditions this transparency and dialogue take place. Some, like Elaine Graham, have argued for the potential which the cyborg and the goddess evoke: 'all sorts of ethical and political ideals and enable new understandings of responsibility, identity and community as envisaged under the posthuman condition of hybrid, nonessential human nature' (422). However, Alison Adam has pointed up the ways in which cyberfeminism precisely avoids ethical questions (2002, 168). This avoidance of ethical questions is largely because cyberfeminism has not engaged with the material and historical conditions of the human/technological interface. Because the cyborg and the cyber-goddess validate (any and all) activity by women online, the result is that 'all' woman-centred online activity is authenticated. This apolitical and dehistoricised cyberfeminism has, as Judith Squires puts it, 'become the distorted fantasy of those so cynical of traditional political strategies, so bemused by the complexity of social materiality, and so bound up in the rhetoric of the space flows of information technology, that they have forgotten both the exploitative and alienating potential of technology' (369). To follow on from Squires, this apolitical and dehistoricised understanding uses 'internet' as metaphor, rather than providing a materialist examination of the Internet. Just as third wave feminism is excoriated by 'real' feminists for its apparent inability to politicise women, cyberfeminism – which is articulated as ultra-activist by its main proponents – can also be dismissed from histories of feminisms because it is not able to adequately locate itself within the history of women and technology. Indeed, for Bela Bonita Chatterjee, to bother tracing 'cyberfeminism is to implicitly suggest that it is, in fact, traceable – that it had a discernable and developmental history and can be set neatly into sequential context with prior developments in feminism' (199).[2] Cyberfeminism needs very quickly to find out how it works in relation to other feminisms and, in doing so, must move beyond the seduction of the monstrous cyborg and the cyber-goddess.

Sex/Gender ≠ Body

The information and communication technologies which have emerged since the computer revolution have also enabled new ways of thinking about the Enlightenment body. The great promise of the Internet has been that it would dissolve gender and sex boundaries, allowing for a free mingling of minds. There are three versions of this promise:

(1) the consumer relationship has reduced the relevance of the demographic complication of sex;
(2) we regard any form of technology as eliding sex;
(3) with the repudiation of the 'body' in cyberspace, the phenomenological equation of 'body equals woman' is erased.

This thesis often goes untested and masquerades as demonstrative 'new' sex by virtue of the kinds of thinking that feed into it. Arthur and Marilouise Kroker aptly demonstrate this sort of thinking: 'Neither male (physically) nor female (genetically) nor their simple reversal, but something else: a virtual sex floating in an elliptical orbit around the planet of gender that is left behind' (18). Why are we so keen to believe that the Internet appears to provide a space in which feminist politics and praxis can take place outside the patriarchal hegemony? Empirical studies have demonstrated that although the potential for gender-fucking whilst online is tempting, it remains largely science fiction. What is important is that the Internet is constructed ideologically as a promise that the dissolution of the sexed body is imminent and although sexed and gendered characteristics can be re-coded at the press of a button, embodied patterns of behaviour resist any revolutionary change, as I have argued elsewhere (2004). The Internet does question the Enlightenment notion of self – as a gendered, raced and psychically sound individual – but the cyber-body retains, for example, characteristics of gender and race because both are a social configuration. The body circulating through cyberspace does not obviate the body at the keyboard: while these may not be exactly the same body, they are both embodied identities, embodied 'within the specifics of place, time, physiology and culture, which together compose enactment' (Hayles 196). The conditions for the cyber-dissolution of the body remain the gendered and racial body, so although the Internet raises questions about the Enlightenment notion of self by silencing once again the very question of embodiment, it also reifies the paradigms that endorse this selfhood.[3]

Moreover, gender online operates in many of the same ways that it operates offline. Kira Hall's empirical research on social interaction online indicates that the post-gender world of the cyborg is certainly not to be found in cyberspace. She notes that 'rather than neutralizing gender, the electronic medium encourages its intensification. In the absence of the physical, network users exaggerate societal notions of femininity and masculinity in an attempt to gender themselves' (167).[4] Susan Herring's work supports this, identifying two types of online posting: adversarial flaming which is used largely by men (e.g. a superior stance, posting long/frequent messages and participating disproportionately) and attenuated and supportive style used largely by women: '[w]omen's messages ... tend to be aligned and supportive in orientation, while men's messages tend to oppose and criticize others' (115). This is not to argue that technology is necessarily masculinised – Nina Wakeford's work on gender dynamics in an Internet café usefully draws the distinction between gendered on- and off-line behaviour of computer users. One, however, need only look to the history of the other communications revolution of the twentieth century – the telephone – for a historical example of this. A radical impact of the telephone was its exponential increase in the identification of the domestic as a locus of consumption. Ideas of predominantly female users, operators and female-coded technology expressed a fantasy of sex evolution that distracted from the degree to which the telephone supplemented existing economic arrangements and the notions of sexed embodiment that expressed and bolstered them (Martin 63–65). Cyberfeminism repeats this model in making the naïve assumption that gender politics do not exist online and that the sexed embodiments materialised by gender are suspended.

Indeed, the relationship of gender and technology has a long history, as Andreas Huyssen notes when he argues that '[a]s soon as the machine came to be perceived as a demonic, inexplicable threat and as the harbinger of chaos and destruction ... writers began to imagine the Maschinenmensch as woman ... Woman, nature, machine had become a mesh of signification which all had one thing in common: otherness' (70). The machine is coded as feminine because technology has been demonised as other; technology is othered because it is feminised, particularly information technology. In the desire to embrace and endorse the web and cyberspace as a new and free space for all women, cyberfeminism denies the long history of technology and gender. Braidotti reminds us that gender boundaries and gender difference become exaggerated in both cyberpunk and the cyborg film genre:

> on the one hand an eroticized fetishization of the technological has pervaded through the imaginary of our societies, on the other hand, the technological is not associated with any sex, let alone the feminine, but rather with a transexual or sexually undecided position. It coincides with a sort of flight from the body. ... In such a context, the female body is constructed as the site of the natural, of *bios* and *zoe*, hence also of procreation. (2002, 233)

Even a cursory examination of the cyberpunk novels and films of the past twenty years – from William Gibson's *Neuromancer* (1984) to Andy and Larry Wachowski's *The Matrix* trilogy (1999–2003) – demonstrates that they explicitly draw upon the *film noir* tradition, speaking the language of hardboiled masculinity.[5] This can be dismissed as merely the masculine relationship with the machine 'which seems to bring out the worst in some men. It's been there with cars (the biggest, the brightest, latest, fastest) and it's there with computers as well' (Spender 183). But rather than enabling the argument that men have an unalterable relationship with technology, those working in the field of gender and technology – which *could* include cyberfeminism if it engaged a political agenda and developed a technologically materialist approach to history – should seek to understand the politics and history of this relationship.

If masculinity is the predominant model of behaviour online, it must also be emphasised that this is a white masculinity. That fewer than twenty per cent of global households have electricity – let alone Internet access – raises the question of whose politics this fantasy obscures and permits. Braidotti points out that gender, age and ethnicity act as major axes 'of negative differentiation' in access and participation in the new high-tech digital world (2002, 176). Indeed, the question of whose cyber-space this is shifts the focus away from gender, something which cyber-feminists have been reluctant to do. While the Internet is used by both men and women, it is predominantly a white and Western activity. Beth E. Kolko, Lisa Nakamura and Gilbert B. Rodman argue that just as 'first and second-wave feminists often failed to include race and the issue of third world women in their politics, so too have many cyberfeminists elided the topic of race in cyberspace' (8). Third wave feminists have noted that the politics of this wave of feminism emerged from the work of those who were excluded by the rhetoric of second wave feminism:

> [t]he term *feminism* is itself questioned by many third world women. Feminist movements have been challenged on the grounds of cultural imperialism, and of shortsightedness in defining the meaning of gender in terms of middle-class, white experiences, and in terms of internal racism, classicism, and homophobia. (Mohanty 7; emphasis in original)

Leslie Heywood and Jennifer Drake acknowledge that third wave feminism looks to U.S. third world feminism for 'languages and images that account for multiplicity and difference, that negotiate contradiction in affirmative ways, and that give voice to a politics of hybridity and coalition' (9). But third wave feminism (particularly in its academic incarnation) is still very white and despite its origin in the work of Rebecca Walker, is only beginning to account for its racial exclusions.[6] Similarly, aside from the work of Kolko, Nakamura and Rodman and work by Radhika Gajjala, cybertheory remains largely white and cyberfeminism certainly still feeds on a sci-fi aestheticisation of whiteness as dominance.[7]

Recent work on the body may provide a way forward for cyberfeminism. For example, Dianne Currier points towards Gilles Deleuze and Felix Guattari's model of assemblage as a way to map how 'assembled bodies and technologies and social spaces and practices intersect with systems of knowledge and power' (535). This model of assemblage could help us to understand the category of woman as understood within the technological and the social, and has direct implications for the study of the body in cyberspace: 'we must understand cyberspace as not simply a technologically generated space or place, but as a series of assemblage comprised of elements of the technical, social, discursive, material, and immaterial' (536). Deleuze and Guattari's reading of the notion of *assemblage* holds that meaning, like all other bodies, is only temporarily stratified, and fragile in its construction out of multiplicitous lines of becoming. Transformation of that meaning is no longer about the teleological product but the interminable and irreducible process of getting towards it: a relationship which is 'neither of imitation nor resemblance, only an exploding of two heterogeneous series on the line of flight composed by a common rhizome that can no longer be attributed to or subjugated by anything signifying' (10). Deleuze and Guattari propose a rhizomatic approach to the world that allows for infinitely increased experiential possibility and a heterogeneity of subjectivity and selfhood. Another way of moving the cyberfeminist debate forward would be to draw upon the work of Judith Butler. For Butler, performativity, while destabilising the notion of any kind of natural gender or subject that emerges from an internal essence, does not mean that one can simply put on new clothes and instantly, on an ontological level, become someone else. Rather, performativity appears as 'a repetition and a ritual, which achieves its effects through its naturalization in the context of a body, understood, in part, as a culturally sustained temporal duration' (xv). In these terms, construction of a (gendered or otherwise) subject happens through 'certain exclusionary practices that do not "show" once the juridicial structure of politics has been produced' (5). While these are necessarily brief sketches of possible ways of thinking about gender, the body and technology they do demonstrate ways in which the seduction of the monstrous cyborg and the cyber-goddess can be negotiated by those interested in studying the body and cyberspace.

Neither cyborg nor goddesses

Consider the differences between those women who work with technology and the self-proclaimed cyberfeminist: the woman working the night shift in a call centre in Bangalore and the woman in London posting her latest creation on YouTube.com are separated by more than geography and bandwidth. If cyberfeminism is broadly concerned with women and cyberspace, can both these women be understood as cyberfeminists? Can the category of cyberfeminism elide the monumental differences between these women and their specific relationships with technology? To put it more bluntly, if you are a woman in cyberspace, are you a cyberfeminist? Although acknowledging the masculinity of technoculture, Braidotti has famously identified the utopic potential of cyberfeminism and called for the need for new utopias (1996, passim). Much of cyberfeminism has been predicated upon utopian imaginings of cyberspace or, as Chatterjee puts it, 'dreams of an uncomplicated and uncritical merging with the matrix for women into a vague postfemale entity' (202). Judy Wacjman picks up on this use of the utopian, arguing that while the 'force of utopian thinking derives precisely from being about a place that does not exist ... cyberfeminism presents the utopian imagining of cyberspace as a more or less adequate description of aspects of what currently exists' (75). Cybertheorists and feminists need to reclaim materialist territory from cyberfeminists, moving away from the utopian towards the materialist. Adam's call for a cyberfeminist ethics goes some way to demanding that this kind of feminism be accountable for itself, its histories and its politics. At the same time, we should bear in mind her point that cyberspace is deeply conservative, resting on 'technological determinism which is uncritical of technological advances, which accepts as inevitable that technology will be used in a particular way' (1997, 20). Cyberspace should never be understood in utopian terms and the promise that we would leave our bodies behind has been proven untenable time and again. Cyberfeminism, in speaking for *all* women in cyberspace, succumbed to an elision of IRL histories and politics – while it appeared to offer a get-out clause in the gender debates of the 1980s and 1990s, it merely reified sex and gender in ways that are all too familiar.

This is not to deny that there is not non-utopian work being done under the label of cyberfeminism. In their Introduction to *Reload: Rethinking Women + Cyberculture* (2002), Mary Flanagan and Austin Booth positively describe cyberfeminism as 'a new wave of feminist theory and practice that is united in challenging the "coding" of technology and in investigating the complex relationships between gender and digital culture. ... [and] is concerned with the ways in which cybertech-nologies affect women's lives in particular' (11). While their collection is largely concerned with readings of feminist science fiction and cyber-punk, it does provide an example of work which could be termed cyber-feminist and which does not succumb to utopian thinking. Along with this sort of work, I would also flag up Deborah Wheeler's work on women and the Internet in Kuwait, Wakeford's work on the cultures of the Internet café, Justine Cassell and Henry Jenkins's collection on gender and computer games and Sarah Kember's work on cyberfeminism and arti-ficial life. Alongside this scholarly work are such websites as feminist.com, which is a 'web-based facilitator of connectedness between girls and women and the many, varied organizations serving their needs and interests worldwide' (par. 1). These are all examples of work on and/or in gender and digital and virtual cultures which *could* be termed cyberfem-inist. However, the usefulness of doing so remains to be seen. Like the term '(post)feminism', the term 'cyberfeminism' may have gone too far in one direction to be recuperated by the feminist community. And if we are to have a new (cyber)feminism, then it will need to interrogate more carefully its politics and its histories: this will involve disentangling cyborg feminism, gender and technology studies, cybertheory and e-activism, as well as moving beyond utopian models of cyberspace. Haraway's polemic ends with the oft-quoted 'I'd rather be a cyborg than a goddess'; however, it is precisely these subject positions which cyberfeminism must learn to move beyond in order to have a sustainable place within current feminist thinking.

Notes

1. Cybernetic developments have undeniably enabled more immediate communication between (geographically as well as ideologically) disparate groups. Ednie Kaeh Garrison coined the term 'technologic' to refer to 'a particular practice of communicating information over space and time, a creation of temporary "unified" political groups made up of unlikely combinations and collectivities ... the combining of diverse technologies to construct powerful cultural expressions of oppositional consciousness' (150).
2. See Judy Wacjman for more on this: 'cyberfeminism needs to be understood as a reaction to the pessimism of the 1980s feminist approaches that stressed the inherently masculine nature of technoscience. ... [Cyberfeminists] accept that industrial technology did indeed have a patriarchal character, but insist that new digital technologies are much more diffuse and open' (63).
3. As Lisa Nakamura summarises, the 'nuanced realities of virtuality – racial, gendered, othered – live in the body' (7).
4. Hall's research in 1996 was conducted largely on electronic bulletin boards. Her findings have been proved time and again with regards to more recent incarnations of electronic communication.
5. See my work on *The Matrix* trilogy (2005).
6. See Kimberly Springer for more on third wave black feminism.
7. See Gajjala for an example of a study on the intersection between cyberspace, race and feminism.

Works cited

Adam, Alison. 'The Ethical Dimension of Cyberfeminism.' *Reload: Rethinking Women + Cyberculture*. Ed. Mary Flanagan and Austin Booth. Cambridge: MIT, 2002. 158–74.
——. 'What Should We Do with Cyberfeminism?' *Women in Computing*. Ed. Rachel Lander and Alison Adam. Exeter: Intellect Books, 1997. 17–27.
Braidotti, Rosi. 'Cyberfeminism with a Difference.' 3 July 1996. Accessed: 1 Sept. 2006. <http://www.let.uu.nl/womens_studies/rosi/cyberfem.htm>.
——. *Metamorphoses: Towards a Materialist Theory of Being*. Cambridge: Polity, 2002.
Butler, Judith. *Gender Trouble: Feminism and the Subversion of Identity*. New York: Routledge, 1999.

180   *Stacy Gillis*

Cassell, Justine, and Henry Jenkins, eds. *From Barbie to Mortal Kombat: Gender and Computer Games*. Cambridge: MIT, 1998.

Castricano, Jodey. 'A Modem of One's Own: The Subject of Cyberfeminism.' *Rhizomes* 4 (Spring 2002). Accessed: 1 Sept. 2006. <http://www.rhizomes.net/issue4/castricano.html>.

Chatterjee, Bela Bonita. 'Razorgirls and Cyberdykes: Tracing Cyberfeminism and Thoughts on Its Use in a Legal Context.' *International Journal of Sexuality and Gender Studies* 7.2–3 (2002): 197–213.

Currier, Dianne. 'Assembling Bodies in Cyberspace: Technologies, Bodies, and Sexual Difference.' *Reload: Rethinking Women + Cyberculture*. Ed. Mary Flanagan and Austin Booth. Cambridge: MIT, 2002. 519–38.

Deleuze, Gilles and Guattari, Felix. *A Thousand Plateaus*. Trans. Brian Massumi. Minneapolis: University of Minnesota Press, 1987.

DeLoach, Amelia. 'Grrrl sites defined ... .' *Computer-Mediated Communication Magazine* 1 Mar. 1996. Accessed: 1 Sept. 2006. <http://www.december.com/cmc/mag/1996/mar/delgrrl.html>.

feminist.com. 1995–2006. Accessed: 1 Sept. 2006. <http://www.feminist.com/whatsnew>.

Flanagan, Mary, and Austin Booth. Introduction. *Reload: Rethinking Women + Cyberculture*. Ed. Mary Flanagan and Austin Booth. Cambridge: MIT, 2002. 1–24.

Gajjala, Radhika. 'An Interrupted Postcolonial/Feminist Cyberethnography: Complicity and Resistance in the "Cyberfield".' *Feminist Media Studies* 2.2 (2002): 177–93.

Garrison, Ednie Kaeh. 'U.S. Feminism-Grrrl style! Youth (Sub)cultures and the Technologics of the Third Wave.' *Feminist Studies* 26.1 (2000): 141–70.

Gillis, Stacy. 'Cyber *Noir*: Cyberspace, (Post)Feminism and the *Femme Fatale*.' *The Matrix: Cyberpunk Reloaded*. Ed. Stacy Gillis. London: Wallflower, 2005: 74–85.

——. 'Cybersex.' *More Dirty Looks: Gender, Pornography and Power*. Ed. Pamela Church Gibson. London: British Film Institute, 2004. 92–101.

Graham, Elaine. 'Cyborgs or Goddesses? Becoming Divine in a Cyberfeminist Age.' *Information, Communication & Society* 2.4 (1999): 419–38.

Hall, Kira. 'Cyberfeminism.' *Computer-Mediated Communication: Linguistic, Social and Cross-Cultural Perspectives*. Ed. Susan Herring. Amsterdam: Benjamins, 1996. 147–70.

Haraway, Donna. *Simians, Cyborgs and Women: The Reinvention of Nature*. New York: Routledge, 1991.

Hawthorne, Susan, and Renate Klein. 'Cyberfeminism: An Introduction.' *CyberFeminism: Connectivity, Critique and Creativity*. Ed. Susan Hawthorne and Renate Klein. Melbourne: Spinifex, 1999. 1–16.

Hayles, N. Katherine. *How We Became Posthuman: Virtual Bodies in Cybernetics, Literature and Informatics*. Chicago: University of Chicago Press, 1999.

Herring, Susan. 'Posting in a Different Voice: Gender and Ethics in CMC.' *Philosophical Perspectives on Computer-Mediated Communication*. Ed. Charles Ess. New York: SUNY Press, 1996. 115–45.

Heywood, Leslie, and Jennifer Drake. Introduction. *Third Wave Agenda: Being Feminist, Doing Feminism*. Ed. Leslie Heywood and Jennifer Drake. Minneapolis: Minnesota University Press, 1997. 1–20.

Huyssen, Andreas. *After the Great Divide: Modernism, Mass Culture, Postmodernism*. Bloomington: Indiana University Press, 1987.

Keifer-Boyd, Karen. *The Cyberfeminist House*. 2002. Accessed: 1 Sept. 2006. <http://sva74.sva.psu.edu/~cyberfem/>.

Kember, Sarah. *Cyberfeminism and Artificial Life*. London: Routledge, 2002.

Kolko, Beth E., Lisa Nakamura, and Gilbert B. Rodman. Introduction. *Race in Cyberspace*. Ed. Beth E. Kolko, Lisa Nakamura and Gilbert B. Rodman. London: Routledge, 2000. 1–13.

Kroker, Arthur, and Marilouise Kroker. *The Last Sex: Feminism and Outlaw Bodies*. New York: St. Martin's, 1993.

Martin, Michèle. 'The Culture of the Telephone.' *Sex/Machine: Readings in Culture, Gender, and Technology*. Ed. Patrick D. Hopkins. Bloomington: Indiana University Press, 1999. 50–74.

Miller, Melanie Stewart. *Cracking the Gender Code: Who Rules the Wired World*. Toronto: Second Story, 1998.

Mohanty, Chandra Talpade. 'Cartographies of Struggle: Third World Women and the Politics of Feminism.' *Third World Women and the Politics of Feminism*. Ed. Chandra Talpade Mohanty, Ann Russo and Lourdes Torres. Bloomington: Indiana University Press, 1991. 1–47.

Nakamura, Lisa. *Cybertypes: Race, Ethnicity and Identity on the Internet*. New York: Routledge, 2002.

Plant, Sadie. 'The Future Looms: Weaving Women and Cybernetics.' *Body and Society* 1. 3–4 (1995): 45–64.

——. 'On the Matrix: Cyberfeminist Simulations.' 1996. *The Gendered Cyborg: A Reader*. Ed. Fiona Hovenden *et al*. London: Routledge, 2000. 265–75.

Pollock, Scarlet, and Jo Sutton. 'Women Click: Feminism and the Internet.' *CyberFeminism: Connectivity, Critique and Creativity*. Ed. Susan Hawthorne and Renate Klein. Melbourne: Spinifex, 1999. 33–50.

Spender, Dale. *Nattering on the Net: Women, Power and Cyberspace*. Melbourne: Spinifex, 1995.

Springer, Kimberly. 'Strongblackwomen and Black Feminism: A Next Generation?' *Different Wavelengths: Studies of the Contemporary Women's Movement*. Ed. Jo Reger. New York: Routledge, 2005. 3–21.

Squires, Judith. 'Fabulous Feminist Futures and the Lure of Cyberculture.' 1996. *The Cybercultures Reader*. Ed. David Bell and Barbara Kennedy. London: Routledge, 2000. 360–73.

subRosa. N. pub. Accessed: 1 Sept. 2006. <http://www.cyberfeminism.net/>.

Sundén, Jenny. 'What Happened to Difference in Cyberspace ? The (Re)Turn of the She-Cyborg.' *Feminist Media Studies* 1.2 (2001): 215–32.

VNS Matrix. 'Brave New Girls.' N. pub. Accessed: 1 Sept. 2006. <http://lx.sysx.org/vnsmatrix.html >.

Wacjman, Judy. *TechnoFeminism*. Cambridge: Polity, 2004.

Wakeford, Nina. 'Gender and the Landscapes of Computing in an Internet Café.' *Virtual Geographies: Bodies, Spaces and Relations*. Ed. Mike Crang, Phil Crang and Jon May. London: Routledge, 1999. 178–201.

Wheeler, Deborah. 'New Technologies, Old Culture: A Look at Women, Gender, and the Internet in Kuwait.' *Culture, Technology, Communication: Towards an Intercultural Global Village*. Ed. Charles Ess. New York: SUNY Press, 2001. 187–212.

Part III
Politics and Popular Culture

14

Contests for the Meaning of Third Wave Feminism

Feminism and Popular Consciousness

Ednie Kaeh Garrison

In the U.S., consciousness of feminism is tightly woven into the cultural and historical consciousness – or lack thereof – of the late twentieth and early twenty-first centuries.[1] This is not the same as saying we live in a feminist culture; rather, it is a claim about feminism – with already constituted and contested meanings – among the repertoire of discursive tools by which we categorise, position, label and understand those who advocate the rights of women, the oppressiveness of patriarchy and the linking of these tools to the ideological and material dominance of any number of unequal social systems, among them racism, capitalism, hetero-normativity, classism and cultural and political imperialism. This accounts for how feminism as ideology and a praxis is simplified and how feminist cohorts and formations are constantly constructed. This thing we call third wave feminism neither is new nor escapes the historical and cultural contexts of its articulation. The very claim to know what third wave feminism means is riddled with contradictions and problems. Few can agree about what and whom it encapsulates – advocates and detractors alike. The only general consensus to have emerged is that it has become a name for young women who identify as feminists (but not the feminists of the sixties and seventies), and, especially among its detractors, it is a name assigned to those who have no real clear sense of what feminist ideology, feminist praxis, feminist movement or feminist identity have meant across time and place. In both cases, the construction of third wave feminist meaning has hinged upon a series of simplifications and mis-conceptions about feminism that circulate in the national popular imaginary.

The media is a central site of consciousness formation and knowledge production in the U.S. and it plays an important role in the cultural knowledge production of feminist consciousness. While work has been done on representations of women in the media and the contradictory uses of feminist and sexist imagery in advertising to convince women to engage in certain relations of consumption, not enough work has been done to examine how representations of feminism – as entirely negative, unfeminine, strident, self-indulgent, threatening to heteronormativity, and also as white and middle-class and straight – obfuscate forms of feminism, different feminist constituencies, sites of feminist consciousness-raising and political activism, its relevance, and the ways feminism can enable us to work our ways out of the traps of racist, capitalist, patriarchal logics. Deborah Rhodes contends that for 'those interested in social movements in general and the women's movement in particular' more attention must be given to the ways 'the media choose to present (or not to present) as news about women and how they characterise (or caricature) the women's movement' (685). Drawing upon the work of Stuart Hall, Rhodes argues for a recognition of the cultural significance of the media as 'increasingly responsible for supplying the information and images through which we understand our lives' and as a cultural institution that 'play[s] a crucial role in shaping public consciousness and public policy' (685). In the case of the production of third wave feminist meaning, our inattentiveness to the power of the media as a source of knowledge and meaning contributes to the relatively limited success of feminist revolution. We fail to fully understand how the media operates to ideologically re/contain the possible meanings attached to feminism.

Mass media matters

One of the most expansive and interpolating of public spheres in the U.S., the media synthesises a constellation of communications genres, including the tripartite 'radio, magazines and television', video, film, Hollywood, newspapers, books, Madison Avenue, billboards, advertising, the Internet, which comprise a hegemonic and seductive public cultural institution dictated by political, economic and cultural ideologies. It also goes by other names: mainstream media; mass media; consumer media; popular media; popular culture; monopoly mass media; corporate media and mass circulation press. This list exposes who and what has power in producing the media. Rather than monolithically blaming 'them' – those faceless, disembodied people in power – these names offer ways to think about how we both collude with and attempt to resist the discursive repertoires that recursively limit what counts as feminism in the dominant and dominating American culture. Those who possess this power are not usually aware of their positions of privilege in relation to the others over whom they have power, nor are they conscious of their protective strategies and manipulations. They already have the (implicit) consent of most of the population, and that population tends to do most of their work for them. They not only benefit absolutely from the system as it exists, but also believe the system, as it exists, works in their best interests.[2]

One way to see the hegemonic power of this cultural-ideological apparatus in operation is to examine the discursive repertoire of tropes deployed as 'so naturalized and overdetermined in American culture' (McDermott 675) that we do not recognise them as socially constructed moralistic contests for cultural and political authority. In her investigation of the cultural authority granted (anti)feminist feminists like Christina Hoff Sommers, Patrice McDermott explains that

> the new critics [of feminist scholarship and women's studies] have derived their credibility from their use of familiar and culturally powerful conventions of rationalist discourse. Rationalist discourse is the defining language of debate in the public sphere, and any serious bid for socially sanctioned entry into public debate must be framed by these linguistic conventions. (675)

While rationalist discourse is commonly deployed in the struggle for recognition and equal access to the public sphere, McDermott argues that anti-feminists like Sommers are granted more authority because they deploy simplified moralistic linguistic codes to discredit the cultural authority of feminism. Besides Sommers, McDermott identifies Daphne Patai and Noretta Koertge, Katie Roiphe, Wendy Kaminer and Karen Lehrman as 'new critics of feminism [who] are not fundamentally engaged in an empirical attack on feminist methodology; rather, they are launching a moral attack on feminist cultural authority' (676).[3] One typical argument is that teachers and students of Women's Studies are ugly girls who have been ignored by men, or are angry lesbians who have been sexually abused by men and are taking it out on society at large by training young women to reject men and traditional family values by becoming feminists and/or lesbians. These homophobic and (anti)feminist critics of feminism and Women's Studies depend on the perception of the logic and reason of discursive tropes that dominate mainstream public conversations and debates about women, the women's movement and feminism.

The efforts of their sponsors and the commercial media (often the same thing) to push and validate their work and ideas on 'the public' reinforces Amy Erdman Farrell's claim that feminists cannot underestimate 'the importance of the media in shaping the public's understanding of feminism' (645).

Despite the transformative goals of feminist ideology and praxis, American feminists exhibit an astounding level of gullibility in their engagement with the media. This gullibility is connected to the attachment feminists have for being 'American', which is cultivated by the media as one of the most powerful interpellating forces producing a sense of shared experience and identity in the U.S. As Benedict Anderson has remarked, the combination of print technology and capitalism has been a primary function of the creation of the 'imagined community' of the nation. Thus, we imbue the media – our late twentieth/ early twenty-first-century site of the merger between print/communications technology, capitalism and 'human linguistic diversity'[4] – with an exponential power by accepting as true its representations of concepts like feminism, women, and issues that are presumed feminist because they are regarded as 'women's' issues. This particularly salient site of cultural transmission, production and articulation in America is at the same time always already a public market of commodities on parade. The double function of the media as a culture market leads to the representation of feminism and its variants as a label or lifestyle or brand as it gets re-constituted as a commodity for sale.[5] In this late-capitalist, consumer society, it is worth recalling Jean Baudrillard's dictum that '[i]n order to become object of consumption, the object must become sign; that is, in some way it must become external to a relation that it now only signifies' (22). The logic of consumption – 'the commercial imperative of popular media' (Farrell 644) – extracts from the object its politics, the substance of its context, so that its representation signifies the satisfaction of needs, but only as a simulation of satisfaction. The object of consumption – feminism – stands in for actual political relations, deferring the political in favour of the idea of the relation between lifestyle practice and political commitment. And, as bell hooks pointed out as early as 1984, '[t]he willingness to see feminism as a lifestyle choice rather than a political commitment reflects the class nature of the movement' (27). hooks' observation that the willingness of some feminist movement participants to reduce feminism to lifestyle choices links bourgeois liberal feminism to the commercial imperative of popular media. The popular cultural dominance of this version – liberal feminism – can only ever have limited success because it is too thoroughly entrenched in the system against which more radical and transformative feminist movements react. This is not to completely reject liberal feminism, but to ask whether it is a good tactic for countering late-capitalist consumerist logics which rely on the commodification of resistance as a hegemonic strategy.[6]

Chela Sandoval re-articulates this 'mode of consciousness in opposition' under the title 'equal rights', explaining that '[o]n the basis that all individuals are created equal, subscribers to this particular ideological tactic will demand that their own humanity be legitimated, recognized as the same under the law, and assimilated into the most favored form of the human in power' (1991, 12). That is, the goal is to assimilate into the form of those in power – to take their shape. This goal does not infer changing the power structure systemically but, rather, changing the specific cohort which is in the position of power within the existing structure. Likewise, in her study of social movement studies of the women's movement, Stacey Young opens with a discussion of the 'grammar of liberalism' (1). Next to the first appearance of liberal feminism in her text is the following foot-note: 'Women's movement activists and feminist theorists often identify liberal feminism with the National Organization for Women, the National Women's Political Caucus, and other organizations engaged in electoral politics' (209). This list makes sense given Young's explanation of the relationship between liberalist ideology and government:

> Liberalism's focus on government at the expense of other levels of society leads feminists who subscribe to liberalism's theory of power to prioritize engagement with institutions of governance as the strategy of choice for feminist change. This is premised on the assumption that women's oppression is merely an accident or an oversight, or a rather superficial, hollow vestige of obsolete social organization, and that the machinery of liberal institutions can be harnessed to effect women's equality with men, since this goal is consistent with 'equality' – a central tenet of liberalism. (4)

The explications of Sandoval and Young reveal that liberalism can be one strategy among many, even though the dominance of the logic of liberalism in the public sphere, with its discourse of rationality, positions those who counter it as unreasonable or aberrant.

Audre Lorde's famous (and often mis-applied) statement – 'the master's tools will never dismantle the master's house' (110) – is instructional here. The cultural dominance of liberal feminism limits the possibilities of a transformative feminism by supporting the belief that we cannot fight the system as it exists outside its own terms. In effect, it does nothing to change 'the master's house' except to allow a few people in who previously were confined to the periphery. Further, a condition of inclusion (and access to the tools) for those few is to maintain the integrity of 'the master's house' by not demanding any substantial structural or institutional changes. Such a position is limited and restricted, and does not represent the width and breadth of feminism, nor will it achieve the goals of the liberatory movements into which I, and many others who believe in the transformative possibilities of critical political consciousness, want and need to include feminism. Just because liberal feminist organisations and projects are the site for the majority of what gets acknowledged as legitimate feminist activism in this country, does not mean that these locations are necessarily, always and/or only, the best locations from which to participate as feminist activists. Nor are definitions of activism that privilege this form of political participation necessarily the best way to be activist. Who determines, and to what ends, the forms of political participation that matter? Because of the tradition promulgated by the corporate, consumer media that recognises political participation only at the level of organisational practice, legislative negotiation and engagement with the 'official' political process, taking action – and having it recognised as legitimate and worthwhile – is frequently determined by what and who gets recognised and covered (and how) by the media.

The popular consciousness of feminism

One way to understand the emergence of third wave feminism is to examine the interrelated simplifications and diversionary discourses of fear, anxiety and discouragement that dominate American mainstream public debates and conversations over feminism, especially the spectres that have become associated with what has been identified as backlash politics. This is the name Susan Faludi has given, in *Backlash: The Undeclared War Against American Women* (1991), for the cultural-ideological apparatus that allows those in power to stay in power by manipulating popular consciousness of the women's movement and feminism, among other volatile radical movements and ideologies. In fact, the rhetoric of backlash broadly coincides with the construction of the 'failures' of the sixties revolutions and the rise in media popularity of conservative groups like the Moral Majority and the Christian Coalition. While Faludi's book is largely a descriptive project, its value is in pointing out the subjectivity of the media and its agents, and for providing specific examples of how 'false images of womanhood' (xv) are used to manipulate, confuse and deter not only women and feminists, but the whole nation.

According to Faludi, in the 1980s the mainstream press pitted liberation against marriage and motherhood. She positions the media as the central perpetrator of the backlash against women through demonstrating the processes by which mass media managers, owners and producers – who believe in the myth of the 'female crises' – repackage it to the public so that the public will also believe it. Her primary sources are the plethora of articles, news stories, television shows and Hollywood films through-out the decade that encouraged women to believe their 'biological clocks' were more powerful than their 'selfish' desires for corporate careers, that childless women were dangerous psychopaths, that women who did not marry by their early thirties were more likely to be killed by terrorists than find husbands and were, therefore, doomed to unfulfilled spinsterhood, that women who tried to balance family and career were doomed to be failed mothers, and so forth. These stories invoke the dis-cursive tropes of 'the family', 'motherhood', and traditional sex roles to feed off anxieties which women and men experience when women do not fulfil the capitalist heterosexual contract. Not only do women get blamed for the kinds of instabilities which post-industrialism and late capitalism have created in our culture, but feminism (usually the version that is only interested in corporate ladder climbing) gets constructed as the enemy, conveniently providing a figure for traditionalist ideologues and 'average' women to target. In this script, the specificities of race, class, sexuality, and so on, are erased to the extent that our national nar-ratives of women fulfilling their civic duties through motherhood and the socialisation of children draw upon racist, heterosexist and clas-sist discourses of Republican motherhood and 'true' womanhood.[7] Likewise, liberal feminism, historically successful at deploying the non-specified discourse of maternal womanhood to advocate for women's rights, can be separated from this version of feminism, which might be more appropriately qualified as corporate or careerist feminism.

A primary discursive technique of backlash deterrence produces and commodifies the categories of 'the feminist' and 'real women/feminin-ity' as opposing perspectives and competing factions. This technique can be witnessed in the popularised conflicts between generational cohorts of 'the feminists' and 'young women', the latter continually labelled as a 'postfeminist' generation. As Suzanna Danuta Walters con-tends, popular conceptualisations of postfeminism '[encompass] the backlash sentiment … as a more complex phenomenon of a recent form of antifeminism' (117).[8] Since at least the early 1980s the terms post-feminism, postfeminist generation, generation gap, inter-generational conflict, young women, and youth apathy have circulated in the media and the U.S. popular imaginary, to be joined in the 1990s by second wave feminism and second wavers in contradistinction to third wave feminism and third wavers. The ways in which these terms empower and constrain popular consciousness are important to understanding American feminism in the 1990s and the early twenty-first century. In other words, the emergence of third wave feminism cannot be explored without also considering the popular construction of 'postfeminism' as a term that discursively (and recursively) distances multiple cohorts of young women after 1980 from those who participated in the 'feminist' decades of the sixties and seventies. I use postfeminism to refer to the mainstreamed discursive repertoire of tropes that combine stereotypes incubated in the popular media about feminism and women who have come of age after the women's movement of the 1960s and 1970s and whose interactions with 'feminism' are influenced by the popular rhetoric of backlash.

In the U.S. this vocabulary of postfeminism requires a particular Oedipal metaphor to keep the crone spectre of the second wave feminist separated from young women, divesting them of the power of feminism and especially of radical feminism, which argues for systemic transformation rather than simply the right of women to participate equally in an intricately oppressive society. This generational metaphor is compelling because Oedipal familial dramas are so culturally sanctioned. Even the terms 'second wave' and 'third wave' are made to echo the metaphor.[9] Gina Dent ascribes part of the blame for this association to descriptions of feminist movement that assume the wave metaphor is itself a generational metaphor, even though '[t]his generational language hides other differences within it – national trajectories, sexual orientation, professional status, etc.' (70). To refer to the third wave refers to generations posed as suspended in conflict or separated by a gap. This presupposes only two conflicting factions,[10] thereby feeding so well into the media's tendency to categorise feminism and feminist conflicts simplistically and oppositionally. The appeal to the family romance is a convention of patriarchal social organisation which sustains itself and perpetuates oppressive hierarchies and aggressive competition. An indication of the investment in this simplistic and oppositional generational conflict model is evidenced in the preference for the term 'postfeminism' over the last twenty years. For example: the 'post-feminist generation' Susan Bolotin wrote about in 1982 in *The New York Times Magazine* becomes a cohort of 'twentysomethings' in Paula Kamen's *Feminist Fatale* (1991), only to explode again into the postfeminist 'post-Pagliaites' described by Ginia Bellafante as representative of contemporary feminism in a *Time* article in 1998 asking (yet again!) if feminism is dead. This longitudinally extensive 'postfeminist generation' facilitates a cynical and apathetic view of youth at any point after the sixties (a time when students and other young people played a particularly important role in liberation movements), and it enables the 'feminist crone' to exist at a safe distance in a mythological past reviled or romanticised, depending on one's investments in feminist ideology and politics.

In addition to constructing two oppositional generations, the vocabulary of postfeminism is also employed in the popular imaginary to reinforce the solipsistic confusion of the category 'women' with 'generic women', which is then confused further by metonymically fusing 'women' to 'feminism'. The consequence of these two semantic moves is that the differences that matter between women and the meanings attached to feminism are simplified and homogenised. It should be clear that the costs of excessively privileging *these* differences among women and feminists is that American popular media representations of feminism continuously reproduce a feminism that is white, straight and middle-class, and that feminists remain incapable of effectively countering these representations. It may be true that it is easier for some feminists to focus on generational difference, especially when anxieties run high about accusations of racism, homophobia and classism among those who sense, even subconsciously, the costs of declaring their experiences of oppression as legitimate. For white, straight and/or middle-class feminist women who claim the authority to speak about oppression on the basis of their subordinate position under patriarchy to complicate this authority by simultaneously recognising privilege and oppression when the dominant cultural logic insists that one is *either/or* and not *both/and* may help to alleviate some of the panic. The diversion into generational difference is such a response and says something about who counts as a feminist in this context. Perhaps this solipsism in popular consciousness helps to explain the similarity of so many of those who get to represent feminism in the media. This is one way, as well, to account for the relative absence of feminists of colour, lesbians and poor feminists who are critically engaging with mainstream media culture.

Indeed, it is telling that more people of colour, lesbians and poor feminists participate in the production and dissemination of popular cultures that are not the mainstream. Across the spectrum, American feminists are affected by these public discursive representations of feminism. They reproduce them; subtly re-enforce and collude with their construction, dissemination and propagation; mis-apply the stereotypes; mistake stereotype for archetype; and consequently make assumptions in their encounters with those outside their age group (assuming all feminists can place themselves in one or the other of these age cohorts). In the formation of third wave feminist meaning, the mainstream pre-occupation with this specific generational conflict tends to become the defining difference that sets 'third wave' apart from 'second wave'. This is not to say that age and generation do not matter; however, to centre them almost exclusively is too simple. American feminists across generational, cohort and political orientations are also products of a particular cultural ideological apparatus, like those who produce, create and disseminate the media. To assign blame only to one or the other does not get at the shared culturally embedded roots of our thinking about oppositional struggle. Such expectations exist within the popular consciousness of 'the people', and thus it is rational for it to be a framing device of the media, but this means it is also an expectation of academics, activists and other advocates of feminism. As the contributors to Devoney Looser and E. Ann Kaplan's *Generations: Academic Feminists in Dialogue* (1997) repeatedly point out, the cultural dominance of the idea of patriarchal descendence pervades the feminist academy as much as any other cultural institution. Despite tendencies to collapse what one might term the third wave brand of feminism into the more publicly familiar vocabulary of postfeminism, feminism in its third wave is far more critically engaged with second wave feminism and the history and cultural legacies of mid-twentieth-century social movements than the popular renderings of it would suggest. We need to refuse to let third wave feminism become just another brand because the strategic usefulness of the name-object is too powerful to be co-opted so completely.

Third wave feminist meanings

As a feminist who has been researching and writing about the emergence of third wave feminism, I am especially concerned with what feminism means and how different cohorts and individuals contest for the power to determine its meaning. I have been both delighted and distressed by what I have seen, and both reactions are the strongest when I have examined the intersections between feminist knowledge production and popular knowledge of feminism in the efforts of those invested in creating a constituency that can be called the third wave. One of the greatest challenges for third wave feminists engaging with the media, moving into media institutions and/or producing alternate media cultures that register outside the mainstream may be to reconstruct the ways the popular consciousness of feminism is conceived and articulated. Coming to feminist political consciousness today involves weeding through disjointed, conflicting and apparently contradictory conversations. This includes contending with the tension between what gets to be establishment feminism in the eyes of the media, subsequent popular consciousness of feminism, and more complex articulations, comprehensions and practices (often expressed as academic or intellectual and therefore suspect and unrealistic). Such a project entails new historiographies of the second wave that do not rein-scribe good feminist/bad feminist, activist feminism/self-indulgent feminism splits, but also ones that take seriously the criticisms of racism, classism, heterosexism and homophobia – and not only of the women's movement and of variously privileged feminists, but also of other movements and constituencies that comprised that mythical time 'the sixties' and, most importantly, of American culture more generally. And today it also means seriously working through the implications of a globalised and transnational feminist consciousness. What has come to count as 'third wave feminism' in the American popular imaginary, and in much of what counts as third wave feminist writing/cultural production, tends to be problematically and insufficiently localised. One of the lessons to be learned is the difference between the self-referential and the self-reflexive.

What made the emergence of a notion of a third wave of feminism in the 1990s so meaningful – when the second wave really was not over, when second wave feminists continue to be very much engaged in the political and cultural life of the country, and when the term 'feminism' (however problematically defined) was a strong force in the popular lexicon – was not that it should signal the willingness of a specific age-cohort to take up the name 'feminist', but that it ought to signal a far more important shift in the strategic consciousness of feminist ideology/praxis. Although it is by no means guaranteed, I do still want to believe the name-object 'third wave feminism' has transformational potential. However, this potential can be realised only when feminists and their allies take the lead in defining and demarcating its content, not in flippant, irreverent, sound-bite versions of intellectual wish-wash palatable to the media and the public, but with careful attention to the messiness, the contradictions, the ambiguities, and the complexities such an endeavour inevitably entails. To initiate such a project, we must adamantly deny that all third wave feminist ideology/praxis does is des-ignate a particular generation of young women to the ranks of an already hegemonic feminist history/genealogy/establishment. This is an intervention into the public sphere and not simply an academic exer-cise. The mass media as public sphere has already done much of the work to solidify such a version, and many well-intentioned feminist identified writers and celebrities have fallen unwittingly into line. If the general consensus has solidified around third wave feminism as just a nifty moniker for a specific age cohort, then I am not one. I refuse to walk such an easy, superficial road.

Notes

1. I am not prepared to speak beyond the boundaries of the U.S., although cognisant that the American media is a dominant global and imperialistic force.
2. Chela Sandoval's re-articulations in *Methodology of the Oppressed* (2000) of Louis Althusser's 'science of ideology' is particularly relevant to the present analysis.
3. See Diane M. Blair and Lisa M. Gring-Pemble for an analysis of the romantic quest narrative used by many of these same authors.
4. While the media comprises far more than print technologies, its discursive quality as a mode of distribution and communication is still dependent upon notions of text, linguistic meaning construction and language. The merger of print technology and capitalism, as Anderson's term 'print-capitalism' infers, is one of the foundations of our contemporary monopoly mass media.
5. For more on this see Baudrillard (10–56) as well as Robert Goldman *et al.*, Shelley Budgeon and Dawn H. Currie, and Bonnie J. Dow.
6. For more on this see Ednie Kaeh Garrison.
7. See Ann DuCille for a powerful critique of this phenomena as appropriated by bourgeois, white American feminists from the mid-nineteenth century through the late-twentieth century.
8. Judith Stacey's work linking the term postfeminism to ideas of post-revolutionary, post-industrial late capitalism and Ann Brooks's work linking it with postmodernism should not be mistaken for the popular appropriations of postfeminism as signifier of a generational cohort who rejects its mothers' feminism. I would not, however, argue that academic treatments of postfeminism fail to understand a vernacular version of postfeminism; instead, I tend to read these efforts as attempts to rescue an evocative word for more political purposes. In this sense, then, the term postfeminism is as much a contested concept as any.
9. For more on this see Stacy Gillis and Rebecca Munford.
10. An exception is Nancy Whittier, who uses the concept of 'political generations' to study the history and persistence of the radical feminist community in Ohio between the 1960s and 1990s.

Works cited

Anderson, Benedict. *Imagined Communities: Reflections on the Origin and Spread of Nationalism.* London: Verso, 1993.

Baudrillard, Jean. *Selected Writings.* Stanford: Stanford University Press, 1988.

Bellafante, Ginia. 'Feminism: It's All about Me!' *Time* 29 June 1998: 54–60.

Blair, Diane M., and Lisa M. Gring-Pemble. 'Best-Selling Feminisms: The Rhetorical Production of Popular Press Feminists' Romantic Quest.' *Communication Quarterly* 48.4 (2000): 360–79.

Bolotin, Susan. 'Voices From the Post-Feminist Generation.' *The New York Times Magazine* 17 Oct. 1982: 28–31; 103; 106–07; 114; 116–17.

Brooks, Ann. *Postfeminisms: Feminism, Cultural Theory and Cultural Forms*. New York: Routledge, 1997.

Budgeon, Shelley, and Dawn H. Currie. 'From Feminism to Postfeminism: Women's Liberation in Fashion Magazines.' *Women's Studies International Forum* 18.2 (1995): 173–186.

Dent, Gina. 'Missionary Position.' *To Be Real: Telling the Truth and Changing the Face of Feminism*. Ed. Rebecca Walker. New York: Anchor, 1995. 61–75.

Dow, Bonnie J. *Prime-Time Feminism: Television, Media Culture, and the Women's Movement Since 1970*. Philadelphia: Pennsylvania University Press, 1996.

DuCille, Ann. 'The Occult of True Black Womanhood: Critical Demeanor and Black Feminist Studies.' *Signs* 19.1 (1994): 591–629.

Faludi, Susan. *Backlash: The Undeclared War Against American Women*. New York: Anchor, 1991.

Farrell, Amy Erdman. 'Feminism and the Media: Introduction.' *Feminism and the Media*. Spec. issue of *Signs* 20.3 (1995): 642–45.

Garrison, Ednie Kaeh. 'US Feminism-Grrrl style! Youth (Sub)cultures and the Technologics of the Third Wave.' *Feminist Studies* 26.1 (2000): 141–70.

Gillis, Stacy, and Rebecca Munford. 'Generations and Genealogies: The Politics and Praxis of Third Wave Feminism.' *Women's History Review* 13.2 (2004): 165–82.

Goldman, Robert, Deborah Heath, and Sharon L. Smith. 'Commodity Feminism.' *Critical Studies in Mass Communication* 8 (1991): 333–51.

hooks, bell. *Feminist Theory: From Margin to Center*. Boston: South End, 1984.

Kamen, Paula. *Feminist Fatale: Voices from the 'Twentysomething' Generation Explore the Future of the 'Women's Movement.'* New York: Donald I Fine, 1991.

Looser, Devoney, and E. Ann Kaplan, eds. *Generations: Academic Feminists in Dialogue*. Minneapolis: Minnesota University Press, 1997.

Lorde, Audre. *Sister Outsider: Essays and Speeches*. Freedom, Ca: The Crossing Press, 1984.

McDermott, Patrice. 'On Cultural Authority: Women's Studies, Feminist Politics, and the Popular Press.' *Feminism and the Media*. Spec. issue of *Signs* 20.3 (1995): 668–84.

Rhodes, Deborah L. 'Media Images, Feminist Issues.' *Feminism and the Media*. Spec. issue of *Signs* 20.3 (1995): 685–710.

Sandoval, Chela. *Methodology of the Oppressed*. Minneapolis: Minnesota University Press, 2000.

——. 'U.S. Third World Feminism: The Theory and Method of Oppositional Consciousness in the Postmodern World.' *Genders* 10 (1991): 1–24.

Sommers, Christina Hoff. *Who Stole Feminism? How Women Have Betrayed Women*. New York: Simon and Schuster, 1994.

Stacey, Judith. 'Sexism By a Subtler Name? Postindustrial Conditions and Postfeminist Consciousness in Silicon Valley.' *Women, Class, and the Feminist Imagination: A Socialist-Feminist Reader*. Ed. Karen V. Hansen and Ilene J. Philipson. Philadelphia: Temple University Press, 1990. 338–56.

Walters, Suzanna Danuta. *Material Girls: Making Sense of Feminist Cultural Theory*. Berkeley: California University Press, 1995.

Whittier, Nancy. *Feminist Generations: The Persistence of the Radical Women's Movement*. Philadelphia: Temple University Press, 1995.

Young, Stacey. *Changing the Wor(l)d: Discourse, Politics, and the Feminist Movement*. New York: Routledge, 1997.

15

'Also I Wanted So Much To Leave For the West'
Postcolonial Feminism Rides the Third Wave

Anastasia Valassopoulos

A 'mobile cohabitation of alliances'

In a strongly polemical opening to *Scattered Hegemonies: Postmodernity and Transnational Feminist Practices* (1994), Inderpal Grewal and Caren Kaplan state that:

> In arguing against a standpoint epistemology, we are not arguing that this is an era of postfeminism. We believe that many white, bourgeois feminists have announced a postfeminist era precisely because their particular definitions of feminism (which often require universalization) have not been able to withstand critiques from women of color as well as the deconstructions of poststructuralist or postmodern theory. (20)

This defensive understanding of postfeminism as a 'white' discourse that upholds divisive borders alerts us to the continuing need for a more flexible and incisive understanding of feminist practice and theory, particularly when, as Winifred Woodhull reminds us, 'even "radical" feminists often turn a blind eye to the situation of women in the third world' (77). However, as Ella Shohat argues in her introduction to *Talking Visions: Multicultural Feminism in a Transnational Age* (1998), ideological borders have no function if we accept the intrinsic 'hybrid culture of *all* communities, especially in a world increasingly characterized by the "travelling" of images, sounds, goods and people' (1; emphasis in original). Shohat advocates dialogical relationships that operate beyond 'liberal-pluralist discourse' (2). Through examining a range of cultural moments where seemingly feminist discourses themselves form the basis of dialogical relationships, this chapter argues that by looking at how concepts 'travel' back and forth, we may be better placed to invoke a model of the feminist wave where influences can appear and disappear, become embedded or subside. Rather than seeking to designate 'subversive acts' that seemingly undo wider hegemonic structures, identified as either 'patriarchal' or 'Western', or to pitch white bourgeois feminists against their subjects, a more productive method may be to untangle the various dialogues at play and to witness emerging feminisms across disciplines. Unwilling to identify moments of 'empowerment' (these remain relative to what they are being measured against), this chapter desires to temporarily suspend groupings and timelines when encountering specific cultural products that do not overtly rely on, yet are not unproblematic inheritors of, a particular Western feminist tradition.

As difficult as this might be for politically committed feminists operating within a discourse of human rights as well as gender and sexual equality, a broader, more humble way of thinking about, for example, the complex relationships between women is required in order to pick up on nuanced alternative forms of feminism that otherwise can go unrecognised, de-politicised and ultimately untheorised. Postcolonial feminism, as practised today, in its desire to represent the needs, concerns and histories of complex situations that have arisen out of colonialism, seems overly keen to reproduce a recognisable and authoritative line-up of contexts and interpretations. Thus, Reina Lewis and Sara Mills's recent collection entitled *Feminist Postcolonial Theory* (2003) moves between bell hooks, Audre Lorde, Angela Davis, Chandra Talpade Mohanty, Gayatri Chakravorty Spivak and Deniz Kandiyoti with little critical evaluation of how the various forms of Western, postcolonial and other feminist theories are in dialogue with each other and at what crossroads they meet. A more flexible way of viewing the collaboration between and among feminist thought may reside in what Shohat has called a 'multicultural feminism [that] challenges a Eurocentric ordering of women's cultures ... [This multicultural feminism] questions the benevolence of "allowing" other voices to add themselves to the "mainstream" of feminism by looking at feminism as *itself* a constitutively multi-voiced arena of struggle' (15–16; emphasis in original).

In order to imagine and act upon a multicultural feminism that has no hierarchical order, one has also to engage with how 'mainstream' feminism has been interpreted globally. To resist 'reducing feminists of color to "native informants" whose contribution to feminism is limited to their authenticating report about their exotic forms of subalternity' we need to, it seems, move away from the 'few star feminists of color' (Shohat 16) and engage with the broader field of postcolonial feminist experience. Though a 'multicultural feminism' appears to stretch the influence and applicability of postcolonial feminist theory, the metaphor of the third wave can also enrich the discussion as it can teach us about the *process* of feminism, in its various formats and endless varieties. The remit of the third wave can also include the questioning of how Western feminist theories still influence postcolonial (and Third World) feminist practice. Without wishing to extend the wave metaphor too far, I will argue that it does allow for a variety of crests to form that are not in competition with each other but which allow for a variegated prominence; a position that changes and subsides as situations change and new ones are formed. Though to an extent I agree with Shohat's argument that 'U.S. women of color and Third World women's struggle over the past decades cannot conform to the orthodox sequence of "first waves" and "second waves," just as multicultural feminism cannot be viewed as simply a recent bandwagon phenomenon' (19), it is still important to accept, as the examples to follow will illustrate, that though not all women's struggles can conform to the wave sequence, many are still negotiating their response and allegiance to this sequence. Whilst we all cannot help but work within particular contexts, and whilst our work is inflected by our own locality and interests, the concept of the third wave may be a meeting point rather than an end point. As Sara Ahmed asks, 'how does the consumption of strangers involve a transformation in the subject who consumes?' (115). Shohat's concept of a 'mobile cohabitation of alliances' (15) can act as the broad umbrella under which various feminisms/strangers can operate, whether at the political level or at the academic level, addressing the 'schism' at the heart of feminist concerns (Gillis, Howie and Munford 4).

'Also I wanted so much to leave for the West'

In *Persepolis* (2000), *Persepolis 2: The Story of a Return* (2001) and *Embroideries* (2003), Iranian author Marjane Satrapi offers a comic-strip autobiography of her memories and experiences. Satrapi moves through the daily lives of the protagonist Marjane and her family, simultaneously charting the history of modern Iran. Whilst *Persepolis* focuses on the young Marjane and pre/post revolutionary Iran, *Persepolis 2* is divided into Marjane's time away from home and her return. We are thus privy to her perspective as, at once, insider and outsider. At the start of *Persepolis 2*, Marjane is sent away by her parents to live in Austria, 'leaving a religious Iran for an open and secular Europe' (1). Open to the new experiences available to her, she attempts to absorb new cultural forms and ideologies. Here, Marjane, unsure of how to deal with the politically radical ideas of her new school friends, decides to read up on their heroes: Mikhail Bakunin, Jean-Paul Sartre and then Simone de Beauvoir. This is a particularly fascinating sequence in the work as it operates to both reveal and consequently question Marjane's relationship to feminist thought. In the first panel, we see Marjane's frenzied new activity, one that ostensibly has to do with fitting in, and arguably educating herself in order to *catch up*. The following six panels allow us to follow a narrative that leads us to her encounter with, and negotiation of, de Beauvoir. Though Marjane appears to have had no encounter with 'feminism' before her discovery of de Beauvoir, Satrapi represents her emerging sense of subjectivity in the first panel by drawing multiple Marjanes, alluding to the significance of de Beauvoir's centrality in relation to feminist ideas surrounding the potential subject positions that are taken up and rejected by women.

In this sequence (Figure 15.1), Satrapi interestingly reveals the inadequacies of a feminist language that has little to offer the modern Iranian women searching for plausible and practical answers to everyday formative queries regarding gendered subjectivity and sexuality. De Beauvoir, in this context, becomes the failed example of feminist possibility, requiring a more unquestioning recipient than the young Marjane who is already at the crossroads of two cultures, two homes. In *Cartographies of Diaspora* (1996), Avtar Brah argues for a *'diachronic relationality'* between the memory of home and the experience of the present (197; emphasis in original). This relationality, depicted in the frames of the graphic novel, allows for a temporal shift that helps to illuminate the negotiation of complex ideas, such as self-awareness and one's relationship to cultural influences. Brah extends her understanding of 'the concept of diaspora' to include a *'multi-locationality* within and across territorial, cultural and psychic boundaries' (197; emphasis in original). What are invoked in the graphic novel form are the multiple and competing relationships to subjectivities across time and space; the depiction of this 'multi-locationality' heightens our understanding of Marjane's experience.[1]

In *Persepolis 2*, Satrapi reveals and privileges the trial and error method of 'feminist' awakening/s and questions the supposed locationality and

Figure 15.1 'Learning to love de Beauvoir'.

authoritative source of feminist principles. This form is important here as not only are we encouraged to sense an awareness and a link between Marjane's mother's experience of de Beauvoir (a work of fiction, *The Mandarins* [1954] in this case), thus locating de Beauvoir as a political and intellectual source for certain Iranian women, but also the '... ??' of Marjane's reaction, coupled with the Iranian words in the mother's speech balloon, work together to form a complex narrative about feminist generations. Whilst Marjane's mother reads a narrative about post-war France, Marjane now reads de Beauvoir's exploration of sexual inequality. Satrapi, in using the frames to enact Marjane's misconception and misunderstanding of de Beauvoir's treatise on the 'urinary functions' of young children (see de Beauvoir 301), reveals the incongruity of feminist ideology and the young Marjane's feminist inclinations. When urinating standing up fails, the only option is to sit back down. What is crucial, though, is that sitting back down does not elicit feelings of inferiority. Rather, the move inaugurates the understanding that even learning to urinate like a man requires a complete change of self-perception. Though, arguably, the example of urination is one that should itself lead to an understanding of de Beauvoir's central feminist ideology, what it actually achieves is a debunking of de Beauvoir for those who do not have a similarly structured feminist history to look back on and who in effect learn through trial and error (here illustrated through the actual attempt to urinate like a man). The symbolic leap necessary in order to engage with de Beauvoir's ideology is absent from Marjane's frame, but only insofar as it is not deemed applicable to her condition. I find this to be a remarkable illustration of current debates concerning the extent to which it is possible to import or advocate wholesale Western feminist practice. Here Satrapi seeks to reveal the ways in which this practice must be negotiated and understood. Not only must the teenage Marjane try to understand the unfamiliar territory of de Beauvoir, but she must also be able to confidently question and critique it rather than be in awe of it because it does not fit her present notions of 'liberation' and 'emancipation' (21). The depiction of Marjane's curiosity, surprise, shock and then bewilderment evocatively illustrates the movement from awe to practicality. Rather than rejecting de Beauvoir's influence, the young Marjane accepts that, as an Iranian woman, she must overcome certain other barriers before making the ideological jump required in order to embrace second wave feminist doctrine (if indeed this jump need ever be made).

This move, however, is profoundly open-ended in terms of its possibility. Later on in the story, on returning to Tehran, Marjane is confronted with old friends who now look 'western' (105). Nevertheless, it soon becomes clear to Marjane that this 'look' is not accompanied by a liberal feminism. Her old friends remain bound to traditional Iranian values, thus highlighting the ease with which one can look 'western' without inhabiting what one might suppose are the Western values of liberation and emancipation. Asked about her sexual encounters, Marjane naïvely makes known that she has 'had a few experiences' (116). Her friends' retort – 'so, what's the difference between you and a whore'– only serves to further frame the movement of her earlier 'feminist' experience (116). In the same way as it is not enough to read *The Second Sex* (1949) in order to become a feminist, dying one's hair blonde and wearing lipstick is no indication of liberal feminism. Yet, importantly, Marjane has to (and does) learn how to be a liberated and emancipated *Iranian* woman in *Iran*. This locality intersects with her experiences abroad and to an extent shapes her search for herself. I propose that this focus on locality is what energises the text and allows us to formatively visualise not only difficulties and challenges inherent in adapting to new ideas but also the ways in which this negotiation (of texts and ideas) itself becomes a new form of engagement.

Embroideries, Satrapi's latest publication, takes this negotiation further but frames women's narratives and coping strategies as something endemic to peaceful relationships between the sexes. Through taking us along a journey of women's narratives or 'gossip', Satrapi allows for a private space of women to be experienced as such – as a space to share stories of private subversions and significant achievements. The 'West', interestingly, is understood as that place/space where things are different, where there exists the possibility to be *something else*. The words 'Also I wanted so much to leave for the West' are spoken by the naïve Azzi who believes that 'life [is] elsewhere' (n. p.), anywhere but Iran. It is *Persepolis 2* that offers the more nuanced alternative to how this elsewhere can be engaged with. It not only questions and critiques Western feminism but also reveals geographically specific strategies at work from which an alternative understanding of feminism can be declared.

The 'rhetoric of development'

As part of what Deniz Kandiyoti in *Gendering the Middle East* (1996) has called a 'painstaking process of critical reflection on the nature and historicity of the contexts within which knowledge is produced' (1), Lila Abu-Lughod's culturally specific observations on the television-viewing practices of lower-class Egyptian women achieves great strides towards this wider project. Abu-Lughod's articulation of viewers of television dramas as performing subjects of the nation looks at the spaces between subaltern subjects' lives and the spaces available to them by competing discourses (as provided by popular culture) (14). The study, *Dramas of Nationhood: The Politics of Television in Egypt* (2005), is not so much concerned with how television programmes reflect local experiences or even how experiences are affected by viewing. Avoiding any supposition that answers to these questions could be provided, Abu-Lughod instead concentrates on how messages circulate between the medium of television and the intended audience. I want to argue here that reading Abu-Lughod's study and involving oneself in the cultural consumption of the 'other' requires that we ask ourselves difficult questions concerning our limitations as readers of contexts and our reliance on certain feminist figures that emerge as authoritative.[2] Abu-Lughod is primarily analysing the way in which certain programming decisions (that take into account intended audiences) often remain beyond criticism and how this is ensured through the detailed subjects of the programmes themselves that often promote a stance of moral and social development based on ostensibly *shared* values that unanimously and unquestioningly relate to all persons. She reveals the extent to which television dramas promote the notion that education guarantees enlightenment, moral awareness and ultimately financial success (the Egyptian channels that she critiques are state-owned and state-run). What Abu-Lughod finds interesting is that the lower-class women working as domestics in Cairo with whom she watched the programmes and talked to did not take issue with the ideology being sold to them through the programmes. Rather, having failed, in their own eyes, to achieve this level of *success*, the women looked elsewhere to realise or acquire some sense of self-importance and pride. Significantly, Abu-Lughod identifies religion as an antidote to the rhetoric of development that works here to reinstate a belief in the self, badly damaged through a perception of failure (105).

Abu-Lughod concentrates on two television dramas, *Nuna al-sha'nuna* (1996) and *And the Nile Flows On* (1991), to show how various narratives and life choices are presented to viewers.[3] Of particular interest is *Nuna al-sha'nuna* (*Noony the Looney*), adapted from the short story of the same name by Salwa Bakr, a well-known Egyptian writer. This is the story of Nuna, a young servant girl working in Cairo whose dreams of escape are fuelled by a somehow instinctive understanding of the value of education, an education that she has no access to. As Hoda El-Sadda notes in her article 'Women's Writing in Egypt' (1996), 'Noony's strength and initiative stem from her innate intelligence, her inquisitive mind that shields her from becoming just another passive recipient of preconceived ideas and values' (134). However, Abu-Lughod perceptively argues that Nuna's interest in the wider possibilities apparently offered through education only reinforces another set of preconceived ideas and values, that of middle-class feminists. In the television drama of the story, once Nuna decides to escape servitude, she flees to the sister of her employer who has thoughtfully taught her to read and have respect for education (90–91). Abu-Lughod argues that this ending reinforces the fact that 'social justice is a moral, not a class problem' (90). To viewers suffering the disappointments of job insecurity and dire financial situations, 'the language of piety may seem more familiar than the secular language of rights and choice used by feminist developmentalists including the writers and directors of television productions like *Nuna al-sha'nuna* or by the family planning enterprise represented by *And the Nile Flows On*' (107). Here, the problem of cross-class feminist practice can be seen to miss its mark and send viewers in an unintended direction. Cultural products and their producers, bound up with a nationalist project, may seek to present a view of the way that political and social life ought to be lived, upheld and underscored by a belief in a teleological map where all persons, through education and will, can achieve this ideal scenario. This places the responsibility squarely in the hands of the individual rather than the fundamentally unequal socio-economic context. Faced with the uncompromisingly difficult situation of low wages, poor family support and a relatively negative worldview, Abu-Lughod argues that these cultural products only serve to patronise (rather than give *choice*). She points out that the mismatched feminist agenda actually only gives one choice – that of a middle-class conformist sensibility. Unfortunately, Abu-Lughod claims, what is refuted is that

the underprivileged, the downtrodden, and the marginal would not in the course of their ordinary lives have rich experiences, mental or emotional. The secular intellectual thus speaks, at least in the short story, for the subaltern in a voice that is ultimately middle class and wedded to a modernist set of values that include education, science and knowledge. (87)

Not wishing to resurrect the conundrum acknowledged by Spivak in 'Can the Subaltern Speak', I do wish to suggest that middle-class modernist feminism in this context is strongly reminiscent of earlier Western feminist practice towards Third World feminism. Keen to continue upholding a particular view that privileges the sites of education, science and knowledge (and I do not here wish to fall into the trap of stating that these are not crucial issues), the question of difference, subjective experience and the various levels at which gender is experienced and understood, do not seem to be part of the feminist agenda at work in the production of popular culture. Where we might see a deeper questioning of gendered identities in Arab women's writing, television programming seems to have at its heart an unwavering pedagogical element.

What Abu-Lughod does is show how her method of intervention (if that is not too strong a word), with its emphasis on context and a multiple view and its respect for the variety of life choices and conditions, cannot be open to one unifying solution. Through the discussion of Salwa Bakr's story, the film version of it, and the reaction of the well-respected scholar Ferial Ghazoul, she critically demonstrates how a particular group of secular intellectuals interpret cultural products. This interpretation provides a model of modernity that we then as feminist scholars working in the West may often indiscriminately accept. Opening up these diverse experiences to critical treatment and allowing them theoretical leverage could stall the rather homogenous view of Middle Eastern postcolonial feminist activity that is at play (which cannot always be uplifting). As Abu-Lughod states:

> Rather than representing what Ghazoul has called 'the eloquence of the downtrodden' (*balaghat al-ghalaba*), I would suggest that Bakr, as an educated intellectual, however radical, feminist, and sympathetic to the socially marginal, cannot escape what we might call instead 'the rhetoric of development' (*balaghat al-tanmiya*). And it is the elements in the story that conform to the rhetoric of development that explain why it could have been taken up by television. (87)

Grewal and Kaplan argue that '[w]hen modernity takes shape as feminism, therefore, it collaborates with nationalism. In its nationalist guise, it cannot be oppositional. The need to free feminism from nationalist discourse is clear' (22). Different and more productive lines need to be investigated in relation to what is considered a *good life*, a *moral life*, and so on. Abu-Lughod's technique and nuanced approach to how difference can be experienced and act pedagogically is enlightening, and her method and openness realise the potential of conditions that may at first seem alien. This line of inquiry appeals to and certainly defines a third wave feminist compulsion to listen to and welcome the diversity of feminist practice but, also, to remain attuned to the hierarchies and agendas within these practices. In other words, a third wave feminism that is both keen to learn but also keen to understand relationships of power between and among women.[4]

'It bothered me that I was always asked to speak about politics'

> If feminist political practices do not acknowledge transnational cultural flows, feminist movements will fail to understand the

material conditions that structure women's lives in diverse locations.

(Grewal and Kaplan 17)

*   *   *

Taking as a starting point Grewal and Kaplan's assertion, together with Woodhull's claim that third wave feminism's 'significance and potential can be grasped only by adopting a global interpretive frame' (78), I would venture to suggest that these two directions might work in tandem to produce a new body of feminist theory and practice. Where possibilities emerge, the unpredictability of reactions and the variability of dialogue reveal the inherent difficulties and perhaps the work that has yet to be accomplished. Notwithstanding the importance of material conditions, concentrating on these can often result in a *lazy* dialogue where the specificity of cultural production is ignored. One such example is BBC Radio 4's *Woman's Hour* host Jenni Murray interviewing Souad Massi, a relatively well-known French-based Algerian born singer and musician, in January 2006. If we acknowledge popular culture and the media as constituting a forum for feminist debate, then certain terms of engagement must be criticised for their lack of thinking through the ways in which relations can be conducted on an equal footing. After a brief introduction, Murray is keen to move quickly to the disapproval that Massi's father expressed at her singing aspirations as a young woman: 'Your father was not so keen, was he?' Murray's questions lead even the keenest listener into the following associations: Arab woman, singer, forbidden, Algeria, Islam, and so on. The questions revolve around how the Algerian civil war in 1992 affected Massi's music (no mention is made of Algeria's troubled colonial history) and what kind of problems she encountered being part of a rock band in Algeria. At no point in the interview does Murray inquire into Massi's musical capabilities, influences, training, band or touring dates.

Towards the close of the interview, Murray is keen to discuss Massi's husband: 'You have, I know, a traditional husband'. Interestingly, Massi describes her life on the road and how difficult this is now that she has a baby daughter. The 'traditional husband' does not appear to be an unreasonable man; in fact, he is not mentioned at all. Murray's failed attempts at questioning reveal that there is in fact no story to tell here in relation to the supposed traditional husband. An attuned listener cannot help but wonder what answer would have been satisfactory? Somehow Massi resists these pitfalls and instead discusses the difficulties of keeping up with her singing career whilst having to breastfeed her baby in the middle of the night. As a closing comment, Murray asks: 'What's it like, as well, being seen as one of the best known performers from the Islamic world? How much of a responsibility does that feel?' Placing Massi's career squarely within the political realm of the 'Islamic world' and evoking a call to responsibility reproduces 'constructed oppositions' (Grewal and Kaplan 17). Massi is here made to stand in for her historical context at the expense of her specific artistic context. In another interview, this time at a Parisian radio station, Massi, in a response to a series of similar questions, retorts that it is best that the interviewer ask the intellectual representatives of her country to respond to questions of political consequence. At ease in French in a way that she is not in English, Massi is quick to reply: 'It bothered me that I was always asked to speak about politics. The artistic part would come up afterwards' (*Algeria in a Smile*).

At the close of the *Woman's Hour* interview, Murray introduces the song that Massi will perform: 'I'm not going to attempt the title in Arabic, no way.' With a little coaxing from Massi, the title (only two words) is repeated in Arabic without great difficulty. This incident encapsulates the problems at the heart of this encounter. If our theoretical practice and our transnational global feminist networks are in place to inform and make us aware of not only political but also cultural contexts, then one might be tempted to call this an opportunity missed. I would argue that, again, a certain approach to these encounters can act as furthering a third wave feminist agenda that is unwilling to re-categorise difference as knowable and finite but, rather, as open-ended and surprising. As Hamid Djahri, one of the musicians in Massi's band puts it,

> [Massi's music] would commonly be called Oriental music but it's really a combination of Western, Arab, Andalusian, and Oriental music. All these styles together make her music interesting because it can be shared by everyone. (*Algeria in a Smile*)

Though Massi herself does speak briefly about the problems of pursuing her career in Algeria, this is by no means the whole story. As works on Arab female performers and entertainers such as Karin Van Nieuwkerk's *A Trade Like Any Other: Singers and Dancers in Egypt* (1995) and Virginia Danielson's *The Voice of Egypt: Umm Kulthum, Arabic Song, and Egyptian Society in the Twentieth Century* (1997) reveal, there is a rich tradition of female artists who have had to contend with the underlying contradictory contexts of their role as performers in an Islamic setting. Their strategies and successes have acted as both deterrents and inspirations to future Arab/Islamic performers. As Massi states: 'It is difficult to express ourselves in my country' (*Algeria in a Smile*). Nevertheless, the documentary accompanying her album *Deb* (2005) is concerned with capturing musical composition, work in the studio and performance. That these elements do not form part of the cross-cultural dialogue at the time of interview is disappointing and points to an impasse that results from a developmental feminist monologue. Third wave feminism, in its present and future, can achieve what its predecessors have not achieved, a 'mobile cohabitation of alliances' made up of women's practices that are attuned to differences, internal agendas and theoretical potential.

To take global cultural products and attempt to contextualise, interpret and theorise them is to take part in this imagined alliance. What the three contexts under discussion here reveal is the complex manner in which interpretation operates, influenced as it is by the form of cultural production (be this a comic-strip autobiography or a radio interview), the intended audience and the crucial matter of self-representation. What a third wave feminist intervention can hope to achieve is a repositioning of these interpretations as inspirational yet also open to challenge. In this way, encounters between feminisms produce unpredictable results that reveal to us as yet unimagined forms of being feminists. That this operates both ways is crucial; otherwise local contexts risk receding into objectively understood moments that do not offer fresh forms of being feminist and doing feminism.

Notes

1. Will Eisner in *Comics and Sequential Art* (2004) reminds us that 'lines drawn around the depiction of a scene, which act as a containment of the action or segment of action, have as one of their functions the task of separating or parsing the total statement' (28).
2. For example, the analysis below on Jenni Murray's interview with Souad Massi reveals that in the act of wanting to make Massi appear as the singer who rises to fame against all adversity, what is missed is a probing of the fascinating way in which Massi and her musicians have been able to produce a multi-layered music open to a variety of complex interpretations.
3. *And the Nile Flows On* foregrounds the role of an enlightened female doctor and an understanding shaykh who tackle the 'population problem' and the benefits of 'family planning' in a considerate and sensitive way. Abu-Lughod describes this television drama as one of the more 'openly pedagogical' ones (92).
4. Though, practically, for a non-Arabic speaker it is not easy to find subtitled versions of the television dramas that Abu-Lughod refers to, it is still possible to immerse oneself in the study itself as an exercise in strategically engaging with the contexts at hand. This utilitarian use of her book is one that I feel is congruous with the wider project of a sustainable and dynamic feminist practice.

Works cited

Abu-Lughod, Lila. *Dramas of Nationhood: The Politics of Television in Egypt.* Chicago: Chicago University Press, 2005.

Ahmed, Sara. *Strange Encounters: Embodied Others in Post-Coloniality.* London: Routledge, 2000.

Algeria in a Smile. DVD. Perf. Souad Massi. Island Records, 2003.

And the Nile Flows On [*Wa ma zala al-nil yajri*]. By Anwar 'Ukasha. Dir. Muhammad Fadil. 1991.

Bakr, Salwa. *Such a Beautiful Voice.* Trans. Hoda El-Sadda. Cairo: General Egyptian Book Organisation, 1992.

de Beauvoir, Simone. *The Second Sex.* 1949. Trans. and ed. H.M. Parshley. London: Vintage, 1997.

Brah, Avtar. *Cartographies of Diaspora: Contesting Identities.* London: Routledge, 1996.

Danielson, Virginia. *The Voice of Egypt: Umm Kulthum, Arabic Song, and Egyptian Society in the Twentieth Century.* Chicago: Chicago University Press, 1997.

Eisner, Will. *Comics and Sequential Art.* Florida: Poorhouse Press, 2004.

El-Sadda, Hoda. 'Women's Writing in Egypt.' *Gendering the Middle East: Emerging Perspectives.* Ed. Deniz Kandiyoti. London: I.B.Tauris, 1996. 127–44.

Gillis, Stacy, Gillian Howie, and Rebecca Munford. Introduction. *Third Wave Feminism: A Critical Exploration.* Ed. Stacy Gillis, Gillian Howie and Rebecca Munford. Basingstoke: Palgrave, 2004. 1–6.

Grewal, Inderpal, and Caren Kaplan. Introduction. *Scattered Hegemonies: Postmodernity and Transnational Feminist Practices.* Ed. Inderpal Grewal and Caren Kaplan. Minneapolis: Minnesota University Press, 1994. 1–33.

Kandiyoti, Deniz. 'Contemporary Feminist Scholarship and Middle East Studies.' *Gendering the Middle East: Emerging Perspectives.* Ed. Deniz Kandiyoti. London: I.B. Tauris, 1996. 1–29.

Lewis, Reina, and Sara Mills, eds. *Feminist Postcolonial Theory.* Edinburgh: Edinburgh University Press, 2003.

Massi, Souad. Interview with Jenni Murray. *Woman's Hour.* BBC Radio 4. 4 Jan. 2006. <http://www.bbc.co.uk/radio4/womanshour/ 2006_01_wed_02.shtml>.

Nieuwkerk, Karin Van. *A Trade Like any Other: Female Singers and Dancers in Egypt.* Austin: Texas University Press, 1995.

Nuna al-sha'nuna [*Noony the Looney*]. By Lamis Jabir. Dir. In'am Muhammad Ali. 1996.

Satrapi, Marjane. *Embroideries.* 2003. Trans. Anjali Singh. London: Jonathan Cape, 2005.

——. *Persepolis: The Story of a Childhood.* 2000. Trans. Mattias Ripa and Blake Ferris. London: Jonathan Cape, 2003.

——. *Persepolis 2: The Story of A Return.* 2001. Trans. Anjali Singh. New York: Pantheon, 2004.

Shohat, Ella. Introduction. *Talking Visions: Multicultural Feminism in a Transnational Age.* Ed. Ella Shohat. Cambridge: MIT Press, 1998. 1–63.

Woodhull, Winifred. 'Global Feminisms, Transnational Political Economies, Third World Cultural Production.' *Third Wave Feminism and Women's Studies.* Ed. Stacy Gillis and Rebecca Munford. Spec. issue of *Journal of International Women's Studies* 4.2 (2003): 76–90. Accessed: 5 April 2005. <http://www.bridgew.edu/SoAS/jiws/ April03/woodhull.pdf>.

16

(Un)fashionable Feminists
The Media and Ally McBeal

Kristyn Gorton*

Popular representations of feminism in the media sell: whether in music, film or television, images of independent women appeal to a wide audience. One has only to look at chart hits such as Destiny's Child's 'Independent Woman' (2000), or Kelly Clarkson's 'Miss Independence' (2003), films such as *Charlie's Angels* (2000) or *Lara Croft: Tomb Raider* (2001), or popular fiction such as *Bridget Jones's Diary* (1996) to appreciate that women's 'liberation' is a marketable commodity. Throughout these representations it is implied that women have achieved the goals of second wave feminism – financial autonomy, a successful career, sexual freedom – and, therefore, that the demands associated with the movement of the 1970s have been superseded. Indeed, this image is so widely acknowledged that the cover of the 29 June 1998 issue of *Time* magazine declared feminism to be dead. One rhetorical mechanism through which the media have articulated this distorted perspective is by the construction of a 'then' and 'now': two distinct feminisms, one representing women 'today', and the other, either labelled 'second wave' or 'seventies' feminism, depicting feminisms of the past. These two interpretations of feminism are set against each other, with an implication that women have either moved to a less politicised and less effective feminism; or, more generally, that there is no more need for feminism.

At the heart of these new representations of women is the claim that contemporary feminist politics, in contrast to the intellectual debates of the 1970s, have been weakened by an increasing attention to fashion and style. Thus, the *Time* article tells its readers: 'In the 70s, feminism produced a pop culture that was intellectually provocative. Today it's a whole lot of stylish fluff' (Bellafante 56). Statements such as this imply that feminism has evolved into a movement concerned with style over substance: the personal apparently has triumphed over the political. Whatever the veracity of this representation of modern feminism, it does aid in the construction of women as consumers, for whom feminism is reduced from a political movement to a certain style that can be bought. However, this representation rests upon an artificial divide between the contemporary feminist movement and its predecessor: it thus elides a whole series of continuities, in both the experiences of women over the last three decades, and feminist responses to those experiences. Interestingly, this elision also tends to increase the consuming audience, as older feminists are constructed as secondary consumers of the new model. If we are to show the viability and relevance of feminism to women today we must address the issues highlighted by third wave feminists, including negotiating the legacy of second wave feminism, critiquing the impact of identity politics and understanding the role the media plays in feminism. For example, in *Manifesta: Young Women, Feminism, and the Future* (2000), Jennifer Baumgardner and Amy Richards suggest that we adopt a 'pro-woman line' in our critique of the media's influence on feminism (112). Crucially, this strategy distinguishes itself from second wave feminist projects in that it 'presumes' a level of feminism in order to critique issues such as pleasure and enjoyment as well as power and equality (Baumgardner and Richards 118–19).

This chapter will examine how Ally McBeal – the show, the character and the actress who portrays her – not only offers a way of understanding how the media uses representations for its own agenda but also demonstrates the enjoyment female viewers take in consuming these representations. This enjoyment is not to be dismissed, as it carries its own political resonance. The pleasures women take in these representations, and the representations themselves, suggest a continuing dialogue with earlier feminist concerns, which cannot be so easily dismissed as it is in *Time*'s simplified account of feminism 'today'. Ally McBeal – both the show and the character – has been used by those in the media and the academy alike to represent a break with earlier second wave feminisms. Simon Heffer, for example, writes in the *Daily Mail*: 'After years of TV programmes that have sought to pretend to the contrary, Ally McBeal herself repudiates the main mantra of feminism: that a high-achieving young woman has no need of a man' (13). Heffer's comment echoes the show's general premise: that a successful career woman in her late twenties/early thirties cannot be fully satisfied without a man.

Amanda Rees similarly argues that

> [l]ack of a partner for the Ally McBeals of this world doesn't just imply the absence of masculine attention, but the presence of very real emotional turmoil and self-doubt; having a husband or a boyfriend, it would seem, is the real mark of success. (365)

Likewise, the show's writer-producer, David E. Kelley proposes that Ally McBeal is 'not a hard, strident feminist out of the 60s and 70s. She's all for women's rights, but she doesn't want to lead the change at her own emotional expense' (qtd. in Bellafante 58). As Kelley suggests, Ally McBeal is characterised as a woman who wants the power to make choices in her life, but does not want to have to fight for them herself – or for them to impinge on her personal expression. That is, she wants the benefits of feminism without running the risk of being associated with the criticisms of feminism. Ally McBeal has come to represent a woman who has achieved some of the goals of second wave feminism, in that she is financially independent, successful in her career, and unafraid to demand sexual satisfaction. Yet, as Rees points out, she is in emotional turmoil over her status as a single woman. Although most of the episodes in *Ally McBeal* take place in a law firm, love and marriage are always foregrounded. Ally is seen as a woman who puts her trust in the possibility of 'true love'. On the one hand, this characterisation reiterates the cultural assumption that women will place sensibility over sense, even in the workplace. On the other hand, Ally's faith in love distinguishes her from her colleagues and has a profound affect on them. As Jane Arthurs argues, she 'doesn't simply fit into a masculinized workplace predicated rationality; in fact her emotional excess becomes the dominant office code for her male colleagues as well' (133). The personal is here inexplicitly linked with the political: personal in the sense that things happen to Ally (she is constantly in the throes of a new love affair, or a new case or a debate about love and marriage), political not only on the show itself but also in the way the show and its main character are portrayed in the media.

I would suggest that this media-defined notion of postfeminism tries to define 'today's' woman in order to legitimate its own history and its shift away from feminism.[1] Instead of wanting to move beyond representations of woman, postfeminism wants to move beyond representations of feminism that 'outdate' its own image. For example, the *Time* cover noted above depicts 'Ally McBeal' as the reason why feminism may no longer be a viable political movement. The cover has three faces in black and white: Susan B. Anthony, Betty Friedan and Gloria Steinem; and one in colour, Calista Flockhart, identified not by her own name, but by the character she portrays on television: Ally McBeal. Beneath Flockhart's photograph is the question: 'Is Feminism Dead?' The *Time* cover, amongst other readings, demonstrates the media's ability to construct icons in a political movement that has struggled against such representation. The media thus reduces the complexities of the feminist movement into a marketable success or disaster story, one that interferes directly with the practice of feminist politics: the faces that line the cover are there to question feminism as a relevant movement. The *Time* cover suggests a linear progression which implies that feminism has moved from a 'we' solidarity of the 1960s and 1970s to a 'me' based feminism in the twenty-first century. The staring faces also appear as reminders of the media's role in turning feminism into a kind of fashion-show politics. There can be no doubt that one of the intentions or underlying readings of the cover is that feminism has changed its style over the years. The shift from the severe matron-like appearance of Susan B. Anthony to the glossy, lip-sticked face of Ally McBeal reinforces the postfeminist argument that women today can be feminist *and* attractive to men. Angela McRobbie argues that the 'cultural space of post-feminism' can be articulated through the 'distance from feminism' that it takes (257). Charlotte Brunsdon refers to this distancing with the phrase 'not like that' indicating that one of the ways feminism is presented through popular culture is through a 'disidentity'. Reading Nigella Lawson as a postfeminist, Brunsdon argues that Nigella's '[I'm] not like that' move away from her earlier counterparts (Martha and Martha) is one of the principal ways feminism appears in popular culture (43). Returning to the *Time* cover, we can read the constitutive link that is implied: because Ally McBeal is 'not like' her earlier counterparts, feminism must be dead.

Although all of the faces and names in black and white correspond directly, the face at the end of the feminist spectrum is incorrectly identified as 'Ally McBeal'. Indeed, most viewers who recognise the face would identify her with this name. However, Ally McBeal is the name of a television character, and of the show itself, not of the actress. Flockhart's 'real' identity has been exchanged for a constructed one. In this example, then, 'today's' feminist is a woman who is identified by the character she represents, not by her own name. Her agency is exchanged for the character she portrays. The metonymic shift may appear trivial but, in a political movement that stresses agency, it is an important one. Notably, it suggests the breakdown of the relationship between the personal and the political. Flockhart does not share the same political agency that her 'foremothers' on the cover possess. She is relegated to the fictionalised version of herself, and deprived of a voice of her own. This identity swapping also highlights the importance of 'celebrity' within feminism.[2] From the Spice Girls to Ally McBeal, there is an elision between popular culture representations of feminism and feminism itself. Nevertheless, despite *Time's* then/now distinction, the celebritisation of feminism is far from new: the media played a similar role in constructing 'role models' for feminism in the 1970s. Indeed, Germaine Greer has recently argued that

> the media identified 'newsworthy' candidates for leadership and massaged their images briefly before setting up cat-fights between them. I was dubbed the 'High Priestess of Women's Liberation, Gloria Steinem was 'The New Woman', and Betty Friedan was 'The Mother Superior'. (228)

In the 1970s, as much as today, feminism was sold to women as a simplified product ready for consumption.

Ally's contemporary position as a female 'role model' is directly addressed in the episode 'Love Unlimited'. While representing a woman whose husband wants to annul their nine-year marriage on the basis of his 'sex addiction' problem, Ally is asked to be the role model for young professional women by Lara Dipson, Executive Vice President of *Pleasure* magazine. Ally's refusal to enter into such a contract results in a battle over identity, feminism and fashion. Lara tells Ally that:

> We are going to have to make a few adjustments in the way you dress. And I'd really like to fatten you up a little bit. We don't want young girls glamorising that 'thin' thing. Now my sources tell me that you feel an emotional void without a man. You're really going to have to lose that if women are going to look up to you.

Dipson's character, dressed in a 'power suit' (complete with shoulder pads), clearly represents a popular image of a 1980s feminist, while Ally, dressed in a small mini skirt is positioned as a postfeminist. The scene thus points up an interesting analysis of the nature of postfeminism, the relationship between (post)feminists, and the demands they *imagine* coming from second wave feminism. In this case, Ally growls at Lara and bites off her nose (to spite her face). The scene then switches, and we, as viewers, realise that this fantastical meeting is Ally's dream.

In constructing this dialogue as part of Ally's dream – or nightmare – there is a suggestion that women unconsciously deal with the effects feminism has in their lives. Indeed, there is an implication that women have inherited the legacy of second wave feminism from their mothers, but have other needs and wants which cannot be satisfied within this paradigm. As Ally tells John, the dream represents her conflicting desires for someone she can 'be totally weak with. Somebody who will hold me and make me feel *held*' (emphasis in original). She pauses and emphasises the 'held'. She adds: 'I think I crave some kind of dependency and that makes me feel like a failure as a woman. You know I had a dream that they put my face on the cover of *Time* magazine as the "Face of Feminism"?' Kelley not only takes on the media's reaction to his character, but also engages with some of the anxieties he perceives within feminism: that is, a desire to be successful in terms of a career and a desire to be dependent upon a man. While most feminists would argue that these two desires are not incompatible, they would appreciate that this is a common assumption made about feminism – as common and as falsely stereotypical as dungarees and bra-burning.

The underlying implication in the fantastical meeting between Lara and Ally, then, is that second wave feminism demands that women subscribe to their ideals, style and politics. Lara tells Ally that she needs to change the way she dresses and to gain some weight – otherwise young girls might glamorise the 'thin thing' – while Ally defiantly states that she does not want to be seen as a role model. As Ally suggests in the analysis of her dream, there is a crisis between the desire for dependency and the desire to be an independent woman. In particular, there is confusion over what it means to be a feminist as well as what it means to be a successful woman. This anxiety has prompted a renewed interest in feminism: from the media, which recognises the commercial marketability of feminism, from second wave feminists such as Gloria Steinem and Kate Millett[3] and from a younger generation of feminists such as Natasha Walter, Jennifer Baumgardner and Amy Richards.[4] For instance, in the foreword to Rebecca Walker's collection, *To Be Real: Telling the Truth and Changing the Face of Feminism* (1995), Gloria Steinem begins her critique of feminism 'today' by returning to a gathering from the 1970s. In setting up the scene, she describes the women largely in terms of what they are wearing. She writes: 'Standing near a table full of food, there is a white writer with long hair and a short skirt, and an energetic, thirtyish black woman in a maid's uniform complete with frilly apron.' Her description of the group of women finishes with the question: 'who is the feminist?'; and, in an attempt to subvert her readers' expectations, she answers: 'all of them' (xiii–xiv). Steinem moves on to explain that this meeting was held in order to raise awareness about household workers' rights. The woman in the short skirt was Steinem, and the woman in the maid's uniform was Carolyn Reed, who organised the event in order to draw the party's attention to the diversity of household workers and to demonstrate the 'tyranny of expectation' (xiv). Steinem effectively uses this example to demonstrate how a 'feminist' has been and continues to be understood largely by her appearance, not by her politics. This 'room-sized' metaphor is also deployed to remind us of the diversity in feminism – as well as the *necessity* for that diversity. Feminists do not all look alike, nor should they. However, as Steinem argues, through the media's influence, images of feminism are being sold as *the* image, rather than as one image amongst many. Her analysis prompts us to question whether an emphasis on fashion or style leads to a de-politicisation of feminism; or, has it changed the way in which feminism is political?

To this end, Natasha Walter's *The New Feminism* (1998) examines the mechanisms through which feminism can be reclaimed for women today. Like Steinem, Walter opens her study by taking notice of the women around her: 'You see women driving sleek cars to work through urban traffic; you see women with dreadlocks arguing for the environment ... They are wearing a minidress one day and jeans and boots the next' (1–2). For Walter, these diverse images of women are evidence that a certain kind of feminism is no longer needed, and that a 'new' feminism is necessary. The ability to wear a minidress one day and jeans and boots the next signifies for Walter an ability to wear what we like and a need to redress issues within feminism. Part of Walter's 'new' feminism, which could be called postfeminism, is to separate the personal and the political – thus dismantling one of the central foundations of second wave feminism. Walter argues that this separation will give 'the social and political demands of feminism more edge' and 'free up the personal realm' (5–6). She continues to argue that '[f]eminism has over-determined our private lives and interpreted too many aspects of our cultural life as evidence of a simplistic battle, patriarchy versus women' (6). This assessment of second wave feminism thus echoes Kelley's characterisation of Lara Dipson. Both Walter's interpretation and Kelley's dramatisation foreground the sense in which postfeminists perceive second wave feminism as a 'tyranny of expectation' rather than as a political foundation. On the one hand, there is a similarity between Steinem's and Walter's arguments: they both locate appearance and diversity as decisive issues in feminist politics, and recognise the way that fashion has been an issue within feminism *and* critiques of feminism. Yet, on the other hand, Steinem continues to recognise the necessary relationship between the personal and the political in her acknowledgement that '[t]he greatest gift we can give one another is the power to make a choice. The power to choose is even more important than the choices we make' (xxvi). The power to choose is distinctly political – as pro-choice campaigns in the U.S. attest to. Whether we wear minidresses or jeans and boots is inconsequential – what is important is the freedom to make that decision.

What the character of Ally McBeal shares with writers such as Walter, then, is an ambivalence about what it means to be a feminist – and this ambivalence sells. In contrast to the one-dimensional Lara Dipson, who Kelley clearly positions as a kind of militant second wave feminist, Ally is struggling with her desires to be independent and to be 'held'. Whereas Dipson clearly knows what she wants and who she is, Ally does not. Is she a postfeminist, or a third wave feminist? Is she a feminist at all? These questions are deliberately left unanswered. We, as viewers, are left to wonder just what side of the fence Ally is on. We are also left wondering what this ambivalence offers us. Perhaps one of the most important aspects of this anxiety is that it has re-engaged debates and discussions about the *need* for feminism. Leslie Heywood and Jennifer Drake, for example, argue that their collection, *Third Wave Agenda*,

> makes things "messier" by *embracing* second wave critique as a central definitional thread while emphasising ways that desires and pleasures subject to critique can be used to rethink and enliven activist work. We see the emphasis on contradiction as continuous with aspects of second wave feminism. (7; emphasis in original)

Heywood and Drake thus make it possible to conceive of a third wave of feminism that can critically negotiate the legacy of second wave feminism as well as the anxieties and uncertainties expressed in postfeminism. This re-engagement also allows us, as feminists, to consider the enjoyment that female viewers experience from popular representations of feminism. It is of no coincidence that the fictional Lara Dipson is from *Pleasure* magazine, as pleasure is a contentious issue in the criticism of soap operas such as *Ally McBeal*. Should women enjoy a character like Ally McBeal with all her snivelling, whining and man problems? Or maybe we should ask *why* women enjoy a character like Ally McBeal?

We need to consider both the pleasure and enjoyment contained within the text and also the ways in which feminist television criticism has sometimes focused on how fictionalised images of women are destructive and counter-productive to feminist issues. The condescending nature of some criticism implies that women are neither able to decipher nor critically engage with the images they see. In the example of the scene between Ally and Lara, some female viewers may feel both repulsion for Ally's 'need to be held' and a deep understanding of that need. In other words, programmes such as *Ally McBeal* become pleasurable insofar as they offer play with some of the conflicting inheritances of feminism: desire for both independence and companionship. Articles in the media and in the academy suggest that Ally represents a woman that other women identify with. Laura Morice, for instance, writes: 'Let's leave the debate over Ally's impact on the women's movement to the critics and allow ourselves a rare guilty: watching a woman we can relate to – flaws and all' (par. 7); while Judith Schroeter argues that Ally 'personifies typical conflicts that arise from an increasingly individualised society – thus, conflicts we all face in our daily lives. ... Ally McBeal can provide support and help us cope with them' (par. 4). These statements suggest not only that women look for some escape from the active experience of being a woman, but also that they find a kind of pleasurable escape in characters such as Ally McBeal. Why do female viewers choose a character like Ally McBeal to identify with or as a means of escape?

Critics such as Tania Modleski and Ien Ang have theorised feminist ways of reading the soap opera from seeing it as a postmodern narrative to offering new versions of the *femme fatale*. In her work on 'melodramatic identifications' (85), Ang argues that as critics we must remember that characters like Ally McBeal are fictional, and for that reason are designed to engage the viewer at the level of fantasy, rather than reality. Ang suggests that these characters 'do not function as role models but are symbolic realisations of feminine subject positions with which viewers can identify *in fantasy*' (92; emphasis in original). The concept of fantasy is central to Ang's argument, and she conceptualises it within a psychoanalytic framework; that is, she does not understand fantasy as an illusion, but as a version of reality – as a fundamental aspect of human existence. She also operates from within poststructural theories on subjectivity, arguing that 'being a woman implies a never-ending *process* of becoming a feminine subject – no one subject position can ever cover satisfactorily all the problems and desires an individual woman encounters' (94; emphasis in original). It can be argued that Ally, as a character, allows women to explore their feelings of anxiety about their position within a male dominated workplace, about being thirty-something and about marriage and having children. What *Ally McBeal* offers some female viewers is an opportunity to escape from what Steinem identifies as the 'tyranny of expectation'. Whether it comes from imagined expectations, such as the ones Ally dreams Lara Dipson to have, or from broader cultural demands, a programme like *Ally McBeal* offers a momentary escape and/or a chance to relate to the hopes and fears many women share.

Another reason why so many female viewers enjoy a programme such as *Ally McBeal* lies in the format and reception of the show. Modleski's influential *Loving with a Vengeance: Mass-Produced Fantasies for Women* (1982) reconsiders the critical positioning of the soap opera as a 'feminine' form in order to undermine its value. Modleski understands the 'feminine' nature of the soap opera as positive, and even subversive, of dominant narrative forms. In particular, she foregrounds how the soap opera's narrative, 'by placing ever more complex obstacles between desire and fulfilment, makes anticipation of an end an end in itself' (88). The structure of most episodes of *Ally McBeal* relies on this very notion of a constant deferral of desire, happiness and a definite ending: although most of the shows centre on Ally's desire to find 'Mr Right', she never manages to find him. Indeed, the fact that Ally never finds 'Mr Right' in the first few seasons may also be why the show enjoyed so much success. In contrast, the fourth and fifth seasons see Ally settling down in a new house with a new man, Victor, and a child, Maddie; not exactly the traditional family, but the more settled Ally's life gets, the more the ratings fell. As Joke Hermes' research on viewers' reactions to *Ally McBeal* suggests: 'The fun in being a woman ... is a matter of extending the best stage of a woman's life: after achieving a career (and income) and before motherhood, with heterosexuality a comfortable given providing for women's needs much like a good shoe department' (86). As Ally settles down her viewers can no longer enjoy the play and ambiguity in her life.

We might best understand the success of *Ally McBeal* and similar programmes as demonstrating the enjoyment viewers experience, not only in representations of femininity, but also in more general representations of the 'personal.' Some women enjoy Ally's fantasies, in part, because the demands of second wave feminism have *not* yet been met: women one-sidedly look to the personal because they are still disproportionately excluded from public power and influence. If apathy is the political response to this form of social exclusion, perhaps the atomised consumption of fantasy is its social consequence. Indeed, while *Ally McBeal*'s success has generally been read within the academy as a representation of the triumph of postfeminism, the contention here is that it demonstrates the continuing salience of the demands of second wave feminism on modern women. Thus, if we are to convincingly defend feminist theory's relevance to the modern world, we should not drop the demands of second wave feminism, but rather integrate these demands with the insights of third wave feminist discourse on pleasure and enjoyment with a view to deepening its critical edge.

Notes

* Thanks to Paul Blackledge for his help with this chapter.
1. Ann Brooks states that there are two competing definitions of postfeminism in circulation: one propagated by the media, and the other an intersection between feminism and poststructuralism (2–4).
2. For more on celebrity see Chris Rojek.
3. Kate Millett claims she is 'out of fashion in the new academic cottage industry of feminism' (G4).
4. In addition to television programmes such as *Ally McBeal* and *Sex and the City*, the phenomenon of Chicklit has sparked new discussions and debates regarding feminism, consumerism and female empowerment which coincide with the renewed interest in feminism reflected by titles such as Rebecca Walker's *To Be Real: Telling the Truth and Changing the Face of Feminism* (1995), Leslie Heywood and Jennifer Drake's *Third Wave Agenda: Being Feminist, Doing Feminism* (1997), Marcelle Karp and Debbie Stoller's *The BUST Guide to the New Girl Order* (1999) and Cameron Tuttle's *The Bad Girl's Guide to Getting What You Want* (2000).

Works cited

Ang, Ien. *Living Room Wars: Rethinking Media Audiences for a Postmodern World*. London: Routledge, 1996.

Arthurs, Jane. *Television and Sexuality: Regulation and the Politics of Taste*. Maidenhead: Open University Press, 2004.

Baumgardner, Jennifer, and Amy Richards. *Manifesta: Young Women, Feminism, and the Future*. New York: Farrar, Straus and Giroux, 2000.

Bellafante, Ginia. 'Feminism: It's All About Me.' *Time* 29 June 1998: 54–62.

Brooks, Ann. *Postfeminisms: Feminism, Cultural Theory and Cultural Forms*. London: Routledge, 1997.

Brunsdon, Charlotte. 'The Feminist in the Kitchen: Martha, Martha and Nigella.' *Feminism in Popular Culture*. Ed. Joanne Hollows and Rachel Moseley. Oxford: Berg, 2006. 41–56.

Greer, Germaine. *The Whole Woman*. London: Doubleday, 1999.

Heffer, Simon. 'Absurd, Tiresome and Far Too Thin (But I'll Still Be Very Sorry to See Ally Go.' *Daily Mail* 19 Apr. 2002: 13.

Hermes, Joke. 'Ally McBeal, Sex and the City and the Tragic Success of Feminism.' *Feminism in Popular Culture*. Ed. Joanne Hollows and Rachel Moseley. Oxford: Berg: 2006. 79–96.

Heywood, Leslie, and Jennifer Drake. Introduction. *Third Wave Agenda: Being Feminist, Doing Feminism*. Ed. Leslie Heywood and Jennifer Drake. Minneapolis: Minnesota University Press, 1997. 1–20.

Karp, Marcelle, and Debbie Stoller, eds. *The BUST Guide to the New Girl Order*. New York: Penguin Books, 1999.

McRobbie, Angela. 'Post-Feminism and Popular Culture.' *Feminist Media Studies* 4.3 (2004): 255–64.

Millett, Kate. 'The Feminist Time Forgot.' *Guardian* 23 June 1998: G4–5.

Modleski, Tania. *Loving with a Vengeance: Mass-Produced Fantasies for Women*. New York: Routledge, 1982.

Morice, Laura. 'Bringing Ally to Life.' *Self Magazine*. Feb. 1998. Accessed: 10 July 2006. <http://allycalista.tripod.com/Self.html>.

Rees, Amanda. 'Higamous, Hogamous, Woman Monogamous.' *Feminist Theory* 1.3 (2000): 365–70.

Rojek, Chris. *Celebrity*. London: Reaktion Books, 2001.

Schroeter, Judith. 'The Ally McBeal in Us: The Importance of Role Models in Identity Formation.' *theory.org.uk*. Jan. 2002. Accessed: 10 July 2006. <http://www.theory.org.uk/ally.htm>.

Steinem, Gloria. Foreword. *To Be Real: Telling the Truth and Changing the Face of Feminism*. Ed. Rebecca Walker. New York: Anchor, 1995. xiii–xxviii.

Tuttle, Cameron. *The Bad Girl's Guide to Getting What You Want*. San Francisco: Chronicle Books, 2000.

Walker, Rebecca, ed. *To Be Real: Telling the Truth and Changing the Face of Feminism*. New York: Anchor, 1995.

Walter, Natasha. *The New Feminism*. London: Little Brown, 1998.

17
'Kicking Ass Is Comfort Food'
Buffy as Third Wave Feminist Icon
*Patricia Pender**

> BUFFY: I love my friends. I'm very grateful for them. But that's the price of being a Slayer ... I mean, I guess everyone's alone, but being a Slayer – that's a burden we can't share.
>
> FAITH: And no one else can feel it. Thank god we're hot chicks with superpowers!
>
> BUFFY: Takes the edge off.
>
> FAITH: Comforting!
>
> *(Buffy the Vampire Slayer*, 'End of Days' 7021)

> I definitely think a woman kicking ass is extraordinarily sexy, always ... If I wasn't compelled on a very base level by that archetype I wouldn't have created that character. I mean, yes, I have a feminist agenda, but it's not like I made a chart.
>
> (Joss Whedon qtd. in Udovitch 110)

* * *

What accounts for the extraordinary feminist appeal of the hit television series *Buffy the Vampire Slayer* and how has its ex-cheerleading, demon-hunting heroine become the new poster girl for third wave feminist popular culture? In this chapter I examine *Buffy* through the problematic of third wave feminism, situating the series as part of a larger cultural project that seeks to reconcile the political agenda of second wave feminism with the critique of white racial privilege articulated by women of colour and the theoretical insights afforded by poststructuralism. I suggest that if one of the primary goals of third wave feminism is to question our inherited models of feminist agency and political efficacy, without acceding to the defeatism implicit in the notion of 'postfeminism', then

Buffy provides us with modes of oppositional praxis, of resistant femininity and, in its final season, of collective feminist activism that are unparalleled in mainstream television. At the same time, the series' emphasis on individual empowerment, its celebration of the exceptional woman, and its politics of racial representation remain important concerns for feminist analysis. Focusing primarily on the final season of the series, I argue that season seven of *Buffy* offers a more straightforward and decisive feminist message than the show has previously attempted, and that in doing so it paints a compelling picture of the promises and predicaments that attend third wave feminism as it negotiates both its second wave antecedents and its traditional patriarchal nemeses.

'Third wave feminism' functions in the following analysis as a political ideology currently under construction. Buffy makes a similar claim about her own self-development when (invoking one of the more bizarre forms of American comfort food) she refers to herself as unformed 'cookie dough' ('Chosen' 7022). Ednie Kaeh Garrison proposes that the name 'third wave feminism' may be 'more about desire than an already existing thing' (165), and Stephanie Gilmore has suggested that, ironically, the defining feature of third wave feminism 'may well be its inability to be categorized' (218). Transforming such indeterminacy into a political principle, Rory Dicker and Alison Piepmeier state that one of the aims of their recent anthology, *Catching a Wave: Reclaiming Feminism for the 21st Century* (2003), is to 'render problematic any easy understanding of what the third wave is' (5). While there are arguably as many variants of third wave feminism as there are feminists to claim or reject that label, the characteristics I have chosen to focus on here are those that provide the most striking parallels to *Buffy*'s season seven: its continuation of the second wave fight against misogynist violence; its negotiation of the demands for individual and collective empowerment; its belated recognition and representation of cultural diversity; and its embrace of contradiction and paradox.

Combining elements of action, drama, comedy, romance, horror, and occasionally musical, *Buffy* sits uneasily within the taxonomies of television genre. Darker than *Dawson*, and infinitely funnier than *Felicity*, *Buffy* was explicitly conceived as a feminist reworking of horror films in which 'bubbleheaded blondes wandered into dark alleys and got murdered by some creature' (Whedon qtd. in Fudge par. 2). From its mid-season U.S. premiere in 1997 to its primetime series finale in 2003, the chronicles of the Chosen One have generated, in the affectionate words of their creator and director, Joss Whedon, a 'rabid, almost insane fan base' (Longworth 211). Subverting the conventional gender dynamics of horror, action and sci-fi serials, as well as the best expectations of its producers, the series has followed the fortunes of the Slayer as she has struggled through the 'hell' that is high school, a freshman year at U.C. Sunnydale, and the ongoing challenge of balancing the demands of family, friends, relationships and work with her inescapable duty to fight all manner of evil. As the voiceover to the show's opening credits relates: 'In every generation there is a Chosen One. She and she alone will fight the demons, the vampires, and the forces of darkness. She is the Slayer'.

Television critics and feminist scholars alike have been quick to appreciate the implicit feminist message of the series as a whole. Buffy has been celebrated as a 'radical reimagining of what a girl (and a woman) can do and be' (Byers 173); as a 'prototypical girly feminist activist' (Karras par. 15); and as a 'Hard Candy-coated feminist heroine for the girl-power era' (Fudge par. 17). Her ongoing battle with the forces of evil is seen as symbolic of several second wave feminist struggles: the challenge to balance personal and professional life (Bellafante 1997, 83), the fight against sexual violence (Marinucci 69), and the 'justified feminist anger' young women experience in the face of patriarchal prohibitions and constraints (Helford 24). More metacritically, the series has been analysed in terms of its 'wayward' reconfiguration of the mind/body dualism (Playden 143), and its refusal of the 'inexorable logic' of binary oppositions (Pender 43). Despite the fact that the series itself has ended, the furore of attention it continues to generate both within and outside the academy assures *Buffy* an active afterlife. The last few years alone have seen at least seven monographs, an online journal, five international conferences and four anthologies devoted to the burgeoning field of 'Buffy Studies', with countless further publications in the academic pipeline.[1]

But what propels such feminist fandom? What inspires this excess of affect? Rachel Fudge addresses this question directly when she writes that the impulse that propels Buffy out on patrols, 'night after night, forgoing any semblance of "normal" teenage life', is identical to the one 'that compels us third-wavers to spend endless hours discussing the feminist potentials and pitfalls of primetime television' (par. 8). Fudge claims that Buffy 'has the sort of conscience that appeals to the daughters of feminism's second wave', women for whom 'a certain awareness of gender and power is ingrained and inextricably linked to our sense of identity and self-esteem' (par. 8). In her examination of Buffy as the third wave's 'final girl', Irene Karras argues that Buffy's appeal lies in her intentional 'slaying [of] stereotypes about what women can and cannot do' (par. 15).

Karras applauds the show's combination of sexuality and what she calls 'real efforts to make the world a better and safer place for both men and women' (par. 15). Blending an exhilarating athleticism with a compulsion to activism, Buffy's spectacular agency – her (literally) fantastic facility for kicking ass – has come to function as feminist comfort food.

When fellow Slayer Faith consoles Buffy with the thought '[t]hank god we're hot chicks with superpowers' (first epigraph), the gesture is offered as sympathy and support; it helps to 'take the edge off' the burden they 'can't share'. In this exchange, the Slayer's burden is assuaged in part by what Whedon refers to as her 'sexiness' (second epigraph); in part by the very exceptional qualities or superpowers that isolate her to begin with; and perhaps ultimately by the sharing of confidences, and by extension, of responsibilities. The 'comfort' offered here is a complex conglomerate, and one that rewards further scrutiny. The title of this chapter, 'Kicking Ass Is Comfort Food', comes from the episode 'The Prom' (3020), which occurs immediately prior to season three's apocalyptic Ascension. Buffy has just been told by her lover, Angel, that – in the event that they survive the imminent end-of-the-world – he will be abandoning their relationship and leaving town. To complicate matters, a jilted senior denied a prom date has secretly been training hellhounds to attack partygoers wearing formal attire. Buffy's mentor Giles attempts to console his devastated charge with the conventional cure for a broken heart:

GILES: Buffy, I'm sorry. I understand that this sort of thing requires ice cream of some sort.
BUFFY: Ice cream will come. First I want to take out psycho-boy.
GILES: Are you sure?
BUFFY: Great thing about being a Slayer – kicking ass is comfort food. ('The Prom')

Kicking ass becomes comfort food for Buffy when her supernatural abilities provide her with an extraordinary outlet for more conventional frustrations. Action – in this case a cathartically violent form of action – serves up a supernatural solace for a range of quotidian, human afflictions.

Kicking ass offers Buffy psychological and physical relief: it allows her to simultaneously redress straightforward social evils and to palliate more personal sorts of demon. For the feminist viewer, the spectacle of Buffy kicking ass is similarly comforting; equally exhilarating and empowering, Buffy provides the compound pleasures of both the hot chick and her superpowers. Recent feminist critiques of the heteronormative assumptions and moral policing that underlie second wave theories of visual pleasure ensure that as feminist viewers, we too can find the spectacle of 'a woman kicking ass ... extraordinarily sexy' (second epigraph).[2] At the same time, as Elyce Rae Helford has argued, Buffy can stand metaphorically for young women everywhere who are angered by having 'their lives directed by circumstances or individuals beyond their control' (24). In an era which can sometimes seem saturated with condemnations of feminism's increasing frivolity, Buffy's indomitable militancy – her unrelenting vigilance – can be consumed by the feminist spectator as primetime panacea. Buffy's predilection towards, and consummate abilities in, the art of kicking ass thus simultaneously soothe and sustain, inspire and incite the compulsion to feminist activism.

While over the last seven years the series has addressed a staggering range of contemporary concerns – from the perils of low-paid, part-time employment to the erotic dynamics of addiction and recovery – it is significant that the final season of *Buffy* makes a decisive shift back to feminist basics. Season seven eschews to a certain extent the metaphorical slipperiness and pop-cultural play that is typical of its evocation of postmodern demons and instead presents a monster that is, quite literally, an enemy of women. The principal story arc pits an amorphous antagonist, The First Evil, against the Slayer and her 'army', a group that has swelled to include in its ranks 'Potential' Slayers from around the globe. Staging the series' final showdown with a demon that is overtly misogynist and creating an original evil with a clearly patriarchal platform, *Buffy*'s season seven raises the explicit feminist stakes of the series considerably.

Unable to take material form, The First Evil employs as its vessel and deputy a former preacher turned agent-of-evil called Caleb. Spouting hellfire and damnation with fundamentalist zeal, Caleb is, of all of the show's myriad manifestations of evil, the most recognisably misogynist: 'There once was a woman. And she was foul, like all women are foul' ('Dirty Girls' 7018). Dubbed 'the Reverend-I-Hate-Women' by Xander ('Touched' 7020), Caleb is a monstrous but familiar representative of patriarchal oppression, propounding a dangerous form of sexism under the cover of pastoral care. 'I wouldn't do that if I were you sweet pea', Caleb at one point warns Buffy; 'Mind your manners. I do believe I warned you once' ('Empty Places' 7019). At other times he calls her 'girly girl' ('End of Days' 7021), a 'little lady' ('Empty Places'), and, once (but only once), 'whore' ('Touched'). Buffy's response (after kicking him across the room) is to redirect the condescension and hypocrisy couched in his discourse of paternal concern: 'You know, you really should watch your language. Someone didn't know you, they might take you for a woman-hating jerk' ('Touched'). In comparison to the supernatural demons of previous seasons, Caleb's evil might seem unusually old-fashioned or even ridiculous, but successive encounters with the Slayer underscore the fact that his power is all the more insidious and virulent for that. Mobilising outmoded archetypes of women's weakness and susceptibility – 'Curiosity: woman's first sin. I offer her an apple. What can she do but take it?' ('Dirty Girls') – Caleb effectively sets a trap that threatens to wipe out the Slayer line. Within the context of the narrative, Caleb's sexist convictions – 'Following is what girls do best' ('Dirty Girls') – and, more importantly, their unconscious internalisation by the Slayer and her circle, pose the principal threat to their sustained, organised, collective resistance.

In its exploration of the dynamics of collective activism, *Buffy*'s final season examines the charges of solipsism and individualism that have frequently been directed at contemporary popular feminism. 'Want to know what today's chic young feminist thinkers care about?' wrote Ginia Bellafante in her notorious 1998 cover story for *Time* magazine: 'Their bodies! Themselves!' (1998, 54). One of the greatest challenges Buffy faces in season seven is negotiating conflicting demands of individual and collective empowerment. Trapped by the mythology, propounded by the Watcher's Council, that bestows the powers of the Slayer on 'one girl in all the world', Buffy is faced with the formidable task of training 'Potential' Slayers-in-waiting who will only be called into their own power in the event of her death. In the episode 'Potential' (7012) Buffy attempts to rally her troops for the battle ahead:

> The odds are against us. Time is against us. And some of us will die in this battle. Decide now that it's not going to be you. ... Most people in this world have no idea why they're here or what they want to do. But you do. You have a mission. A reason for being here. You're not here by chance. You're here because you are the Chosen Ones.

This sense of vocation resonates strongly with feminist viewers who feel bound to the struggle for social justice. However, such heroism can still be a solitary rather than collective endeavour. On the eve of their final battle, after decimating her advance attack, Caleb makes fun of what he calls Buffy's 'One-Slayer-Brigade' and taunts her with the prospect of what we might think of as wasted Potential:

> None of those girlies will ever know real power unless you're dead. Now, you know the drill ... 'Into every generation a Slayer is born. One girl in all the world. She alone has the strength and skill. ...' There's that word again. What you are, how you'll die: alone. ('Chosen' 7022)

Such references make clear that loneliness and isolation are part of the Slayer's legacy. Balancing the pleasures and price of her singular status, Buffy bears the burden of the exceptional woman. But the exceptional woman, as Margaret Thatcher and Condaleeza Rice have amply demonstrated, is not necessarily a sister to the cause; a certain style of ambitious woman fashions herself precisely as the exception that proves the rule of women's general incompetence. In one of the more dramatic and disturbing character developments in the series as a whole, season seven presents Buffy's leadership becoming arrogant and autocratic, her attitude isolationist and increasingly alienated. Following in the individualist footsteps of prominent 'power feminists', Buffy forgoes her collaborative community and instead adopts what fans in the U.S. and elsewhere perceived as a sort of 'You're-Either-With-Me-Or-Against-Me' moral absolutism ominously reminiscent of the Bush administration (Wilcox) – an incipient despotism exemplified by what Anya calls Buffy's 'Everyone-Sucks-But-Me' speech ('Get It Done' 7015).

The trial of Buffy's leadership is sustained up to the last possible moment, and its resolution repudiates recurring laments about the third wave's purported political apathy. 'According to the most widely publicized construction of the third wave', write Leslie Heywood and Jennifer Drake, '"we" hate our bodies, ourselves, our boring little lives, yet we incessantly focus on our bodies, and our boring little lives. ... "We" believe that the glamorization of nihilism is hip and think that any hope for change is naïve and embarrassing' (1997b, 47). Jennifer Baumgardner and Amy Richards respond to such allegations directly when they write 'imagine how annoying it is to hear from anyone (including the media and especially Second Wave feminists) that young women aren't continuing the work of the Second Wave, that young women are apathetic, or "just don't get it"' (85). Baumgardner and Richards state that they have reacted 'by scrambling to be better feminists and frantically letting these women know how much we look up to them'. Ultimately, however, they have 'refused to accept this myth' (85).

Drawing attention to the Slayer's increasing isolation, Caleb highlights the political crisis afflicting her community, but in doing so he inadvertently alerts Buffy to the latent source of its strength, forcing her to claim a connection she admits 'never really occurred to me before' ('Chosen'). In a tactical reversal Giles claims 'flies in the face of everything ... that every generation has ever done in the fight against evil', Buffy plans to transfer the power of the Chosen One, the singular, exceptional woman, into the hands of the Potentials – to empower the collective, not at the expense of, but by force of, the exception. In the series finale, Buffy addresses her assembled army in the following terms:

> Here's the part where you make a choice. What if you could have that power *now*? In every generation one Slayer is born, because a bunch of men who died thousands of years ago made up that rule. They were powerful men. This woman [pointing to Willow] is more powerful than all of them combined. So I say we change the rules. I say *my* power should be *our* power. Tomorrow, Willow will use the essence of the scythe to change our destiny. From now on, every girl in the world who might be a Slayer, *will* be a slayer. Every girl who could have the power, *will* have the power. Can stand up, will stand up. Slayers – every one of us. Make your choice: are you ready to be strong? ('Chosen'; emphases in original)

At that moment – as the archaic matriarchal power of the scythe is wrested from the patriarchal dictates of the Watcher's Council – we see a series of vignettes from around the world as young women of different ages, races, cultures and backgrounds sense their strength, take charge, and rise up against their oppressors. This is a 'Feel the Force, Luke' moment for girls on a global scale. It is a revolution that has been televised.

In transferring power from a privileged, white, Californian teenager to a heterogeneous group of women from different national, racial and socio-economic backgrounds *Buffy*'s final season addresses, almost as an afterthought, the issue of cultural diversity that has been at the forefront of third wave feminist theorising. Garrison has drawn attention to the connections between Chela Sandoval's articulation of 'U.S. Third World Feminism' and U.S. third wave feminism, representing the latter as a movement fundamentally indebted to the feminist critique articulated by women of colour. Garrison claims that, 'unlike many white feminists in the early years of the Second Wave who sought to create the resistant subject "women", in the Third Wave, the figure "women" is rarely a unitary subject' (149). This understanding of third wave feminism is borne out by Baumgardner and Richards, who argue that 'the third wave was born into the diversity realized by the latter part of the second wave', a diversity represented by the works of African American and Chicana feminists, third world feminists of colour and U.S. third world feminists (77). Heywood and Drake make the third wave's debts to third world feminism explicit when they state that the arguments that women of colour scholars introduced into the dominant feminist paradigms in the 1980s 'have become the most powerful forms of feminist discourse in the 1990s' (1997b, 49). They claim that while third wave feminism owes 'an enormous debt to the critique of sexism and the struggles for gender equity that were white feminism's strongest provinces, it was U.S. third world feminism that modeled a language and a politics of hybridity that can account for our lives at the century's turn' (1997a, 13).

From some of its earliest incarnations academic third wave feminism has presented itself as a movement that places questions of diversity and difference at the centre of its theoretical and political agenda. However, as Stacy Gillis and Rebecca Munford have pointed out, the 'extent to which third wave feminism has learned how to incorporate, rather than to exclude' remains an issue for ongoing concern (5). Examining what she sees as the serious limitations of predominantly Western third wave feminism, Winifred Woodhull warns that the third wave risks repeating the exclusionary errors of earlier feminist practices. 'Given the global arena in which third wave feminism emerges', she writes, 'it is disappointing that new feminist debates arising in first world contexts address issues that pertain only to women *in* those contexts' (78; emphasis in original). Woodhull claims that the significance and potential of third wave feminism 'can be grasped only by adopting a global interpretive frame, that is, by relinquishing the old frameworks of the west and developing new ones that take seriously the struggles of women the world over' (ibid.). In its most rigorous and responsible guise, then, third wave feminism's call for cultural diversity is the political response to the critique of white racial privilege articulated by second wave feminists of colour, and the theoretical consequence of incorporating the discourse of difference elaborated by poststructural theory more broadly. In its less careful incarnations, as *Buffy* demonstrates admirably, it can perform the very strategies of occlusion and erasure that its more critical proponents are at pains to redress.

Buffy's racial politics are inarguably more conservative than its gender or sexual politics, a situation pithily summarised by one of the few recurring black characters of the show's first three seasons,

Mr. Trick: 'Sunnydale ... admittedly not a haven for the brothers – strictly the Caucasian persuasion in the Dale' ('Faith, Hope, and Trick' 3003). While the final season of the show has seen an expansion of *Buffy*'s exclusively white, middle class cast with the introduction of character Principal Robin Wood and the international expansion of the Slayer line, such changes can easily be dismissed as mere tokenism. Season seven makes repeated recourse to racial stereotypes – most notably in its primitivist portrayal of the 'First Slayer' and the 'Shadow Men' as ignoble savages, and its use of formulaic markers of cultural difference to distinguish the international Slayers. As Gayle Wald has warned in a slightly different context, feminist scholarship must be wary of uncritically reproducing simplistically celebratory readings of popular culture that focus on gender performance 'as a privileged site and source of political oppositionality', in which 'critical questions of national, cultural, and racial appropriation can be made to disappear' (590). A critical analysis of *Buffy*'s racial representations need not be considered a critique of the palpable pleasures provided by the show, but rather, as Wald suggests, 'a critique of the production of pleasure through gendered and racialized narratives that signify as new, transgressive, or otherwise exemplary' (595).

In extending the Slayer's powers to young girls across the globe, *Buffy*'s season seven can be seen to begin to redress – albeit belatedly and incompletely – the national, cultural, and racial privilege the show has assumed through its seven year cycle. Bringing ethnic diversity and racial difference to the Slayer story, a generous reading of *Buffy*'s finale might see it as an exemplary narrative of transnational feminist activism. A more critical reading might see it as yet another chapter in a long, repetitive story of U.S. imperialism. I would suggest that these readings are not as inimical as they might initially seem; season seven's narrative implies that *both* of these readings are admissible, perhaps even mutually implicated. In her analysis of what she calls 'the globalization of Buffy's power', for instance, Rhonda Wilcox has argued that '*Buffy* can be seen as both a metaphor for and an enactment of globalization', one that contemplates both its negative and positive aspects. Wilcox claims that the series celebrates capitalist institutions such as the mall at the same time that it recognises and critiques the 'cultural presumption' inherent in the idea of 'all-American domination of the world ... through the spread of technological goods and through governmental aggression'. Similarly, I would suggest that the idealised vision of universal sisterhood with which *Buffy* concludes needs to be read against the immediate political context in which its final season screened, a context that illuminates some of the same gestures of cultural imperialism that the series elsewhere successfully critiques. *Buffy*'s celebration of what is effectively an international military alliance under ostensibly altruistic American leadership demands special scrutiny in our current political climate. In the context of the indefensible arrogance of Bush's 'War on Terror' and the spurious universalism of his 'Coalition of the Willing', *Buffy*'s final gesture of international inclusivity is imbued with unwittingly inauspicious overtones.

It would be a mistake, I think, to underestimate or to collapse too quickly the contradictions embedded in *Buffy*'s cultural politics, contradictions that are in turn indicative of the crosscurrents that distinguish the third wave of feminism. The refusal of misogynist violence, the battle against institutionalised patriarchy, and the potential of transnational feminist activism are issues that remain at the forefront of the third wave agenda, and themes that *Buffy*'s final season explores with characteristically challenging and satisfying complexity. The fact that its success in critiquing its own cultural privilege is equivocal should be read less as a straightforward sign of failure than as a reflection of the redoubtable contradictions that characterise third wave feminism itself. Fudge has suggested that *Buffy* 'constantly treads the fine line between girl-power schlock and feminist wish-fulfillment, never giving satisfaction to either one' (par. 17). Adopting one of the signature rhetorical and political strategies of feminism's third wave, *Buffy* has consistently welcomed such apparent contradiction with open arms. I suggest that in its examination of individual and collective empowerment, in its ambivalent politics of racial representation, and its willing embrace of contradiction, *Buffy* is a quintessentially third wave cultural production. Providing a fantastic resolution – in both senses of the word – to some of the many dilemmas confronting third wave feminists today, *Buffy* is comfort food for girls who like to have their cake and eat it too.

Notes

* I would like to thank the editors of this volume for their helpful suggestions for revision and the students in my 'Girls on Film' classes at Stanford and Pace for their creative and critical engagement with this material. Thanks also to Caitlin Delohery and Falu Bakrania who provided invaluable comments on earlier versions of this chapter.

1. See the *Buffy Bibliography*, the *Encyclopaedia of Buffy Studies* and David Lavery's '"I Wrote My Thesis on You": *Buffy* Studies as an Academic Cult'.
2. For more on this see Debbie Stoller.

Works cited

Baumgardner, Jennifer, and Amy Richards. *Manifesta: Young Women, Feminism, and the Future*. New York: Farrar, Straus and Giroux, 2000.

Bellafante, Ginia. 'Bewitching Teen Heroines.' *Time* 5 May 1997: 82–85.

——. 'Feminism: It's All About Me.' *Time* 29 June 1998: 54–62.

Buffy Bibliography. Ed. Derik Badman. 20 Apr. 2005. Accessed: 1 Sept. 2006. <http://www.madinkbeard.com/buffyology.html>.

Buffy the Vampire Slayer. By Joss Whedon. Perf. Sarah Michelle Gellar, Alyson Hannigan and Nicholas Brandon. Twentieth Century Fox, 1997–2003.

Byers, Michelle. 'Buffy the Vampire Slayer: The Next Generation of Television.' *Catching a Wave: Reclaiming Feminism for the 21st Century*. Ed. Rory Dicker and Alison Piepmeier. Boston: Northeastern University Press, 2003. 171–87.

Dicker, Rory, and Alison Piepmeier. Introduction. *Catching a Wave: Reclaiming Feminism for the 21st Century*. Ed. Rory Dicker and Alison Piepmeier. Boston: Northeastern University Press, 2003. 3–28.

Encyclopaedia of Buffy Studies. Ed. David Lavery and Rhonda V. Wilcox. 1 May 2003. *Slayage: The Online Journal of Buffy Studies*. Accessed: 1 Sept. 2006. <http://www.slayage.tv/EBS>.

Fudge, Rachel. 'The Buffy Effect: Or, A Tale of Cleavage and Marketing.' *Bitch: Feminist Responses to Popular Culture* 10 (1999). Accessed: 20 June 2000. <http://www.bitchmagazine.com/archives/08_01buffy/buffy.htm>. [No longer available].

Garrison, Ednie Kaeh. 'U.S. Feminism-Grrrl Style! Youth (Sub)Cultures and the Technologics of the Third Wave.' *Feminist Studies* 26.1 (2000): 141–70.

Gillis, Stacy, and Rebecca Munford. 'Harvesting Our Strengths: Third Wave Feminism and Women's Studies.' *Third Wave Feminism and Women's Studies*. Ed. Stacy Gillis and Rebecca Munford. Spec. issue of *Journal of International Women's Studies* 4.2 (2003): 1–6. Accessed: 22 Sept. 2003. <http://www.bridgew.edu/SoAS/jiws/April03/introduction.pdf>.

Gilmore, Stephanie. 'Looking Back, Thinking Ahead: Third Wave Feminism in the United States.' *Journal of Women's History* 12.4 (2001): 215–21.

Helford, Elyce Rae. ' "My Emotions Give Me Power": The Containment of Girls' Anger in *Buffy*.' *Fighting the Forces: What's at Stake in* Buffy the Vampire Slayer.' Ed. Rhonda Wilcox and David Lavery. Lanham: Rowman and Littlefield, 2002. 18–34.

Heywood, Leslie, and Jennifer Drake. Introduction. *Third Wave Agenda: Being Feminist, Doing Feminism*. Ed. Leslie Heywood and Jennifer Drake. Minneapolis: Minnesota University Press, 1997a. 1–20.

——. 'We Learn America Like a Script: Activism in the Third Wave; Or, Enough Phantoms of Nothing.' *Third Wave Agenda: Being Feminist, Doing Feminism*. Ed. Leslie Heywood and Jennifer Drake. Minneapolis: Minnesota University Press, 1997b, 40–54.

Karras, Irene. 'The Third Wave's Final Girl: *Buffy the Vampire Slayer*.' *thirdspace* 1.2 (2002). Accessed: 1 Sept. 2006. <http://www.thirdspace.ca/articles/karras.htm>.

Lavery, David. '"I Wrote My Thesis on You": *Buffy* Studies as an Academic Cult.' Sonic Synergies/Creative Cultures Conference. University of South Australia, Adelaide. 21 July 2003.

Longworth Jr., James L. 'Joss Whedon: Feminist.' *TV Creators: Conversations with America's Top Producers of Television Drama*. Ed. James L. Longworth Jr. Syracuse: Syracuse University Press, 2000. 197–220.

Marinucci, Mimi. 'Feminism and the Ethics of Violence: Why Buffy Kicks Ass.' *Buffy the Vampire Slayer and Philosophy: Fear and Trembling in Sunnydale*. Ed. James B. South. Chicago: Open Court, 2003. 61–75.

Pender, Patricia. '"I'm Buffy and You're ... History": The Postmodern Politics of *Buffy the Vampire Slayer*.' *Fighting the Forces: What's at Stake in* Buffy the Vampire Slayer. Ed. Rhonda Wilcox and David Lavery. Lanham: Rowman and Littlefield, 2002. 35–44.

Playden, Zoe-Jane. '"What You Are, What's to Come": Feminisms, Citizenship and the Divine.' *Reading the Vampire Slayer: An Unofficial Critical Companion to Buffy and Angel*. Ed. Roz Kaveney. London: Tauris Parke, 2002. 120–47.

Stoller, Debbie. 'Introduction: Feminists Fatale: BUST-ing the Beauty Myth.' *The BUST Guide to the New Girl Order*. Ed. Marcelle Karp and Debbie Stoller. New York: Penguin, 1999. 42–47.

Udovitch, Mim. 'What Makes Buffy Slay?' *Rolling Stone* July 2000: 40–41, 110.

Wald, Gayle. 'Just a Girl? Rock Music, Feminism, and the Cultural Construction of Female Youth.' *Signs: Journal of Women in Culture and Society* 23.3 (1998): 585–610.

Wilcox, Rhonda. '"Show Me Your World": Exiting the Text and the Globalization of *Buffy*.' Staking a Claim: Global Buffy, Local Identities Conference. University of South Australia, Adelaide. 22 July 2003.

Woodhull, Winifred. 'Global Feminisms, Transnational Political Economies, Third World Cultural Production.' *Third Wave Feminism and Women's Studies*. Ed. Stacy Gillis and Rebecca Munford. Spec. issue of *Journal of International Women's Studies* 4.2 (2003): 76–90. Accessed: 22 Sept. 2003. <http://www.bridgew.edu/SoAS/jiws/April03/woodhull.pdf>.

18

'My Guns Are in the Fendi!'
The Postfeminist Female Action Hero

*Cristina Lucia Stasia**

The female action hero has received significant popular and academic attention. Whether gracing the posters of academic conferences on postfeminism[1] or the cover of *Vogue* (April 2002), she is a catalyst for discussions of feminism, female agency and femininity. Images of girls 'kicking ass' proliferate in magazines and marketers have exploited the market potential of postfeminist girls who think it is cool that girls can kick ass – but are more interested in purchasing the designer stiletto the girl is kicking ass in. Stephanie Mencimer boasts that

> the muscle-bound stars of the action-film blockbusters of the '80s and '90s have found themselves ungraciously drop-kicked out of the genre by, of all things, a bunch of girls. Girl power flicks like *Charlie's Angels*, *Crouching Tiger*, and *Tomb Raider* are topping the $100 million mark once dominated by men like Schwarzenegger. (15)

The *Lara Croft: Tomb Raider* (2001; 2003), *Charlie's Angels* (2000; 2003), *Miss Congeniality*[2] (2000; 2005) and *Kill Bill* (2003; 2004) franchises are complemented by single entries into the female action genre including *The Long Kiss Goodnight* (1996), *Double Jeopardy* (1999), *Enough* (2002), the Jodie Foster films *Panic Room* (2002) and *Flight Plan* (2006), the story of model-turned-body hunter *Domino* (2006), crossover hits like *House of Flying Daggers* (2004) and *Sympathy for Lady Vengeance* (2005) and numerous action/comic and action/sci-fi hybrids including *Catwoman* (2004), *Electra* (2005) and *Aeon Flux* (2006). While these films showcase different heroes – the hyperfeminine Angels and Croft, the mother-hero of the Foster films, the superhero, the sci-fi mutated hero – they all showcase an active femininity which responds directly to the historical moment of postfeminism.

The gender of mass-mediated heroism – and its means of production and consumption – has changed. Distantly related to the female action hero of the 1970s and the cute kid sister of the action heroine of the 1980s, this girl power action hero is also her own woman – or, most often, her own girl. She is as different from the action heroine of the 1980s, typified by the hardbodied Ripley (Sigourney Weaver) in *Aliens* (1986) and Sarah O'Connor (Linda Hamilton) in *Terminator 2* (1991), as she is from the male action hero of today. This new female action hero not only manifests anxieties about changing gender roles, but indicates a lack of anxiety as popular culture fulfils the prophecy of the term post-feminism: convincing women they live in a post-patriarchy. This model resonates with the female action film and the triumph of the fittest body/mind – a body which is almost exclusively white and middle-class and a mind which is free of political concerns. Terms for the postfeminist action hero index key aspects of her appeal and her limitations: 'tough girls' and 'action chicks' (Inness), 'action babes' (O'Day), and 'violent femmes' (Mencimer) all position this hero as strong but also as unthreatening, described in infantilised or sexualised terms. Sherrie Inness uses the term 'action chick' as an umbrella term to describe heroes from Ripley to Lara. While she critiques the way that 'tough women are still expected to be feminine, attractive, and heterosexually appealing' (14), the use of descriptors like 'action chick' and 'tough girl' endorses a specific account of femininity. Similarly, Marc O'Day coins the term 'action babe cinema' to characterise female action films: 'combinations of "eye candy" and "the ride", those elements of cinematic spectacle which make us go "wow!"' (201–02). The criticism of these films reinforces some of the limitations: terming them babes/girls/action chicks instead of heroes continues to skew the focus from their heroics to their sexualised bodies. Despite the spectacularisation of male heroes they are still called heroes, not babes/boys/action dicks.

The way the female action hero is softened, not hardened, by these labels parallels the management of women's agency in both the historical moment of postfeminism and postfeminist popular culture. These labels epitomise the problematic which this figure personifies: women are allowed to be violent only within the parameters allowed by patriarchal discourse. That is, they may be threatening but are always heterosexually attractive. With particular reference to *Lara Croft: Tomb Raider*, the *Charlie's Angels* films and the *Miss Congeniality* films, this chapter argues that the postfeminist action hero is symptomatic of larger issues in postfeminism. Reading these films against popular texts provides insight into the relationship between second wave feminism and post-feminism, and the problematic status of femininity, politics and history in postfeminism. This chapter has two objectives: the first is to explain why young women today are both resistant to and ignorant of feminist history by reading the messages given to them about feminist history in postfeminist action films. The second is to illustrate the limits of postfeminism as personified in its female action heroes.

Victim feminism/power feminism

The complexity of the post-second wave feminist period is often elided and simplified, and the postfeminist catchphrase 'girls kick ass' is too often used to refer to the new kinds of active femininity emerging in this period. Even a cursory comparison of the Angels, for example, with their contemporary male action heroes demonstrates the fallacy of this claim and that the female hero is sexualised and infantilised in ways the male hero is not – for example, Vin Diesel has yet to lipsynch in his under-wear. The problem of analysing female action films is that post-second wave feminism is often collapsed into a monolithic movement that defaults to girl power. Catherine M. Orr notes that second wave femi-nism 'offers today's young women the most important of feminist lega-cies: a sense of entitlement' (33). Accounts of post-second wave feminism have often endorsed the politics of individual preoccupations, as numerous qualifying prefixes attest: babe, lipstick, do-me, girlie, vic-tim, power. Moreover, postfeminism and third wave feminism are, too often, used interchangeably. Although, as Joanne Hollows and Rachel Moseley argue 'post-feminism and third-wave feminism are used in a range of different ways in different historical and national contexts' (7), both third wave feminism and postfeminism engage with both popular culture and the contradictions of women's lives in late capitalism. Unlike third wave feminism, however, postfeminism rejects the institu-tional critique made by second wave feminism.

The value of third wave feminism is that it 'contains elements of second-wave critique of beauty culture, sexual abuse and power structures' (Heywood and Drake 3) while, especially in the Girlie model, celebrating (white) femininity: 'Most Girlies are white, straight, work outside the home and belong to the consumer class' (Baumgardner and Richards 138). Appealing in its advocation of femininity and all its accoutrements, third wave Girlie feminism has been mainstreamed into postfeminist girl power.

Angie Manzano cautions that 'when feminism is disseminated by and interpreted through capitalist-controlled institutions, you get a clash of ideologies and interests. Something's gotta give' (10). Both third wave feminism and postfeminism privilege conventional femininity and individualism; however, in the translation of Girlie to girl power, what gives is both a complete dismissal of past feminisms and any sense of the need for gender equality: we are always already equal, it is just a matter of exercising one's girl power. As much as Girlies see femininity as a powerful site of personal power, they do not advocate girlieness instead of political agitation. While the postfeminist action hero's femininity and individualism are resonant with third wave 'Girlie' culture, she reifies third wave feminism into postfeminist visuals and girl power sound bites. Although postfeminism was initially conflated with antifeminism (Faludi 72; Braithwaite 337) it is more closely related to power feminism while girl power mirrors power feminism's optimism and elitist ideas about power. Power feminism was popularised by the It Girls of 1990s feminism: Naomi Wolf, Katie Roiphe and Christina Hoff Sommers.[3] The central tenet of power feminism is 'that the gains forged by previous generations of women have so completely pervaded all tiers of our social existence that those still "harping" about women's victim status are embarrassingly out of touch' (Siegel 75). Dismissing second wavers as 'victim feminists' who need to realise that, today, equality is achieved by seizing power not changing power structures, Wolf argues that 'while women certainly suffer from a lack of power, women also suffer from a fear of power' (235). Articulating the primary barrier to equality as women's reticence to embrace power facilitates an ideology that looks suspiciously like patriarchal capitalism.

Postfeminism occludes patriarchal power in favour of a focus on the various ways that second wave feminism has empowered women to act – and buy – on their own behalf while ignoring that the ability to act/buy is circumscribed by race/class/age/sexuality: 'For power ... is hardly, unshakably male; we can make it female with ease: with votes, with voices and with a little money from a lot of wallets' (Wolf 142). But access to voting, voicing and financial solvency is mitigated by the markers of race/class/sexuality; thus re-gendering power so all women are equal is not easy. While power feminists 'explicitly define themselves against and criticize feminists of the second wave' (Drake 8), identifying second wave feminism as both the originator of victim feminism and the obstacle to equality (Henry 39), it is the whiny women of the second wave – victims of patriarchy instead of agents of change – who are villainised. Astrid Henry argues that 'the attention on generational differences has dramatically shifted feminism's focus from external enemies to internal ones' (183). Postfeminism's aggressively antagonistic relationship with second wave feminism is highlighted in a number of postfeminist action films through the trope of generational conflict.

Feminism, femininity and the action hero

In the postfeminist action film, the shift from fighting bad guys to fighting older women both inflects and is inflected by the shift in cultural understandings of what oppresses women – not patriarchy, but the women who paved those roads the postfeminist action hero chases them on. In *Miss Congeniality*, FBI agent Gracie Hart (Sandra Bullock) is initially resistant to posing as a beauty pageant contestant in order to stop a murder: 'What could possibly motivate anybody to enter a beauty pageant? ... It's like feminism never even happened. Any woman that does this is catering to misogynistic Neanderthal mentality'. Although Gracie begins the film championing feminism and articulating a second wave critique of beauty pageants, after a makeover, and bonding with the contestants, she realises that she has been misinformed:

> ANNOUNCER: There are many who consider ... the Miss United States pageant to be outdated and antifeminist. What would you say to them?
>
> GRACIE: I used to be one of them. And then I came here and I realised that these women are smart, terrific people who are just trying to make a difference in the world. For me, this experience has been one of the most rewarding and liberating experiences of my life.

Gracie finds liberation and reward not in her work as an FBI agent, but in achieving the conventional (white, middle-class) femininity that eluded her until she was made over. It is post-makeover that Gracie finally gets the guy – who did not notice her until her heels were as high as her IQ. Moreover, the villain is not the male serial killer police initially suspected, but the older woman, Kathy Morningside (Candice Bergen), who created the pageant and guided the girls. As revenge for impending dismissal because the producers want a 'newer, hotter show', she has a bomb planted in the winner's crown. The threat to women has migrated from male violence to intergenerational, female jealousy. In this film, second wave feminism is as outdated and deadly as Kathy and postfeminism as new and hot as the made-over Gracie. Offering its action hero significant physical freedoms and an independent mind only to rein them in with makeovers and men, Gracie's transformation proves that even if you are a successful *action hero*, trading your sweats for couture and your single status for an arrogant man makes you a successful *woman*. Pointedly, the film works overtime to non-hierarchise what qualities make a heroic woman. Henry argues that in the focus on individualism, 'feminism has frequently been reduced to one issue: choice' (44). The contestants' choice to apply for scholarships via swimsuit in a pageant is celebrated *because* it is a choice and, as the conclusion makes explicit, femininity is power. In the end, young women do not need collective activism, they just need a sleepover so they can understand each other and respect each other's choices. In postfeminism, choice is so powerful that exercising it in any direction is empowering – whether choosing a lipstick or a political platform.

Charlie's Angels: Full Throttle similarly functions to distort second wave feminism from a diverse movement into monolithic victim feminism, encouraging a reading of feminism as outdated and, literally, a threat to national security. The villain is a former 1970s Angel, Madison (Demi Moore), who spouts feminist rhetoric and is tired of working for the man – in her case a literal man, Charlie. The young Angels first admire Madison. Upon meeting her, Natalie (Cameron Diaz) exclaims: 'I've heard so many stories about you! You're my favourite Angel!' The Angels acknowledge that they would not be Angels today if it were not for her, appearing to point to a valorisation of the work of the 1970s' Angels. When Madison is revealed as the villain, the Angels ask how she could turn against Charlie. Madison announces: 'I don't take orders from a speaker-box anymore. I work for myself'. While Madison paved the way for the younger Angels, she is villainised because she wants autonomy. The Angels ask Madison why she changed sides and she replies: 'Why be an Angel when I can play God?' In the postfeminist action film, power is a zero-sum game. In order for Madison/feminists to have power, she/they must take it away from the benevolent patriarch Charlie and his obedient Angels. Despite their initial admiration of Madison, when she reminds them of her accomplishments before their final showdown the Angels protest: 'We know already!' They are weary of hearing about how women fought – and need to continue to fight – for equality. When Charlie worries about his Angels, Madison acknowledges the complicity of women with patriarchy: 'I'm sure there's three more where they came from. You've never had trouble finding someone willing to give their life for you'. Charlie counters: 'Madison, you've never been able to accept that this agency is about teamwork. We're a family'. Madison interrupts: 'I've heard the sales pitch, it was very seductive. Once. But being an

Angel wasn't fulfilling my destiny it was keeping me from it'. In the patriarchy, teamwork is code for 'working for the Man'. The end of the film shows what the girl power generation can do if they work together: get rid of all traces of feminist history. It is the Angels who do Charlie's dirty work and kill Madison: Alex (Lucy Lui) yells 'She's so fired' and tosses Madison into a fiery pit. Clearly, women who articulate critiques of institutionalised sexism are not only unwelcome in the post-feminist sisterhood, but they literally need to go to hell.

One of the priorities of postfeminism is 'reclaiming' femininity – an odd project since second wave feminism was marked by a celebration of the feminine.[4] Where both the *Alien* and *Terminator* sequels hardened their female action heroes at the apex of 'muscular cinema' (Tasker 1), the postfeminist action hero is less hard body than hot body, combining conventional femininity and traditionally male activities. Yvonne Tasker argues that 'the pleasures of the action cinema are primarily those of spectacle rather than dialogue' (6). This emphasis on spectacle is borne out in *Lara Croft: Tomb Raider*, which fundamentally comprises four long action sequences. On the one hand, these sequences function to showcase Lara's (Angelina Jolie's) body, thus reinforcing a conventional configuration of the 'to-be-looked-at-ness' of woman within the cinematic (Mulvey 436). However, the spectacle that is privileged here is not just Lara's body, but her ability to use it to perform intense physical tasks. She is the driving force behind the action sequences and, in this way, Lara has agency, moving around dangerous spaces, outperforming the other characters and driving the plot. Her agency is, however, (re)incorporated as spectacle. The action heroine of the 1980s might have presented the muscular female body 'first and foremost as a functional body, a weapon' (Brown 56), but the postfeminist action hero underscores woman-as-spectacle. Unlike the 1980s action heroine, who was shot in ways which emphasised her muscles and not her (lack of) breasts, the camera focuses on three parts of Lara's body: breasts, thighs/groin and buttocks. The male action hero is objectified, but the camera focuses on his muscles, not his groin. Almost every shot of Lara is framed by her breasts and she keeps her guns strapped to her thighs, thus excusing countless thigh/groin shots. Lara is figured as a primarily sexualised object before subject.

In her discussion of the 1980s action heroine, Tasker notes that muscles 'become appropriated for the decoration of the *female* body' (142; emphasis in original). The postfeminist action hero, however, is neither masculinised nor muscularised – she is toned, not bulky. Rather, she is hyperfeminised – Jolie wore fake breasts and hair extensions for the role.

The postfeminist action hero is also distinguished from the 1980s action hero because she is a girl – a positioning which further counters the threat of her agency by offering the hope that she will 'settle down'. Lara's youthfulness is played up through costuming and she is infantilised through her relationship with her father (Jon Voight), whom she calls 'Daddy'. Likewise, the Angels wear Spiderman underwear, break out in dance routines and screech 'daddy!' at their fathers – imagine The Rock doing the same. Gracie snorts and stumbles, an awkward tomboy in a woman's body. Unlike the mature 1980s action heroine, the postfeminist action hero is young and girlish. 'As a girl who has not accepted the responsibilities of adult womanhood' (Tasker 15) there is the possibility that things will change when she does. The postfeminist action hero also sells traditional notions of women's power. Although she enjoys unlimited mobility in the public sphere she is reassuringly returned to the private sphere. Lara's first encounter with villains takes place in her home: as she performs a bungee ballet, they crash through her windows. This intrusion into her private sphere is the catalyst for her action. Lara's 'public' action is also motivated in the 'private' sphere through the father-daughter relationship; it is her (dead) father who authorises the quest (like Charlie authorises the Angels' quests and the male FBI director authorises Gracie's mission). Having pleased her father, Lara signals her exit from tomboyish girlhood into traditional 'womanhood' by appearing in the white dress she had earlier rebuffed, ready to embrace her role as Lady Croft. She picks up a gun, thus potentially destabilising this image but it is to battle with a robotic monster within the safety of the private sphere. She has been returned to playfully exercising her action within the confines of the private sphere and in the safety and marital index of a white dress. O'Day explains that the female action hero's masculine threat is allayed by 'stressing the heroine's sexuality and availability in conventional feminine terms' (203). The postfeminist action hero is not threatening because she is an impossible ideal – super beautiful, super sexy and super heroic: underscoring woman-as-spectacle.

These women's ability to occupy the role of hero, personify ideal femininity and move freely in the public and private spheres owes as much to their race and class as their athletic ability. When the postfeminist action hero is not white, she attains mobility only when her race is ignored. When her race is acknowledged, she is unable to occupy the role of hero and is either used as a foil to white femininity or her race is identified (indirectly) as the reason she cannot dominate both the public and private spheres as an action hero must. The disappearance of the black female action hero evinces not only the whitening of the genre but of feminism. Race and class occupy different places in third wave feminism and postfeminism. Third wave feminism is 'defined by the challenge that women-of-color feminists posed to white second wave feminism' (Heywood and Drake 1). While third wave feminism comes out of and retains the critique of race found in third world second wave feminisms, Postfeminism is exclusively a white, middle-class movement. Siegel critiques postfeminists' myopia: 'these authors position themselves as harbingers of a new order, a new order, that is, for middle-class, heterosexual, white women' (64). The postfeminist action film illustrates this 'new order' and the way that race and class are ignored, portrayed as exotic and/or marginalised. In the *Charlie's Angels* films, Alex's ethnicity is never mentioned and she never encounters racism, although she does assume costumes that reference such Asian stereotypes as the geisha girl, masseuse and dominatrix. She is whitened with a non-Asian last name (Lundy), a white boyfriend and a white father. In the Croft films, race is featured only in the the 'exotic' locales Lara visits where she receives help from locals who recognize her heroism. The one film which explicitly acknowledges race is *Miss Congeniality 2: Armed and Fabulous*. Gracie, now the face of the FBI and a 'role model for women' is teamed with a black female partner, Sam Fuller (Regina King). The move of the black woman from hero to buddy, from epitome of femininity to foil to white femininity, mirrors not only important generic shifts in action film, but also the movement of race from the centre to the periphery of popular feminism. The opposite of the passive black buddies exemplified by Martaugh (Danny Glover) in *Lethal Weapon* (1998), Sam is violent, angry and has such a bad attitude that no one will work with her.

In the male buddy film, the feminisation of the black buddy brings the (white) masculinity of the hero into sharper relief. In the female buddy film, Sam is initially masculinised only to be feminised through her relationship with Gracie. Sam is not only masculinised in both name and costume in order to assert Gracie's embodiment of (white) femininity, but Gracie even reprimands a weak male to be a man 'like Fuller'. Sam wears makeup and a dress when she is impersonating a drag queen: the black female's embodiment of femininity is not 'natural' and must be mediated through performance. Black femininity is not only in service of white femininity but Sam's role as Gracie's bodyguard further ensures that she protects (white) femininity with her life, just as in the male buddy film the black buddy 'ends up willingly sacrificing himself' (Tasker 36). This is a far cry from the Blaxploitation female action hero who valued and protected her own life. Like in the male buddy film in which 'racial difference is redistributed' (Willis 36), racial difference becomes the unspoken as femininity is positioned as the battleground between Sam and Gracie. After Sam saves Gracie (who saves Miss America), Gracie returns to work as an agent and their differences dissolve into a happy partnership. Further, the conclusion of the film presents a 'world beyond race' (Wiegman 140). Postfeminism similarly envisions a world where racial difference is reconciled without dialogue – where the only issue preventing racial harmony is women of colour's refusal to work their (girl) power. In the postfeminist action film, active femininity is limited to white heroes or heroes who ignore their race. This parallels the way that postfeminists are 'accepting' of racial/class difference, but are not concerned with it. The marketing of postfeminism has eclipsed the popularisation of third wave feminism and the focus on how the postfeminist action heroes embody feminism's achievements reifies the diversity of the contemporary feminist movement into the safety of postfeminism.

Third wave heroes?

The popularisation of girl power draws attention away from third wave feminism. Leslie Heywood and Jennifer Drake, amongst others, have highlighted how U.S. Third World feminisms, women of colour feminisms, working-class feminisms and queer feminisms are all integral to third wave feminism. 'A third wave goal that comes directly out of learning from these histories and working among these traditions is the development of modes of thinking that can come to terms with the multiple, constantly shifting bases of oppression' (Heywood and Drake 3). However, in the commodification of Girlie to girl power, this multiplicity is not taken up by postfeminists or the postfeminist action hero. In postfeminist discourse, women are empowered if they say they are – no matter what their choices – and their ability to say they are is proof enough that they are empowered. This circular logic dominates postfeminism. Although Naomi Wolf insists that 'every woman has the right to own herself' (127), bell hooks clarifies that 'the willingness to see feminism as a lifestyle choice rather than a political commitment reflects the class nature of the movement' (29). In a disturbing reversal of a second wave slogan, Karen Lehrman maintains that '[u]nder real feminism, women have ultimate responsibility for their problems, happiness, and lives. The personal, in other words, is no longer political' (5). Not only is the personal no longer political, in postfeminism, the personal is all that matters. Postfeminism and its action hero, along with other popular postfeminist texts, index a conservative agenda. Power feminism 'has been co-opted by the media and labeled *the* "new" feminism because it shores up competitive individualism, the American work ethic, consumerism, and catfighting, all in feminism's name' (Drake 107; emphasis in original). The postfeminist action hero works in tandem with the Manhattan singletons, reality bachelorettes and desperate housewives to articulate female empowerment as an individualised and personal act located in the 'achievement' of conventional femininity through consumerism.

The (white) postfeminist heroes have unlimited resources and depend on the right outfit to get the job done – which provides an opportunity to showcase the material goods that define a liberated woman. Postfeminism, which assumes that we are all on a level playing field, is the premise but girl power is the product. Susan Hopkins writes that 'Girl Power effectively encapsulates the newly aggressive and confident girl cultures – cultures which have been opened up for aggressive commodification ... (Post)feminism has been embraced as a fresh strategy for stimulating consumption' (3). Ultimately, the postfeminist action hero is limited by girl power's championing of feminism-by-purchase. Marketers have recognised that women will put money where 'liberation' appears. Girl power becomes synonymous with purchasing power. Wolf asserts that 'power feminism has little heavy base ideology beyond the overarching premise "More for women"' (138). Unfortunately, more of the same does not change anything and marketers have reified 'more' to more girl power products not equality. In the postfeminist action film, girls do not get heroes that reflect changing ideas of women's power because, as these films illustrate, ideas about women's power are not changing as much as they are being managed to look like they are. My concern is that these postfeminist action heroes provide images of an equality that has not been achieved and that they mitigate their viewers' interests in exploring inequalities. Despite the complex history between the female action film and feminism, and the way the female action film has offered at least a mitigated resistance to dominant gender norms, the postfeminist action film offers no resistance to white heteropatriarchy because it cannot: postfeminism, particularly the heavily marketed girl power, is complicit with maintaining the institutional structures of patriarchy by advocating personal change instead of critical activism. As Natasha Walter cautions: 'If we want to crack the powerlessness of women in this generation we must look not just at how women can change themselves, but also at how women can change the places in which they live and work' (71). But the postfeminist action heroes, like postfeminists, are not interested in that kind of work. Which is why, thirty years after second wave feminism, the patriarch Charlie can still accurately state about his postfeminist Angels: 'They have three things in common; they're brilliant, they're beautiful and they work for me'.

Notes

* For my mother, Vera, one of two women in the first Canadian police graduating class that assigned women to regular patrol duties.

1. *Interrogating Postfeminism: the Politics of Gender and Popular Culture* Conference, University of East Anglia, 2–3 Apr. 2004.
2. 'My guns are in the Fendi', Gracie Hart in *Miss Congeniality 2: Armed and Fabulous* (2005).
3. The publication of works by these women 'roughly coincides with the pronouncement by the mainstream media and by conservative pundits that we are living in a "postfeminist" era' (Siegel 75).
4. See Baumgardner and Richards (134–35) for more on the gynefocal aesthetic in second wave feminism.

Works cited

Baumgardner, Jennifer, and Amy Richards. *Manifesta: Young Women, Feminism, and the Future*. New York: Farrar, Straus and Giroux, 2000.

Braithwaite, Ann. 'The Personal, the Political, Third Wave, and Post Feminism.' *Feminist Theory: An International Interdisciplinary Journal* 3.3 (2002): 335–44.

Brown, Jeffrey A. 'Gender and the Action Heroine: Hardbodies and *The Point of No Return*.' *Cinema Journal* 35.3 (1996): 52–71.

Charlie's Angels. Dir. McG. Perf. Drew Barrymore, Lucy Liu, Cameron Diaz. Columbia Pictures, 2000.

Charlie's Angels: Full Throttle. Dir. McG. Perf. Drew Barrymore, Lucy Liu, Cameron Diaz. Columbia Pictures, 2003.

Drake, Jennifer. 'Review Essay: Third Wave Feminisms.' *Feminist Studies* 23.1 (1997): 97–108.

Faludi, Susan. *Backlash: The Undeclared War Against American Women*. New York: Crown Publishers, 1991.

Henry, Astrid. *Not My Mother's Sister: Generational Conflict and Third-Wave Feminism*. Bloomington: Indiana University Press, 2004.

Heywood, Leslie, and Jennifer Drake. Introduction. *Third Wave Agenda: Being Feminist, Doing Feminism*. Ed. Leslie Heywood and Jennifer Drake. Minneapolis: Minnesota University Press, 1997. 1–20.

Hollows, Joanne, and Rachel Moseley. *Feminism in Popular Culture*. Ed. Joanne Hollows and Rachel Moseley. Oxford/New York: Berg, 2006.

hooks, bell. *Feminist Theory: From Margin to Center*. 2nd Ed. Cambridge: South End Press, 2000.

Hopkins, Susan. *Girl Heroes: The New Force in Popular Culture*. Annadale: Pluto, 2002.

Inness, Sherrie. *Tough Girls: Women, Warriors and Wonder Women in Popular Culture*. Pittsburgh: University of Pennsylvania Press, 1999.

Lara Croft: Tomb Raider. Dir. Simon West. Perf. Angelina Jolie, Jon Voight, Iain Glen. Paramount, 2001.

Lara Croft Tomb Raider: The Cradle of Life. Dir. Jan de Bont. Perf. Angelina Jolie, Ciaran Hinds, Gerard Butler, Noah Taylor. Paramount, 2003.

Lehrman, Karen. *The Lipstick Proviso: Women, Sex and Power in the Real World*. New York: Doubleday, 1997.

Manzano, Angie. 'Charlie's Angels: Free-market Feminism.' *Off Our Backs* 30.11 (Dec. 2000): 10.

Mencimer, Stephanie. 'Violent Femmes.' *Washington Monthly* (Sept. 2001): 15–18.

Miss Congeniality. Dir. Donald Petrie. Perf. Sandra Bullock, Candice Bergen, Benjamin Bratt. Warner Bros., 2000.

Miss Congeniality 2: Armed and Fabulous. Dir. John Pasquin. Perf. Sandra Bullock, Regina King, William Shatner. Warner Bros., 2005.

Mulvey, Laura. 'Visual Pleasure and Narrative Cinema.' 1975. *Feminisms: An Anthology of Literary Theory and Criticism*. Ed. Robyn R. Warhol and Diane Price Herndl. New Brunswick: Rutgers University Press, 1993. 432–42.

O'Day, Marc. 'Beauty in Motion: Gender, Spectacle and Action Babe Cinema.' *Action and Adventure Cinema*. Ed. Yvonne Tasker. London: Routledge, 2004. 210–18.

Orr, Catherine M. 'Charting the Currents of the Third Wave.' *Third Wave Feminisms*. ed. Jacquelyn N. Zita. Spec. issue of *Hypatia: A Journal of Feminist Philosophy* 12.3 (1997): 29–45.

Siegel, Deborah L. 'Reading between the Waves: Feminist Historiography in a "Postfeminist" Moment.' *Third Wave Agenda: Being Feminist, Doing Feminism*. Ed. Leslie Heywood and Jennifer Drake. Minneapolis: Minnesota University Press, 1997. 55–82.

Tasker, Yvonne. *Spectacular Bodies: Gender, Genre and the Action Cinema*. New York: Routledge, 1993.

Walter, Natasha. *The New Feminism*. London: Virago, 1999.

Wiegman, Robyn. *American Anatomies*. Durham: Duke University Press, 1995.

Willis, Sharon. *High Contrast: Race and Gender in Contemporary Hollywood Films*. Durham: Duke University Press, 1997.

Wolf, Naomi. *Fire with Fire: The New Female Power and How to Use It*. Toronto: Vintage Books, 1994.

19
Sexing It Up?
Women, Pornography and Third Wave Feminism

Melanie Waters

In *Third Wave Agenda* (1997), Leslie Heywood and Jennifer Drake describe third wave feminism in terms of its engagement with the legacy of questions that have been overlooked, oversimplified or unresolved by the work of the second wave (1997, 23). There are few questions that present themselves to a new generation of feminist thinkers quite as forcefully as that of pornography. Despite the current reinvigoration of academic interest in the politics of pornographic representation – as well as the questions of sexuality, identity and personal autonomy that circulate around it – third wave feminism's contribution to the pornography debate remains largely unexcavated. In this chapter, I will analyse the vexed issue of pornography through the lens of contemporary feminist thought, evaluating the extent to which the diversified approach of third wave feminism might function as a corrective to 'prescriptive' second wave accounts of female sexuality and its construction within Western culture.

Given the third wave's 'links with political activism', which 'should ensure that [it] is more than just a theory, but an approach that will actively work against the social injustices which still form part of the everyday experiences of many women', its accentuation of individuality, diversity and plurality sometimes militates against the coherence of its political agenda (Gamble 2001, 53). This has led some critics to perceive contemporary, 'popular' feminism, with its ethic of liberal individualism, as a depoliticised movement. In *What Are We Fighting For?* (1998), for example, Joanna Russ contends that the voraciously political mode within which the feminism of the 1960s and 1970s tended to operate has been replaced in the 1990s by a feminism that places a disproportionate and depoliticised emphasis upon the personal lives of women. In this 'movement from activism to internal debate' (Whelehan 1995, 238) – epitomised by the third wave's unquestioned pro-porn stance and its proven endorsement of sexual confessionalism – some feminists have expressed concern that feminism's 'political edge' may have been lost (ibid.).

Defining pornography

Historically, the feminist pornography debates have been complicated by disputes over how pornographic materials might be objectively classified. At the radical edge of second wave feminism, Andrea Dworkin and Catherine MacKinnon famously described pornography as 'the graphic sexually explicit subordination of women, whether in pictures or in words' – a definition which formed the basis of the anti-pornography civil rights ordinance that they sought to pass in the 1980s (1988, 36).[1] More recently, however, feminist scholarship has worked to foreground the fluid dimensions of pornographic texts: as Drucilla Cornell argues in her introduction to *Feminism and Pornography* (2000), pornography is 'not one clearly designatable pedagogical object', but a 'dynamic construct' that is perpetually redefined in accordance with shifting socio-cultural mores and, to some extent, by ongoing debates within feminism concerning sexuality, identity, power, and censorship (1). A similar, if more comprehensive, account of pornography's categorical instability is found in *Hard Core* (1990), where Linda Williams finds that the mutation of the meaning of 'pornography' within and across cultures, combined with variations in the enforcement of censorship laws, significantly problematises the identification of a 'coherent' pornographic tradition (9–16).

Furthermore, given that the representational praxes of pornography are increasingly convergent with the aesthetic operations of Western visual cultures, the process of identifying pornographic materials is becoming evermore fraught. For Imelda Whelehan in *Overloaded* (2000), the conspicuous overlap of the popular and the pornographic is significant enough to dramatically reconfigure the shape of feminist responses to representations of female sexuality:

> [Many feminists now] feel that the boundaries defining what is pornography are too restrictive, and that there is a need to address the representation of women in more general terms since 'softer' images ... borrow conventions directly from porn and, arguably, tell us far more about the way the female body, and by extension femininity,

is used in society. Following on from this, some would prefer to deny porn its single-issue status by placing studies in relation to a wider consideration of how women are depicted and why. (2000, 31–32)

Whelehan's work, alongside that of Linda Williams, Drucilla Cornell, Lynne Segal, and Judith Butler, speaks to the need to extend the terms of the pornography debate beyond the perceived anti-porn/anti-censorship dialecticism that so forestalled second wave discussions of sexual representation. Although the third wave's reorientation of the pornography debate is clearly influenced by this recent feminist scholarship, it focuses less on the political implications of pornographic representation than on the personal ambivalences to which it gives rise. In this way, third wave feminism eschews the intricacies of the issues that pornography raises: instead of questioning what pornography *is*, it questions what pornography *does* – and how successful it is at doing it. This shift of emphasis from the political to the personal – as demonstrated in the third wave's emphatic valorisation of female sexual pleasure – marks out the extent to which the legacy of the second wave 'sex wars' has weighed upon contemporary conceptualisations of women's sexuality.

In order to evaluate this legacy, it is first necessary to examine the ways in which sexuality has been configured within the debates about pornography that have taken place within feminist circles since the 1960s. Whilst I have already alluded to second wave feminism's perceived 'anti-porn/anti-censorship dialecticism' in the previous paragraph, I am necessarily hesitant about the straightforward opposition that this characterisation implies. As many feminists have pointed out, after all, this account of the second wave woefully simplifies the complexity of feminist discussions about sexual representation, reducing a network of interlocking and divergent theories to a straightforward showdown between the sexual libertarians and their prudish counterparts (Whelehan 1995, 166). It is, however, this facile, mass-mediated version of second wave feminism, rifted along the lines of female sexuality, which has weighed most heavily upon third wave approaches to sexual representation. Premised on the assumption of pornography's acceptability to a generation of feminists who have grown up in the 1970s and 1980s, third wave feminism works to situate itself *beyond* second wave analyses of pornography. Still, in doing so, it falsely suggests that pornography has ceased to be relevant to contemporary feminism. At a time when the visual and textual vocabulary of pornography is being speedily absorbed into the West's cultural mainstream – within which 'the near-pornographic depictions of women and sex' are easily accessible through print, audio-visual, and technological media – third wave feminism's assessment of, and contribution to, the pornography debate seems long overdue (Whelehan 2000, 62). Whilst the third wave's apparent reluctance to directly address the politics of pornography might be understood in terms of the movement's progressive approach to sexuality, it is more clearly explicable through reference to the historically antagonistic relationship between second wave feminism and popular representation.

The spectre of radical feminism

In the contemporary Western imaginary, the radical, anti-pornography polemic of Andrea Dworkin and Catherine MacKinnon, which dominated feminist dialogues about sexuality throughout the late 1970s and early 1980s, has been popularly (mis)represented as the voice of the second wave. In *Pornography*, published in 1981, Dworkin attempts to install sexuality or, more accurately, *hetero*sexuality, as the originary source of all gender inequality: '[T]he power of sex manifested in action, attitude, culture, and attribute is the exclusive province of the male, his domain, inviolate and sacred. ... The woman is acted on; the man acts and through action expresses sexual power, the power of masculinity' (22–23). For Dworkin, as for MacKinnon, sexuality functions within patriarchal cultures as a unidirectional strategy of control, a way of maintaining a system of male privilege and female subordination. The pornographic text, with its bald, sexualised depictions of empowered masculinity, is, by extension, the site at which this strategy of control is most efficiently, and threateningly, expressed. As Lynne Segal argues, however, by 'reinscribing old patriarchal "truths" centred on the polarizing of male and female sexuality – his: predatory, genital, exploitative and dominating; hers: gentle, diffuse, nurturing and egalitarian' – this 'forceful feminist writing' runs contrary to the project of other, more liberal, feminisms and their various attempts to deconstruct the essentialising binary logic upon which patriarchy has, for so long, thrived (61).

Whilst the persuasive rhetoric of anti-pornography feminism usefully focalises the cultural eroticisation of violence against women, its automatic interpretation of all pornographic texts as evidence of patriarchy's misogynistic brutality has had the effect of obstructing open discussions around pornography's dynamic representational politics. '[A]ll pornography', MacKinnon argues, 'is made under conditions of inequality based on sex', and these conditions 'are *what it takes* to make women do ... pornography', even that which 'shows no overt violence' (103; emphasis in original). In the context of sexual inequality, then, female consent – let alone agency – is little more than false consciousness. Women cannot autonomously participate in the production or consumption of pornography, and if they claim to, then it is only because they are under the sway of a patriarchal ideology that seeks to indoctrinate and exploit them. This question of female agency – or, more specifically, anti-pornography feminism's vehement denial of its possibility – has been a mainstay of contemporary debates about sexuality and is still popularly conceptualised as the impasse at which feminist dialogues inevitably stall. For Nina Hartley, described in one third wave magazine as a 'fiercely feminist porn star' (Boob 1999b, 329), anti-pornography feminism's well-intentioned eagerness to understand female sex workers as victims has resulted in the disempowerment of women whose experiences do not cohere to this narrow outlook: 'MacKinnon really does feel like she is helping women, while at the same time, she and Dworkin and their ilk silence women. They won't listen to our stories, our truths. Somehow a woman's ability to tell her own story, to talk about her own life, the teller of her own truth, is a no-go' (ibid. 339). As Hartley here remarks, anti-pornography feminism is beset by a major contradiction: in the attempt to speak up for women who have been 'silenced' by pornography, Dworkin and MacKinnon inhibit the free speech of other women, or, when these women speak, simply deny the truths that they have to tell about their own experiences.

If the anti-pornography position is ideologically and analytically myopic, then it is also unapologetic in its divisive, judgemental politics: anti-censorship feminists, by refusing to accept the inexorable destructiveness of pornography, are often accused of being wholly complicit with operations of the sex industry. In an extreme example, MacKinnon warns that '[i]f pornography is part of your sexuality, then you have no right to your sexuality' (qtd. in Strossen 161). MacKinnon's verdict is based on the precarious assumption that pornography is passively consumed, that a woman's experience of pornography will always only confirm her status as a 'victim'. For Kegan Doyle and Dany Lacombe, a vital aspect of the third wave project lies in acknowledging the complex ways in which women (and men) interact with pornography: 'We must recognize that women actively consume mainstream porn – resisting, twisting, and sometimes subverting it. Mass culture does not simply victimize women, and anybody that claims it does belittles the vast majority of women, whose desires, fantasies, and subjectivities are irretrievably bound up in it'

(195–96). In the effort to deprive women who produce or consume pornography the right to their sexuality, MacKinnon, alongside other self-identifying anti-pornography feminists, pursues an unappealing politics of exclusion, and generates a scenario in which feminism – though never a monolithic movement – seems to fracture along the fault line of sexual representation.

(Mis)representing sex and feminism

Given the prescriptive dimensions of Dworkin and MacKinnon's reading of sexuality, from which any acknowledgement of its subversive potential are conspicuously absent, it is perhaps unsurprising that their approach to pornography is similarly inflexible; it is not merely a mode that represents, for the most part, the sexual debasement of women, but, as Dworkin explains, something 'real', 'objective' and 'central to the male system' (1981, 200–201). For MacKinnon,

> [t]he most elite denial of the harm is the one that holds that pornography is 'representation', when a representation is a nonreality. ... The effect is to license whatever is done there, creating a special aura of privilege and demarcating a sphere of protected freedom, no matter who is hurt. ... If, by contrast, representation *is* reality, as other theorists argue, then pornography is no less an act than the rape and torture it represents (107–108; emphasis in original).

Within the terms of this literalising manoeuvre, the 'representational' is awkwardly absorbed into the structures of the 'real'. Moreover, this 'real' is understood, and fixed, as the sexual degradation of women; a degradation in which the fact of women's socio-political and economic exploitation is perceived as being dramatically embodied. By stabilising women's oppression as the uniform 'real', anti-pornography feminism problematically elides the subversive potential of pornography: after all, if the 'victim' status of women is pornography's only possible referent, then its capacity to challenge conventional, gendered modes of sexual interaction through strategies of performance is necessarily suppressed.

It is this conflation of the real and the representational, and its political implications, with which Butler takes particular issue in 'The Force of Fantasy' (1990). Here, she argues that Dworkin and MacKinnon's attempts to control the representation of women through the blanket censorship of pornography are counter-productive: 'Feminist theory and politics cannot regulate the representation of "women" without producing that very "representation": and if that is in some sense a discursive inevitability of representational politics, then the task must be to safeguard the open productivity of those categories, whatever the risk' (504). Whilst Dworkin and MacKinnon advance censorship as the single valid feminist response to pornography, Butler believes that it 'can only displace and reroute the violence it seeks to forestall' by increasing the currency of the very images it is designed to suppress; after all, prohibition necessarily eroticises that which it purports to forbid (502).[2] Instead of censorship, then, Butler advocates a program of 'proliferation' as a countermeasure to the violent and/or sexual debasement of women in pornography. 'It is in the very proliferation and deregulation of such representations', she claims, 'that the authority and prevalence of the reductive and violent imagery produced by ... pornographic industries will lose ... the power to define and restrict the terms of political identity' (504). In other words, it is the *expansion* of the pornographic imaginary, rather than its constriction, that will elicit the displacement of dominant modes of sexual representation. As pornographic representations of male and/or female sexuality are allowed to proliferate, the diversity of these representations will summarily increase with the effect that the integrity and stability of all identity categories will be undermined. This, in Butler's view, will eventually give way to a scenario in which identity – and the power which may or may not be associated with it – will be understood in terms of its fluidity, not its fixity. Rather than singular, authoritative accounts of sexual identity there will develop, over time, 'multiple and open possibilities for identification' (503).

Butler's approach corresponds broadly to that of Pamela Church Gibson and Roma Gibson, the editors of *Dirty Looks*, a landmark collection of essays published in 1993. Described by critics as heralding 'a paradigm shift in feminist responses to pornography' (Gibson and Gibson, back matter) the essays mark a deliberate break with the anti-porn/anti-censorship binarism, foregrounding instead the complexity and ambiguity of the issues that surround sexual representation, and arguing, like Butler, for more context-based analyses of pornographic texts. By situating women as both producers and consumers of sexually explicit materials, moreover, *Dirty Looks* introduces the factor of female pleasure into the pornography debate: the relationship between women and pornography is no longer understood as immobile and invariable, but as diverse and dynamic. Released in 2004, the second edition of *Dirty Looks* – entitled *More Dirty Looks* – works to focalise the diversity within pornographic representation and sexual response yet further. Alongside essays from the original collection exploring the construction of sadomasochism, cybersex, trans-vestism and masculinity within the pornographic imaginary, the new collection features academic analyses of gay, non-Western and internet pornographies, which roundly undermine the heterosexist assumptions upon which the arguments of anti-pornography lobbyists rely.

Whilst many third wave feminists might subscribe to the logic that underpins the essays in the *Dirty Looks* volumes – placing similarly heavy emphases on sexual diversity, the politics of representation and issues of personal pleasure – they are simultaneously resistant to the aca-demic prose style that characterises these works. In an attempt to make feminism accessible to a majority of women, therefore, third wave accounts of pornography have openly eschewed the 'exclusive and elab-orate professional jargon' of the academy in favour of more anecdotal narrative modes (Wolf 1993, 125). If this strategy was originally intended to function as a corrective to the 'exclusive' theoretical discourses of earlier feminisms, then its success is limited by the fact that confessional writing – however readable – does, in this context, give the impression that 'feminism is about how the individual feels right here, right now, rather than the bigger picture' (Viner 22). It is the 'bigger picture' that is at stake in many third wave accounts of pornography, in which pornography tends to be valorised or dismissed on the basis of its capac-ity to generate personal arousal, and not as a result of its political implications.

Female sexuality and the third wave

Described in a collection of articles from its first six years as '[b]oth a literary magazine and a chronicle of girl culture' *BUST* was launched by editors Marcelle Karp and Debbie Stoller in 1993 and is now routinely cited as evidence of third wave feminism's popular presence (back matter). In its emphatic focus on all things 'girlie', *BUST* strives to reconstruct feminism 'for a culture-driven generation' (Baumgardner and Richards 2000, 134). As Jennifer Baumgardner and Amy Richards explain in *Manifesta*, 'Girlie encompasses the tabooed symbols of women's femi-nine enculturation – Barbie dolls, makeup, fashion magazines, high heels – and says that using them isn't shorthand for "we've been duped"' (136). More pertinently, however, the girlie brand of feminism that *BUST* promotes is seen to constitute an important 'rebellion against the false impression that since women don't want to be sexually exploited, they don't want to be sexual; against the necessity of brass-buttoned, red-suited seriousness to infiltrate a man's world; against the anachronistic belief that because women could be dehumanized by porn ... they must be; and the idea that girls and power don't mix' (137). As sexuality and its various expressive modes figure prominently within third wave feminism, so these issues occupy positions of similar importance within the pages of *BUST*. This is confirmed by the contents page of *The* BUST *Guide to the New Girl Order* (1999), a collection of writings from the first six years of BUST magazine, which features titles including 'Me and My Cunt', 'More Than a Blow Job: It's a Career', 'How to Be as Horny as a Guy' and the interview with the porn star Nina Hartley discussed above. In their magazine form these articles, as Baumgardner and Richards have noted, are 'juxtaposed with buxom images from vintage soft-core porn, images now in the control of women'. In this way, they argue, porn is 'demystified, claimed for women, debated' (133). Rather than standing as evidence of *BUST's* facilitation of feminist discussions about pornography, however, the magazine's use of soft-core, 'cutesy' imagery suggests precisely the opposite; that the debate has already happened, and that a pro-porn, pro-sex stance has been adopted as third wave feminism's default position.

Whilst Stoller recognises in 'Sex and the Thinking Girl' that feminism has made, and still needs to make, huge advances in terms of increasing employment opportunities for women, she suggests that we temporarily 'set aside' the problem of gendered income differentials in favour of addressing 'an orgasm gap ... that hasn't budged since the days when *Donna Reed* actually believed that *Father Knows Best*' (76). With this clear prioritisation of female sexual pleasure comes an emphasis on practice over theory; an emphasis that tends to typify these types of third wave texts: 'In our quest for sexual satisfaction', Stoller claims, 'we shall leave no sex toy unturned and no sexual avenue unexplored' (84). In foregrounding pleasure over the *politics* of pleasure, third wave feminism edges away from the discursive, theoretical engagements which, as I have already established, are now inextricable from popular conceptualisations of the second wave. This process of distancing is, to some extent, the result of the third wave's attempt to make feminism more agreeable to a generation of young women who have been fed the myth that feminists are the fat, man-hating, no-fun lesbians to whom Whelehan refers, and who are not, besides this unappealing stereotype, convinced of the movement's continued relevance. Distinguishing this revamped version of feminism from that of her feminist 'foremothers', Stoller promises that third wavers do not dare to assume that they 'know what "female sexuality" is all about', and are therefore unwilling to make judgements about the appropriateness of its manifestations (84).

As one contributor to *BUST* puts it, 'if it feels good downstairs and no one gets hurt, girlfriend, fuck morals' (Lust 109). Inclusive and non-judgmental though this feminism is, it nonetheless promotes an ethic of acceptance that is hostile to the flourishing of politicised feminist debate.

Given Stoller's ideologically unfettered approach to the pursuit of erotic fulfilment, it is perhaps unsurprising that the 'sexual avenue' of pornography is regarded as one that can be accessed freely and without guilt: 'We don't have a problem with pornography, unless, of course, it doesn't turn us on. With X-rated movies available for rent at every local video store and Hooters considered a family restaurant, we realize that American porn culture is here to stay' (84). Here, the overwhelming ubiquity of explicit imagery is the pretext upon which feminist objections to pornography are abandoned. Because pornography is everywhere, because it has made the successful transition from the marginal to the mainstream, it is no longer functional as a site of feminist protest. Whilst this gesture of dismissal would seem to imply that pornography has changed its ways by 'correcting' and/or diversifying its approach to female sexuality, this is categorically not so. Rather, Stoller's refusal to acknowledge the continued contentiousness of pornography speaks to the third wave's desperation to expel the spectre of anti-pornography feminism from the contemporary landscape and claim pornography as a site of female empowerment: instead of 'trying to rid the world of sexual images we think are negative, we're far more interested in encouraging women to explore porn, to find out whether it gets them hot or merely bothered' (82). Contradicting the empowering claims that she makes on behalf of pornography, however, Stoller goes on to acknowledge that it is still 'ruthlessly sexist', containing 'very little in it to appeal to women' (82). If this is the case, then surely feminists have not yet reached the point at which they can claim, unequivocally, that they 'don't have a problem with pornography'? With porn culture and its 'ruthlessly sexist' imagery 'here to stay', the questions and ambivalences that it raises are, if anything, more pressing than ever.

Pornographic confessionalism?

Although a number of third wave feminists identify pornography as a site of sexual complexity that forces women to interrogate the politics of their own desire, these observations are organised, almost exclusively, into personal confessions that speak to the vagaries of individual pleasure but often shy away from its broader implications. Whilst the validity of this confessional work is not in question – these confessions do, after all, address the ambiguities of female sexuality in very powerful ways – the focus of these works is, in many cases, problematically narrow. Merri Lisa Johnson is closely attuned to the problems that self-disclosure has presented to feminists in her introduction to *Jane Sexes It Up* (2002), where she argues that the confessional writing of 'sex–positive spokeswomen' is 'often anti-intellectual in tone' and has so far failed 'to give women new ways of thinking about fucking, new ways of understanding what's happening in our beds and in our bodies'. In her view, however, it is still 'individual women's stories, narrow in scope and deep in reflection' that 'aid in advancing the complexity of feminist social theory' (5). Johnson is confident that her collection, subtitled *True Confessions of Feminist Desire*, provides a useful corrective to these other 'anti-intellectual' discourses about sexuality. Her explicit designation of the contributions to her volume as 'confessions' at once invokes and exploits the complex relationship between confession, intimacy, sexuality and feminine forms of expression in Western culture. Historically, confession has played a vital role in the development of women's writing: letters and diaries, with their heavy reliance on acts of confession are, in Shari Benstock's theorisation, 'private modes of writing [that are] commonly associated with women' (254). As I have already hinted, confession is also, perhaps paradoxically, a staple of the pornographic text. Johnson's explicit synthesis of 'confession' and 'feminist desire' thus gestures towards discrete traditions of female and pornographic representation, whilst reconstructing the terms of these representational fields as definitively 'feminist'.

In a 2002 collection of feminist writing entitled *Inappropriate Behaviour*, 'po-faced feminist analysis' is conspicuously discarded in favour of 'humour and attitude'; a prioritisation that is particularly discernible in the essays that deal with female sexual desire (qtd. in Redfern, par. 8). One of the most startling chapters in this collection is entitled 'Squiddly Diddly' and purports to theorise 'the relationship of the octopus to female sexuality'. Despite its attempts to contextualise 'octopus sex' in relation to rape fantasies, phallic symbolism and 'the thrill of the perverse', Penny Birch's essay makes sense primarily as an intimate confession, inspired by the force of her personal erotic fantasies: 'I imagine that having a live squid in my vagina would be quite an experience, but it's not really fair on the squid' (37). Similarly, in 'Bullets for Broads' from the same collection, Katherine Gates and a handful of female interviewees admit to a sexual fascination with guns and describe their involvement in erotic gunplay. 'Bonnie', a 'prominent bisexual West Coast SM player' relates an experience with her female lover in the following way: 'I have my left hand in her cunt and she's wrapped around my hand, and I reach for her weapon. It's loaded. ... I put the muzzle in my mouth. And she's looking into my eyes. Not wavering, not blinking, and neither defiant nor fearful. And without blinking she looks up and undoes the safety' (Gates 147, 150). Undeniably, this type of writing works to break some of the cultural taboos that stubbornly circulate around female sexuality. More interestingly, however, these texts not only deal in a subject matter that is broadly classifiable as pornographic, but also take recourse to pornography's favoured discursive mode: confession. By describing sexual experiences and fantasies in their own words, but in an established pornographic rhetoric, it might be argued that the authors of these works successfully utilise the tools by which anti-pornography feminists claimed women were oppressed in order to subvert the gendered power differentials that were suspected to underlie this oppression. In the case of 'Bullets for Broads', Bonnie's confession – although 'violent' in the strict sense – is one of lesbian desire, and as such it is not easily explicable in terms of Dworkin and MacKinnon's account of pornography, in which sexual violence is inexorably tethered to *male* fantasies of heterosexual domination. These short essays thus unsettle gendered theorisations of sexual dominance and submission that either equate femininity to erotic passivity or, when it takes a more 'feminist' form, aggression. According to Amy Richards, these 'feminist' sexual confessions exemplify the third wave's valorisation of sexual plurality. Positing this as a corrective to second wave feminism's indexical approach to female sexuality, Richards opines that now 'there's more than one way to be sexual. Historically, there was only one way, at least it was perceived that way, and that's what people were resisting. And I think now there are many ways to be sexual – athleticism is sexy, different body types are sexy, androgyny is sexy' (Richards qtd. in Strauss, par. 20).

Even if feminist disclosures of the type found in *BUST* or *Inappropriate Behaviour* are subversive, the impact of these texts beyond the third wave community is surely negligible. Although in Richards's view 'there are many ways to be sexual' and 'different body types are sexy', her conviction is not supported by evidence in the popular media. As Naomi Wolf asserts in *The Beauty Myth* (1990), it is images of the 'gaunt, youthful model' of femininity that preside over Western visual space. This 'beauty pornography' – which 'artificially links a commodified "beauty" directly and explicitly to female sexuality' – has 'invaded the mainstream to undermine women's new and vulnerable sense of sexual self-worth' (11). If there are places in which it is okay to be athletic or androgynous or merely 'different', then they do not seem to be in mainstream popular culture where, according to Wolf, thinness, whiteness and youth are relentlessly upheld as the primary constituents of female 'beauty' and sexual desirability. Here, then, the empowered rhetoric of third wave feminism often rings a little hollow.

Within third wave feminism, pornography functions problematically in relation to these questions of sexual desirability, representation and female self-esteem. Whilst the optimistic, 'empowered' rhetoric of Richards rings a little hollow in the midst of such arguments, some third wavers have tried to address the representational complexities of pornography through (yet further) reference to personal experience. For Marcelle Karp, writing as 'Betty Boob' in 'Betty and Celina Get Wired', pornography – or, more specifically, 'femme porn' – provides a space in which mainstream versions of sexual desirability might be contested. Flouting the third wave's usual ethic of acceptance, Karp blasts that she does not 'hate' the women who appear in girl-on-girl scenes like she hates models 'who are freaks of nature'. For her, 'the bodies of porn stars are specifically designed for aesthetically stimulating pleasure. These chicks are short, tall, white, black, bleached; they're natural, flat, siliconed beyond belief. ... Each lady is sculpted in her own special way' (91). Although Karp's account is wholly subjective, and her observations unsupported by any point of reference beyond personal opinion, its presentation of pornography as a democratic form of representation seems to demand a more comprehensive, informed analysis. Perhaps it is the very fact of Karp's bold claims, unconfirmed by theory or evidence and described as personal digressions, that demonstrates the problem with the third wave's eschewal of pornographic politics. Without a social or political context, feminist statements about pornography and its effects are destined to be dismissed as little more than personal conjecture. In 'Fear of a Black Cat', Doreen Hinton, writing under the pseudonym 'Hapa Wahine', responds to the evacuation of racial diversity from the pornography of her youth, in which 'all [vaginas] were generally of the same size, shape, symmetry, and perfect shade of pink'. The absence of other Black and Asian women from the popular pornographic imaginary has perpetuated myths about non-white genitalia, 'from Asian women having horizontal vaginal openings to Black women having an unusual amount of sweat glands so as to produce an inordinate amount of stench' (114). Although Hinton eschews political contextualisation in favour of personal lamentation, it is fair to say that her short essay gestures towards the types of political discourses that might arise from a third wave reinvigoration of the pornography debate.

Whilst the relationship between the personal and the political has always been characterised by tensions, the recognition of these tensions has played a key role in advancing and complicating feminist arguments. If third wave feminism is to contribute to ongoing discussions within feminism, then it must first engage with and examine these tensions, instead of assuming that the delineation of personal experience is always and automatically a political act. Essentially, then, third wave articulations of sexual desire or experience require a context: in order for these texts to have any political impact at all, the reader needs to have some sense of why they have been written; how they intersect with, and diverge from, other feminist theory or praxis; what the broader implications of the desires or experiences they detail might be. It is in this way that third wave feminism might begin to acknowledge the continued relevance of pornography to discussions of sexuality, and to take account of its role in reflecting and shaping contemporary gender identities.

Notes

1. For more information on the anti-pornography civil rights ordinances see Dworkin, 'Against the Male Flood' (1994) and Dworkin and MacKinnon, *In Harm's Way* (1998).
2. For Butler 'limits are, in a sense, what fantasy loves most, what it incessantly thematizes and subordinates to its own aims' (493).

Works cited

Baumgardner, Jennifer, and Amy Richards. *Manifesta: Young Women, Feminism, and the Future.* New York: Farrar, Strauss and Giroux, 2000.

Benstock, Shari. 'Afterword: The New Woman's Fiction.' *Chick Lit: The New Woman's Fiction.* Ed. Suzanne Ferris and Mallory Young. London: Routledge, 2005. 253–56.

Birch, Penny. 'Squiddly Diddly: The Relationship of the Octopus to Female Sexuality.' *Inappropriate Behaviour: Prada Sucks and Other Demented Descants.* Ed. Jessica Berens and Kerri Sharp. London: Serpent's Tail, 2002. 29–38.

Boob, Betty [Marcelle Karp]. 'Betty and Celina Get Wired: Part I: Betty's Story.' *The BUST Guide to the New Girl Order.* Ed. Marcelle Karp and Debbie Stoller. London: Penguin, 1999a. 88–93.

——. 'She's Gotta Have It: An Interview with Nina Hartley.' *The BUST Guide to the New Girl Order.* Ed. Marcelle Karp and Debbie Stoller. London: Penguin, 1999b. 329–40.

Butler, Judith. 'The Force of Fantasy: Feminism, Mapplethorpe, and Discursive Excess.' 1990. *Feminism and Pornography.* Ed. Drucilla Cornell. Oxford: Oxford University Press, 2000. 487–508.

Cornell, Drucilla. Introduction. *Feminism and Pornography.* Ed. Drucilla Cornell. Oxford: Oxford University Press, 2000. 1–18.

Doyle, Kegan, and Dany Lacombe. 'Porn Power: Sex, Violence, and the Meaning of Images in 1980s Feminism.' *Bad Girls/Good Girls: Women, Sex and Power in the Nineties*. Ed. Nan Bauer Maglin and Donna Perry. New Brunswick: Rutgers University Press, 1996. 188–204.

Dworkin, Andrea. 'Against the Male Flood: Censorship, Pornography, and Equality.' 1994. *Feminism and Pornography*. Ed. Drucilla Cornell. Oxford: Oxford University Press, 2000. 19–38.

——. *Pornography: Men Possessing Women*. London: Women's Press, 1981.

Dworkin, Andrea, and Catherine A. MacKinnon. *In Harm's Way: The Pornography Civil Rights Hearings*. Cambridge: Harvard University Press, 1998.

——. *Pornography and Civil Rights*. Minneapolis: Organizing Against Pornography, 1988.

Gamble, Sarah. 'Postfeminism.' *The Routledge Companion to Feminism and Postfeminism*. Ed. Sarah Gamble. London: Routledge, 2001. 43–54.

Gates, Katherine. 'Bullets for Broads.' *Inappropriate Behaviour: Prada Sucks and Other Demented Descants*. Ed. Jessica Berens and Kerri Sharp. London: Serpent's Tail Publishing, 2002. 139–52.

Gibson, Pamela Church, ed. *More Dirty Looks: Gender, Pornography and Power*. London: British Film Institute, 2004.

Gibson, Pamela Church, and Roma Gibson, eds. *Dirty Looks: Women, Pornography, Power*. London: British Film Institute, 1993.

Heywood, Leslie, and Jennifer Drake. Introduction. *Third Wave Agenda: Being Feminist, Doing Feminism*. Ed. Leslie Heywood and Jennifer Drake. Minneapolis: Minnesota University Press, 1997. 1–24.

Johnson, Merri Lisa. 'Jane Hocus, Jane Focus.' *Jane Sexes It Up: True Confessions of Feminist Desire*. Ed. Merri Lisa Johnson. New York: Thunder's Mouth Press, 2002. 1–11.

Karp, Marcelle, and Debbie Stoller, eds. *The BUST Guide to the New Girl Order*. London: Penguin, 1999.

Lust. 'One Sick Puppy.' *The BUST Guide to the New Girl Order*. Ed. Marcelle Karp and Debbie Stoller. London: Penguin, 1999. 109–12.

MacKinnon, Catherine A. 'Only Words.' *Feminism and Pornography*. Ed. Drucilla Cornell. Oxford: Oxford University Press, 2000. 94–120.

Redfern, Catherine. Rev. of *Inappropriate Behaviour: Prada Sucks and Other Demented Descants*. Ed. Jessica Berens and Kerri Sharp. *The F-Word: Contemporary UK Feminism*. 16 June 2002. Accessed: 31 May 2006. <http://www.thefword.org.uk/reviews/2002/06/inappropriate_behaviour_prada_sucks_and_other_demented_descants>.

Russ, Joanna. *What Are We Fighting For?: Sex, Race, Class, and the Future of Feminism*. New York: St. Martin's Press, 1998.

Segal, Lynne. 'Only the Literal: The Contradictions of Anti-Pornography Feminism.' *More Dirty Looks: Gender, Pornography and Power*. Ed. Pamela Church Gibson. London: British Film Institute, 2004. 59–70.

Stoller, Debbie. 'Sex and the Thinking Girl.' *The BUST Guide to the New Girl Order*. Ed. Marcelle Karp and Debbie Stoller. London: Penguin, 1999. 75–84.

Strauss, Tamara. 'Lipstick Feministas.' *MetroActive*. 29 Nov. 2000. Accessed: 31 May 2006. <http://www.metroactive.com/papers/cruz/11.29.00/feminism-0048.html>.

Strossen, Nadine. *Defending Pornography*. New York: Scribner, 1995.

Viner, Katharine. 'The Personal is Still Political.' *On the Move: Feminism for a New Generation.* Ed. Natasha Walter. London: Virago, 2000. 10–26.

Wahine, Hapa [Doreen Hinton]. 'Fear of a Black Cat.' *The* BUST *Guide to the New Girl Order.* Ed. Marcelle Karp and Debbie Stoller. London: Penguin, 1999. 113–14.

Whelehan, Imelda. *Modern Feminist Thought: From the Second Wave to 'Post-Feminism.'* Edinburgh: Edinburgh University Press, 1995.

——. *Overloaded: Popular Culture and the Future of Feminism.* London: Women's Press, 2000.

Williams, Linda. *Hard Core: Power, Pleasure, and the 'Frenzy of the Visible.'* London: Pandora Press, 1990.

Wolf, Naomi. *The Beauty Myth.* London: Vintage, 1990.

——. *Fire with Fire: The New Female Power and How It Will Change the 21st Century.* London: Chatto and Windus, 1993.

20

'Wake Up and Smell the Lipgloss'
Gender, Generation and the (A)politics of Girl Power
Rebecca Munford

> In *BUST*, we've captured the voice of a brave new girl: one that
> is raw and real, straightforward and sarcastic, smart and silly,
> and liberally sprinkled with references to our own Girl Culture –
> that shared set of female experiences that includes Barbies and
> blowjobs, sexism and shoplifting, *Vogue* and vaginas ... So wake
> up and smell the lipgloss, ladies: The New Girl Order has
> arrived.
>
> (Karp and Stoller xiv–xv)

*   *   *

In her discussion of 'girl power' in *The Whole Woman* (1999), Germaine
Greer laments the 'catastrophic career of "girls", "girls behaving badly",
"girls on top"' (399). Beginning with the Buffalo Girl, Vivienne
Westwood, Greer maps out a lineage of career girls, through Madonna,
Courtney Love and Björk, who have acted as figureheads for 'succeeding
generations of aggressively randy, hard-drinking young females, who
have got younger with every passing year, until they are now emerging
in their pre-teens' (400). Having denounced the 'relentless enculturation'
(92) and stereotypes of female passivity and modesty to which girls were
subjected three decades earlier in *The Female Eunuch* (1970), here she
identifies an equally, if not more, insidious form of indoctrination in the
construction and marketing of 'girl power' – that is, of the paraphernalia of *sexualised* femininity – to girls and young women by the media.
'The propaganda machine that is now aimed at our daughters is more
powerful than any form of indoctrination that has ever existed

before ... To deny a woman's sexuality is certainly to oppress her but to portray her as nothing but a sexual being is equally to oppress her' (410–11). The trajectory of Greer's analysis thus highlights a discursive shift from the decorous 'good girl' to the sexually aggressive 'bad girl' in popular constructions of girlhood and its representations – a Madonna/whore dichotomy that is all too familiar.

Like Greer, many feminist critics have been quick to position 'girl power' and its 'bad girl' icons as a form of popularised post-feminism – a depoliticised product of 'backlash' rhetoric (Faludi 14).[1] The extent to which girl power might be understood as a post-feminist discourse is substantiated by the ways in which its purported icons have perceptibly distanced themselves from the political agendas of second wave feminism. Advocating 'girl power' as a popular philosophy based on the virtues of Thatcherism and the Wonder Bra, the Spice Girls, for example, offer a simultaneous extrication from, and identification with, feminism in their 1997 autobiography *Girl Power!*: 'feminism has become a dirty word. Girl Power is just a nineties way of saying it. We can give feminism a kick up the arse' (The Spice Girls 48). As Imelda Whelehan has remarked, at the same time as offering an ostensible, albeit vague, nod to their feminist inheritance, the Spice Girls are complicit with the view that 'feminism (or feminists) deserve a kick up the arse – rather than the anti-feminists and backlashers who made the word dirty in the first place' (45). In the U.K., the girl power mantle has been picked up, somewhat awkwardly, by Girls Aloud, the winners of reality television show *Popstars: The Rivals* in 2002. In an interview for *Observer Magazine* in July 2003, Barbara Ellen asked the members of the band whether they would describe themselves as 'feminists'. She recalls: 'For the first time in the interview, five faces look totally blank. "We're girls' girls," says Kimberley, eventually. "But we're not feminists, we're not man-haters or anything"' (par. 11). Not even the 'nod' to a feminist inheritance imparted by the Spice Girls, the baffled silence offered by Girls Aloud betrays girl power's propinquity with anti-feminist sentiment. In such articulations, then, 'girl power' is positioned as 'a postfeminist movement, in the sense of coming after and perhaps overcoming feminism' (Hopkins 2). In its popular configuration, it volunteers an updated replacement for – and displacement of – second wave feminism.[2]

Nevertheless, this understanding of girl power as post-feminism – in both Greer's account and the Spice Girls' vapid championing of the slogan – conflates mass-mediated representations and celebrations of the 'bad girl' with the eclectic manifestations of girl culture that have been central to self-proclaimed third wave feminists' formulations and contestations of (post-)feminist identities since the beginning of the 1990s. As Jennifer Baumgardner and Amy Richards – journalists, activists and advocates of girl culture – describe:

> The Third Wave of the movement doesn't have an easily identifiable presence but, if you're looking, you can't help running into hubs that are unique to this generation. ... All are expanding feminism, and reclaiming the word *girl*, but in very different ways. (79–80; emphasis in original)

For in spite of its homogenised media representation – too frequently metonymically represented by the Spice Girls' brand of 'girl power' – girl culture is a far more eclectic and politically grounded phenomenon. In addition to the Third Wave Foundation and the San Francisco-based Young Women's Work Project, Baumgardner and Richards identify the writers of zines such as *Bitch, BUST* and *HUES* as well as female musicians including the Riot Grrrls, Queen Latifah, Courtney Love and Me'shell Ndege'ocello as occupying part of that intersection of culture and contemporary feminism called 'Girlie' (135–36). While second wave feminist critiques, exemplified by that of Greer above, have foregrounded the ways in which popular culture disseminates hegemonic gender representations, third wave feminists have refocalised the traditionally fraught relationship between feminism and popular culture to re-examine the politics of subjectivity. This re-examination often includes a celebration of popular modes of femininity, including 'the tabooed symbols of women's feminine enculturation – Barbie dolls, makeup, fashion magazines, high heels – and says using them isn't shorthand for "we've been duped" ' (Baumgardner and Richards 136). For these young women the discursive shift from the patriarchal 'good girl' to the post-feminist 'bad girl' is not so clearly demarcated. Rather, these opposing identities foreground the instability and contradiction of patriarchal definitions of femininity[3] – as well as the 'tyranny of expectation' (Steinem xiv) imposed by their second wave foremothers.

Nevertheless, third wave feminists' attention to, and engagement with, the popular has been dismissed as a privileging of style over politics – of individual over collective empowerment.[4] What is entangled in third wave formulations of girl identity, and mirrored in Greer's concerns about '[t]he propaganda machine that is now aimed at *our daughters*' (emphasis added), therefore, is the trope of mother-daughter conflict. As Shelley Budgeon describes: '[t]he consequences of generational difference for a unified feminist movement are often framed within the context of an antagonistic relationship between younger and older women in which references are made to "bad daughters" and "lifestyle" feminists vs "victim" feminism' (11). Foregrounding on the one hand a slippage between mainstream notions of post-feminism and third wave feminism and, on the other, an intergenerational dialogue between second and third wave feminisms, this chapter interrogates the politics of gender and generation in two key manifestations of third wave 'girl power' in Western culture – Riot Grrrl and Girlie. In so doing, it will locate girl culture as a crucial site for an interrogation of the ways in which young women are negotiating the tensions between individual and collective empowerment to en/gender feminist identities within and against dominant (post-)feminist discourses.

Third wave grrrls: 'Revolution girl-style, now'

Although the term 'girl power' entered the mainstream popular cultural imagination with the arrival, in 1996, of the Spice Girls in Britain, it had been coined some years previously by members of U.S. Riot Grrrl – 'a recent young feminist (sub)cultural movement that combines feminist consciousness and punk aesthetics, politics and style' (Garrison 142).[5] Through the circulation of girl-centred zines (for example, *Riot Grrrl* and *Girl Germs*) and the creation of all-female record labels (for example, Ani DiFranco's Righteous Babe Records), the 'do-it-yourself' ethos of early Riot Grrrl challenged conventional conceptualisations of the necessarily gendered relationship between (male) production and (female) consumption within the corporate music industry. Ednie Kaeh Garrison, for example, explores the ways in which the members of Riot Grrrl deploy democratised technologies to 'produce hybrid political texts such as zines and music through which they disseminate knowledge and information about subjects such as (but not limited to) feminism in local-national distribution networks' (144). Thus, Riot Grrrl provides a response to dominant representations of patriarchal girlhood by forging spaces in which girls and young women are empowered to resist and, moreover, to produce their own self-representations.

In foregrounding age as a key signifier of difference in formulations and understandings of young feminists' identities, Riot Grrrl, however, not only points up a politics of gender, but also of generation. Riot Grrrl might be influenced by both punk and feminism but it is also, as one of the contributors to *Riot Grrrl* 5 (1993) writes, 'about *not* being the girlfriend of the band and *not* being the daughter of the feminist' (qtd. in Duncombe 66; emphasis added).[6] Central to its pro-girl ethos is a reclamation of girlhood as a space from which to negotiate speaking positions for girls and young women whose experiences and desires are marginalised by the ontological and epistemological assumptions of a feminism that speaks for them under the universalising category of 'woman'.[7] Mary Celeste Kearney proposes that in order to readdress the contradictions of female adolescence 'riot grrrls appropriate the accoutrements of girlhood, femininity, and alternative youth culture for an ironic (dis)play and disruption of the signifying codes of gender *and generation*' (158; emphasis added). Here, the aesthetics of style proffer a response not only to the misrepresentations of patriarchal girlhood, but also to what is often perceived as the rigidity of second wave identity politics. This notion that young women's 'paradoxical identity with traditional feminism began in childhood' (Klein 208) is borne out by the model of hybridity and contradiction vital to the 'kinderwhore' aesthetic propounded by Courtney Love, a grrrl icon who was embraced by third wave feminists both inside and outside of the Riot Grrrl movement prior to her Versace 'outing' in 1997. Leslie Heywood and Jennifer Drake, for example, position Love's transgressive performance of femininity in the 1990s as emblematic of the contradictions brought together by third wave feminism.

> Glamorous and grunge, girl and boy, mothering and selfish, put together and taken apart ... Love bridges the irreconcilability of individuality and femininity within dominant culture, combining the cultural critique of an earlier generation of feminists with the backlash against it by the next generation of women. (1997a, 5)

In this respect, Love's performance of 'ironic femininity' is highlighted as decentring dominant configurations of both patriarchal femininity (across the Madonna/whore binary) and feminist identity (across the victim/power dichotomy).

Insofar as this playful reconfiguration of the signifiers of 'femininity' and 'girlhood' destabilises traditional categories of gender it is resonant with Judith Butler's conceptualisation of the performativity of gender – a theorisation that has held sway in contemporary feminist theory (albeit contentiously) in the period concurrent with the emergence of girl power. 'The effect of gender', Butler proposes, 'is produced through the stylization of the body and, hence, must be understood as the mundane way in which bodily gestures, movements, and styles of various kinds constitute the illusion of an abiding gendered self' (179). Nevertheless, the parodic reiteration of these acts can destabilise notions of normative gender by exposing 'the phantasmatic effect of abiding identity as a politically tenuous construction' (ibid.). Drag, she famously suggests, plays 'upon the distinction between the anatomy of the performer and the gender that is being performed' to implicitly reveal that 'the original identity after which gender fashions itself is an imitation without an origin' (175). In its parodic recontextualisation of girlhood and playful severing of signifier and signified, Riot Grrrl similarly points up the possibilities of resignification; it foregrounds a possible analysis and disruption of both normative (patriarchal) constructions of gender, and 'a stable subject of feminism, understood as a seamless category of women' (Butler 7). Still, if, as Kate Soper suggests, 'politics is essentially a group affair' (234–35), then Butler's post-structuralist critique of gendered subjectivity is troubled by Riot Grrrls' claims for a politics of agency and empowerment that is rooted in a notion of a collective 'girl' identity. The contention here, however, is that while Riot Grrrl proffers a performative recontextualisation of girlhood which reveals the inauthenticity of normative gender roles, it is unwilling to surrender a conception of women – or, specifically, *girls* and *young women* – as social subjects and agents. By yoking together thrift-store dresses with heavy combat boots, luminescent red lipstick with Hello Kitty hairclips and backpacks, and emblazoning the words 'slut' and 'whore' across their bodies, the members of Riot Grrrl deploy performative strategies that rely less on a dissonance between anatomical sex and gender identity (as in the instance of drag), than on a tension between opposing discourses of gender *within* female-embodied sexed identity – in particular the Madonna/whore and girl/woman binaries.

Kearney goes further in her claim that Riot Grrrl represents a reconfiguration of second wave identity politics.

Reaffirming adolescent girlhood as a radically marginal and therefore powerful position from which to act, riot grrrls foreground distinctions between girls and women that are effaced in the blanket universalist notions of 'females' 'femininity' and 'feminism'. But instead of bonding as 'girls', these female youth have appropriated the word 'girl' from its dominant connotations and reformulated that social category by creating a new identity that better represents their revolutionary spirit. (156)

Drawing on Linda Alcoff's 'politics of positionality', Kearney proposes that Riot Grrrl's reconfiguration of identity politics posits a notion of group identity created through the group members' 'similar external relations to the dynamic social processes of history, economics, and politics' (169). Indeed, insofar as Riot Grrrl both contests normative constructions of gender and locates – and recuperates – a notion of 'girl identity' as lived experience it demonstrates Alcoff's assertion that 'the position women find themselves in can be actively utilized (rather than transcended) as a location for the construction of meaning' (452). Locating the underground music community as a third wave reconfiguration of second wave consciousness-raising groups, Melissa Klein similarly highlights the ways in which Riot Grrrl reformulates (rather than rejects) the politics and praxis of second wave feminism – even if it applies them 'to third wave forms' (215).[8] Likewise, the proliferation of Riot Grrrl zines highlights the importance of communication and community as sites of (self-)representational empowerment – by both 'subvert[ing] standard patriarchal mainstream media ... and [giving] girls a safe place to say what they feel and believe' (Rosenberg and Garofalo 811).[9] Crucially, then, Riot Grrrl's emphasis on style can be understood as part of a politics of *identification* that is vital to both individual and collective empowerment.

But is this formulation of girl power establishing another hegemonic girlhood? In spite of its aims to create 'a heterogeneous community of adolescent girls which crosses local, regional, and even national boundaries' (Kearney 154), Riot Grrrl has been positioned as a largely white, middle-class movement. In her discussion of Riot Grrrl and 'white privilege', Kristen Schilt describes how 'many young feminists of color initially felt very supportive of Riot Grrrl because it brought the sexism in the punk scene under close scruitiny', but the 'attraction ended quickly, brought to a close by white girls' failure to investigate their own whiteness, address the critiques leveled by women of color, and discuss how racism and classism often work in concert with sexism' (44).[10] One of the dangerous paradoxes of Riot Grrrl, then, is that while its challenge to universalist notions of 'feminism' and 'women' reiterates the 'critiques of the white women's movement initiated by women of color, as well as from the many instances of coalition work undertaken by US third world feminists' (Heywood and Drake 1997a, 8), by constructing another hegemonic narrative of girlhood it risks repeating the very same exclusions for which it condemns second wave feminism.

Girlie girls: Fashioning feminism

Girlie feminists, identified with the writers of zines such as *BUST* and *Bitch*, have similarly located 'girl power' as a site of agency and resistance.

In their glossary to *Manifesta*, Baumgardner and Richards offer the following definition:

> Girlies are adult women, usually in their mid-twenties to late thirties, whose feminist principles are based on a reclaiming of girl culture (or feminine accoutrements that were tossed out with sexism during the Second Wave), be it Barbie, housekeeping, or girl talk. (400)

For example, while Marcelle Karp and Debbie Stoller, the editors of *BUST*, announce the arrival of 'The New Girl Order' (see epigraph) the 'girl-centric' zine *Bitch* (subtitled *Feminist Responses to Popular Culture*) proposes that its mission is about 'formulating replies to the sexist and narrow-minded media diet that we all – intentionally or not – consume' ('About Bitch' par. 3).[11] The replies to this quotidian sexism take the form of both celebration and critique – with interrogations of Martha Stewart and Barbie featured alongside articles on breasts and hair removal. According to Baumgardner and Richards, these zines offer 'new avenues into feminism for women who might not have found their way to a NOW meeting' (150). Girlie culture thus positions itself as a meeting place – a virtual community – for a generation of young women who self-identify as feminist, but do not necessarily relate to second wave feminist institutions.

By reappropriating the accoutrements of girlhood as *adult* women, Girlie presents another model of contradiction and conflict that destabilises traditional categories of gender and generation. In particular, it responds to the friction between second wave feminism and popular culture by creating a space 'that makes being an adult woman who calls herself a feminist seem thrilling, sexy, and creative' (Baumgardner and Richards xx). While it is tempting to quickly dismiss this shift as a simplistic symptom of the apolitical 'individualism' of the Spice Girls-style girl power described by Katharine Viner – '[s]uddenly feminism is all about how the individual feels right here, right now, rather than the bigger picture' (22) – it can be better understood as crucial to third wave feminists' reconfigurations of the politics of subjectivity. For, like Riot Grrrl, Girlie celebrates traditional 'feminine' trappings not only to abjure patriarchal definitions of femininity, but to challenge the 'inflexibility' of second wave identity politics described by Rebecca Walker:

> For us the lines between Us and Them are often blurred, and as a result we find ourselves seeking to create identities that accommodate ambiguity and our multiple positionalities: including

more than excluding, exploring more than defining, searching more than arriving. (xxxiii)

According to Helen Wilkinson, Girlie thus presents a challenge to both 'the "feminine mystique" so comprehensively analysed by earlier feminist writers such as Betty Friedan, as well as the equally constraining "feminist mystique" of sexual difference' (39). For Girlie girls, 'femininity' is not opposed to feminism, but is positioned as central to a politics of agency, confidence and resistance.

Nevertheless, the extent to which this celebration of 'girliness' really challenges dominant discursive structures remains questionable. 'With Girlie, there is danger that Spice Girls Pencil Set Syndrome will settle in: girls buy products created by male-owned companies that capture the slogan of feminism, without the power' (Baumgardner and Richards 161). The dangers of colonisation and recirculation are perhaps best exemplified by *The Girlie Show* (launched on Channel 4 in the U.K. in 1996) and the Spice Girls – two phenomena which highlight the dangerous slippage between feminist agency and patriarchal recuperation. Created by David Stevenson and fronted by arch-ladette Sara Cox, Clare Gorham and Rachel Williams, *The Girlie Show* represented the ascendance of 'babe feminism' – of 'women dressing like bimbos, yet claiming male privileges and attitudes' (Gamble 43).[12] Meanwhile, the positioning of the individual members of the Spice Girls into five clearly delineated and marketable categories of femininity – Baby, Scary, Posh, Sporty and Ginger – demonstrates the extent to which this 'brand' of girl power represents the commodification and *containment* of feminism – the triumph of 'image power' over 'political power' (Hopkins 18) so manifestly apparent in the (ironic) silence of Girls *Aloud* when pressed on the subject of feminist practice. The alacrity with which the media has embraced 'girl power' and its icons indicates the precarious boundary between the '(re)fashioning' of feminism proposed by the third wave Girlies and the 'fashionable' (post-)feminism propounded by the Spice Girls and *The Girlie Show*. In short, Girlie highlights the extent to which the politics of subjectivity require an understanding of the agency within self-representation as well as the appropriation of that agency.

It is no surprise, then, that the 'fashion statements' of this lipgloss-coated form of 'girlie' feminism have been received with suspicion by second wave feminists. For example, while Debbie Stoller positions the Ur-girl, Madonna, as 'a poster girl for postmodern fashion' ('Feminists Fatale' 44), Margaret Marshment asks whether she 'offers a mockery of conventional femininity, or just another way to be fashionable and "sexy"?' (147). Moreover, while Riot Grrrl presents a politics of identification and activism evidenced by self-defence and skill-sharing workshops, the extent to which Girlie's critique of dominant social forms translates into action at an institutional level has not been fully articulated. Can the meditations on blow jobs and mini-backpacks included in *The* BUST *Guide to the New Girl Order* really comprise part of the 'foundation of the personal ethics upon which a political women's movement will be built' (Baumgardner and Richards 20)? By focusing its critique on cultural manifestations of dominant social forms rather than the institutions and economic structures which maintain them, Girlie risks reinforcing a binary between culture and politics that privileges individual over collective empowerment. There is a radical difference between embracing lipgloss to revalorise traditional paradigms of 'femininity' and lobbying for changes in legislation and public policy. As Baumgardner and Richards put it, Girlies need to 'know the difference between saying we want equal pay and knowing how to go about getting it' (162). The problem with Girlie is that, unlike Riot Grrrl, too often the lipgloss, high heels, Barbies and vibrators are more visible than a body of politics – rendering it a ready site for post-feminist colonisation.

Bad girls and rebellious daughters

'[T]here have always been, and will always be, differing versions of what feminism is about, with the "new" or latest trajectories invariably keen to mark their distance from the "old"' (Segal 205). The extent to which Riot Grrrl and Girlie have positioned themselves – and been positioned – in an antagonistic relationship with second wave feminism bears out Lynne Segal's suggestion that intergenerational conflict has been embedded in accounts of feminist histories and, crucially, the wave paradigm. In her critique of gender as performance, Nicole Ward Jouve proposes that without 'male and female, masculine and feminine – there would be nothing: no generation (the root is the same for gender). No meaning' (10). It is thus one of the paradoxes of girl culture that while it refuses to surrender a prediscursive structure for girls' and young women's subjectivity, it positions itself in an antagonistic relation to generation. In this light, third wave configurations of girl culture can usefully be understood as dramatising one of the central contradictions confronting young feminists – that is, how to reconcile 'the discursive destabilization of the humanist notion of "a" feminist self and the historic mobilization of a politically engaged feminist "we"' (Siegel 61). It is this tension, this blending of (third wave) poststructuralist strategies with (second wave) identity politics, that provides a space for a reconsideration of the political viability of configurations of 'ironic femininity' as allowing for a notion of feminist agency. Nevertheless, the domineering mother and the rebellious daughter are destructive caricatures. The danger in girl culture – and in the wave paradigm more generally – is that it reiterates the trope of mother-daughter conflict. Reinforcing this intergenerational schism – and ghettoising feminist histories – opens up a space for patriarchal recuperation as girl power emerges as the site of that dangerous and deceptive slippage between third wave feminism and post-feminism.

Notes

1. This media-defined notion of post-feminism should be distinguished from academic feminism's deployment of the term in relation to postmodernist and post structuralist theoretical developments. In the latter, it is understood 'as an expression of a stage in the constant evolutionary movement of feminism ... encompassing the intersection of feminism with a number of other anti-foundationalist movements including postmodernism, post-structuralism and post-colonialism' (Brooks 1).
2. In this respect 'girl power' is strategically aligned with the much publicised strand of 'power feminism' associated with those prominent post-feminist writers who have been acclaimed by the U.S. media as ambassadors for a new generation of young women – Naomi Wolf, Katie Roiphe, Rene Denfeld and Christina Hoff Sommers. Underpinned by a differentiation between 'victim feminism' and 'power feminism', the configuration of post-feminism propounded by these writers suggests that 'the gains forged by previous generations of women have so completely pervaded all tiers of our social existence that those still "harping" about women's victim status are embarrassingly out of touch' (Siegel 75).
3. This resonates with Simone de Beauvoir's understanding of the contradiction and instability of female identity which comes 'from not regarding woman positively, such as she seems to be, but negatively, such as she appears to man. ... And her ambiguity is just that of the concept of the Other: it is that of the human situation in so far as it is defined in its relation to the Other. ... And here lies the reason why woman incarnates no stable concept' (175).
4. As Leslie Heywood and Jennifer Drake put it: 'Our hybrid engagement with culture and/as politics sometimes looks problematic to second wave activists, who might accuse us of exchanging engagement with institutional and economic inequities for a self-referential politics that overestimates the power of critiquing, reworking and producing pop- and subcultural images and narratives' (1997b, 52).
5. For more on the history of Riot Grrrl see Melissa Klein (213–17).
6. The dual resonance of 'generation' as an underlying principle of Riot Grrrl is captured in the title of a recent symposium – 'Sisterhood, Riot Grrrl, and the Next Wave: Feminist Generations/Generating Feminisms' – which took place at The Sallie Bingham Center for Women's History and Culture at Duke University

in October 2005. The Sallie Bingham Center holds a number of archival collections on 'generational feminisms', including zines.

7. Debbie Stoller, for example, argues that (second wave) feminism 'was prepared to celebrate everything about womanhood – everything but the girl' (Stoller 1999b, 184); while, with yet more sinister implications, Baumgardner and Richards question whether second wave feminism's involvement with the Girl's Movement has become 'an excuse to overlook the young women who are making strides right beside them' (186).

8. For instance, while the girl-only moshpit provides a 'safe-space' for young women, Riot Grrrl music 'often functions as a form of CR' (Klein 215). See also Jennifer L. Pozner's analysis of Ani DiFranco's lyrics (pars 9–11).

9. For more on the history of zines and third wave feminism see Dawn Bates and Maureen C. McHugh and on Riot Grrrl zines see Klein (217–18).

10. The issue of 'white privilege' has similarly been taken up in discussions of 'girl identity' in the mainstream music industry. In her analysis of Gwen Stefani's deployment of 'girliness' in the 1990s, for example, Gayle Wald points towards the ways in which the strategy of (re)appropriating girlhood 'signifies ambiguously' (588) in that it effaces 'critical questions of national, cultural, and racial appropriation ... under the sign of transgressive gender performance' (590). In particular, Wald highlights the ways in which Japanese all-female bands Shonen Knife and Cibo Matto challenge Western stereotypes of Asian femininity in their engagement with 'the cultural and racial specificity of hegemonic girlhood' (593). Wald's comments are particularly resonant in light of Stefani's more recent appropriation of Japanese subculture and, especially, her representation of 'Harajuku girls' on her solo album *Love, Angel, Music, Baby* (2004) and its accompanying music videos. For more on Japanese girl culture and 'Girl Orientalism' see Catherine Driscoll (287–301).

11. In a previous (though now unavailable) mission statement, the zine claimed that '[t]he much-touted "girl power" and "girl culture" have the potential to counteract the now-documented plunge in girls' self-esteem during their pubescent years ... *Bitch* is about formulating replies to the sexism that we see every day' ('So What are We Doing Here' par. 1).

12. The programme included features on faking orgasms, 'Reader's Husbands' and 'Toilet Talk'. See Greer (2000, 408) and Imelda Whelehan (50–51).

Works cited

'About Bitch.' *Bitch: Feminist Responses to Popular Culture*. Accessed: 12 July 2006. <http://www. bitchmagazine.com/about.html>.

Alcoff, Linda. 'Cultural Feminism Versus Post-Structuralism: The Identity Crisis in Feminist Theory.' *Feminism and Philosophy: Essential Readings in Theory, Reinterpretation, and Application*. Ed. Nancy Tuana and Rosemarie Tong. Boulder: Westview, 1995. 434–56.

Bates, Dawn, and Maureen Carter McHugh. 'Zines: Voices of Third Wave Feminists.' *Different Wavelengths: Studies of the Contemporary Women's Movement*. Ed. Jo Reger. New York: Routledge, 2005. 179–94.

Baumgardner, Jennifer, and Amy Richards. *Manifesta: Young Women, Feminism, and the Future*. New York: Farrar, Straus and Giroux, 2000.

Beauvoir, Simone de. *The Second Sex*. 1949. Trans. and ed. H. M. Parshley. London: Pan-Picador, 1988.

Brooks, Ann. *Postfeminisms: Feminism, Cultural Theory and Cultural Forms*. London: Routledge, 1997.

Budgeon, Shelley. 'Emergent Feminist(?) Identities: Young Women and the Practice of Micropolitics.' *European Journal of Women's Studies* 8.1 (2001): 7–28.

Butler, Judith. *Gender Trouble: Feminism and the Subversion of Identity*. 2nd ed. New York: Routledge, 1999.

Driscoll, Catherine. *Girls: Feminine Adolescence in Popular Culture and Cultural Theory*. New York: Columbia University Press, 2002.

Duncombe, Stephen. *Notes from Underground: Zines and the Politics of Alternative Culture*. London: Verso, 1997.

Ellen, Barbara. 'Aloud and Kicking.' *The Observer*. 27 July 2003. Accessed: 4 March 2004. <http://observer.guardian.co.uk/magazine/story/0,,1006558,00.html>.

Faludi, Susan. *Backlash: The Undeclared War Against American Women*. New York: Doubleday, 1991.

Gamble, Sarah. 'Postfeminism.' *The Routledge Companion to Feminism and Postfeminism*. Ed. Sarah Gamble. London: Routledge, 2001. 43–54.

Garrison, Ednie Kaeh. 'U.S. Feminism – Grrrl Style! Youth (Sub)Cultures and the Technologics of the Third Wave.' *Feminist Studies* 26.1 (2000): 141–70.

The Girlie Show. By David Stevenson. Pres. Sara Cox, Clare Gorham, Rachel Williams. Channel Four. Rapido TV, 1996.

Greer, Germaine. *The Female Eunuch*. 1970. London: Paladin, 1991.

——. *The Whole Woman*. 1999. London: Anchor, 2000.

Heywood, Leslie, and Jennifer Drake. Introduction. *Third Wave Agenda: Being Feminist, Doing Feminism*. Ed. Leslie Heywood and Jennifer Drake. Minneapolis: Minnesota University Press, 1997a. 1–20.

——. 'We Learn America Like a Script: Activism in the Third Wave; Or, Enough Phantoms of Nothing.' *Third Wave Agenda: Being Feminist, Doing Feminism*. Ed. Leslie Heywood and Jennifer Drake. Minneapolis: Minnesota University Press, 1997b. 40–54.

Hopkins, Susan. *Girl Heroes: The New Force in Popular Culture*. Annadale: Pluto Press, 2002.

Karp, Marcelle, and Debbie Stoller. 'The Birth of *BUST*.' *The* BUST *Guide to the New Girl Order*. Ed. Marcelle Karp and Debbie Stoller. New York: Penguin, 1999. xii–xv.

Kearney, Mary Celeste. '"Don't Need You": Rethinking Identity Politics and Separatism from a Grrrl Perspective.' *Youth Culture: Identity in a Postmodern World*. Ed. Jonathan Epstein. Malden: Blackwell, 1998. 148–88.

Klein, Melissa. 'Duality and Redefinition: Young Feminism and the Alternative Music Community.' *Third Wave Agenda: Being Feminist, Doing Feminism*. Ed. Leslie Heywood and Jennifer Drake. Minneapolis: Minnesota University Press, 1997. 207–25.

Marshment, Margaret. 'The Picture is Political: Representation of Women in Contemporary Popular Culture.' *Introducing Women's Studies*. Ed. Victoria Robinson and Diane Richardson. 2nd ed. Basingstoke: Palgrave, 1997. 125–51.

Pozner, Jennifer. 'Makes Me Wanna Grrrowl.' *Feminista!* 2.1 (1998). Accessed: 12 July 2006. <http://www.feminista.com/archives/v2n1/pozner.html>.

Rosenberg, Jessica, and Gitana Garofalo. 'Riot Grrrl: Revolutions from Within.' *Signs: Journal of Women in Culture and Society* 23.3 (1998): 809–41.

Schilt, Kristen. '"The Punk White Privilege Scene": Riot Grrrl, White Privilege, and Zines.' *Different Wavelengths: Studies of the Contemporary Women's Movement.* Ed. Jo Reger. New York: Routledge, 2005. 39–56.

Segal, Lynne. *Why Feminism?* Cambridge: Polity, 1999.

Siegel, Deborah L. 'Reading between the Waves: Feminist Historiography in a "Postfeminist" Moment.' *Third Wave Agenda: Being Feminist, Doing Feminism.* Ed. Leslie Heywood and Jennifer Drake. Minneapolis: Minnesota University Press, 1997. 55–82.

'So What are We Doing Here, Anyway?' *Bitch: Feminist Reponses to Popular Culture.* Accessed: 12 Nov. 2003. <http://www.bitchmagazine.com/mission.html>. [No longer available].

Soper, Kate. *Troubled Pleasures: Writings on Politics, Gender and Hedonism.* London: Verso, 1990.

The Spice Girls. *Girl Power!* London: Zone-Chameleon, 1997.

Stefani, Gwen. *Love, Angel, Music, Baby.* Interscope Records, 2004.

Steinem, Gloria. Foreword. *To Be Real: Telling the Truth and Changing the Face of Feminism.* Ed. Rebecca Walker. New York: Anchor, 1995. xiii–xxviii.

Stoller, Debbie. 'Feminists Fatale: BUST-ing the Beauty Myth.' *The* BUST *Guide to the New Girl Order.* Ed. Marcelle Karp and Debbie Stoller. New York: Penguin, 1999a. 42–47.

——. 'Growing up Girl.' *The* BUST *Guide to the New Girl Order.* Ed. Marcelle Karp and Debbie Stoller. New York: Penguin, 1999b. 183–88.

Viner, Katharine. 'The Personal is Still Political.' *On the Move: Feminism for a New Generation.* Ed. Natasha Walter. London: Virago, 1999. 10–26.

Wald, Gayle. 'Just a Girl? Rock Music, Feminism, and the Cultural Construction of Female Youth.' *Signs: Journal of Women in Culture and Society* 23.3 (1998): 585–610.

Walker, Rebecca. 'Being Real: An Introduction.' *To Be Real: Telling the Truth and Changing the Face of Feminism.* Ed. Rebecca Walker. New York: Anchor, 1995. xxix–xl.

Ward Jouve, Nicole. *Female Genesis: Creativity, Self, Gender.* Cambridge: Polity, 1998.

Whelehan, Imelda. *Overloaded: Popular Culture and the Future of Feminism.* London: Women's Press, 2000.

Wilkinson, Helen. 'The Thatcher Legacy: Power Feminism and the Birth of Girl Power.' *On the Move: Feminism for a New Generation.* Ed. Natasha Walter. London: Virago, 1999. 27–47.

In Dialogue

21
Interview with Luce Irigaray

Gillian Howie

GH: *Do you think that the wave metaphor is a helpful way to understand stages in feminist theory/the woman's movement?*

LI: Is it really a metaphor or an image that tries to suggest an affinity of women with water, with fluid, with sea? If the stages in feminist movement correspond to waves, this could suggest a moving ceaselessly without ever changing the bottom which supports such a movement. And also: that the movement is caused by things other than itself, by things in part external with respect to itself: a star outside it, the ground on which it takes place, etc. Thus, the matter would be of a permanent but instable and not autonomous movement which could never assume a definitive meaning or form. Waves in some way refer to a mythical time and not to historical times. How could we articulate mythical time with historical times? Certainly, it is a question that the entry of women into Western culture raises. And the problem is not to substitute a kind of temporality for another but to overcome this opposition and dichotomy.

GH: *You have refused to belong to any one faction within the woman's movement but continue to define yourself as a feminist. Can you explain why it is important to you to be a feminist rather than, say, a 'post-feminist'?*

LI: Where did you see that I define myself as 'feminist'? On the contrary, I have many times protested against the fact that I could be called a feminist. I have repeated that I do not want to belong to any 'ism' category, be it feminism, post-feminism, post-modernism, etc. Other people designate me as feminist, but not myself. Perhaps because these words ending in 'ism' allude to something both too rigid and too evanescent. The relation between the foundation and the manifestation is not the relation in which I take interest. I would also like to remind you that I work towards woman's liberation and more generally human liberation. And this requires us to favour singularity with respect to all sorts of gregariousnesses that, in my opinion, the words ending in 'ism' presuppose.

GH: *It seems that the cessation of your contract at the University of Vincennes was related to the content of your second doctorate* Speculum of the Other Woman. *Do you think that feminists still face such challenges within the Academy today?*

LI: It is difficult for me to answer this question. I am not a feminist within the Academy. I think that the reactions are various and ambiguous. Today, women are promoted on the condition that they remain respectful of academic customs, context and traditional culture. Now, for a woman, having access to the Academy represents such an important promotion that she forgets the necessary change of traditional culture. It is also very difficult for her to realise both the gestures in the same time: entering the academic world and modifying it. Indeed, it could happen that women become more formally academic than men are, because they stay in the Academy without really sharing the culture which takes place there. Stressing formalism, then, could be their way of belonging to the Academy and of being welcomed into it. The problems begin when, in this place, a woman challenges the manner of thinking and of acting that the Academy has not, or not yet, made its own. And this was the case with *Speculum*.

GH: *You have separated your work into three distinct stages: a critique of masculine subject identity; the problem of defining female subjectivity; and the problem of defining a relationship between two (sexed) subjects – a 'double subjectivity'. Would you say that this latter stage sets you apart from other 'philosophers of difference'?*

LI: First, I would like to specify that the first stage is rather a criticism of Western culture as being founded by only one subject who claims to be neuter, neutral and universal while in fact it is masculine. What I intended to construct in *Speculum* is a culture of and between two different subjects. From the beginning my work is devoted to sexuate difference. I try to promote a difference which is not the same as that present in the majority of discourses of Western thinkers and of all of us. Generally, difference is understood as quantitative and not qualitative. Of course, 'quantitativity' can assume various meanings. The difference in Hegel's work and in Marx's work refers to a relation to quantity that is not the same, even if it remains quantitative, as is generally the case in a culture of only one subject.

Man and woman are irreducible the one to the other: they cannot be substituted the one for the other, not because of a quantity – one would be better than the other, one is the first and the other the second, for example – but because of a difference in being and existing, that is to say a qualitative difference. Agreeing with this and putting it in practice constrain us to enter another logic. Without understanding this necessity, it is not possible to approach my work. In my work, the negative is endowed with an other sense and function with respect to our tradition. In Hegel, for example, the negative works in order to reduce the all in the one, the One. To the contrary, I use the negative to maintain the duality of subjectivities. And this is possible, starting each time from two subjects who belong to different worlds as is the case for man and woman. The difference I implement in my thinking cannot take place between the one and the multiple, as is generally the case in Western thought. It refers to a real and concrete difference between two subjectivities, a real that can be elaborated but without abolishing the two and the difference between the two. Contrary to other philosophers of difference, I start from a real and concrete difference that is, as such, a universal, which cannot be overcome without abolishing the universal itself.

GH: *You have previously suggested that although you and Simone de Beauvoir were in agreement that women are 'the other sex', she responded to this by refusing to be Other, whilst you embraced the difference in order to transform the relationship. How might that relationship be transformed?*

LI: I prefer to say that woman represents the emergence of the other with respect to Western tradition. To designate such an otherness as 'the other sex' runs the risk of reducing the difference to the sex, strictly speaking, without considering the global identity. For this reason, I increasingly use the word 'sexuate difference' and not 'sexual difference'. Similarly, I do not use the words 'the Other' to refer to woman. I consider that it is important to maintain the difference between vertical transcendence and horizontal transcendence, and to keep the capital letter to designate vertical transcendence. In a way, the absolute and perfect same: the Same. My interpretation of woman as other differs from that of Simone de Beauvoir. According to her, woman is second with respect to man. Simone de Beauvoir remains in a culture of only one subject in relation to which the others are quantitatively different. My idea of otherness is more radical. The difference now is qualitative, and the negative is not used to compare two subjects: it maintains the duality of the subjects and of their worlds. This requires entering an other logic as I claim in *Speculum*. The misunderstandings about my work testify to the difficulty of accomplishing the passage from one logic to an other.

GH: *Does sexual difference act as a model for the appreciation and recognition of other differences?*

LI: It is not a question of being a model. Sexuate difference is the most basic and the most universal difference. It is also the difference which operates, or ought to operate, each time, the connection between nature and culture for everyone. This connection is specific to girl and woman in comparison with boy and man. The feminine subject does not relate to the self, to the other(s), to the world as a masculine subject does. This does not depend only on bodily morphology and anatomy or on social stereotypes, as many people imagine. Rather, it is a question of relational identity that precisely realises the original connection between body and culture. I am afraid that people who claim to be materialist cannot agree with the crucial role of our sexuate body in the construction of a cultural world. Now, it is not the same to make love in oneself or outside oneself, to engender in oneself or outside oneself. Neither is it the same to be born from the same gender as one's own or from another gender, and to be able to or not able to engender as one's mother did. These basic original givens determine a psychic and cultural identity peculiar to each sex, whatever could be the differences between a man and a woman.

GH: *You have indicated that feminisms have tended to get lost in saying 'I' whereas you would prefer to make visible that the 'I' is a subject that is two (je indice elle); both subject and object. Can you explain what you mean by 'object' in this context?*

LI: I do not understand your question very well. Of course, if feminisms or feminists use 'I' as is usual in our tradition, they cannot make a subject or a world emerge different from those that men have promoted. Could such subjects or worlds contribute towards women's liberation? In my opinion, they rather contribute towards women's repression, even though they are assumed by women themselves. It could be important here to clarify what I wrote about mimicry as a strategy and what is said about my supposed favour for mimicry. The question is: How can we leave a culture of only one subject to enter a culture of two different subjects? In some analyses, I propose to allocate to each subject a clue which indicates their sex. If this clue refers to an objectivity of the subject – who is male or female, masculine or feminine – it is not, for all that, a question of reducing the subject to an object.

GH: *In* I Love to You, *you write that '[i]t's not as Simone de Beauvoir said: one is not born but rather becomes a woman (through culture) but rather that: I am born a woman, but must still become this woman that I am by nature'. Could you clarify how this is not an essentialist claim?*

LI: For Simone de Beauvoir, becoming a woman amounts to submitting oneself to sociocultural stereotypes in relation to woman. For her, a positive becoming in the feminine does not exist, and entering a cultural world signifies adopting the culture in the masculine which, for centuries, has corresponded to our tradition. The cultivation of the self for a woman in a way implies becoming a cultivated man. The woman then becomes split into a female and a masculine belonging. Furthermore, entering our traditional culture, women share its values, including its essences. The essences remain in a culture of one subject, whatever the strategy of ambiguity – or ambivalence? – for destabilising them, which can result in a worse nihilism.

For my part, I think it is better for a woman to cultivate herself in a feminine way; that is, to cultivate her female belonging through feminine values. Of course, this needs us to leave our past culture – of only one subject – to enter a really different culture based on the relation between two subjects not subjected to one another. In my thought and practice, the way of defining these subjects is already relational, and it takes into account, from the beginning, body and spirit or soul without separating them. The scission between female and feminine identity thus no longer exists. Moreover, the relations between the two subjects are found from their different ways of relating to the self, to the other(s), to the world. They then exclude the existence of immutable values or essences which could be shared by all people. It is all the more so since each subject, even if specific, is each time changing because of the relation(s) with an other subject who does not share the same world, the same values.

GH: *It has been said that you advocated strategic essentialism, especially in works such as* This Sex Which is Not One. *Would you agree with this, and, if so, would you still recommend it?*

LI: I am often surprised to hear the comments concerning my work! Could it be the lack of essences which allows people to say anything and everything about my thinking? It is certainly a lack of perception with respect to the transcendental at work in it. I return to your question. From *Speculum*, I said that I intended to define a culture of two subjects, but this needed to elaborate a means to construct a culture in the feminine. *This Sex Which is Not One* belongs to both the stage of criticism in my work, the first stage, and the stage of searching for specific ways of cultivating a feminine identity. Could it be this task which is confused with essentialism by some people? It was realised in order to reach the possibility of being two.

GH: *Michel Foucault described this century as Deleuzian and both you and Gilles Deleuze talk about 'becoming-woman' as a way to move beyond (masculine) subject-identity. Could you say how your concepts differ?*

LI: As far as I am concerned, 'becoming woman' or 'becoming a woman' correspond to cultivating my own identity, the identity which is mine by birth. For Deleuze, it amounts to becoming what he is not by birth. If I appeal to a return to nature, to the body – that is, to values that our Western culture has scorned – Deleuze acts in the opposite way: according to him it would be possible and suitable to become someone or something which is without relation with my original and material belonging. How could this be possible above all from the part of a man with respect to becoming woman? Putting on the stereotypes concerning femininity? Deleuze would want to become the woman who Simone de Beauvoir did not want to become? It would be amusing to present a dialogue between the masculine identity of Simone de Beauvoir and the feminine identity of Deleuze! Of course, I can imagine why Deleuze wanted to become a woman, but also an animal, to shake his traditional masculine identity. But I would like to stress that he adopted such an idea at the successful time of women's liberation. I thus have some doubts about the intention of such a becoming feminine. Could it not happen to appropriate the success that women were gaining? Is it not then the same gesture as men made during our whole tradition? Why, in this time, have some distinguished thinkers suddenly wished for becoming women or feminists instead of trying to reach a neither neutral nor universal but masculine identity? The least one could say is that they have created a great confusion in relation to a budding culture in the feminine. It was not really respectful of the efforts of women to liberate themselves from the subjection to a culture in the masculine!

GH: *In your influential essay 'Divine Women', inspired by Feuerbach's* The Essence of Christianity, *you argue that 'as long as woman lacks a divine made in her image she cannot establish her subjectivity.' Is it possible or even desirable to understand God as a way to reflect the ideals of female or male subjects?*

LI: In many traditions the divinities are sexuate, as humans are, and they offer help to human becoming at the different stages of its journey.

Monotheism intends to enter another era. But if monotheism represents an accomplishment of humanity, it can quietly tolerate the other stages of the journey towards the divine. I am afraid that many people pretend to reach monotheism without having covered the other stages towards deification. They then contrast the radical otherness of God with the otherness of the other, in particular the sexuate other; that is vertical transcendence with horizontal transcendence. I could agree with difficulty with such an alternative, which precisely has been used to subject woman to man. It is also important to notice that God, amongst other masculine attributes, is called 'the Father', thus is sexuated even in monotheism – as in the Trinity. Could it happen that women project onto God the otherness that they feel with respect to man because she cannot recognise him as radically other, and he cannot maintain his status of other?

GH: *In works such as* I Love to You, *you call for the 'spiritualisation of bodies'. Could you clarify what this means and how it connects to the idea of the 'sensible transcendental'?*

LI: Instead of the repression of spirit on body, which is usual in our tradition, I prefer the transformation of body as living matter into spiritual matter. There exist some phenomena in our religious culture that can evoke what I am trying to say, for example the transfiguration of Christ. But they are quoted as exceptional phenomena and not as a normal way of spiritualisation. Eastern cultures have disclosed to me one other path. There is no longer a question of dividing spirit and body, the one having to lay down the law on the other, but of transforming a vital energy into a spiritual energy at the service of breathing, of loving, of listening, of speaking and of thinking. Such a process transforms, one could say transmutes or transfigures, little by little, our original bodily matter into spiritualised bodily matter, as I explained notably in *Between East and West* (2002). I consider such a spiritual journey as being more adult and also more religious. The division into body and spirit results from a philosophical Western logic which is not especially religious. Transforming or transmuting the matter, keeping it as matter, makes possible the existence of a sensible transcendental, whereas the split between body and spirit renders it impossible because the transcendental then corresponds to a removal from sensibility.

GH: *How do you think a feminist vision of God could help us to move beyond religious fundamentalism – Islamic, Christian, Judaic – and find peace?*

LI: I think that to move beyond religious fundamentalisms, a culture of two different subjects is necessary, that is a culture in which we have to coexist in difference and to accept that our own values are not the sole and unique values. The worse conflicts happen between those who are the same and confront each other about their values, each one claiming to have reached the top. Thus inside all the 'ism' systems or groups – including feminism, which moreover and fortunately is not one – and between all the 'ism' systems of groups, peace remains unlikely. Contrary to what many people think, sameness, equality, identity, etc., do not prepare for peace but for conflicts, because people then remain in a quantitative viewpoint. Difference – of course not hierarchical, thus quantitative – is more able to pave the way towards peace. It could also allow us to avoid fundamentalisms, keeping the horizon of the truth open, including religious truth. Difference, as I try to practice and promote, is also a means of each time respecting the otherness of the other, a thing that prepares for peace and coexistence with everyone. In fact, it is an excellent regulator for keeping democratic behaviour.

GH: *How might you respond to the concern that your emphasis on 'sexual difference' as the key with which to unlock 'differences' simplifies the complexity of our contemporary political world, underplaying, for example, questions of race, sexuality and culture?*

LI: My way of approaching sexual and sexuate difference is really difficult to understand and put in practice because it is different from that which is usual in our tradition. It requires us to change our habits of thinking and of acting. Many people who take an interest in it grasp only certain elements without considering the foundation of such a thought. This brings about many misunderstandings, even amongst people who claim to share such a prospect. One of these consists in contrasting my way of conceiving thought and practice concerning sexuate difference with that of treating other differences: of race, of culture, of generation, etc. I know that it is fashionable today to divide the problem of sexuate difference and the problem of difference of race, of culture, of generation, etc., and to affirm that the first concerns intimate life and the second the political world. I cannot agree with this separation, as I explain in *Democracy Begins between Two* (2000) and 'The Path Towards the Other' in *Beckett, after Beckett* (2005). I am afraid that this opposition contributes to the reduction of attention and efforts to change our customs and habits relative to sexual and sexuate difference. Now our behaviour with respect to difference of races, of cultures, of generation, etc., often results from a lack of cultivation of our sexual instincts, our most basic instincts in relating with the other(s). Another thing: the cultures and traditions are, in great part, constructed starting from sexual and sexuate difference, at the level of genealogies or marriages and alliances. How could it be possible to distinguish a culture with respect to our own without taking into account the difference of treatment of sexes or genders in this culture? And, for example: Are not the problems about the Islamic veil sexual or sexuate problems? And could not the separation of private and public life contribute to the subjection of women, as women working towards their liberation in the 1960s and 1970s claimed?

22
Interview with Elaine Showalter
Stacy Gillis and Rebecca Munford

sg and rm: *What do you understand by the terms 'third wave feminism' and 'post-feminism'?*

es: Third wave feminism is just another way of talking about the contemporary moment rather than calling it post-feminism. Third wave feminism implies a movement, a wave suggests movement, whereas I am very dubious about the existence of a new feminist movement. I think of the wave as more temporal than revolutionary. Post-feminism is a term open to a lot of different, and conflicting and problematic interpretations. One way of thinking about it that has been very common is to interpret post-feminism as meaning after feminism or what you have left when feminism is over. That kind of negativism is extremely prevalent everywhere, not only in the popular press – which is not interested in feminism – but within second wave feminism itself. A lot of the people who participated in the women's liberation movement think that we are going through a very bad patch, and feminism is in a mess, and feminism is in decline and feminism has failed, etc. I am much more literal about it. Post-feminism means after a women's movement. Now one of the ambiguities there is whether you could say we are between women's movements and my own suspicion is that we are not. I think that it is unlikely that there will be another women's movement.

sg and rm: *Why do you feel that there will not be another women's movement?*

es: Because of what it takes to make a movement. Movements, by their nature, are infrequent and localised events and they have certain conditions. You cannot predict when one is going to start exactly but you can understand the historical framework and what it takes to create a revolutionary movement. First, it takes a specific and attainable goal, a goal that is clear so that everyone can see what it is and everyone can agree on what it is. And people need to believe that it is possible to get it by action, so they are willing to give up their divisions, their differences, their competitions and their hierarchies, in the interests of obtaining this goal. If you look at women's movements in the past, although feminism has always been complex in what it wanted, they had very specific goals – whether it was the vote, or rights to abortion, or equal pay for equal work, or access to education, or any of the many things that have motivated the various movements. They were clear and specific. The ideals behind feminism now are much more diffuse and controversial. Second, a movement needs leadership. There is a real dearth of charismatic feminist leaders right now, at least in the U.S. and the U.K. Feminism has been very uncomfortable with leadership. It has not been a goal of feminism to develop leaders. Indeed, you might say that is was quite the opposite. Some revolutionary movements will have a specific goal to educate and develop and train leaders. But not the women's movement. The idea was that leaders were temporary and would give way to a universal sisterhood as soon as the problems were solved. So, women who do assume leadership find themselves dealing with a lot of hostility as well as a lot of support.

SG and RM: *What happened to second wave feminism? Where did it start to fall apart as a movement?*

ES: I think that a radical movement, by its very definition, is not going to last very long. Movements are short-lived entities, like a chemical that has a lot of complex elements but a very short half-life. But I do not think that the absence of a movement as such is a matter of concern. Feminism can go on independently of a woman's movement.

SG and RM: *You have talked about the lack of leadership at the moment. The women's movement has tended to put forward people who will lead for a short while and then the movement almost devours them through mythologisation (e.g. the Pankhursts, Gloria Steinem). Do you think that the feminist movement is crippled by what it does with its leaders?*

ES: No more so than any other revolutionary movement. Leaders of other revolutionary movements have not fared that well either. But, at the beginning of the twenty-first century, if feminism is really going to expand and develop and gain power in the world, Western feminism needs to re-examine some of the premises that have been around for generations – some of the baggage from earlier phases – and really think about whether it continues to be meaningful to insist on these assumptions. Some of the ideals that were exhilarating are now confining. It is easy to get trapped in some of these old methods of thinking. For example, the women's liberation movement, because it was so connected with leftist politics and a certain kind of utopian socialist thought, had an automatic belief that one did not want to look for women exercising leadership and achieving power in social spaces of which it did not approve. But if we want to look at leadership, big business, government, and the military are some of the places that you find women with the strongest leadership abilities. Rather than demanding a pure political space where feminism develops its leaders we should think about where female leadership exists and what we can learn from it. Feminism has operated for several decades on an ethics of powerlessness, and we need to investigate an ethics of power. In the twenty-first century you cannot pretend anymore that no women have power. I am very interested in women in the business world. There are quite a number in the U.K. who are achieving prominence. Look at Laura Tyson of the London Business School or Nicola Horlick – or any of these women who have been very successful in business and politics. I am very struck by the fact that in a lot of feminist discussions these women are not mentioned. You still get women who are speaking out of the authority of failure.

SG and RM: *What do you think feminism should be doing at this point in history?*
ES: The big area where I would like to see feminism engaged in an entrepreneurial, effective and power-orientated way is in childcare. It is the kind of issue around which women could organise, although it is somewhat more problematic than, say, the vote, because you do not worry about the quality of a vote – but you do worry about the quality of childcare. You cannot exactly agree to it until you know exactly what it is you are going to get. A lot of the attitude of feminism towards childcare is passive – 'Give it to us, we demand it, we are entitled to it'. I know that when I was in the women's movement we were more active. One of the things we did in my group, which had seventeen people in it, was start a day-care centre. We just started it. We said we do not just want childcare, we *have* to have it, we *must* have it. So, five of the seventeen of the women took responsibility for it. And they tried to think of different ways that they could get it – and they found a space, and they got the university to sponsor some of it, and they found ways to get money. They played various angles so that they could get some of the space and costs subsidised, and they had various fund-raising sales, and eventually they launched it. That day-care centre is still running – both of my kids went to it. A *fait accompli* is one of its own best arguments politically. It

would be interesting now to see women who have money and leverage thinking about how to make childcare work. Could we set it up as a business? Why does it always have to be the government providing it? Commercial childcare does not have to be a shameful enterprise, a Kentucky Fried Children. Yet too many feminist conferences on childcare include academics, social workers, welfare mothers and so on, none of whom has any real leverage although they have good ideas. I would invite some rich women to these discussions. There are different kinds of alliances that feminism could look to now, and I think feminism could adopt a more active attitude: We will make what we need, we are determined that we are going to have what we need, and we are not just going to go around begging. I do not want to take a high moral ground because there is too much moralism in feminism already but I think there needs to be a reconsideration of these old taboos about power, and we need to have discussions with women who represent all different kinds of experiences and backgrounds. Often second wave feminists regard anything that subsequent generations do – whether that is activism, organising and/or theorising – with a real resentment and anger. There is a real sense that many second wavers do not think that subsequent generations are 'doing it right.' This generational conflict is not exclusive to feminism. When I talked at the Third Wave Feminism conference at the University of Exeter, I suggested that feminist tension is partly an accident of timing. At the beginning of the twentieth century there was enormous optimism among women because feminism was really a very young movement and young women were joining it. But at the millennium, many women who had come out of the women's liberation movement were aging. They did not see the millennium as a new beginning; they saw it as an ending, they saw it in terms of decline. Many of them certainly sound as if they are very embittered, very negative and very pessimistic. I also think that the women's liberation movement was extremely successful in its time and place. I am continually impressed when I think how much was accomplished by relatively small groups of extremely committed women in the right place at the right time. We really seized the day. With the new generation in the twenty-first century, I do not see that the issues have emerged with sufficient force and I do not think that enough leaders have come forward. I personally do not feel any resentment towards it, but I do not think that third wave feminism has really gelled. If anything, it seems that it is still trying to accommodate the feminism of the 1970s in some of its leftist shibboleths. In addition, many new issues have not been forcefully engaged.

SG and RM: *You have talked about feminist leaders. How much do you think we need feminist icons?*

ES: I do not know how many feminist icons there are. There are certainly some female icons. But again, when I did *Inventing Herself*, people were so annoyed with me, not just that I said Princess Diana had been an icon for women but that I said Oprah Winfrey was an icon for women. As many people objected to Oprah Winfrey as to Princess Diana. I gave a talk in London about the book and that was what I was most denounced for. People said, oh Oprah Winfrey, she is just a creature of the media. But she is also now a powerful and socially engaged woman – albeit with some very different ideas than second wave feminism had. The issue is not just claiming women as feminist icons, but working with them or getting them to work with you. Gloria Steinem was such a person for the women's liberation movement. There are a lot more strong female figures right now but they are not often given the sense of feminist support that would make them interested in taking leadership. So I do not think that we need feminist icons, but we do need women who are powerful economically and politically as well as women who make things happen. There are also the schisms within academic feminism which alienate some people.

SG and RM: *The women's studies/gender studies/feminist studies debates can be invigorating but are also marked by acrimony and, at times, deception. In contrast to this, we feel that we should celebrate feminism being in other places than feminist or women's studies. We need to celebrate letting go of feminism.*

ES: That is a very good way to put it. And I think that is exactly what it is – letting go of it; letting go of it because that is the foundational step in making alliances. You really have to ask what it is that you want, and how much you want it. If you really want something to happen then you are willing to give up some of the pleasures of ownership, so to speak, in terms of making alliances with other people who can work with you. It would be very interesting to get some of the women who are in business and government to work on women's leadership centres, to work with undergraduates in order to give them the mindset and the tools to make things happen, and training in everything from money management to public speaking.

SG and RM: *In what ways can we make an individual difference? How do we give leadership skills to women? Most women have to learn anew in a vacuum, whereas men are given this sort of training almost as a birthright.*

ES: Structured mentoring is very important. I think there should be a lot more of it. Maybe some of these very powerful women could be encouraged to take half a dozen younger women to mentor, and to show them how to master some of these skills. I try to do that myself on a very small scale with various students who I have had working for me. They do some research work for me, but I also involve them in the various kinds of activities that are part of my career, and help them learn how to write a book review, a lecture, a recommendation.

SG and RM: *There is a second wave perception that self-proclaimed third wave feminists (e.g. the writers of zines like* BUST *and* Bitch) *do too much playing, too much popular culture and not enough doing, not enough politics. This sense of moral superiority between generations is aggravating but how can we resolve the accusations of too much popular culture?*

ES: Women are not given the right to play, and popular culture is a form of women's play. I am quite fond of English football, but I do not put the amount of time into it that men do into various sports. I do not play golf. I am not interested in cars. I think that you get a feeling for a place and for people by participating in popular culture. I do not know why I should feel guilty about it. These lines around popular culture are much too rigidly drawn and I do not see why it is necessary for women to deny themselves pleasure.

Afterword: Feminist Waves

Jane Spencer

There's something seductive about the number three. Third time lucky. Thesis, antithesis, synthesis. And we all want progress. Even Julia Kristeva's famous essay 'Women's Time' (1979), which divided feminism into three 'attitudes' or 'generations' while invoking the possibility of 'the *parallel* existence of all three in the same historical time, or even that they be interwoven one with the other' (209; emphasis in original), ended up strongly implying that third comes last and is best. First attitude: the pursuit of equality. Second attitude: the claim of difference. Third attitude: undermining the kind of fixed identity on which the first two have been based: 'In this third attitude, which I strongly advocate – which I imagine? – the very dichotomy man/woman as an opposition between two rival entities may be understood as belonging to *metaphysics*' (209; emphasis in original). It is this third attitude which the work collected here also imagines, and contests, and places in new contexts. Since Kristeva's essay a new generation of women has grown up, and a new terminology of feminist waves has emerged. As she predicted, there has been a focus of struggle 'in personal and sexual identity itself', a concentration on 'the multiplicity of every person's possible identifications' (210), but the result has rather been a proliferation of identities than a deconstruction of identity itself. Class difference, racial diversity, the multiplicities of sexual orientation and gender identity, have all been made the bases of different kinds of identity politics. Feminism has moved towards related forms of oppositional politics while being itself repeatedly declared dead by the media; and as the essays collected in this volume demonstrate, there is no clear agreement as to what third wave feminism is even about. As Amanda Lotz points out in her chapter, the term is often used interchangeably with postfeminism, and both terms can be co-opted for the anti-feminist end of implying that feminism as a political movement is obsolete. If we resist such appropriation, and attempt to make feminist use of the term 'third wave', we are necessarily defining it as what came after the second wave (itself understood in retrospect as what came before the third): 'there have always been, and will always be, differing versions of what feminism is about, with the "new" or latest trajectories invariably keen to mark their distance from the "old"' (Segal 205). To this extent the third wave is a generational phenomenon, raising the question of what can or should be passed on from one set of feminists to the next, and to what extent the rising generation must rebel against the earlier.

Female to female inheritance has, of course, always been problematic in a patriarchal society in which the legacy passed from male to male is understood as natural and of central importance. Even today men can be unselfconsciously honoured as the fathers of artistic movements, scientific fields, inventions, ideas. Advances in thought are reified into systems by being named for their male founders: so we have Marxism, Freudianism, Darwinism. It is no accident that feminism was not named after an individual woman. If, sometimes, a mother for feminism is mooted – Mary Wollstonecraft, for example – it is always tentatively, with irony, or in the spirit of daughterly insurrection. Culture – including the culture of political organisation – is still subliminally understood as a male property passed on from father to son. Sons may need to rebel against their fathers, but in the interests of eventually taking on their power and inheriting a structure that remains intact, though its content may change. A daughter's place in culture – and a mother's place – have always been more difficult to interpret. Women have certainly yearned for cultural mothers. Twentieth-century feminist literary critics constructed a female literary tradition in a clear attempt to discover and honour our foremothers. At the same time mothers have been the focus of anxiety and ambivalence. Diane Elam argues that

> Feminism needs to take account of the fact that it does not simply stand outside of institutional power structures at the same time that it tries to imagine new ways of standing together. The problem with actually doing this seems to revolve around a lack of specifically feminist models of power and tradition. Patriarchal power structures of the family – imagining relationships between women as always those of mothers and daughters, for instance, stay in place by default. (64)

In a patriarchal society the mother's role of subordination and self-sacrifice is what the daughter does not want to inherit; and the unwritten commandment 'Thou Shalt Not Become Thy Mother' has now exerted an effect on generations of feminist-influenced women, militating against the odds of turning feminism into a cultural inheritance to be passed on from metaphorical mothers to their daughters. This has its advantages – the revolutionary feminism of one generation does not get the chance to become the repressive orthodoxy of the next – and its disadvantages. In her chapter, Lise Shapiro Sanders quotes Jennifer Baumgarnder and Amy Richards, pointing out that sometimes it seems as if the feminism of one generation gets completely lost and that feminists 'need to reinvent the wheel every fifty years or so' (68).

The debate about essentialism is certainly one area of feminism where we see, if not a reinvented wheel, at least a battle constantly revisited. This is partly because, as Susan Stryker shows here, new forms of politics, such as transgenderism in the 1990s, invite us to consider anew the relationship between the anti-foundationalist critique of identity and the political struggle in the name of women. Equally the vexed question of men's relation to feminism, explored here by Andrew Shail, poses anew the question of what it is to de-essentialise sex. The essentialist issue, surely, foams up in all feminist waves. Alison Stone sees the third wave as the generation that delivers 'a widespread rejection of essentialism' and her chapter concentrates on finding a truly anti-essentialist anti-essentialism to inform a feminist politics that works not with identity but with coalition. But not all putative coalition members are convinced by the anti-essentialist position. Its dominance in current feminist thought, argues Mridula Nath Chakraborty, 'merely reinscribes the racist and ethnocentric assumptions of hegemonic feminist theorising', and she provocatively states her wish to 'claim back the essentialism that makes me a woman of colour in the first place'. Niamh Moore situates the challenge to essentialism as a crucial part of second wave feminism and points to the dangers of an entrenched and suspicious anti-essentialism, arguing that it leads to out-of-hand dismissal of eco-feminist attempts to reopen the question of women and nature. Such attempts in empirical fact, she argues, show that feminist activism is neither dead nor essentialist, but alive and evolving in environmental organisations such as the Friends of Clayoquot Sound.

Perhaps we are more able to distinguish between second and third wave feminisms if we concentrate on other features. Within Western feminism, the revalorisation of all things bright, beautiful and girlie in popular culture is perhaps the most immediately obvious feature differentiating second and third wave generations, and this is investigated by several of the contributors. From Cristina Lucia Stasia's critique of the continuing sexual objectification of women in the new female action hero, to Patricia Pender's celebration of Buffy as 'a quintessentially third wave cultural production', the political valence of girl power is scrutinised. But whether girlie-ness is seen as a liberating force or a capitulation to consumerism, it is arguably less significant than the different conditions facing new generations. Educationally and economically, young Western women now are nearer to equality with their male contemporaries than their mothers were with theirs. As the economic disadvantages of femaleness set in later in life, overwhelmingly with motherhood itself, feminism has a different significance to women at different stages of life. In their chapter, Leslie Heywood and Jennifer Drake show that third wave feminism is not a case of daughterly rebellion for its own sake. They chart some of the economic conditions arising from globalisation that have particularly shaped the experiences of those born after the 1970s. For Heywood and Drake, younger Americans' experience of 'relative gender equality in the context of economic downward mobility' is likely to foster generational rather than gender solidarity. The greater authority enjoyed by some women, in part the legacy of second wave feminism, can also be seen, they argue, as the unintended by-product of the general collapse of traditional authorities in an economic globalisation that has as its most salient feature a huge concentration of wealth, massively widening the gap between rich and poor and bearing disproportionately on the majority of the world's women. The third wavers Heywood and Drake locate contemporary feminism as enmeshed within a broad field of environmentalism and anti-corporate movements whose activists are deeply opposed to many of the institutions within which women's previous gains have been made.

In this context it is not surprising that there is no agreement about how to think of, much less use, what power is now in female hands. In her interview, Elaine Showalter – now firmly identified with the second wave feminist tradition – urges us to make use of those women now in positions of power in politics, corporations, or the military, envisaging a benign culture of female mentoring that will enable women to transform social institutions from within. Other chapters in this volume call for a geographical rethink. Agnieszka Graff points out that to take into account Eastern European feminism is to reconsider the chronology of second and third waves altogether. Winifred Woodhull, by contrast finding the third wave a globally meaningful construction, sees it as emerging with the late 1980s/early 1990s financial globalisation, and as urgently in need of developing a correspondingly global, feminist strategy. Anastasia Valassopoulos raises the question of globalisation differently, by exploring the possibilities for postcolonial feminism of engagement with Western feminist debates, looking forward to the ideal of 'a feminism that is not owned by anyone and can be used by all'. Such a movement would be irreducibly plural. Evidently, the third wave is not going to give us our synthesis. There is some doubt as to whether it exists at all beyond a contentious label. In their chapter, Ashley Tauchert and Gillian Howie argue against the simplistic opposition of second and third wave feminism and send out a call for renewal and return – a return to materialist feminist analysis, and to argument. They remind us of the significance of substantive disagreements within feminism, and that we need to have the arguments, not to avoid them by explaining different positions as the characteristics of different phases, generations and waves. Lise Shapiro Sanders calls for a different return – to utopian thinking – while, similarly, stressing that arguments have to be had: utopia is not a 'conflict-free zone'.

The talk of waves, in fact, can obscure our recognition of how far we are engaged in a long-standing argument. The debate between the advocates of making feminist gains within the current system and those who argue that radical change is needed has been going on for a long time. If we try to make it a generational one, where do the lines fall? Between young advocates of girl power and old lefties hankering after a lost socialism? Or between older women now in government or on company boards and young anti-capitalist activists? Recognising the problem of a generational reading, the editors of this collection and many of its contributors are frankly sceptical about the whole idea of the third wave. While Mary Orr suggests that thinking in waves may not do justice to contemporary women's issues, Rebecca Munford argues that the idea of third versus second wave locks us into the unhelpful notion of fundamental mother-daughter conflict. Maybe we should, as she and Stacy Gillis have argued elsewhere, ditch the wave paradigm altogether, to avoid the generational notion of feminism which distorts its history, threatening to trap us in repetitive struggle and to aid the anti-feminist backlash (178). So why, finally, this collection – revised, enlarged and improved – a second edition of *Third Wave Feminism*? Because the term is doing its job as a focus for widespread debate, forging new connections among feminists within and outside academia, and fostering a recovering sense of feminist urgency. Never mind which number we are on, we need to be making waves.

Works cited

Baumgardner, Jennifer, and Amy Richards. *Manifesta: Young Women, Feminism, and the Future*. New York: Farrar, Straus and Giroux, 2000.

Elam, Diane. 'Sisters are Doing It to Themselves.' *Generations: Academic Feminists in Dialogue*. Ed. Devoney Looser and E. Ann Kaplan. Minneapolis: Minnesota University Press, 1997. 55–68.

Gillis, Stacy, and Rebecca Munford. 'Genealogies and Generations: The Politics and Praxis of Third Wave Feminism.' *Women's History Review* 13.2 (2004): 165–82.

Kristeva, Julia. 'Women's Time'. 1979. Trans. Alice Jardine and Harry Blake. *The Kristeva Reader*. Ed. Toril Moi. Oxford: Basil Blackwell, 1986. 187–213.

Segal, Lynne. *Why Feminism? Gender, Psychology, Politics*. Cambridge: Polity, 1999.

Index

CPSIA information can be obtained at www.ICGtesting.com
Printed in the USA
LVOW012236020113

314088LV00031B/2714/P